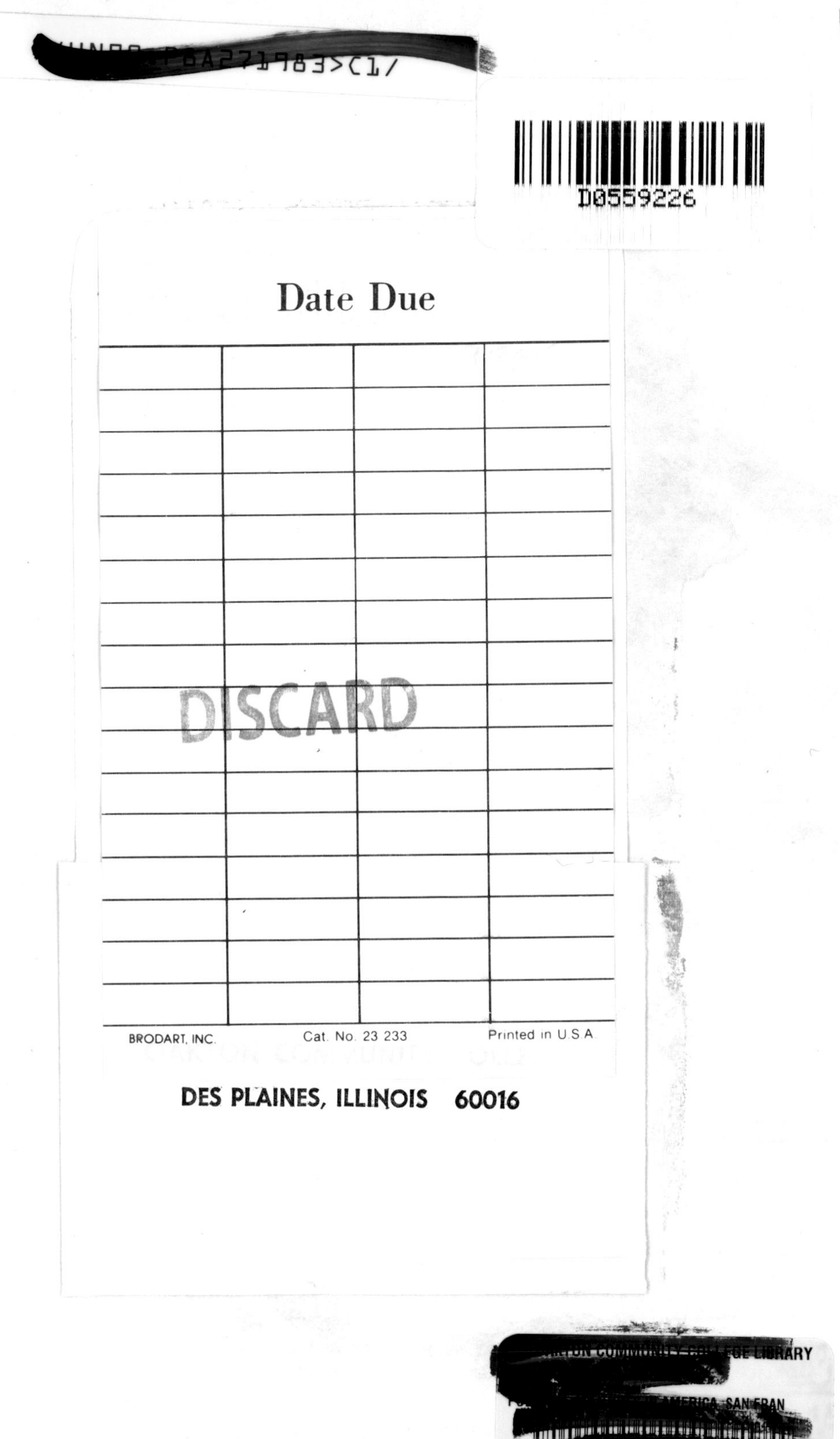

D0559226
Date Due
DISCARD
BRODART, INC.
Cat. No. 23 233
Printed in U.S.A.
DES PLAINES, ILLINOIS 60016

Political Attitudes in America

Political Attitudes in America

[FORMATION AND CHANGE]

Paul R. Abramson

Michigan State University

W. H. FREEMAN AND COMPANY

San Francisco

Project Editor: Pearl C. Vapnek
Designer: Eric Jungerman
Production Coordinator: Bill Murdock
Illustration Coordinator: Richard Quiñones
Compositor: Graphic Typesetting Service
Printer and Binder: The Maple-Vail Book Manufacturing Group

Library of Congress Cataloging in Publication Data

Abramson, Paul R.
Political attitudes in America.

Bibliography: p.
Includes indexes.
1. Public opinion—United States. 2. United States—Politics and government—1945–
I. Title.
HN9O.P8A27 1983 306′.2 82-13508
ISBN 0-7167-1420-5 (pbk.)

Printed in the United States of America

1 2 3 4 5 6 7 8 9 0 MP 0 8 9 8 7 6 5 4 3 2

To Janet

Contents

VI. Implications and Conclusions

Figures

Tables

Preface

Since World War II, the American electorate has lived through two unpopular wars and has witnessed the assassination of one president and the forced resignation of another. Black Americans in the South gained political and social rights that had been denied them earlier. And although the postwar years began relatively quietly, they eventually witnessed urban riots and campus rebellions, only to return to a period of political quiescence.

There have been other tumultuous periods in American history, but the postwar years can be studied in ways that cannot be applied to earlier periods. For since the early 1950s, public opinion researchers have continually monitored the political attitudes and behaviors of the electorate. Thus, we now have far better data with which to examine how the public reacts to political and social change. Moreover, during the last two decades, a growing number of social scientists have studied the political attitudes of preadults, so we now have data on the origins of political attitudes. In addition, several studies have now examined individuals at more than one point in time, allowing us to study the way individuals' political attitudes and behaviors change.

The goal of this book is to synthesize the research to better understand the way electorates change over time. Despite some comparisons with other countries, this study is confined to a single electorate for a limited period in its history. The American electorate is the only mass public that can be studied over so long a period, and there is far more extensive research on American political attitudes than on any other. Moreover, although the three decades we study represent only about a seventh of the life of the republic, they represent over half the adult political life of most individuals. Thus, as we shall see later, we can trace the attitudes of some birth cohorts over half their adult political life.

Part I of this book provides an introduction to the study of political attitudes. Chapter 1 is an overview of some of the major changes in political behaviors and attitudes during the postwar years, the decline of electoral participation since 1960, the erosion of partisan loyalties since 1964, and the decline of political trust since 1964. Chapter 2 explains how surveys of the American electorate are conducted. It compares the advantages and disadvantages of alternative survey methods and describes the sampling procedures employed by the University of Michigan Survey Research Center. Chapter 3 briefly describes how political attitudes are measured and explains how data are presented in this book. Chapters 2 and 3 provide a useful introduction to survey research methods that should enable readers who are not familiar with the logic of survey research to follow the remaining chapters.

Chapter 4 examines the importance of generational replacement. It defines some of the basic terms used in cohort analysis, explains how generational replacement occurs, and shows the speed at which replacement has occurred among both the white and the black electorates. It provides a concrete example of the effects of generational replacement to illustrate how we can measure the impact of replacement processes. The chapter spells out the six basic effects that generational replacement can have on the distribution of attitudes and behaviors among mass electorates.

Part II examines continuity and change in partisan loyalties, Part III discusses continuity and change in feelings of political effectiveness, and Part IV studies change in feelings of political trust. These three sections follow the same basic logic. The first chapter of each section (Chapters 5, 8, and 11) explains the concept to be studied, shows how it is measured, and examines the importance of the attitude for political behavior. The second chapter (Chapters 6, 9, and 12) shows how these attitudes are learned among preadults. These chapters examine the impact of parents, as well as other sources of political learning. In each of these chapters, we examine differences in political learning between whites and blacks; and in Chapters 9 and 12, we evaluate systematically the way subcultural differences in political attitudes develop. The third chapter of each section (Chapters 7, 10, and 13) examines attitude change among adults. Each chapter begins with panel studies that examine the same individuals more than once and attempts to determine how and why individuals change their political attitudes. We then see how attitudes have changed among the electorate as a whole, paying careful attention to racial differences in political attitude trends. By studying each attitude, we determine the effects of generational replacement on the distribution of attitudes among the electorate and ultimately provide concrete illustrations of the basic effects of generational replacement.

Part V studies a variety of trends, some of which are the subject of considerable controversy. Chapter 14 analyzes change in feelings of tolerance toward ideological nonconformists. This chapter parallels the basic structure of Parts II, III, and IV, although, given the absence of extensive research on the preadult origins of tolerance and the absence of extensive panel studies of tolerance, a fully developed section on tolerance is unwarranted. Still, the study of tolerance provides one of the clearest examples of the effects of generational replacement on political attitudes and allows us to comment briefly on a fascinating debate over the meaning of recent tolerance trends.

Chapter 15 examines changes in levels of conceptualization among the electorate, possible changes in issue consistency, attitude stability, and issue voting. We evaluate the claims of scholars who argue that there have been changes in these attitudes and behaviors among the electorate, as well as those of observers who maintain that little change has occurred.

Part VI explores the implications of attitude change for American political behavior. Chapter 16 shows that two of the attitude trends we study—the decline of partisan loyalties and eroding beliefs that the government is responsive—can account for about seven-tenths of the decline in electoral participation. We thus shed light on one of the major puzzles of postwar American politics, by explaining why electoral participation has declined despite major changes that should have increased participation among the electorate. The final chapter summarizes our main conclusions, reviews the effects of generational replacement, and spells out some of the major gaps in our knowledge. Lastly, we use the data we have examined to speculate on the future of American politics.

November 1982 Paul R. Abramson

Acknowledgments

My study of attitude change among the American electorate during the past three decades was possible only because of the pioneering efforts of scholars who began to collect data back in the early 1950s. My primary debt, therefore, must be to the late Angus Campbell, and to his collaborators, especially Philip E. Converse, Warren E. Miller, and Donald E. Stokes. The task of storing and disseminating these data, along with data collected during the subsequent quarter century, fell to the Inter-University Consortium for Political and Social Research. Unless otherwise indicated, all of the data presented in my figures and tables are based on my analyses of data provided by the Consortium. The Consortium bears no responsibility for my analyses and interpretations of these data.

I am grateful to M. Kent Jennings for providing me with analyses of the panel data for the University of Michigan Survey Research Center study of high school seniors and their parents. Clyde Z. Nunn provided me with additional information about his study of tolerance, and Ruth S. Jones and William S. Maddox provided additional information about their research on American preadults. My own study of preadult political attitudes, based on a survey of Saginaw, Michigan, tenth graders, was funded by an All-University Research Initiation Grant from Michigan State University. I am grateful to the officials of the City of Saginaw school district for their cooperation and to Rick E. Rollenhagen for his assistance with the field work and data analysis.

My colleagues, Cleo H. Cherryholmes, Ada W. Finifter, Robert W. Jackman, Joseph A. Schlesinger, and Brian D. Silver, commented on portions of this manuscript, as did two former colleagues, John H. Aldrich and Terry M. Moe. I learned a great deal about the political-trust measure through collaborative work with Ada Finifter and a great deal about the dynamics of political participation through collaborative work with John Aldrich. Fred G. Abramson provided insights about the alternative effects of generational replacement. George I. Balch, Walter Dean Burnham, Jack Citrin, William Claggett, and Howard L. Reiter commented on my research on electoral participation. Harriet Dhanak and the staff of the Politometrics Laboratory at Michigan State University provided extensive assistance with the data analysis.

I am grateful to Richard J. Lamb for encouraging me to undertake this project, to John H. Staples for editorial suggestions, and to Pearl C. Vapnek for her assistance with the production of this book. William J. Crotty, of Northwestern University; Edward C. Dreyer, of the University of Tulsa; and Richard G. Niemi, of the University of Rochester, provided extensive reviews of the entire manuscript.

I am once again grateful to my wife, Janet, for her editorial assistance and for helping me see this book through to completion.

November 1982 Paul R. Abramson

Political Attitudes in America

I

An Introduction to the Study of Political Attitudes

[CHAPTER 1]

Recent Political Change

It is easy to overdramatize recent events. Still, seen from 1982, the events of the 1960s and 1970s appear to be among the most dramatic in American history. Even those events that were not quite unprecedented may have been magnified by the impact of television.

John F. Kennedy's assassination in November 1963 was not unprecedented. There was strong public reaction to Lincoln's assassination in 1865 and to McKinley's in 1901. (Garfield had been president only four months when he was shot in 1881.) Still, the massive media coverage of Kennedy's death, the televised slaying of Lee Harvey Oswald, and the continuing controversy over Kennedy's assassination—as well as the murder of his brother Robert five years later—left an indelible impression on American political memories.

Scandal, like assassination, is not new to American politics. Yet the Watergate scandal had unprecedented consequences. Beginning with the break-in of the Democratic party headquarters in the Watergate Hotel in June 1972, the scandal gradually widened to implicate President Nixon himself. The Senate Watergate Committee began its nationally televised hearings in the spring of 1973, and, in the summer of 1974, the House of Representatives' Judiciary Committee began its nationally televised hearings. By the end of July, the House committee passed its first article of impeachment against President Nixon. On August 9, 1974, Nixon became the only American president to resign from office.

America's involvement in the Vietnam War also led to unprecedented results. America had engaged in other foreign wars with less than unanimous support. There was opposition to the War of 1812 and to the Mexican War, and the Korean War proved unpopular. But the protracted, costly, and ultimately unsuccessful American involvement in Vietnam left far deeper wounds than had any previous foreign conflict. Beginning with the rapid escalation of American involvement in 1965, the United States eventually had over half a million troops in Vietnam. While popular support for the war was high at the outset, support waned as the conflict dragged on year after year. The war forced Lyndon B. Johnson's retirement from the White House in 1968. Nixon's gradual disengagement from the war contributed to his landslide victory over George S. McGovern four years later. Ultimately, however, our military disengagement produced an untenable "peace," leading to the military defeat of our South Vietnamese ally in April 1975. While America had not been defeated on the battlefield, many Americans—regardless of their previous position on the war—may have concluded that 55,000 American lives had been sacrificed for little apparent purpose.

While change for America as a whole was dramatic, change for black Americans was even more striking. Between 1940 and 1970, black Americans experienced rapid social and geographic mobility, largely resulting from the modernization of American agriculture. More than 20 million Americans left the land during those decades, and about one in five who left the farms was black. Blacks moved not only from the farms to the cities, but from the South to the North and West. In 1940, only 23% of the blacks lived outside the South; by 1970, 47% did. By 1970, four out of five blacks lived in metropolitan areas, and blacks were more urbanized than whites.

Paralleling this social and geographic mobility, blacks experienced great gains in social and political rights. The 1954 Supreme Court desegregation decision ended the legally sanctioned policy of racial segregation of schools in Southern and many border states. The Civil Rights Act of 1964 outlawed racial segregation in restaurants and lodging, and the Voting Rights Act of 1965 restored the vote to Southern blacks. Black expectations may have outstripped black gains, contributing to the wave of urban riots that began in the summer of 1965 and peaked in the summer of 1967. By 1968, George C. Wallace—appealing largely to antiblack sentiments—gained nearly 10 million votes, nearly one out of seven of the total votes cast. Since 1968, there have been few urban riots, and antiblack feelings have ebbed, but these events of the 1960s have led to a distinctive black electorate that often reacts quite differently to political events than the white electorate does. For this reason, the analyses in this book usually examine the white and the black electorate separately.

The events described above appear to have contributed to major changes in the political behavior and attitudes of the American electorate, and our goal is to examine and explain these changes. Perhaps the major change in political behavior has been the decline of electoral participation. Two of the major changes in political attitudes have been a decline in party loyalties and an erosion of political trust. Let us look briefly at these changes.

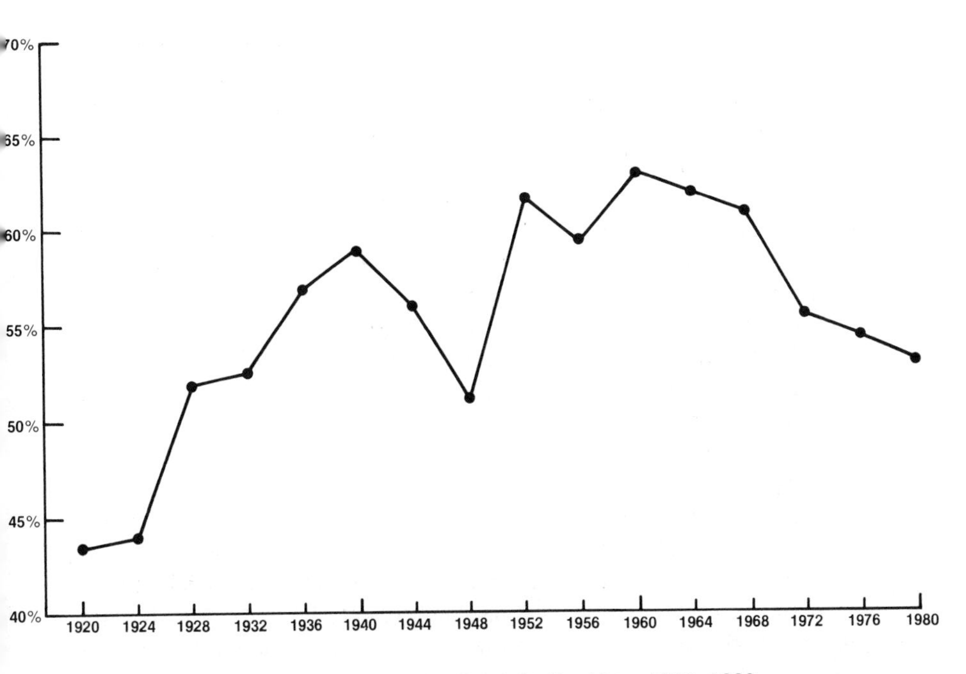

Figure 1.1 Percentage of Adults Who Voted for President: 1920–1980.
[*Source:* U.S. Bureau of the Census (1972, 1981b).]

The Decline of Turnout

The decline of electoral participation should be placed in historical context. As the Nineteenth Amendment, granting women the right to vote, was ratified shortly before the 1920 presidential election, we use that year as our starting point. Figure 1.1 shows the percentage of the adult population that voted for president in each election between 1920 and 1980.[1]

Turnout was very low in 1920, the year of Warren G. Harding's (Republican) landslide win over James M. Cox, but this is scarcely surprising, since women had gained the right to vote only a few months before the election and since turnout was very low among women. Turnout grew only slightly in 1924, but jumped markedly in 1928, when Alfred E. Smith (Democrat), the first Roman Catholic candidate of a major political party, ran for office. Turnout grew slightly in 1932, when Franklin D. Roosevelt was elected for his first term and began a two-decade period of Democratic dominance. Turnout

[1] Data for 1920 through 1928 are based on Table 597 of U.S. Bureau of the Census (1972); data for 1932 through 1980 are based on Table 824 of U.S. Bureau of the Census (1981b). The estimate for the voting-age population for the 1980 election is based on a count as of April 1980. As the voting-age population grew somewhat between April 1980 and November 1980, the percentage voting is probably somewhat below the 53.2% reported by the Bureau.

increased considerably in 1936, when Roosevelt, as the incumbent president, mobilized new voters into the electorate. Turnout rose once again in 1940, when Roosevelt won an unprecedented third term as president. It was not until 1944, when Roosevelt ran for reelection during World War II, that turnout dropped—mainly because of the social dislocations caused by the war.

Turnout was again low in 1948, the year of Harry S Truman's (Democratic) upset over Thomas E. Dewey. But turnout jumped in 1952, when Dwight D. Eisenhower (Republican) ran against Adlai E. Stevenson, reaching its highest level since 1920. While voting dropped in 1956—a fairly dull rerun between the incumbent Eisenhower and Stevenson—it grew again in 1960, when Kennedy (Democrat) became the first Roman Catholic to be elected president. While the 63% turnout was low compared with that of other democracies, it was the highest in America since women were enfranchised.

Despite some fluctuations, there was a fairly consistent increase in turnout during the four decades between 1920 and 1960. Brody estimates that turnout increased at an average rate of 1.63 percentage points per election during this period (1978, p. 291).[2] Had turnout continued to increase at the same rate, 71% of the adult population would have voted in the 1980 presidential election. Instead of rising, however, turnout declined consistently in the next five elections, registering its biggest drop between 1968 (the Nixon–Humphrey–Wallace election) and 1972 (the Nixon–McGovern contest). In 1980, only 53% of the adult population voted for president.

A similar pattern may be seen by examining turnout in off-year congressional elections. Turnout was only 32% in 1922 and 30% in 1926. But it rose consistently from 1926 through 1938, when 44% of the adult population voted for Congress. Turnout dropped in the wartime election of 1942, but rose consistently from 1942 through 1962. In 1962 and 1966, 45% voted.

Since 1966, turnout has consistently declined, and, in the 1978 off-year election, only 36% of the adult population voted for Congress.[3] A recent study of congressional voting participation by Burnham traces turnout back to 1834 and concludes: "Beginning in the mid-1960s and continuing down to the most recent elections, turnout has continually and severely declined. By 1978, non-Southern congressional turnout, at 40.4% of the estimated potential electorate, had fallen to very near the all-time low achieved in 1926" (1981, p. 19).

As we shall see, the decline of turnout occurred in spite of many factors that might well have increased participation, especially the rise in educational levels among the electorate. Not all Americans have followed the same trend. Blacks, for example, have higher levels of turnout than they had in 1960, mainly because the Voting Rights Act of 1965 reenfranchised Southern blacks. Even though the entire electorate has not followed the same trend, the very

[2] Actually, Brody's estimates are not based on an average, but on the form of trendline analysis briefly discussed in Chapter 3.

[3] Data for 1922 through 1930 are based on Table 597 of U.S. Bureau of the Census (1972); data for 1934 through 1978 are based on Table 824 of U.S. Bureau of the Census (1981b).

low level of turnout in the United States has concerned politicians, journalists, and political scientists.

President Carter, for example, warned about low levels of turnout. In his "crisis of confidence" speech, he lamented: "Two-thirds of our people do not even vote" (*New York Times*, July 17, 1979). Other politicians have proposed reforms that might increase turnout, such as the further easing of registration requirements, voting by mail, and declaring Election Day a national holiday—although such reforms have received little congressional support in recent years.

Journalists and political commentators have also lamented the low level of participation. Shortly after the 1978 congressional election, *Time* wrote: "Americans' unwillingness to vote has long been something of a scandal, and last week's election drew the lowest percentage of the electorate for a non-presidential election since World War II" (November 20, 1978). Gans argues: "The crucial difference between democracy and other forms of government, it is said, is that in a democracy the leadership of the nation derives its legitimacy and support from the consent of the governed. Perhaps the principal problem facing the United States today is the degree to which that consent is being withdrawn—the degree to which fewer and fewer Americans believe it necessary, important, or even worth their while to cast their ballots" (1978, p. 27).

Hadley attempts to explain why 70 million Americans do not vote, arguing: "The effect this great mass of nonvoting people will have on our democracy depends on who they are and why they don't vote" (1978, p. 16). While Hadley does not reach alarmist conclusions, he nonetheless argues that a large number of nonvoters are a "great mass of refrainers, disconnected from the process of democracy, but able at any moment to dominate our future" (p. 126).

The continued decline of turnout in the 1980 presidential election led to continued concern. As the *New York Times* editorialized: "For a long time during the campaign, it seemed as if the true people's choice was None of the Above. It can even be maintained, without disrespect to Ronald Reagan, that None of the Above finally won." The *Times* estimated that 75 million Americans voted for neither Reagan nor Carter. "In other words, it looks as though only 53 percent of the voting age population turned out to vote. If that's correct, American voter turnout contrasts sadly with that in other democracies" (November 24, 1980).

Political scientists, too, have expressed concern over the low level of turnout. Burnham points out that turnout is lowest among the relatively disadvantaged and argues that this fact may have especially severe consequences for democracy (1978, 1981). Janowitz sees the decline of electoral participation as an important indicator of the weakening of social-control mechanisms in the United States. Janowitz argues that elections are important mechanisms for providing governmental legitimacy: "[A]n effective competitive electoral system does more than the specific task of selecting leaders and creating political conditions for making legitimate decisions. If effective, it serves to reinforce the norms of rule by consent" (1978, pp. 90–91). In this light, the decline of turnout is seen as especially significant: "[S]ince 1952, the long-term secular increase in voting participation has not been effectively maintained. Given the increasing levels of education, wide exposure to the mass media, and politicalization of minority groups, the persistence of a high level of nonvoting and even specific increases in nonvoting is particularly noteworthy. This trend can be perceived as a direct measure of the electoral process's ineffectiveness as a mechanism of social control" (p. 102).

My goal here is not to be an alarmist. The implications of the decline in turnout have been debated, and some scholars argue that the decline has few policy consequences (Wolfinger and Rosenstone, 1980, pp. 108–114), while others emphasize that the total number of elections has increased (Boyd, 1981; W. Miller, 1980). Regardless of the importance of the decline of turnout, the decline presents a major puzzle for students of political behavior, for there were social forces at work during this period that might well have *increased* turnout. The study of attitude change over time provides a partial explanation for this major trend in American political behavior.

The Decline of Party Loyalties

The weakening of the American political party system is among the most widely recognized trends in postwar American politics. Students of this trend have examined the organizational, behavioral, and attitudinal basis of the decline. From an organizational perspective, politicians, journalists, and political scientists have discussed the weakening of formal party structures—from the breakdown of the big-city political machines to the declining importance of national party organizations. There are behavioral changes among the electorate—such as the increasing tendency for voters to disregard party labels and to split their ballot between candidates of both the Democratic and the Republican party. The most important attitudinal change has been a weakening of party loyalties among the American electorate.

Although we examine this trend in detail later (Chapter 7), paying careful attention to the way different segments of the electorate have changed, we may briefly outline the decline of party loyalties by examining two data sources: Gallup polls that have been conducted since 1937, and polls conducted since 1952 by the University of Michigan Survey Research Center and the Center for Political Studies.[4] Figure 1.2 shows the percentage of the electorate that claimed to be Republican or Democratic from 1937 through 1980.

In their broad outlines, the data are clear and follow the same general trend regardless of which data set is used. The Gallup data suggest that party loy-

[4]For more detailed reports on Gallup results, see Mueller (1973, pp. 4–7), and *Public Opinion* (April/May 1981, pp. 30–31).

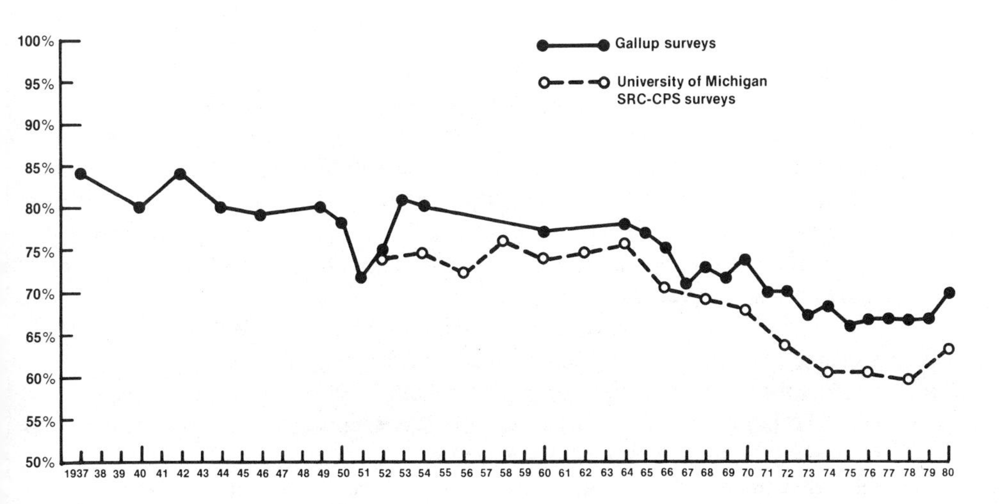

Figure 1.2 Percentage of Electorate Who Are Republicans or Democrats: 1937–1980.

[*Source:* Gallup surveys based on *Gallup Opinion Index* (July 1979, August 1980). SRC–CPS data based on codebooks provided by Inter-University Consortium for Political and Social Research.]

alties may have been greatest in the late 1930s and early 1940s.[5] Both data sources suggest that party loyalties were fairly stable between 1952 and 1964, but that they began to decline after that—sometime between 1964 and 1966. The Gallup data suggest that party loyalties stopped declining after 1974 and show a slight rebound in recent years. While the Gallup organization considers this increase in partisan loyalties "significant" in a statistical sense, they nonetheless conclude: "Probably the most significant trend is the unrelenting increase in the proportion of Independents, most notably in the past 20 years. This development may be a reflection of the broader phenomenon of increasing fragmentation in American politics—weaker parties, the increasing influence of parochial interests—discerned by numerous media observers and political scientists alike" (*Gallup Opinion Index,* August 1980, p. 30). More recent Gallup data show a slight increase in the percentage of Republicans, as well as a marginal increase in the percentage of Independents. In Gallup polls conducted in late November 1981, 67% of the electorate identified as either Republican or Democratic, and 33% were Independents (*Public Opinion,* December/January 1982).

[5]Given biases in early Gallup surveys, however, the results for the 1930s and early 1940s should be interpreted with caution. Given the tendency for these early surveys to oversample persons in upper-socioeconomic categories, and the nonsampling of Southern blacks, there might be a tendency for these surveys to overestimate the percentage of party identifiers.

The Michigan SRC data consistently show a smaller proportion of party identifiers, probably because of differences in the way their basic party-identification question is worded. The SRC data suggest that, between 1952 and 1964, three out of four Americans were either Republicans or Democrats. By 1966, this proportion declined to seven out of ten, and the decline of party loyalties continued fairly consistently through 1978, by which time just under six out of ten Americans identified with the two major parties. Since then, there has been a slight rebound in partisan loyalties, and, in 1980, 63% identified as either Republicans or Democrats.

Two observations should temper our discussion of this decline. First, a majority of Americans still claim to be either Republican or Democratic. Second, the Michigan surveys suggest that about three out of five Independents (as of 1980) said they felt "closer" to either the Republican or the Democratic party. Despite these qualifications, the erosion of party loyalties is a clearly identified trend and one that, as we shall see, may have important consequences for American electoral behavior.

Politicians, journalists, and political scientists are keenly aware of the decline of partisan loyalties. President Ford, for example, voiced concern about the growing number of Americans who rejected the two major parties. The concern about the growth of Independents may have been especially great among Republicans, since they are actually outnumbered by self-proclaimed Independents. Despite a recent surge in Republican strength, several polls show that Americans are more likely to claim to be Independents than to identify as Republicans (*Public Opinion,* December/January 1982).

Journalists, too, have voiced similar concerns. Broder reflects this concern in his book *The Party's Over,* subtitled *The Failure of Politics in America*. He notes that "[m]illions of voters have been cast adrift from their old allegiances" and argues that they could contribute to a new party alignment (1972, p. 201). In an article on the "Challenges of the '80s," *U.S. News and World Report* asks whether the decade would witness a " 'Last Hurrah' for Old-Time Politics?" The author projects that American political parties will continue to be weak during the 1980s. As the article reports, the percentage of Independents has doubled during the past four decades. "Many analysts . . . are skeptical that political parties will be able to regain much, if any, of the influence they have lost recently. A Gallup Poll indicates that the proportion of voters who regard themselves as independents has increased from one fourth to one third since 1970" (October 15, 1979, p. 70).

Hebers echoes Broder's concerns in an article entitled "The Party's Over for the Political Parties" (*New York Times Magazine,* December 9, 1979). Hebers notes the decline in party loyalties among the electorate and focuses on the weakening of national and state party organizations. As he argues: "[A] growing number of scholars and political leaders are alarmed that a system stripped of its parties may ultimately be more damaging to the political process than the powerful party machines that in times past have produced such manipulators as the Tammany Hall bosses and the Chicago Democratic organization headed by the late Mayor Richard Daley" (p. 159). As Hebers reports: "Those who see the disturbing effects of the decline in party leadership cite as examples the inability of national leaders to obtain a consensus for broad national goals, such as a strong energy policy; the disproportionate influence of special interests that are able collectively to tie the hands of Presidents; the low turnout at elections . . . and general apathy about politics" (p. 159).

Numerous political scientists have discussed the decline of party loyalties. For example, Sundquist points to public-opinion data on the decline of partisan loyalties and concludes: "The loosening of party attachments all across the electorate and the movement of masses of voters from party identification to independence has been the most striking development within the party system in the past decade" (1973, p. 332). Burnham, after analyzing both public-opinion data and voting results, goes even further: "If 'partisan decomposition' continues under these conditions of pervasive public discontent, democracy will be progressively emptied of any operational meaning as executive–bureaucratic imperatives come to dominate the political system" (1975, p. 272). Nie, Verba, and Petrocik conclude: "Perhaps the most dramatic political change in the American public over the past two decades has been the decline of partisanship" (1976, p. 47). And Janowitz argues that one of the "master trends" in American politics has been "the gradual but persistent increase in the proportion of the electorate who consider themselves to be independents" (1978, p. 169).

Some political scientists have argued that the decline of party loyalties is also related to other trends in American political attitudes and behaviors, such as the tendency of voters to become more politically sophisticated, to think more systematically about political issues, and to vote according to issues. As we shall see, however (Chapter 15), these other trends are not as clearly documented as the decline of party loyalties—although they merit our attention.

As with the discussion of the decline of participation, I am not trying to make alarmist predictions. As we shall see, some of the claims about the decline of party loyalties are not fully warranted. For example, we will discover that the decline of partisanship plays a relatively small role in the decline of electoral participation. Moreover, projections about the future decline of partisan loyalties depend very much on the assumptions we make about the way party loyalties develop and change among individuals. Yet the careful study of the decline of party loyalties sheds a great deal of light on the processes through which attitudes form and the way they change.

The Decline of Political Trust

A third major trend has been a decline of popular trust in government. The exact meaning of this downturn is a subject of considerable controversy, but

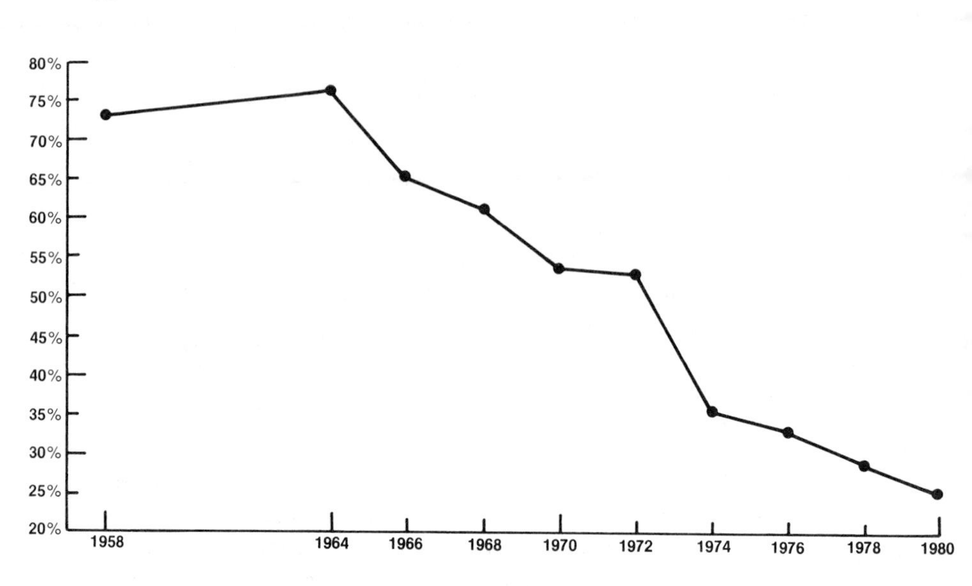

Figure 1.3 Percentage of Electorate Who Trusted Government in Washington Just About Always or Most of the Time: 1958–1980.
[*Source:* Based on codebooks provided by Inter-University Consortium for Political and Social Research.]

politicians, journalists, and political scientists all recognize that public confidence in American political leaders has eroded.

While there are many measures that point to this erosion of confidence, one of the clearest is the set of political-trust questions developed by the University of Michigan Survey Research Center. The most frequently asked question has been "How much of the time do you think you can trust the government in Washington to do what is right—just about always, most of the time, or only some of the time?" Figure 1.3 shows the percentage of Americans who said the government could be trusted just about always or most of the time in all the SRC surveys conducted between 1958, when the question was first asked, and 1980. Back in 1958 and 1964, more than seven out of ten Americans thought the government could be trusted most or all of the time. Since 1964, political trust has declined continuously, with the biggest drop between 1972 and 1974. By 1980, only one out of four Americans trusted the government to do what is right. As we shall see, political trust also declined on the other four SRC political-trust questions. In addition, questions developed by the Michigan SRC to measure feelings about the responsiveness of the government also registered a sharp decline, although with these questions the decline began somewhat earlier (Chapter 10).

In addition to the questions used by the Michigan SRC, questions developed by the Harris poll show a marked decline in confidence in social and governmental institutions between 1966 and 1971, with confidence remaining low after that. For example, in 1966, 42% of the American electorate had "a great deal of confidence" in the "people in charge of running Congress." By 1971, only 19% did, and, in late 1980, this figure stood at 18%. In 1966, 41% had "a great deal of confidence" in the "people in charge of running the executive branch of the federal government"; in 1971, only 23% did, and, in late 1980, only 17%.[6]

According to Ladd: "Literally every measure that public opinion research has come up with—and in poll-conscious America there are many of them—shows that there has been a steep decline in popular satisfaction with important aspects of national performance since 1966" (1979, p. 27). Ladd concludes: "In record numbers Americans see government as getting too powerful, as run for a few interests, as untrustworthy, as indifferent to popular needs, and as profligate" (p. 27).

Politicians have been concerned with this decline in popular confidence. In 1973, for example, the U.S. Senate Committee on Government Operations commissioned a poll to measure citizens' views of the American government (U.S. Senate, 1973). As a candidate for the presidency in 1976, Jimmy Carter pledged that one of his goals would be to restore trust in government. But Carter apparently concluded that he had failed to achieve this goal. Drawing heavily from public-opinion polls conducted by Caddell, President Carter concluded that there was a "crisis of confidence" that "strikes at the very heart and soul and spirit of our national will. We can see this crisis in the growing doubt about the meaning of our own lives and in the loss of a unity of purpose for our nation" (*New York Times,* July 19, 1979). In part, this crisis of confidence resulted from the pessimistic view Americans had about the future. It also resulted from the lack of confidence in public institutions. "As you know," Carter told his television audience, "there is a growing disrespect for Government and for churches and for schools, the news media and other institutions."

While President Reagan has been far more optimistic in describing the American electorate, he, too, seems aware of this discontent. For example, in his televised address urging public support for his tax-cut program, he asked the audience to "put aside any feelings of frustration or helplessness about our political institutions" and to contact their senators and congressmen (*New York Times,* July 28, 1981).

Whether there actually is a crisis of confidence is a subject of debate. According to Caddell, there is a growing crisis; he argues: "In many different polls on many different fronts—economic, political, social—the public registers a higher degree of pessimism and disaffection than it did earlier in the

[6]Figures for 1966 and 1971 are from *Public Opinion* (October/November 1979, p. 30). Figures for November 1980 are from *ABC News–Harris Survey* (November 24, 1980, p. 2).

seventies" (1979, p. 4). But Warren Miller argues that several measures show that the decline of confidence has leveled off since 1974 and that Carter restored confidence among his fellow Democrats (1979). Analyzing these same surveys, Arthur Miller reports that "Americans' confidence in government has been slowly crumbling over the past decade and a half, and is now at the lowest level recorded at any time during the past 20 years" (quoted in *Institute for Social Research Newsletter,* Autumn 1979, p. 4). Since the Caddell–Warren Miller exchange, political trust, as measured by the Michigan surveys, has declined even further, although there is some evidence that optimism about the future has increased.[7]

The debate between Caddell and Warren Miller focuses largely on whether there was a meaningful change during the last four years of the 1970s. There is no doubt that political trust, as well as some other measures of support for the government, have registered a marked decline since the mid-1960s. Since Arthur Miller first analyzed the decline of political trust (1974a), there has been controversy over the meaning of these attitude changes, but little dispute over whether public attitudes toward the government have changed. Janowitz, in his analysis of change over the last half century, argues that "an increased distrust of the electoral process" (1978, p. 111) is among the major trends in recent American politics, although, as he acknowledges, there is little empirical evidence that would allow us to examine this trend before the 1950s. Reviewing the SRC political-trust questions, the Harris confidence-in-institutions questions, and Gallup's questions on satisfaction with the government, presidential "popularity," and prestige in elected officials, Janowitz concludes: "Distrust is not a sudden development of the Nixon regime; it has been an aspect of the emergence of 'weak' political regimes" (p. 113).

In spite of these gloomy reports, some scholars see the decline in trust as having few direct implications for political behavior. Although political scientists have widely discussed the decline of political trust, there are greater behavioral implications in the decline of feelings that the government is responsive to the people—an attitude that we label "feelings of 'external' political effectiveness." But we can learn a great deal about the way attitudes form and change through a careful examination of both feelings of political trust and feelings of political effectiveness.

Conclusions

In reviewing recent changes in American politics, we have relied on public-opinion data. Such data are so widely used that they have taken on a reality of their own. Poll results themselves are viewed as indicators of political

[7] Based on surveys conducted by *New York Times*/CBS News Polls. See *New York Times* (July 1, 1981).

success or failure, as the crisis-of-confidence debate reveals. Moreover, some important changes in postwar American politics can only be assessed—even in a preliminary way—by reference to public-opinion data.

Up to now, however, we have not explained how such data are collected, how political attitudes are measured, or how such data are presented. Chapter 2 and 3 address these matters. Then, before we move on to the study of specific political attitudes, we will discover that the political attitudes of the electorate can change even if individuals never change their attitudes. Individuals need not change their attitudes for attitudes to change among the electorate, since the electorate itself is continuously changing. Individuals continuously leave the electorate through death, while others enter through birth. Birth, aging, and death create an ongoing process that we label "generational replacement." That process, the speed at which it occurs, and the effects it can have on political attitudes is examined in Chapter 4. After examining this process, we turn to the actual study of political attitudes among the American electorate.

[CHAPTER 2]

Survey Research

Throughout this book, we rely primarily on information collected through surveys, that is, studies based on asking individuals about their political attitudes and behaviors, as well as factual information about their lives. No social scientist has the time or the money to measure the political attitudes of all 230,000,000 million Americans, so researchers must select individuals to be studied. To properly evaluate the results of data collected from surveys, one must understand the procedures used to sample the American population.

A Brief History of Survey Research

Throughout the nineteenth century, "straw polls" were used to predict election results. The most famous effort, however, was the series of presidential polls conducted by the *Literary Digest,* which began its polling operations in the 1916 contest between Woodrow Wilson and Charles Evans Hughes. By 1924, the *Digest* began a nationwide poll in which over 16 million straw ballots were mailed to persons listed in telephone directories and in automobile-registration lists. These polling procedures correctly predicted the 1924, 1928, and 1932 presidential election results. For example, in 1932, the final *Digest* straw poll showed that 1,150,000 persons favored Herbert Hoover, the Republican incumbent; 1,700,000 favored Roosevelt, the Democratic challenger; while nearly 200,000 favored other candidates. The poll predicted that Roosevelt would receive 56% of the popular vote. In fact, he received 57%.

In 1936, the *Digest* repeated similar polling procedures, again drawing names from telephone books and lists of automobile owners. In its final report, 1,300,000 favored Alfred M. Landon, the Republican candidate; 970,000 favored Roosevelt; while 100,000 supported other candidates. According to these figures, Roosevelt would receive 41% of the popular vote, and Landon would win handily. In fact, Roosevelt received 61% of the popular vote, which was, at the time, the greatest popular-vote landslide in American history.

What had gone wrong? While there can be no definitive answer to this question, it appears that the *Digest* polls systematically overrepresented members of upper-income groups, who were more likely to have telephones and to own automobiles. Up through 1936, however, these biases did not affect the *Digest* forecasts, since upper-income groups did not vote disproportionately for the Republican party. But by 1936, Roosevelt, as an incumbent president, was supporting social policies that polarized the electorate along social-class lines. Upper-income groups swung heavily toward the Republican party, while lower-income groups swung heavily Democratic. Under these conditions, the biases in the *Digest* polls profoundly influenced the results. The *Digest* went out of business in 1938, partly as a result of its embarrassment in predicting a Landon victory. One basic lesson emerged from the *Digest's* mistake: Polls that are not designed to be representative of the overall population should not be used to describe the distribution of opinions among the overall population.

In 1936, the same year that the massive *Literary Digest* poll was forecasting a Landon win, far smaller polls, based on several thousand respondents, correctly predicted Roosevelt's reelection, although his margin of victory was underestimated. One poll, conducted by *Fortune* magazine, was the forerunner of the Roper polls; another survey, conducted by the American Institute of Public Opinion (AIPO), is more popularly known as the Gallup poll. These polls relied on quota techniques, which were designed to yield a sample that represented the U.S. adult population. Such polls employed census information about the demographic characteristics of the population; for example, the percent male and female, the percent in different age groups, and the percent at different occupational levels. Persons were selected so that the total number of persons sampled would match the actual distribution along these basic demographic characteristics. These polls did exclude one large demographic group—Southern blacks—but as Southern blacks were disfranchised, excluding them did not affect the ability to predict election results. In a quota sample, the researcher set a quota in advance to determine how many persons of each demographic characteristic were to be included. The interviewers were given instructions about the types of people they were to interview so that the end result of all the interviews would match the key demographic characteristics of the adult population. Interviewers had some discretion about which actual persons to interview, although the degree of discretion varied from survey to survey.

Quota samples were a vast improvement over nonrepresentative surveys, and both the Roper and the Gallup poll developed a good track record of predicting election results. The Gallup poll, for example, correctly predicted Roosevelt's 1940 win over Wendell L. Willkie and his 1944 win over Thomas E. Dewey, although in both elections it underestimated Roosevelt's margin of victory. But in 1948, all the major commercial polls erred by predicting that Dewey would defeat Harry S Truman. For example, the final Gallup poll, conducted between October 6 and October 20, 1948, found that 1282 respondents favored Dewey, 1096 were for Truman, and 220 favored other candidates. According to these estimates, Truman would receive only 42% of the vote, while Dewey would gain 49%. In fact, Truman received almost 50% of the popular vote, while Dewey received 45%.

What had gone wrong? Certainly, the polls had erred by ending their surveys early, thus failing to capture the switch to Truman during the final weeks of the campaign. But some of the problems with the commercial polls lay with the nature of quota sampling itself. Given the social dislocations caused by World War II, the 1940 census, the main basis for establishing the quota characteristics, may have been dated. Moreover, the freedom of interviewers to select respondents almost certainly led to some oversampling of upper-income groups. Even when an interviewer is sampling in a poor neighborhood, she (and most interviewers are women) may tend to select the better-off residents of the neighborhood. These biases may have been especially important in 1948, a year when the working class moved heavily to the Democratic party and the middle class voted heavily Republican (Abramson, 1975; Berelson, Lazarsfeld, and McPhee, 1954; Lubell, 1956.)

Since 1948, Gallup and other commercial polling agencies have greatly improved their sampling methods. Commercial polling agencies now combine some of the principles of probability sampling (described below) with quota techniques. Moreover, the discretion of the interviewer about whom to interview has been greatly reduced.

By 1948, social scientists, many of whom had done government-related research during the war, began to engage in systematic social science research (Boyd with Hyman, 1975). The two major academic agencies for conducting national surveys are the National Opinion Research Center (NORC), which was founded at the University of Denver in 1941 and since 1947 has been located at the University of Chicago, and the Survey Research Center of the University of Michigan (SRC), founded in 1946. Indeed, in 1948, the Michigan SRC conducted a small election survey (only 662 respondents) that was more accurate than the larger commercial polls and that, at least in its post-election survey, accurately reflected Truman's margin of victory. As this book relies primarily on surveys conducted by the SRC, we should understand the techniques it uses to conduct a systematic sample of the American electorate.

Neither the SRC nor any other academic survey-research organization can conduct a simple random sample of the American population. In such a sample, every adult American would have an equal chance of being selected. If

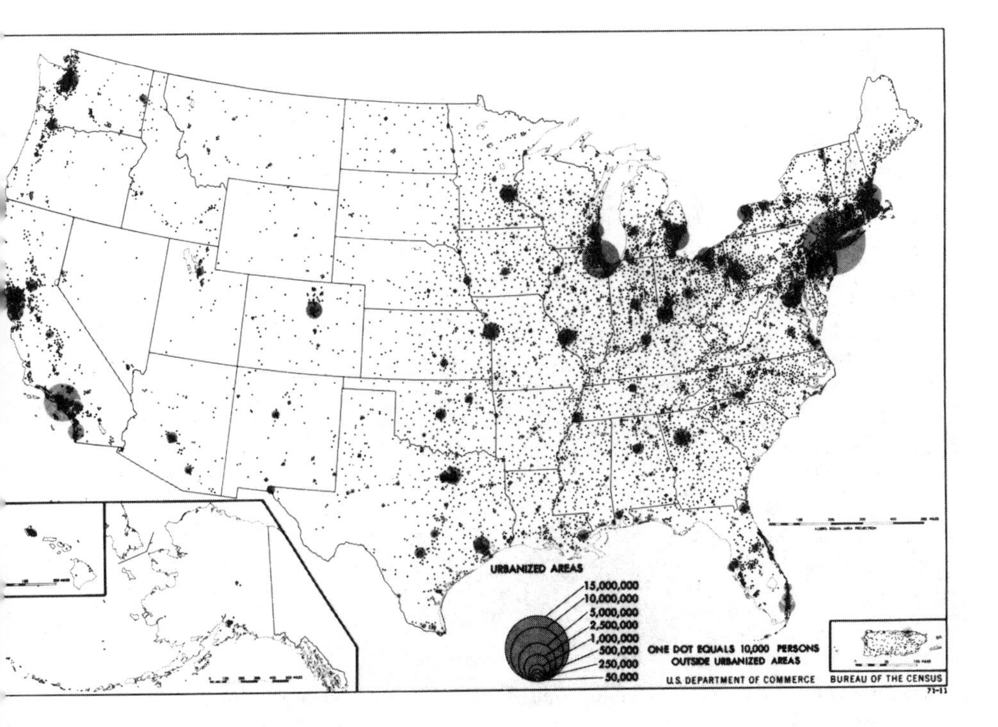

Figure 2.1 Population Distribution of United States: 1970.
[*Source:* U.S. Bureau of the Census (1971, p. 15).]

one had a list of all adult Americans, one could randomly select the persons to be interviewed. But there is no such list.[1] Even if such a list existed, the persons selected to be interviewed would be widely scattered throughout the entire country. Figure 2.1 shows the population distribution of the United States in 1970. Many of the persons chosen through a simple random procedure would live in major metropolitan centers, but some would reside in lightly populated areas. Tracking down these widely scattered names would be extremely expensive, and some people could never be located.

Survey researchers have developed procedures that greatly reduce the cost of sampling the American adult population. The SRC uses what is called a "multistage probability sample."[2] The SRC begins by designating some primary sampling units (psu's) throughout the United States. Figure 2.2 shows the location of psu's for the 1972, 1974, and 1976 election studies. By estab-

[1] In a country where the government has the responsibility for maintaining the electoral rolls, registration lists might be used; but in the United States, about a third of all adults are not registered to vote.

[2] For a more detailed description of the SRC sampling procedures, see Weisberg and Bowen (1977, pp. 21–35). For a still more detailed description, see Survey Research Center (1976).

Figure 2.2 Primary Sampling Units Used by Survey Research Center: 1972, 1974, and 1976.

[*Source:* Based on codebooks provided by Inter-University Consortium for Political and Social Research.]

lishing psu's, which are changed after every census, the SRC can have a trained field staff at each location, greatly cutting costs. A major national survey is conducted from about 75 psu's. The dozen major metropolitan areas of the United States are chosen for every national sample, and other psu's are chosen according to region and population size. Based on the total size of the sample, which usually ranges from about 1500 to 2500, the SRC decides how many interviews to conduct within each psu.

Beginning with the psu as the basic sampling unit, the SRC uses probability-sampling techniques to designate smaller and smaller units. Figure 2.3 illustrates this process. For example, a psu may be a metropolitan region; within that region, a city would be selected as a "sampling location." A list of city blocks may be chosen as a "chunk" within each city. The research staff would then make up a list of housing units, and randomization procedures would be used to draw up a list of these units. To further reduce costs, housing units may be located on the same block; this smaller area would be called a "segment." The interviewer would be assigned the specific housing units that he or she must enter. The housing unit may be a specific house or a specific apartment within an apartment building.

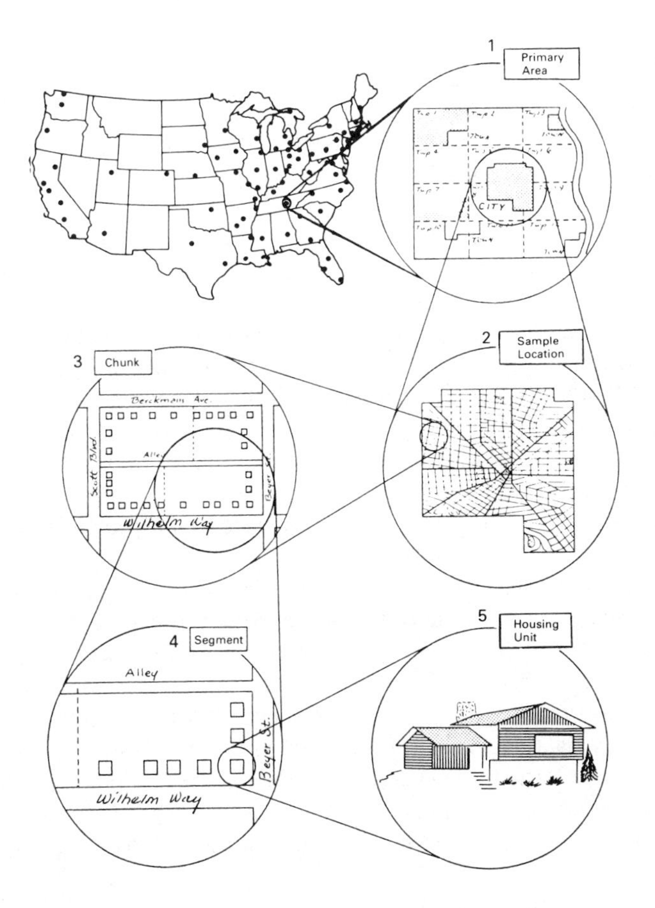

Figure 2.3 Sampling Methods Used by Survey Research Center.
[*Source:* Survey Research Center (1976, p. 36). Reprinted with permission.]

It is only at this stage that the interviewer actually contacts the people within the households. The interviewer first determines whether the dwelling unit is actually just one household (a house may turn out to be subdivided), and newly identified households must be included in the sampling procedures. Once the household is identified, the interviewer makes up a list of all the adult residents of the household. The interviewer then turns to a selection table to determine the specific person to be interviewed within the household. (Different selection tables are used to further randomize the process.) Once the specific person is chosen, that individual becomes the only person who can be interviewed. The particular person chosen may not be at home, and, in principle, unlimited callbacks would be made to locate the "designated respondent" chosen by this procedure.

The SRC, as well as other survey-research agencies, generally restrict their interviews to persons living in private households. Persons living in institutions, such as college dormitories, prisons, rest homes, and nursing homes, or on military reservations, are not included. In spite of this limitation, the stratified sampling conducted by academic survey organizations provides the best possible samples of the electorate.

The procedures used for national surveys may also be applied for local-level surveys. For example, one can conduct quota or probability samples within a single state or within a single metropolitan area. Telephone surveys are useful for some purposes, but they typically use a smaller number of questions and must use procedures (such as random-digit dialing) to sample persons with unlisted phones. In recent years, newspapers and television networks have also begun to engage in systematic surveys. In 1980, both CBS News/*New York Times* and ABC News conducted major samples by interviewing voters after they had left the polling stations. Such "exit polls" may represent the voting population, but cannot sample the sizable percentage of adults who do not vote.

Both the NORC and the SRC have become ongoing research operations that have been collecting politically relevant data for the past three decades. Moreover, the Gallup and Roper polls have been collecting data for over four decades. These survey organizations not only collect data, but publish the results of their surveys. In recent years, however, most of the published analyses of survey data have been by scholars who were not involved with the data-collection efforts. After a survey is conducted, the results are transformed into coded responses that can be stored on magnetic tapes and other storage devices. With appropriate "codebooks" and with access to these data, researchers may come along decades later to address problems that may have been overlooked by the original researchers.

The task of storing, maintaining, and disseminating previously collected survey data is the responsibility of data archivists. The largest archive is the Roper Public Opinion Research Center, established at Williams College in 1957 and now based in Storrs, Connecticut. The Roper center houses the data cards and codebooks for some 15,000 surveys, many of which were conducted outside the United States. The Roper center is the primary repository for data collected by the Roper polls, but it also houses Gallup polls, as well as NORC surveys. The NORC also operates a data archive, which mainly houses its own data. For political scientists, however, the major data archive is the Inter-University Consortium for Political and Social Research (ICPSR), which was founded at the University of Michigan in 1962. The ICPSR stores all the major SRC election studies and makes these surveys available to some 200 member colleges and universities that belong to the consortium. (It also houses some survey data from other countries, historical data based on voting statistics, as well as U.S. Bureau of the Census data.) Surveys provided by the ICPSR provide the major data source for this book, but they also provide a major data source for the entire political science community.

Whether secondary analysis has contributed very much to our knowledge is a subject of debate. Certainly, heavy reliance on data collected by the SRC narrows our range of concerns. However, the ability of scholars to reanalyze data collected by major survey-research agencies has provided an opportunity to challenge many of the prevailing conclusions of political science. Most importantly, it provides an opportunity to study change. We are now able to analyze some political attitudes over the course of nearly three decades. Without the continuing data provided by survey research, and the opportunity for scholars to gain access to these data through major survey archives, we would know far less about the political behavior of the American electorate. (For the most ambitious effort to discuss the past and potential uses of secondary analyses of survey data, see Hyman, 1972b.)

Advantages and Disadvantages of Different Techniques

Given our emphasis on national probability samples conducted by the SRC, one might conclude that there were no advantages to other techniques. But even nonrepresentative surveys have their uses, if they are employed with caution. While massive straw polls, such as those conducted by the *Literary Digest,* have no credible use, many scholars still use nonrepresentative surveys, especially to study preadults. The early classic studies of preadult political attitudes, conducted by such scholars as Greenstein (1965) and Easton and Hess (Easton and Dennis, 1969; Hess and Torney, 1967), were based on nonrepresentative surveys. Of all the studies of preadult political attitudes, only a few have been based on national probability samples.

Nonrepresentative survey

Scholars who use nonrepresentative surveys often use the term "purposive survey," reminding the reader that the researcher had some special purpose other than describing the attitudes of the total population. Such surveys, whatever they are called, have some advantages, as indicated in Table 2.1. Most importantly, they are the least expensive type of survey to conduct. Many scholars who carry out such surveys are graduate students conducting their dissertation research (as Greenstein was, back in 1958, when his New Haven study was conducted). They need free time to conduct their surveys, but little other support. Once the researcher gains access to schools (and nearly all such surveys sample children in schools), the costs are limited mainly to printing the questionnaire. Given the low cost, the scholar can often collect a large number of cases—an advantage that may prove useful when analyzing the data.

Table 2.1 Advantages and Disadvantages of Three Basic Survey Methods

Type of survey	Advantages	Disadvantages
Nonrepresentative survey (also called purposive survey)	1. Least expensive. 2. Can collect large number of cases at relatively small cost. 3. Subsidiary advantage (but not inherent in method): social scientists can utilize questions that reflect their theoretical interests. 4. Subsidiary advantage (but not inherent in method): small subcultural groups or other special populations can be studied.	1. Cannot generalize from survey to make inferences about distribution of attitudes in total population.
Quota sample	1. Relatively inexpensive. 2. Can collect relatively large number of cases at relatively small cost. 3. Can conduct surveys at many points in time. 4. Can make loose statements about way sample represents overall population.	1. Cannot use probability theory to estimate likelihood that results obtained represent population. 2. May have built-in biases that lead to oversampling some segments of population. 3. Subsidiary disadvantage (but not inherent in method): commercial polling agencies that employ quota samples seldom ask large number of questions.
Probability sample	1. Can use probability theory to estimate likelihood that sample represents overall population. 2. Subsidiary advantage (but not inherent in method): academic survey agencies that use probability samples usually ask large number of questions.	1. Very expensive. 2. Can collect relatively small number of cases. 3. Cannot conduct frequent surveys.

By using nonrepresentative surveys, scholars with little financial support have the opportunity to develop new questions and to build new measures of political attitudes that reflect their theoretical interests. Not all scholars develop new questions, and new questions may yield uninteresting results. But the opportunity for creative research exists. Moreover, nonrepresentative surveys may yield an opportunity to study subcultural groups that are difficult to study through national quota or probability samples. Studies of blacks, Hispanics, and Appalachian residents have utilized special-purpose surveys to study a large number of minority-group children, whereas national samples usually yield fewer than 200 blacks and too few members of other minority groups to permit meaningful analyses. Other special populations, such as the elderly, can be studied through special-purpose surveys. These latter advantages, however, are not directly inherent in the technique. In principle, one could use a national probability sample to develop better measures, and a national-level sample could be designed to sample minority groups. However, it takes far greater resources to use national-level probability samples for such ends.

Nonrepresentative surveys have one main disadvantage. They cannot be used to make inferences about the distribution of attitudes or behaviors in the total population. For example, back in 1958, Greenstein found that 71% of his New Haven school children thought that President Eisenhower was doing a "very good" job. But we have no way of knowing what percentage of all American school children thought Eisenhower was doing a good job.

Nonrepresentative surveys can be a valuable source of information and may be especially valuable for generating hypotheses about the way political attitudes develop. However, three cautions are in order when reading the results of nonrepresentative surveys.

1. The reader should always remember that the researcher does not have a representative sample. Usually, authors remind the readers of this fact, but there is a tendency, as authors proceed, to forget this basic limitation. Often, authors make inappropriate statements about their results—statements that would be appropriate only if they actually had a representative sample.

2. The reader should give little credence to the distribution of responses. For example, if you read that 75% of the elementary school children surveyed in Jackson, Michigan, think President Reagan can be trusted, you should pay little attention to this figure. The result might be quite different in Detroit, Grand Rapids, or in Jackson, Mississippi. Indeed, unless the author had a representative sample of students in Jackson, Michigan, the results may not represent the attitudes of the student population of Jackson itself.

3. The reader should focus mainly on the relationships among variables within the nonrepresentative survey. For example, if a researcher reports that children who think President Reagan can be trusted are more likely to feel that politicians will listen to their parents' complaints, the researcher is pre-

senting a relationship that may provide clues about the way feelings of political effectiveness develop. By focusing on the relationship among variables within the study, the author can point to hypotheses that future scholars may test.

There are entire academic disciplines, such as psychology, that rely almost exclusively on studies of nonrepresentative populations. The cumulative knowledge yielded by theoretically grounded studies of nonrepresentative populations has led to considerable understanding about the way attitudes develop. It would be foolish for political scientists to disregard the cumulative knowledge that nonrepresentative surveys of preadult populations can yield. But such results must always be regarded with caution.

Quota sample

Surveys that use quota techniques have four major advantages. First, while they are not nearly as inexpensive as nonrepresentative surveys, they are relatively inexpensive compared with the probability-sampling techniques used by the SRC. Even though current Gallup polls employ some probability procedures, they are still relatively inexpensive, although the Gallup organization does not reveal its actual costs of conducting a national sample.

The low cost of a Gallup survey leads to a second major advantage, for this means that Gallup has collected a very large number of interviews. Nationwide Gallup surveys are conducted about twice a month. By pooling the results of several Gallup surveys, a scholar can analyze a large number of cases. This can be a major advantage in studying subgroups of the population. For example, the average Gallup survey interviews about 165 nonwhites, and, by pooling the results of ten such surveys, one may have a sample of close to 1500 blacks. The average Gallup survey samples about 35 Jews, but, by pooling together the results of several surveys, even such a small group as Jews could be studied. Gallup polls have been successfully employed to study age-group differences, for, by pooling the results of several studies, scholars can examine a large number of cases within each age group.

The frequency with which Gallup surveys are conducted can also provide a third advantage for scholars who are studying attitude change over time. For example, probability studies conducted by the Michigan SRC demonstrate that feelings of party identification declined dramatically between the fall of 1964 and late 1966 (Table 7.2, Figure 7.4). In attempting to identify more precisely when this decline began, Converse turned to Gallup data (1976, p. 72). The frequency of Gallup surveys has also been a major asset for scholars studying changes in presidential "popularity," for, since 1938, Gallup has consistently asked questions measuring public approval of the president's performance.[3]

[3]For examples of research that utilizes the Gallup surveys to study presidential "popularity," see Brody and Page (1975), Kenski (1977), Kernell (1978), Monroe (1979), Mueller (1973), and Stimson (1976).

A fourth advantage of Gallup surveys is that they allow us to make generalizations about the likelihood that the results represent the total adult population. A *Gallup Report,* for example, provides a table for estimating the extent to which a reported percentage is likely to differ from the total population, as well as a table for estimating the likelihood that the difference between two subgroups within the sample are likely to have occurred by chance.

Samples that employ quota techniques have two inherent disadvantages. Technically, we cannot use standard-probability theory to estimate the likelihood that the results represent the overall population. In addition, because interviewers still have limited discretion in selecting households to be sampled, there may be hidden biases. It is generally argued that allowing the interviewer discretion leads to a tendency to oversample persons who are better-off economically. Gallup surveys do not employ callbacks to interview persons who are not at home. This may introduce biases in the opposite direction, by leading to oversampling women, the elderly, and persons with low levels of education.

These two disadvantages, by themselves, do not account for the relatively infrequent use of Gallup data in analyzing political attitudes. The main disadvantage of most commercial surveys is not directly inherent in their sampling methods. In practice, most of these surveys ask too few questions to allow us to explain how political attitudes develop. Gallup, Roper, and Harris polls often ask politically relevant questions, but they seldom ask the extensive battery of questions necessary to permit careful analysis of the way attitudes are interrelated.

These polling agencies sometimes administer a lengthy series of questions. But it is easy to see why they usually do not. Gallup, Harris, and Roper conduct polls largely for commercial purposes. Their political questions are used to report results in newspaper articles, and such reports do not involve detailed analyses of data. Such stories, or the results Gallup publishes in the *Gallup Report,* usually present fairly simple demographic breakdowns of the responses to single questions. The authors of these reports want to present recent results, usually only a few weeks old, and do not have time to engage in detailed analyses. More detailed analyses—especially of Gallup and Harris data—have been used by scholars in secondary analyses, often with insightful results. But the limitations of the data have made these surveys less important for political scientists than the academic surveys conducted by the SRC and NORC.

Probability sample

In principle, the main advantage of probability samples is that they allow one to employ probability theory to estimate the likelihood that results represent the population being studied. Kish has provided a useful table that allows us to evaluate the chance that a given SRC result represents the total

Table 2.2 Allowance for Sampling Error of a Percentage by Size of Sample or Subsample for Stratified Probability Samples Conducted by Survey Research Center

Reported percentage near:	Number of interviews					
	2000	1000	700	500	300	100
5	1	2	2	3	4	
10	2	3	3	4	5	8
20	2	4	4	5	6	11
30	3	4	5	6	7	13
50	3	4	5	6	8	14
70	3	4	5	6	7	13
80	2	4	4	5	6	11
90	2	3	3	4	5	8
95	1	2	2	3	4	

Note: The chances are 95 in 100 that the actual value for the population lies within a range of the reported percentage plus or minus this percentage point.
Source: Adapted from Kish (1965, p. 576). Used with permission of publisher.

noninstitutionalized U.S. adult population. Because we rely so heavily on SRC data, I have reproduced his estimates in a somewhat modified form in Table 2.2 (Kish, 1965). Kish presents the sampling error for SRC samples and for subgroups within SRC samples. If sampling error is 3%, this means that the survey results are very likely (95 chances in a 100) to be within ±3% of the distribution of responses if the entire noninstitutionalized U.S. adult population had been interviewed.

Let us take two concrete examples. In 1978, 54% of the 2304 persons interviewed said that "hardly any" or "not many" government officials were crooked; in 1980, 50% of the 1614 persons interviewed gave this response. We can say that, if the entire noninstitutionalized adult population of the United States had been interviewed in 1978, somewhere between 51% and 57% of the population would have provided this response; in 1980, somewhere between 47% and 53% would. The possibility for sampling error grows as the size of the sample decreases or when we look at subsets of the population. For example, in 1978, 45% of the 234 blacks interviewed said hardly any or not many government officials were crooked; in 1980, 48% of 187 blacks gave this response (see Table 13.2 for responses by race). As the number of blacks is much smaller than the total sample, sampling error rises to about 10%. We can say with confidence that, if all noninstitutionalized blacks had been surveyed in 1978, somewhere between 35% and 55% would have provided this response; while in 1980, the result would have been between 38% and 58%.

As Table 2.2 shows, increasing the size of the sample can reduce sampling error. However, one must quadruple the sample to cut sampling error in half. It should also be noted that the range of sampling error is partly a function of the distribution of the response. Percentages that yield close to a 50–50 division have a wider range of probable sampling error than responses that are less evenly distributed.

Kish has also presented calculations that allow us to determine whether a percentage difference between two subgroups within an SRC sample is likely to result from sampling error. I have reproduced his estimates in Table 2.3.[4] Again, let us turn to our two concrete examples. In the 1978 sample, 56% of the 2016 whites said that hardly any or not many government officials were crooked; in 1980, 50% of the 1406 whites did. In 1978, therefore, blacks were 11 percentage points less trusting on this question than whites were; in 1980, they were only 2 percentage points less trusting. According to Kish's estimates, when we compare percentages in this range and compare one subgroup of 2000 respondents with another of 200 respondents, a difference of 9 percentage points is needed for us to be reasonably confident that there is a real difference between the groups. As the difference in the 1978 sample is greater than this, we can be reasonably confident that whites were more likely to think government officials were honest than blacks were. In 1980, however, differences between whites and blacks could easily have occurred by chance.

The estimates in Table 2.3 can also be used to estimate the likelihood that differences between surveys occurred by chance—as long as the same sampling procedures were used for both surveys. For most surveys, a difference of 4 percentage points is sufficient. As whites make up about 90% of the respondents, a 4-point difference is sufficient when comparing white subsamples. But as there are about 200 blacks in most SRC samples, a difference of 12 percentage points is necessary before we can be reasonably confident that differences between two subsamples did not occur by chance. Thus, we can be reasonably confident that the drop of 4 percentage points in trust on the "crooked" question reflects a real drop in trust among the electorate, and we can be somewhat more confident that the 6-point drop among whites reflects real change. However, the 3-point rise in trust among blacks could easily have resulted from sampling error.

Our comparisons over time are usually based on many surveys. For example, the question about government officials' honesty has been asked in nine separate SRC surveys. In surveys conducted in 1958, 1964, and 1968, seven

[4]For most comparisons, the lower of the two percentages is usually adequate. But for comparisons involving blacks, it may be better to use the higher of the two percentages, since blacks are more geographically clustered. I am grateful to Leslie Kish for this insight (personal communication, July 10, 1981).

Table 2.3 Estimated Sampling Error for Differences Between Two Percentages for Stratified Probability Samples Conducted by Survey Research Center

Part A For Percentages from 35 to 65

Number of interviews	2000	1000	700	500	400	300	200	100
2000	3.2–4.0	3.9–4.9	4.4–5.5	5.0–6.2	5.5–6.9	6.2–7.8	7.4–9.2	10–12
1000		4.5–5.6	4.9–6.1	5.5–6.9	5.9–7.4	6.6–8.3	7.7–9.6	10–13
700			5.3–6.6	5.9–7.4	6.3–7.9	6.9–8.6	8.0–10	11–13
500				6.3–7.9	6.7–8.4	7.3–9.1	8.4–10	11–13
400					7.1–8.9	7.6–9.5	8.7–11	11–14
300						8.2–10	9.1–11	12–14
200							10–12	12–15
100								14–17

Part B For Percentages Around 20 and 80[a]

Number of interviews	2000	1000	700	500	400	300	200	100
2000	2.5–3.1	3.1–3.9	3.5–4.4	4.0–5.0	4.4–5.5	5.0–6.2	5.9–7.4	8.2–9.8
1000		3.6–4.5	3.9–4.9	4.4–5.5	4.7–5.9	5.3–6.6	6.2–7.8	8.4–10
700			4.3–5.4	4.7–5.9	5.0–6.2	5.5–6.9	6.4–8.0	8.6–10
500				5.1–6.4	5.4–6.8	5.8–7.2	6.7–8.4	8.8–11
400					5.7–7.1	6.1–7.6	6.9–8.6	9.0–11
300						6.5–8.1	7.3–9.1	9.2–11
200							8.0–10	9.8–12
100								11–14

Note: The values are the differences between two subgroups in a sample (or subgroups in two different samples) necessary for considering the difference between the two subgroups to be significant. Significance is defined here by Kish as results that are two standard errors apart. For most comparisons in this book, the lower of the two percentages is sufficient to conclude that differences between groups are significant. For comparisons involving blacks, it may be safer to use the higher percentage.

[a]For differences around 10% or around 90% the percentage difference for a "significant" difference between two subgroups is smaller. For percentages near 5% or 95%, the percentage difference needed for a "significant" difference is smaller still. See Kish (1965, p. 580) for details.

Source: Kish (1965, p. 580). This table appeared earlier in Freedman, Whelpton, and Campbell (1959, p. 457). Reprinted with permission of publishers.

out of ten blacks said that hardly any or not many government officials were crooked; while in surveys conducted in 1970, 1972, 1974, 1976, 1978, and 1980, less than half gave this reply (Table 13.2). With these many comparisons, and given the extent of the differences, it is extremely unlikely that the decline in trust among blacks could have resulted from sampling error.

The ability to use probability theory to estimate the likelihood that observed results occurred by chance is a major asset, but it does not account for the extensive use of multistage probability surveys in political science research. The main advantage of such surveys is not directly inherent in the technique. Surveys conducted by academic survey agencies usually contain far more questions than those conducted by commercial polling agencies. Since each person interviewed is asked a large number of questions, political scientists are better able to answer questions about why people behave as they do, how political attitudes develop, as well as the conditions under which attitudes relate to behavior.

It is easy to see why researchers who use probability samples usually ask a large number of questions. They have different goals from those of researchers who conduct commercial polls and often spend years analyzing their results before publishing them. They have the time to engage in the extensive analyses that a large number of questions permits. Asking a large number of questions is partly a function of the sampling procedures. Given the cost of locating the specific "designated respondent" selected through a multistage probability sample, the sunk costs of the interview are great even before the first question is asked. Given these sunk costs, the additional costs of a lengthy interview are warranted. Indeed, the SRC interview during a presidential election survey may last over an hour, and each respondent may be asked several hundred questions before and after the election.

Probability samples have several limitations, however. For one, they are very expensive to conduct. SRC election surveys now average between $130 and $170 per interview (including costs of sampling, interviewing, and coding).

These costs lead to two additional limitations. First, only a relatively small number of interviews can be conducted. This can lead to serious problems in studying subgroups of the population. For example, a sample of 1500 respondents usually contains only 150 blacks. One can still study blacks, but it is very difficult to examine subgroups within the black population. For example, it becomes highly problematic to compare young blacks with older blacks, because the number of cases within each subset is too small to allow for reliable estimates. One can partly solve this problem by deliberately oversampling subgroups of the electorate. For example, in 1964, 1968, and 1970, the SRC election surveys oversampled blacks, but they have never oversampled other minority groups. On the other hand, the large number of Gallup surveys would allow analysts to pool a large number of quota samples conducted within a given year and thus to examine the attitudes of relatively small groups of the American population.[5]

Lastly, and also following from the high costs, politically relevant SRC surveys are conducted infrequently, usually every other year. This limitation can impose severe problems in studying trends. For example, the SRC questions measuring party identification were used in a national sample in the fall of 1964, but were not used again until late 1966. We know that the party loyalties of the American electorate fell markedly during this period, but the SRC national probability samples do not allow us to identify when this decline began. In attempting to answer this question, Converse turned to Gallup surveys, for, although they did not ask the best possible questions about party loyalties, they were conducted at least once a month during this period.

This limitation poses a more severe problem in studying political trust. We know from SRC surveys that political trust declined greatly between late 1972 and late 1974, presumably because of the impact of Watergate. But we cannot pinpoint when this sharp decline began. Possibly, trust reached its nadir in August of 1974, just before Nixon resigned, rose after his resignation, and declined again after he was pardoned by Ford. Knowledge about such short-term fluctuations might prove valuable in assessing the meaning of the political-trust questions. In this case, however, no quota samples exist to aid us, since the trust questions were not employed by commercial polling agencies, which conduct more frequent surveys.

Conclusions

As we saw in this chapter, three basic survey techniques can be used to study political attitudes. Nonrepresentative surveys can be employed to study the way attitudes develop, but they cannot be used to make generalizations about the distribution of attitudes among the electorate. Quota techniques can be used to gain representative samples of the electorate and to describe loosely the distribution of attitudes. However, surveys conducted by commercial polling agencies generally are not very helpful in explaining *why* people behave as they do and *how* political attitudes develop.

The probability surveys conducted by academic survey agencies clearly provide the best data to study attitude formation and change, and this book relies heavily on studies conducted by the Survey Research Center of the University of Michigan. We examined the SRC sampling procedures and explained how to judge the likelihood that the results obtained with a given

[5]In the 1980 census, 6.4% of the population report that they are of Spanish origins (U.S. Bureau of the Census, 1981a). Because of the unsystematic way information about ethnic origins has been collected, national surveys of the electorate (whether based on probability or quota sampling) provide little information about political attitude change among Chicanos or other Hispanic groups (see Glenn and Frisbie, 1977, p. 97, for a discussion).

survey are likely to represent the electorate as a whole. Unfortunately, the SRC procedures are very expensive. These costs limit the number of persons who can be interviewed and prevent the SRC from conducting frequent politically relevant surveys.

On balance, students of political attitudes must turn to whatever evidence they can to understand the way political attitudes form and change. Despite their limitations, we cannot afford to ignore the large number of nonrepresentative surveys of American preadults. Likewise, we must draw on the evidence from quota samples when they provide useful information—especially information about change. And, of course, we rely on probability samples of the American electorate.

[CHAPTER 3]

The Study of Political Attitudes

This book is concerned primarily with the way political attitudes develop and the way they change. There are many definitions of *attitude* (Oskamp, 1977, pp. 7–11), but Allport has advanced a particularly useful, comprehensive definition. According to Allport, an attitude is "a mental and neural state of readiness, organized through experience, exerting a directive or dynamic influence upon the individual's response to all objects and situations with which it is related" (1935, p. 810). Generally, an attitude is viewed as a fairly stable mental state, not highly changeable. The term *opinion* is sometimes used interchangeably with *attitude,* but some scholars argue that opinions are narrower in scope than are attitudes and that opinions are less emotion-laden.

An attitude is not a behavior. The attitudes we study in this book—especially feelings of party identification and feelings of political effectiveness—do appear to influence behavior. For example, persons with strong party loyalties are likely to behave differently than weak partisans when both are confronted with similar political conditions. Likewise, persons who feel politically effective tend to behave differently than those who feel politically powerless.

Why do we focus mainly on political attitudes, and not directly on behavior? The main reason is that a primary goal of this book is to examine change throughout the life cycle. When we ask how attitudes are learned, we can meaningfully compare the extent to which preadults have the same political attitudes as their parents. But because preadults have virtually no opportunity to participate in politics, we cannot compare their political behavior with that of their parents. Once we try to study behaviors, we are forced to abandon our attempt to track change throughout the life cycle. We will, however, discuss the way in which attitude change can contribute to behavioral change, and we will demonstrate that one of the major changes in postwar American politics—the decline of electoral participation—may have resulted largely from attitude change among the electorate. Before turning to the study of attitudes, however, we must first see how they are measured and how data measuring political attitudes can be presented.

Types of Questions

The most fundamental distinction is between *open-ended questions,* in which the person being interviewed provides his or her own responses, and *closed-ended questions,* in which responses are prestructured. The questions used by the University of Michigan Survey Research Center to measure likes and dislikes about the political parties and presidential candidates (p. 261) provide an excellent example of open-ended questions. For example, respondents are asked, "Is there anything in particular that you *like* about the Democratic party? [If yes:] What is that?" Such questions (along with the seven others in this series) provide an extensive opportunity for respondents to express their partisan attitudes at length.

Open-ended questions have several advantages. By avoiding a structured response, there is less danger that respondents will answer even if they have no real attitudes. By examining verbatim replies to such open-ended questions, we may gain unanticipated insights about the political concerns of the electorate. Moreover, reading the verbatim responses conveys some of the flavor of political life that is lost in statistical analyses of survey-research data.

The problem with such open-ended questions is that, once the answers are recorded, the researcher has more information than he or she can digest. After all, a national sample of the electorate yields some 1500 sets of responses. (Given that there are eight questions in this particular series, the analyst has verbatim responses to 12,000 questions.) To handle this mountain of words, one must somehow reduce them to a simpler, coded format, which reduces the responses into a set of categories that can be punched onto computer cards. For example, in 1952, when this series of questions was first used, the SRC used some 900 codes to translate the open-ended responses into a form that could be stored on data cards.

The cost of coding these open-ended questions is immense. So many coding decisions are necessary, many of which involve subtle judgments by coders, that some error is introduced, and procedures to minimize coding error create additional expense. Moreover, the data are coded into so many categories that the results are difficult to analyze. Often, the data are analyzed in such a simple way that the complex, expensive coding procedures seem to have been unnecessary. For example, several scholars, including the SRC authors, have merely added up the number of positive and negative responses for each political party to create a measure of "partisan attitudes" (e.g., Campbell et al., 1960, pp. 68–77; Trilling, 1976, pp. 19–42). Even though there has been a great interest in these open-ended questions and even though they have been asked for eight presidential election surveys, few studies have analyzed the verbatim responses to the questions (see pp. 273–276 for a discussion).

Open-ended questions can play an important role in exploratory studies of a small number of respondents. The use of open-ended questions by Smith, Bruner, and White (1956) and by Lane (1962, 1969) demonstrate the value of this strategy. (The three books cited used 10, 15, and 24 respondents, respectively.) Open-ended questions may prove valuable for studying preadults, as it is important to avoid forcing children to reply to questions that may have no meaning to them (Greenstein, 1975; Greenstein and Tarrow, 1970). But most studies of the political attitudes of the mass electorate, as well as most studies of preadults, have relied primarily on closed-ended questions, which allow only for prestructured responses.

Examples of the three basic types of closed-ended questions are provided in Table 15.1, where we examine the questions used to measure issue consistency. The questions that measure attitudes toward the government's role in economic welfare provide an excellent example. The first format presents a statement and asks respondents whether they agree or disagree.[1] This format is used to measure feelings of political efficacy (pp. 135–136), usually using a simple agree–disagree format.

Social scientists now recognize that the agree–disagree format is prone to error. Some respondents tend to agree with most statements (an "acquiescence response"), so analysts should be careful to test for the possibility that findings result from such acquiescence. Replies to such questions may require too little attention on the part of the respondent, since it is easy merely to state the word "agree" or "disagree." This might introduce additional error. Valuable measures have been developed using these questions, but they should be used today only to maintain comparability with earlier surveys that employed this format.

The second format presented in Table 15.1 may be termed a *forced-choice question*. Two positions on the issue are presented, and the respondent is asked to choose between them. Even though such questions may force some respondents to choose between alternatives they dislike, responses to such questions should yield a more accurate measure of political attitudes. The danger of acquiescent responses is eliminated, and, since respondents must give a more extensive verbal reply, they may consider their answers more carefully. Anal-

[1]For this particular question, using a format developed by Likert (1932), respondents are asked whether they strongly agree, agree, are not sure, disagree, or strongly disagree; but many analyses of such questions ignore the distinction between "strong" agreement and agreement, and between "strong" disagreement and disagreement.

yses by political scientists suggest that the forced-choice format may lead to more accurate measurement of political attitudes than does the agree–disagree format (Bishop, Oldendick, and Tuchfarber, 1978; Sullivan, Piereson, and Marcus, 1978).

The questions used in this book to measure party identification and feelings of political trust generally provide respondents with three alternative responses. Respondents are asked whether they are Republicans, Democrats, or Independents, and whether they trust the government "just about always," "most of the time," or only "some of the time." Other questions, such as the follow-up questions on party identification, as well as two of the political-trust questions, provide two basic replies. Such questions should generally be less prone to response error than are the efficacy questions that use the agree–disagree format.

Since 1970, the SRC–CPS has used many questions that locate each respondent in an *issue space* for a series of policy questions. For example, with the economic-welfare question (see the third column of Table 15.1), the respondent selects a score of 1 if he or she thinks that "the government in Washington should see to it that every person has a job and a good standard of living" and a 7 if he or she thinks "the government should just let each person get ahead on his own." Intermediate replies are also possible. In addition to placing themselves on the issue scale, respondents are asked to say where major candidates and parties stand on each issue. These measures have some useful statistical properties, for we can compare each respondent's position on each issue with his or her perception of where candidates and parties stand (Aldrich and McKelvey, 1977). The relative amount of error introduced by the issue-space format is difficult to determine, but it may lead to less accurate responses than does the forced-choice format (Bishop, Oldendick and Tuchfarber, 1978).

These issue-space questions play a major role in Arthur Miller's analysis of the decline of political trust, which we discuss at length in Chapter 11. They have also been used in the debate on issue consistency, in the analysis of the stability of issue preferences, and in the study of issue voting—all of which are discussed in Chapter 15.

The three types of questions displayed in Table 15.1 do not exhaust the types of closed-ended questions used by political scientists. The Survey Research Center, for example, uses *thermometer rating* to measure feelings toward political candidates and social groups. Survey researchers sometimes use *semantic-differential questions,* in which respondents rate individuals or groups according to a wide range of value-laden words. However, the research we summarize and present has made little use of either of these two techniques.

Regardless of which type of closed-ended format is employed, some respondents will choose a response only because they feel socially pressured to reply. Closed-ended questions are unlikely to pick up nuances that may be recorded in the answers to open-ended questions. But the vast majority of questions employed by survey-research agencies are closed-ended, because they are easy and inexpensive to code. Moreover, since it is easy to analyze the responses to these questions, they have played a major role in the analysis of political attitudes. They are especially important in analyzing change over time, because so many surveys must be analyzed that the cost of relying on open-ended questions tends to become prohibitive.

Indices and Scales

Even the best questions used by survey researchers entail a lot of error. Respondents may misunderstand the question or answer carelessly, or their answers may be misunderstood by the interviewer. Because of the possibility of error, it is usually advisable not to rely on responses to a single attitude question alone, but to combine responses to form cumulative measures. Especially when a large number of questions is used to form a measure, some of the error in any single question may be canceled out by error in measuring other questions. Moreover, combining the responses to several questions allows the analyst to present the data in a more manageable way. Rather than presenting results for a large number of separate questions, the analyst can present results for a single measure that combines the responses to these questions.

The responses to several attitude questions should not be combined to form a single measure unless those questions measure the same basic attitude. Thus, it may be useful to combine the results from the five questions used to measure political trust (p. 194), because they all measure some aspect of political trust. But it would not make any sense to combine the responses to these questions with questions measuring attitudes toward political parties.

How do we know whether any given set of questions does, in fact, measure the same basic attitude? Merely reading the questions to decide what they measure is inadequate. Social scientists have developed a variety of procedures to test whether a given set of questions does in fact measure the same basic attitude dimension, although there is considerable controversy about which procedures are the most appropriate.

Assuming that a given set of questions can be combined meaningfully to form a single measure, two basic procedures can be used. Throughout this book, I rely mainly on simple additive indices. Most of my measures simply sum up the responses to a series of separate questions. For example, in developing the political-trust index, I examined the answers of each respondent to each of the separate political-trust questions. A score was assigned to each answer, and the respondent's score on the index was the sum of the values assigned to the responses to each of the separate questions (see the appendix).

An alternative scoring procedure combines responses to a larger number of questions on the basis of the pattern of responses to these questions. The main example of such a measure in this book is Stouffer's (1955) scale of "willingness to tolerate nonconformists" (see Table 14.1 for a description of this measure). In Stouffer's measure, 15 questions about civil liberties were divided into five groups, each composed of 3 questions. Respondents who were willing to grant civil liberties for 2 of the first 3 questions were scored "most tolerant of all." Given the nature of Stouffer's measure, respondents who were tolerant on 2 of these 3 questions were very likely to be tolerant on the remaining 12 questions. Stouffer labeled his measure a "scale" because the responses to the 15 questions he used met specific criteria of association with one another.

Political scientists seldom clearly distinguish between the terms *index* and *scale,* and there is disagreement about what such a distinction should be. I call most of my own measures "indices," to underscore the simple additive procedures I used to create them. When discussing the work of other scholars, I employ their terminology. The important point to remember is that both indices and scales combine the responses to two or more questions and that the responses to different questions should be combined only if the questions do in fact measure the same basic attitude.

Reliability and Validity

With any form of measurement, there is the danger of error. In measuring political attitudes, we face two separate problems: Are the measures reliable? Are the measures valid?

Generally, we say that an attitude is *reliable* if it evokes consistent answers across repeated measurements. If a person answers a question in one way in one interview, he or she should, if the results are reliable, answer the question the same way if reinterviewed shortly thereafter. Many factors can cause low measurement reliability. The respondent may misunderstand the question, the interviewer may misunderstand the response, the respondent may be untruthful, or there may be clerical error in coding the respondent's reply. In fact, most attitude measures register considerable change even when they are repeated for the same individual over a brief time period. But such change does not necessarily demonstrate that the measures are unreliable. Some of the change may result from actual changes of political attitudes, while some results from unreliable measurement. It is difficult to determine the extent to which such change results from actual attitude change and the extent to which it results from measurement error. It seems reasonable to conclude, however, that most political attitudes have a considerable level of unreliability.

The presence of measurement unreliability complicates any analysis of attitude change among individuals. But measurement unreliability does not prevent us from comparing different subsets of the electorate. For example, we often compare young adults with their elders. Many studies have found that young Americans have much weaker party loyalties than older Americans have. Let us suppose that we have unreliably measured the partisan loyalties of some young adults and of some older Americans. We would still have no reason for supposing that we had systematically underestimated the partisan loyalties of young adults while systematically overestimating the partisan loyalties of older Americans. We might still have a fairly good estimate of the party loyalties of each age group, even though some individuals within each group may have provided unreliable answers. Thus, we could still conclude that the attitudinal differences between young Americans and their elders were real.

Generally speaking, we say a measure is *valid* if it actually measures the concept that the researcher claims to be measuring. Some scholars would argue that a measure cannot be valid unless it is reliable. But it may be more useful to think about reliability and validity separately (Shively, 1974, p. 54). Regardless of the reliability of a measure, Shively argues, we can claim it is valid if it mirrors the concept it is supposed to be measuring. For example, whatever error there may be in measuring political trust, do the questions asked measure "support" for the political system in the way some researchers claim?

In discussing the validity of their attitude measures, political scientists often rely mainly on a careful reading of what the attitude questions appear to be asking. They merely ask what the questions, on their face, appear to be measuring. This procedure tests the *face validity* of a measure. A more useful test, usually called a test of *construct validity,* may be conducted by determining whether persons with different scores on a given attitude measure respond in the hypothesized way to other questions that we predict should be related to a given attitude. For example, are people who score high on the political-trust index more supportive of the American form of government than respondents who score as politically cynical? Are people who score as politically trusting more likely to feel that politicians respond to popular demands? The debate over the meaning of political trust between Arthur Miller and Jack Citrin, discussed in Chapter 11, provides an excellent example of the problems of determining the validity of a measure.[2]

Data Presentation

Throughout this book, we systematically present the results of surveys of American political attitudes. This leads to an examination of many tables, including many which show attitude change over time. These tables rely mainly on percentages. However, we will often be forced to present the data in a condensed form that does not present the full distribution of responses.

[2]Questions about construct validity may bring us full circle to questions of reliability. If a concept is not reliably measured, we cannot expect persons with differing scores to respond in different ways to other attitude questions or to questions about their behavior.

Let us take, for example, a table on political trust presented in Chapter 13. Table 13.2 compares the responses of whites and of blacks to five separate political-trust questions, used between 1958 and 1980. In this single table, 46 separate comparisons between whites and blacks are presented.

Here we examine the responses of whites and of blacks to a question that asks whether the government in Washington can be trusted to do what is right "just about always," "most of the time," or "only some of the time," and we look at the responses for a single year, 1972. Table 3.1 shows three ways of presenting these results. Part A shows the actual distribution of responses of whites and of blacks to this basic political-trust question. It is from such basic distributions of responses that percentage tables are constructed and from which other statistical calculations are carried out.

To better compare the responses of the two races, we can contrast the percentage of blacks and of whites who give each response. Part B shows the ideal way to display such comparisons. The full array of percentages for each race is presented, and the total percentage is presented to help the reader see how the raw numbers in Part A have been transformed into percentages. Moreover, the total number of whites and of blacks is presented at the bottom of each column. This total number helps the reader interpret the table, for the likelihood that racial differences resulted from chance is largely a function of the total number of whites and of blacks sampled. (One can refer to Table 2.3 and see that even a 9% difference is unlikely to occur by chance when comparing groups of this size.) Moreover, the numbers at the bottom of each column allow the reader to come fairly close to reconstructing the actual distribution of responses to this question through multiplication. This allows the reader to conduct other statistical analyses that he or she deems appropriate.

Unfortunately, tables that provide the full array of results consume too much space. The actual Table 13.2 presents 46 racial comparisons. For these many comparisons, we must condense the data presentation into the format of Part C. Here we show only the percentage of whites and of blacks that said the government can be trusted to do what is right just about always or most of the time. How much information have we lost by condensing the data in this way?

First, we no longer see the full range of responses. The distinction between trusting the government just about always and trusting it most of the time is lost, and we no longer see the 1% that gratuitously answered "none of the time." "Don't know" responses have, in effect, been combined with the distrusting responses.[3] However, the loss of information is not very costly, since

[3]One could, however, exclude respondents who answer "don't know" from the table. This would be preferable if there were a large number of "don't know" responses, especially if the groups being compared differ substantially in their percentage of "don't know" replies. Unfortunately, researchers sometimes fail to indicate how they have classified "don't know" and other ambiguous responses.

Table 3.1 Whether Respondent Trusts Government in Washington to Do What Is Right, by Race: 1972

Part A Distribution of Respondents on Political-Trust Question

Extent to which respondent says government in Washington can be trusted	White	Black
Just about always	112	6
Most of the time	1014	63
Some of the time	853	142
None of the time	11	2
Don't know	38	8
Total	2028	221

Part B Whether Respondents Trust Government in Washington to Do What Is Right

Extent to which respondent says government in Washington can be trusted	White	Black
Just about always	6%	3%
Most of the time	50	29
Some of the time	42	64
None of the time	1	1
Don't know	2	4
Total %	101%	101%
Total *N*	(2028)	(221)

Part C Percentage That Trust Government in Washington to Do What Is Right Just About Always or Most of the Time

White	Black
56%	31%

there were few racial differences in the "just about always," "none of the time," or "don't know" categories. In some cases, valuable information would be lost through such a condensing procedure, so this procedure should not be used when it yields misleading results.

We also lose some information in the Part C format by not totaling the results to 100%. This is not a serious problem if the reader understands how such tables are read. When the table says that 56% of the whites said the government could be trusted most or all of the time, it also tells us that 44%

(100% − 56%) did not give this response. If 31% of the blacks said the government could be trusted most or all of the time, we know that 69% (100% − 31%) did not give this answer. In most cases, the remaining responses were "only some of the time," although some were "none of the time" and "don't know."

Finally, the condensed table format does not show the total number of cases on which the percentages are based. This poses a problem for readers who wish to reconstruct the actual numbers in order to conduct additional analyses. Throughout this book, wherever I use the condensed table format, I always provide information that allows readers to at least approximate the numbers on which percentages are based. In some cases, I show the total number of cases on which percentages are based in parentheses after the percentage.

Occasionally, we examine the way individuals change their political attitudes over time by using *panel studies,* in which the same individuals are interviewed more than once. There are several ways to present the results of such surveys; a brief example will explain how they are reported throughout this book.

Let us again take an example from the study of political trust. In Table 3.2, we examine the way feelings of political trust changed among white Americans between 1972 and 1976. The table examines over 1100 respondents who were surveyed in both these years, and shows their scores on a five-item political-trust index (see the appendix for a description of this measure). Part A shows the actual distribution of responses in the various political-trust categories. As we have divided respondents into three basic categories and as we have two data points, there are nine possible combinations. As we can see, there are some respondents in each of the nine cells. For example, 460 respondents scored low on political trust in both 1972 and 1976, 131 scored medium in both years, while only 66 scored high in both surveys.

There are two basic ways that the numbers in Part A can be transformed into percentages. One format is a complete turnover table, which shows the percentage of respondents in each of the nine cells possible. Part B presents the results of this format. It clearly shows that the most frequent result was to score low on political trust in 1972 and to remain low in 1976. This format has one major advantage: it clearly shows the percentage of respondents who had similar levels of trust in both surveys.[4] Reading across the diagonal of Part B—from the top left-hand cell, through the middle cell, to the bottom right-hand cell—we can quickly see that nearly 57% of the total sample had similar political-trust scores in both surveys. The table also clearly shows that only a small percentage of the total sample moved from a high score to a low score and that even fewer moved from a low score to a high score.

[4] I say similar, not identical, because the low, medium, and high, categories are based on collapsing a measure that actually ranges from 0 to 10. The statistical calculations reported in Chapter 13 are based on the full distribution of responses.

Table 3.2 Political Trust of Whites in 1976, by Political Trust in 1972

Part A Distribution of Political-Trust Scores

		1972		
		Low	Medium	High
	Low	460	221	54
1976	Medium	96	131	85
	High	9	33	66
Total N = 1155				

Part B Percentage Distribution of Political-Trust Scores

		1972		
		Low	Medium	High
	Low	39.8%	19.1%	4.7%
1976	Medium	8.3	11.3	7.4
	High	0.8	2.9	5.7
Total % = 100%				
Total N = 1155				

Part C Political Trust in 1976, by Political Trust in 1972

		1972		
		Low	Medium	High
	Low	81%	57%	26%
1976	Medium	17	34	41
	High	2	9	32
	Total %	100%	100%	99%
	Total N	(565)	(385)	(205)

Note: Based on five-item political-trust index. For a description of the procedures used to construct this index, see the appendix.

An alternative calculation presents panel results by dividing respondents into subsets based on their scores during the first wave of the survey and showing attitude scores of respondents among each subset during the last wave of the panel. Part C employs this format. It first divides respondents according to their scores on political trust in 1972 and then shows the scores among each subset four years later. For example, it reveals that, among the 565 respondents with low levels of trust in 1972, 81% had low levels in 1976. Among the 205 respondents with high levels of trust in 1972, only 26% scored low four years later. While Part C does not demonstrate the changing distribution of scores as clearly as Part B, it has two virtues. First, it allows us to see more clearly the extent to which feelings of political trust in 1976 were related to earlier feelings of trust, as measured in 1972. Second, most readers find it easier to understand tables of the Part C format. This second consideration leads me to use the format of Part C when presenting panel tables.

A similar logic is employed when we directly compare the political attitudes of children with those of their parents. I present such data by dividing children into subsets according to their parents' attitudes and then show the attitudes of children among each of these subsets. Such a format allows us to see the extent to which parents with given attitudes are likely to have children with similar attitudes. For example, we can see the extent to which parents who score high on political trust are more likely to have children with high trust scores than are parents who score low.

Measures of Association

We occasionally present statistics that express the degree of association between two variables. For example, to what extent is the tendency to identify as a Democrat related to voting for the Democratic party and to identify as a Republican related to voting Republican? To what extent do the attitudes of children correspond with those of their parents? To what extent do individuals have stable political attitudes over time? (For example, to what extent were political-trust scores in 1976 related to political-trust scores in 1972?) While percentages can be used to make all these comparisons, it is also helpful to employ summary statistics that measure how strongly attitudes and behaviors (or one attitude and other attitudes) are related to each other.

In making such estimates, we usually use *ordinal-level statistics*. That is, we use statistics that assume we can rank respondents according to their scores. For example, we assume that persons who score high on political trust are more trusting than those who score low. But we usually avoid statistics that assume we have measured the degree to which persons with different attitude scores differ from each other. For example, we assume that a person who scores 10 on the political-trust index is more trusting than a person who scores 5 and that a person who scores 5 is more trusting than a person who scores 0. But we do not assume that the difference in trust between the person who scores 10 and the one who scores 5 is necessarily the same as that between the person who scores 5 and the one who scores 0. The two main summary statistics used in this book, the Kendall's tau and the gamma, both rely only on the assumption that the data can be considered as ordinal.

The actual formulas for computing these statistics can be found in many statistics textbooks and need not concern us here. Both the tau and the gamma can range from a low of −1.0 to a high of 1.0. A score of 0 indicates that there is no association between two variables. A score of −1.0 indicates a perfect negative association; a score of 1.0, a perfect positive association. If, for example, all the respondents interviewed in 1972 had identical attitudes four years later, both the tau and the gamma would register 1.0. The tau and the gamma employ somewhat different assumptions, and the gamma generally yields a higher score than does the tau.[5] In the actual example of Table 3.2, the degree of association yields a tau of .41 and a gamma of .64.

We occasionally report the research of other scholars who have used *interval-level statistics,* which assume that the distances between scores on a measure are equal. While this assumption is not valid for the attitude measures we use, there is usually little danger in using such statistics. The most commonly used interval measure is the product–moment correlation, or Pearson's *r,* which is often used to measure the degree of association between two attitudinal variables. Like the tau and the gamma, this measure can also range from a low of −1.0 to a high of 1.0, with a score of 0 indicating no association between two variables.

From time to time, we also use other interval-level statistics. Sometimes we employ a *mean score,* a computation based on the sum of the scores for all respondents on a given measure divided by the number of respondents. The mean score is extremely simple, but it is based on the assumption that the distance between scores can be precisely measured.

When we analyze change over time, we sometimes compute a *trendline,* using least-squares regression analysis to determine the rate at which scores on a measure have changed. For example, let us suppose we wish to calculate the rate at which turnout has declined since 1960. Drawing directly from the data presented in Figure 1.1, we can plot levels of turnout in the last six presidential elections. The line that best fits these data is the one for which the sum of the squares of the distance of the line from the actual observations is lowest. The change with time is the slope estimate, or regression coefficient. While the formula for computing this line is fairly complicated, the actual computation can be done quite easily with many desk calculators. The actual scatter plot, along with the line that best fits the data points, is presented in Figure 3.1. As we can see, the rate of decline is .54 percentage points per annum, or 2.18 points per election.

The slope estimate is a very useful summary statistic for describing change over time, especially when a large number of data points must be assessed. Technically, this calculation rests on the assumption that the data have been measured intervally—probably a reasonable assumption when we calculate

[5]When a table has an identical number of columns and rows, as in Table 3.2, we use a tau-b to report the results; when there are more columns than rows or more rows than columns, a tau-c is used.

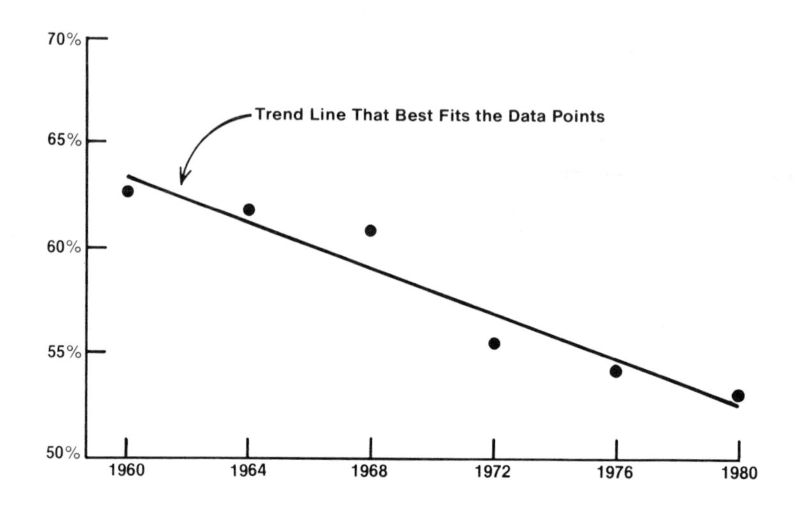

Figure 3.1 Percentage of Adults Who Voted for President: 1960–1980.
(Per annum change = −.54 percentage points. Per election change = −2.18 percentage points.)
[*Source:* U.S. Bureau of the Census (1981b).]

the rate of change in turnout, but not valid when examining attitude change. However, even when such an assumption is not fully warranted, simple least-squares regression analysis may provide a useful summary statistic.

Conclusions

Most studies of political-attitude change rely on measures constructed from closed-ended questions. Regardless of the type of question used, some measurement error is unavoidable. For this reason, it is usually best to rely on measures that combine the responses to several questions, and we employ several indices and scales to measure attitude change.

For the most part, we rely on percentages, although to conserve space we can seldom report the full distribution of responses. In analyzing panel data in which the same respondents are interviewed more than once, we divide respondents according to their attitudes during the first interview and present the distribution of responses among each subset according to their attitudes when they were last interviewed. A similar logic is used to compare the attitudes of children with those of their parents.

In addition to percentages, we also employ measures of association that assess the extent to which attitudes are related to behavior or the extent to which different attitudes are related to one another. The main summary statistics used in this book, the tau and the gamma, merely supplement the basic results, which may be followed through the presentation of percentages.

[CHAPTER 4]

Generational Replacement

One of the major goals of this book is to examine the way the political attitudes of the electorate change. Rapid change almost always results from events that cause nearly all segments of the electorate to change their attitudes in the same general direction. The very rapid decline in political trust between 1968 and 1974, for example, resulted from events that caused every subset of the electorate to become more cynical. While some individuals may have become more trusting, every social and demographic subset of the electorate was more cynical in 1974 than it had been six years earlier. But change among the electorate can occur even if both individuals and groups retain their political attitudes, for the electorate itself is constantly changing.

On an average day, about 5000 Americans die and about 9500 are born.[1] Eighteen years later, most of these 9500 enter the electorate. The electorate also changes as a result of emigration and immigration. Several hundred Americans emigrate from the United States each day, although only a small percentage actually give up their citizenship. About 1200 immigrants enter the United States legally on an average day, and an unknown, larger number enters illegally. Some of these legal immigrants, and doubtless a small number of illegal immigrants, eventually enter the electorate. However, the vast majority

[1]Figures on births and deaths are based on 1979 data reported in Tables 85 and 108 in U.S. Bureau of the Census (1981b). The number of immigrants varies greatly from year to year, so my estimate is based on the average number between 1970 and 1979 as reported in Table 128 in U.S. Bureau of the Census (1981b). The U.S. government does not maintain systematic records on emigration, but Finifter and Finifter (1980) estimate that emigration reached at least 60,000 a year in the early 1970s, although it has declined since then.

of persons enter the electorate as a result of birth within the United States, and the overwhelming majority who leave the electorate depart as a result of death.

The natural biological processes through which the electorate is continuously changed can be labeled "generational replacement." As we shall see in this book, the continuous processes of birth, aging, and death can have a profound impact on the way political attitudes among the electorate change—or on how they *fail* to change. Before we examine the possible consequences of generational replacement, a few definitions are in order.

Generation and Cohort

According to *Merriam Webster's Third New International Dictionary,* the term *generation* has a basically biological meaning: "a body of men, animals, or plants having a common parent or parents and constituting a single degree or step in the line of descent from an ancestor." Brothers and sisters make up one generation, their parents another. This simple biological meaning is sometimes used in the study of political attitudes, and we use it in this book. For example, we frequently examine studies in which parents and their children were interviewed. With such studies, we can directly determine whether parents and children have the same political attitudes, so that we can speak of the intergenerational transmission of such attitudes.

However, the term *generation* has other meanings, such as "the whole number of human beings born and living contemporaneously" and "a particular category of individuals born and living contemporaneously." It can refer to the average length of time between the birth of parents and that of their children. And it can also refer to "a group of individuals having contemporaneously a status (as that of students in a school) which each one holds for a limited period."

Mannheim greatly influenced the study of generations through his classic essay, "The Problem of Generations" (1952). Mannheim argues that generation is both a biological and a sociological concept. Generations are produced through the "biological rhythm in human existence," but "[i]ndividuals who belong to the same generation, who share the same year of birth, are endowed, to that extent, with a common location in the historical dimension of the social process" (p. 290).

Mannheim maintains that historical experiences are most likely to influence persons in their late adolescence and early adulthood, postulating that "personal experimentation with life" usually begins at about the age of 17. Whether young persons are actually influenced by historical events depends on social and historical conditions. For example, young adults living in different cultures may experience quite different events, and, even within a single society, some persons may be relatively isolated from the mainstream of social events and thus be unaffected by major historical movements. Nor do all historical periods produce conditions that influence young adults in distinctive ways. As Mannheim writes: "Whereas mere common 'location' in a generation is of only potential significance, a generation as an actuality is constituted when similarly 'located' contemporaries participate in a common destiny and in the ideas and concepts which are in some way bound up with its unfolding" (p. 306). Mannheim argues that distinctive generations are most likely to be formed in periods of rapid social change. But his basic point is that there is no guarantee that socially or politically distinctive generations will emerge. "Whether a new *generation style* emerges every year, every thirty, every hundred years, or whether it emerges rhythmically at all, depends entirely on the trigger action of the social and cultural process" (p. 310).[2]

A political generation may be defined as "a group of human beings who have undergone the same basic historical experiences during their formative years" (Rintala, 1979, p. 8). Following Mannheim's cautions, we do not label a group of persons born during the same years a "political generation" unless we can actually establish that they are distinctive in their attitudes and behaviors. Therefore, we need a term that describes persons born during the same years, but that makes no other assumptions about their distinctiveness. The term *cohort* is used for just this purpose. Historians may object that a cohort was a military unit within a Roman legion. But *Webster's* also tells us that the word means "a group of individuals . . . having a statistical factor in common in a demographic study (as year of birth)." There are many common "factors" that can define a cohort: the entry class of a school, persons married during the same period, persons who vote for the first time in the same election. But the most basic human experiences are birth and death, and the former is usually used to define a cohort. Throughout this book, the term always refers to a group of persons born during the same years.

But how many years should a cohort include? In other words, how "wide" should a cohort be? Political scientists might want to examine cohorts that are two years wide, since most major surveys of the electorate are conducted every two years. Or four-year cohorts could be utilized, since presidential elections are held every four years. However, to simplify data presentation, I present results according to eight-year cohort divisions.[3]

[2]Mannheim argues that common historical experiences do not necessarily affect all young adults the same way, for they may have differing impacts on different social groups. Persons within a generation who are affected the same way are termed a "generational unit." Rintala (1979) also emphasizes that historical experiences can have differing effects on different social groups. As an example, the political experiences of the Depression created strong Democratic loyalties among working-class youths, but led to Republican loyalties among middle-class youths (Abramson, 1975, pp. 29–34).

[3]All these results were originally based on four-year cohort divisions, and I sometimes briefly report the results of four-year cohorts.

The Basic Cohort Matrix

In examining the effects of generational replacement, we usually begin by presenting the relationship of political attitudes to age within each of the fourteen cross-sectional surveys (surveys conducted at a single point in time) conducted by the Survey Research Center and the Center for Political Studies of the University of Michigan. We then examine political change within cohorts as they move through the life cycle. Lastly, we can make a series of estimates about what the attitudes of the electorate would have been if no generational replacement had occurred. By comparing these estimates with the actual change among the electorate, we can then estimate the effects of generational replacement.

The standard table used to present these results shows the relationships of age and year of birth to political attitudes for all fourteen surveys (or for all the surveys that can be used to study a particular attitude). Because the table allows us to examine simultaneously the relationship of attitudes to age within each survey and to examine the way attitudes within cohorts change over time, it can be called a *cohort matrix* (N. Cutler, 1977b; Glenn, 1977). The basic format of such a table is presented in Table 4.1, which shows the relationship of age to years of birth for all the even-numbered years (except 1954) between 1952 and 1980.[4] By reading down each column, we can see that age increases with years of birth within any given survey. A careful reader will note, however, that the age categories vary slightly from survey to survey. By reading across each row, one sees that any given cohort ages as it moves across time. The year-of-birth categories remain fixed, so, with the exception of the four-year jump between 1952 and 1956, there is a perfect progression of age across each row.

Table 4.1 will aid readers in interpreting subsequent cohort matrices. It allows readers to determine the age of any given cohort for any given survey. For example, it tells us that persons born between 1924 and 1931 were between the ages of 21 and 28 when the 1952 survey was conducted. In 1980, this cohort was between the ages of 49 and 56.

Generational Replacement and the Electorate

The U.S. Bureau of the Census estimates of the age distribution of the U.S. population provide the best data source for calculating the speed of generational replacement.[5] My calculations based on these data reveal the very fast rate at which generational replacement has transformed the electorate during

[4]The 1954 SRC survey does not provide detailed information about age.

[5]Data on the age distribution of the U.S. population were compiled from the following sources: U.S. Bureau of the Census (1965, 1974, 1977, 1978, 1979, 1981a).

Table 4.1 Age, by Years of Birth: 1952–1980

Years of birth	1952	1956	1958	1960	1962	1964	1966	1968	1970[a]	1972	1974	1976	1978	1980
1956–1962												18–20	18–22	18–24
1948–1955									18–22	18–24	19–26	21–28	23–30	25–32
1940–1947					21–22	21–24	21–26	21–28	23–30	25–32	27–34	29–36	31–38	33–40
1932–1939		21–24	21–26	21–28	23–30	25–32	27–34	29–36	31–38	33–40	35–42	37–44	39–46	41–48
1924–1931	21–28	25–32	27–34	29–36	31–38	33–40	35–42	37–44	39–46	41–48	43–50	45–52	47–54	49–56
1916–1923	29–36	33–40	35–42	37–44	39–46	41–48	43–50	45–52	47–54	49–56	51–58	53–60	55–62	57–64
1908–1915	37–44	41–48	43–50	45–52	47–54	49–56	51–58	53–60	55–62	57–64	59–66	61–68	63–70	65–72
1900–1907	45–52	49–56	51–58	53–60	55–62	57–64	59–66	61–68	63–70	65–72	67–74	69–76	71–78	73–80
1892–1899	53–60	57–64	59–66	61–68	63–70	65–72	67–74	69–76	71–78	73–80	75–82	77–84		
1884–1891	61–68	65–72	67–74	69–76	71–78	73–80	75–82	77–84						
1876–1883	69–76	73–80	75–82	77–84										

Note: There will actually be a perfect correspondence between age and year of birth only on December 31 of each year.

[a]Beginning in 1970, the SRC included 18-, 19-, and 20-year-olds in their national samples.

the postwar years. For example, we know that anyone born after 1931 was too young to have voted in the Eisenhower–Stevenson contest of 1952.[6] In 1956, the percentage of the white electorate too young to have voted in 1952 was only 8%; by 1960, it was 16%; by 1964, 24%; by 1968, 33%; and by 1972, with the enfranchisement of 18-, 19-, and 20-year-olds, it was 47%. By 1976, a majority (54%) of the white electorate was too young to have voted in 1952. And by 1980, 62% was too young to have voted in the first Eisenhower–Stevenson contest.

Let us take one other example. Persons born after 1939 were too young to have voted in the Kennedy–Nixon election of 1960.[7] In 1964, the percentage of the white electorate too young to have voted in 1960 was only 9%; by 1968, it was 19%; by 1972, it was 34%; and by 1976, it had grown to 43%. By 1980, half (exactly 50%) of the white electorate was too young to have voted in the Kennedy–Nixon contest.

The speed at which the electorate is replaced results from the combined effect of both death and birth. Older voters are continuously leaving the electorate through death; whereas newer cohorts, born two decades earlier, are continuously entering the electorate. The actual replacement rate will vary as a function of the age distribution of the population, the death rates, and the birth rates, so it will vary from election to election. However, during most of the postwar era, nearly half the white electorate has been renewed every two decades. That is, if we take a given electoral contest, we find that about half the electorate was too young to have voted two decades earlier.

Generational replacement is faster for blacks than for whites. The black birth rate is about half again as great as the white birth rate, and, even though a smaller percentage of blacks reach voting age, blacks are entering the electorate at higher rates than are whites. Moreover, even at age 21 (the voting age for most of this period), black life expectancy is about four years less than white life expectancy. During the postwar years, more than half the black adult population has been renewed every two decades. But we cannot speak of the replacement of the black "electorate" during the entire postwar period, because, until the mid-1960s, half the black population was disfranchised.

Census data clearly demonstrate the speed of generational replacement, but they cannot be used to estimate the effect of replacement on political attitudes. For such estimates, we must turn to representative samples of the electorate that measure political attitudes, and the surveys conducted by the University of Michigan Survey Research Center and the Center for Political Studies provide the single best data source. Table 4.2 presents the basic distribution of whites according to years of birth for the fourteen major political surveys

[6]Except for 18-, 19-, and 20-year-olds living in Georgia.

[7]Except for 18-, 19-, and 20-year-olds living in Georgia and Kentucky, 19- and 20-year-olds living in Alaska, and 20-year-olds living in Hawaii.

Table 4.2 Number of Whites Sampled, by Years of Birth: 1952–1980

Years of birth	1952	1956	1958[a]	1960[a]	1962	1964	1966	1968	1970	1972	1974[a]	1976[a]	1978	1980
1956–1962											30	116	193	198
1948–1955									124	342	436	500	386	268
1940–1947				2	26	104	141	225	236	420	368	401	356	223
1932–1939	3	98	155	192	183	230	156	189	186	313	239	289	230	140
1924–1931	249	293	275	310	195	222	196	240	199	330	277	278	259	151
1916–1923	320	345	320	346	201	243	188	230	188	288	276	293	218	170
1908–1915	289	279	305	297	192	213	165	181	184	290	264	278	189	140
1900–1907	236	227	219	256	159	166	114	157	139	219	201	201	108	82
1892–1899	212	160	167	173	104	122	113	104	97	135	99	102	56	27
1884–1891	141	119	120	127	70	73	52	47	31	41	31	21	12	5
1876–1883	97	60	73	51	33	18	5	8	9	6	1	1	0	0
Before 1876	49	10	9	6	6	4	0	1	0	1	0	0	0	0
Total *N*[b]	1618	1610	1643	1764	1175	1399	1138	1388	1398	2397	2249	2494	2016	1406

Note: Beginning in 1970, the SRC included 18-, 19-, and 20-year-olds in their national samples.

[a]Weighted *N*s.

[b]Including respondents for whom year of birth was not ascertained.

conducted between 1952 and 1980. Once we divide a national sample of the electorate into subsets of eight or nine cohorts, the number of respondents for each cohort becomes fairly small, usually between 150 and 300 cases. In principle, a representative sample of the electorate should yield a representative sample of each cohort. But each cohort sample is relatively small, and thus sampling error is greater. While we may be reasonably confident (.95) that the distribution of responses for the total sample is within 3% of the entire electorate, the range of confidence for a single cohort is about three times as great. Thus, when we examine the relationship of age to political attitudes within any single survey or when we track a cohort across time from survey to survey, we must expect some erratic results simply from sampling error alone. We must not impute very much meaning from any single result, but must be concerned with the general pattern of results.

I have compared the age distribution in the SRC samples with the age distribution revealed by the census enumeration. These comparisons suggest that the SRC data accurately represent the actual population distribution, but with one systematic difference. The SRC data always underrepresent the youngest cohort. These underestimates result from the SRC sampling procedures. As pointed out in Chapter 2, the SRC bases its sample on persons living in private households. As Converse points out, the SRC surveys do not sample youths living in college dormitories, military installations, or prisons (1976, pp. 49–50). We do not know the extent to which these unsampled youths differ in their attitudes from those who are sampled, but we should be especially cautious in interpreting the results for cohorts below the age of 25.[8] There may also be some biases in sampling older respondents, for those living in rest homes and nursing homes are not sampled.

Despite these biases, the SRC data do show about the same rate of generational replacement as the census data reveal. The SRC data are certainly adequate for estimating the effects of generational replacement on political attitudes, as long as we do not attach too precise a meaning to such estimates.

An Example of Generational-Replacement Effects

As our example, we examine the effects of generational replacement on changing levels of education among the electorate. Table 4.3 uses the fourteen SRC–CPS surveys to show the educational attainment of the white electorate from 1952 through 1980 according to five broad educational categories. As we can see, educational levels have risen gradually throughout the entire period. Of course, a gradual rise in educational levels is also revealed through census

[8] For this reason, I usually do not report the results for a cohort until the full eight-year cohort has entered the electorate. I violate this rule for the youngest cohort in 1976, 1978, and 1980 in order to present the most recent survey results for these youths.

Table 4.3 Levels of Education Among Whites: 1952–1980

Level of education	1952	1956	1958	1960	1962	1964	1966	1968	1970	1972	1974	1976	1978	1980
College graduate	7%	8%	10%	11%	13%	12%	11%	14%	12%	14%	15%	16%	17%	17%
Some college	9	11	10	12	13	13	14	15	16	16	18	18	20	21
High school graduate	25	31	32	30	29	33	33	33	35	34	35	36	38	37
Some high school	21	20	19	19	20	19	17	17	15	17	19	14	14	14
Eight grades or less	38	29	28	28	25	23	25	21	22	19	14	15	11	11
Total %	100%	99%	99%	100%	100%	100%	100%	100%	100%	100%	101%	99%	100%	100%
Total *N*	(1613)	(1603)	(1624)[a]	(1763)[a]	(1169)	(1391)	(1133)	(1384)	(1394)	(2393)	(2225)[a]	(2482)[a]	(1999)	(1402)

[a]Weighted *N*s.

data. The SRC data and the census data reveal the same general trend, although the SRC data consistently overestimate levels of educational attainment.[9]

Table 4.4 uses the condensed data format to show the percentage of whites who graduated from high school (including those who attained higher levels of education) among each birth cohort from 1952 through 1980. By reading down each column, we see a very strong tendency for older persons to have lower levels of education than younger persons have.

We know that a person's level of formal education does not decline with age, so the decline in educational levels with age cannot have resulted from aging. The lower level of education among the older age groups results from social conditions at the time these cohorts were in their teens. The opportunities for, and the pressures to attain, a high school diploma have grown throughout the twentieth century, and these changed social conditions are reflected in the higher educational attainment of cohorts born during more recent years.

We know that very few persons receive a high school diploma once they become adults. Of course, there are some persons who acquire a high school equivalency diploma, but, for most adults, levels of formal education are fixed. We would therefore expect educational levels for any given cohort to remain fairly constant as the cohort moves through the life cycle, and this is precisely what the data reveal. All of the cohorts show a gain in educational attainment between 1952 and 1956, which may result from slightly different coding of educational attainment. But if we track cohorts from 1956 onward, we find very little change in levels of educational attainment. In all cases, the observed change could easily have resulted from sampling error.[10]

Despite the static levels of educational attainment within cohorts, the overall educational levels of the American electorate have risen dramatically. In 1956, just over half the white electorate had graduated from high school; by 1980, three out of four had. (The continuous rise in educational levels among the electorate can be seen by reading across the bottom row.)

Given that few Americans attain a high school diploma after they reach adulthood, why did overall levels of education increase? The answer is to be found in the continuous transformation of the electorate. Throughout the entire period, older cohorts with low levels of education were leaving the electorate through death; newer cohorts, with higher levels of education, were entering the electorate. The combined impact of these two forces led to increasing levels of formal education for the electorate as a whole.

[9]These overestimates may partly result from respondents overreporting their educational attainment. In addition, the SRC surveys are not as successful in sampling the lower social strata as is the U.S. Bureau of the Census.

[10]If we continue to track these cohorts into old age, differential death rates would affect our estimates. Women have lower levels of educational attainment than men, and women tend to live longer. On the other hand, among both men and women, persons with higher levels of education tend to live longer than those with lower levels. By not tracking cohorts once the youngest members have passed the age of 70, we reduce such biases.

Table 4.4 Percentage of Whites Who Graduated from High School, by Years of Birth: 1952–1980

Years of birth	1952	1956	1958	1960	1962	1964	1966	1968	1970	1972	1974	1976	1978	1980
1956–1962											*	79	83	89
1948–1955									*	*	86	90	89	89
1940–1947					*	*	*	82	84	81	85	84	90	86
1932–1939		*	*	71	78	77	74	81	73	77	75	77	79	78
1924–1931	59	69	68	69	63	68	68	70	70	73	67	74	74	77
1916–1923	52	60	68	62	66	66	62	67	56	58	62	65	65	62
1908–1915	45	52	53	56	54	49	52	53	48	44	53	50	49	53
1900–1907	36	39	40	38	33	38	35	38	41	36	37	38	**	**
1892–1899	29	36	36	43	32	38	39	30	**	**	**	**	**	**
1884–1891	18	25	23	21	**	**	**	**	**	**	**	**	**	**
1876–1883	23	**	**	**	**	**	**	**	**	**	**	**	**	**
All whites	41%	51%	53%	53%	55%	58%	58%	62%	63%	64%	67%	71%	75%	75%

Note: For the numbers on which these percentages are based, see Table 4.2. Actual *N*s are slightly smaller, since the small percentage of respondents for whom level of education was not ascertained has been excluded from these analyses.

*Not included because the full eight-year cohort had not yet entered the electorate.

**Not included because the advanced age of the cohort makes it nonrepresentative for comparisons across time or because there are too few cases remaining.

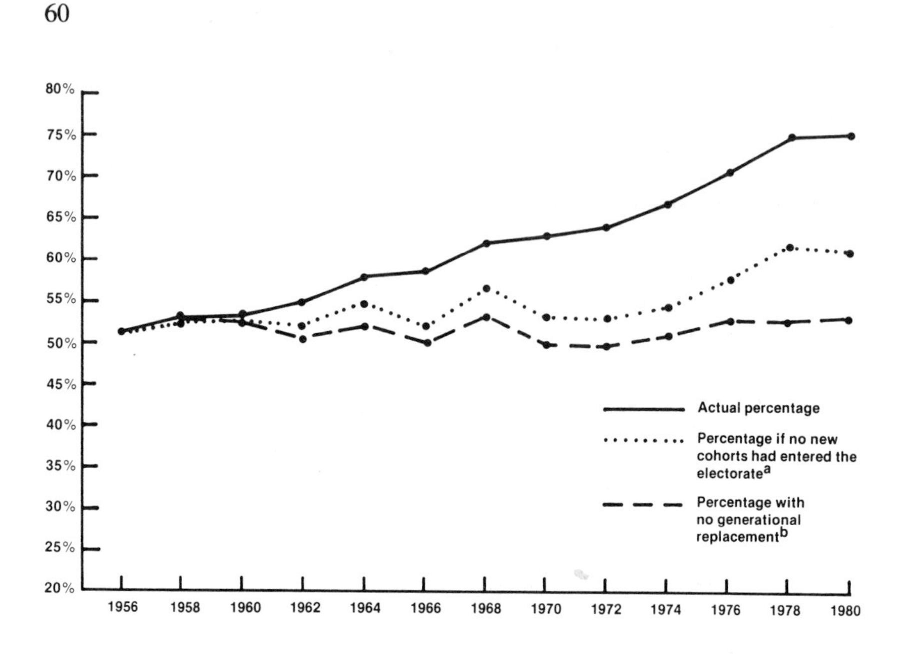

Figure 4.1 Percentage of Whites Who Graduated from High School: 1956–1980. (*Note:* For the numbers on which the percentages for the solid line are based, see Table 4.3. To approximate the numbers on which the percentages for the dotted line and the broken line are based, see Table 4.2. Actual *N*s are marginally smaller, since respondents for whom level of education was not ascertained have been excluded from the analysis. Also note that the 1932–1939 cohort presented in Table 4.2 includes respondents born between 1936 and 1939 who are not included in these calculations. [a]Assuming that no persons born after 1935 entered the electorate. [b]Assuming that no persons born after 1935 entered the electorate and that older cohorts did not diminish through death.)

Let us imagine that, in 1956, political leaders declared that no new voters could enter the electorate. If you were old enough to vote in the second Eisenhower–Stevenson election, you would be allowed to vote in all future elections. If you were too young to vote in 1956, you would never be allowed to vote!

What would have happened to the educational levels of the electorate? Figure 4.1 allows us to answer this question. The solid line shows the actual level of educational attainment among the white electorate between 1956 and 1980, while the dotted line shows the percentage of the electorate that would have graduated from high school if no persons born after 1935 had been allowed to enter the electorate. These computations are derived easily by excluding all respondents born after 1935 from the calculations.[11] This is a simple exercise to carry out on paper, as it does not lead to the revolutionary consequences of disfranchising millions of young adults. As Figure 4.1 reveals,

[11]For example, the percentage for 1980 is based on the 635 whites born before 1936.

overall levels of education would still have risen, even if no new birth cohorts had entered the electorate. We have statistically removed the effects of new cohorts entering the electorate, but not the effects of differential death rates. Older cohorts with lower levels of education were dying at faster rates than the relatively young cohorts that had higher levels of formal education.

Eliminating cohorts born after 1935 from our calculations does not allow us to estimate the full impact of generational replacement. To do this, we must calculate levels of education as if no differential death rates had occurred. We must "immortalize" the older cohorts.[12] No political leaders can accomplish this goal, but we can achieve it through imagination if we employ simple algebra. We use the overall distribution of respondents in 1956 as our base, and we do not change this distribution for our subsequent calculations. We take the number of respondents in each cohort in 1956, multiply this number by the percentage of whites who were high school graduates among this cohort in subsequent surveys, total these products, and divide the sum of the products by the total number of respondents back in 1956.[13] The broken line in Figure 4.1 shows the results of these calculations.[14] While the percentages in this line do fluctuate slightly as a result of sampling error, the results reveal just what we expected all along. If there had been no change in the composition of the electorate, the overall level of education among the electorate would have been unchanged. Put differently, once we remove the effects of generational replacement through our algebraic estimates, we find that there would have been almost no change among the electorate. The change that actually occurred, therefore, must have resulted from generational replacement.

[12]I am grateful to Crewe, Särlvik, and Alt (1978) for this term.

[13]For older cohorts that have too few cases to estimate levels of education, we are forced simply to insert a percentage based on our knowledge about the levels of education of these cohorts in earlier surveys.

[14]For example, we calculated our estimate for 1980 as follows:

Years of birth	*Size of cohort (set at 1956 size)*		*Percentage who graduated from high school*		*Product*
1932–1935	(93)	×	76%	=	70.68
1924–1931	(293)	×	77%	=	225.61
1916–1923	(345)	×	62%	=	213.90
1908–1915	(279)	×	53%	=	147.87
1900–1907	(227)	×	38%	=	86.26
1892–1899	(159)	×	35%	=	55.65
1884–1891	(116)	×	23%	=	26.68
1876–1883	(60)	×	22%	=	13.20
Before 1876	(8)	×	22%	=	1.76
Total	(1580)				841.61

The percentage that would have been high school graduates with no generational replacement is the sum of the products divided by the size of the white electorate in 1956: 841.61 ÷ 1580 = 53.3%.

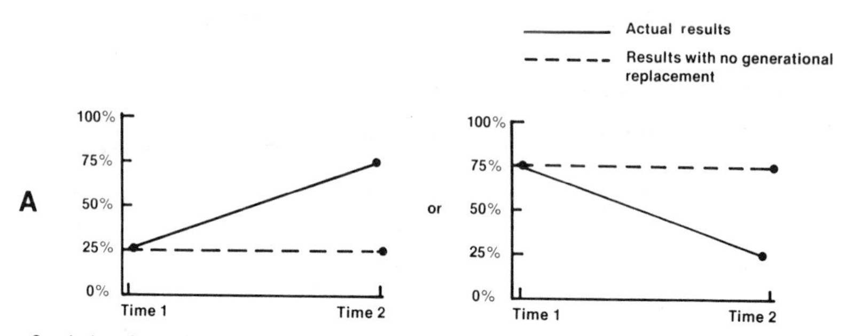

Conclusion: Generational replacement creates a trend. Without generational replacement there would have been no change.

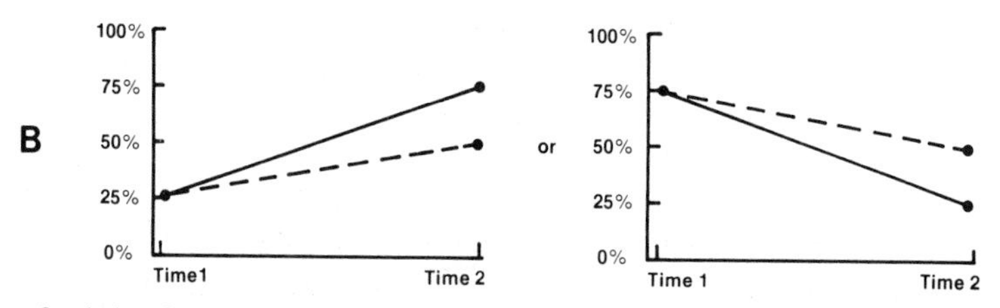

Conclusion: Generational replacement contributes to a trend. Without generational replacement there would have been less change.

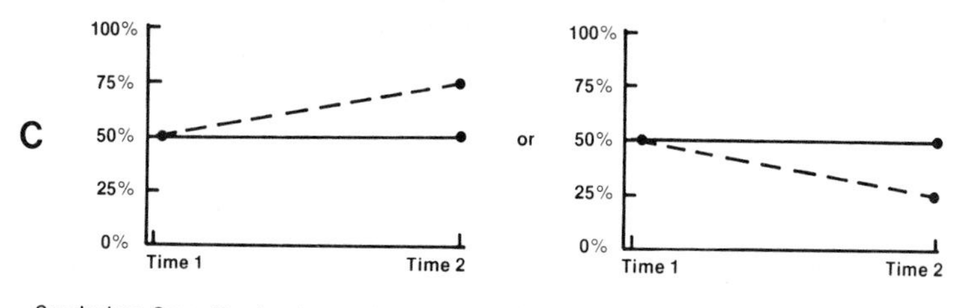

Conclusion: Generational replacement prevents a trend. Without generational replacement change would have occurred.

Figure 4.2 Possible Effects of Generational Replacement.

Possible Effects of Generational Replacement

While the results of Figure 4.1 demonstrate the obvious, it is important to clarify the simple calculations necessary to estimate the impact of generational replacement. Whenever generational replacement affects attitude change among the electorate, surveys conducted over time include those effects. To determine the impact of generational replacement, we must algebraically remove the effects of replacement and then compare these estimates with the actual results.

Figure 4.2 illustrates the possible effects of replacement. Case A is comparable to our results analyzing changing educational levels among the elec-

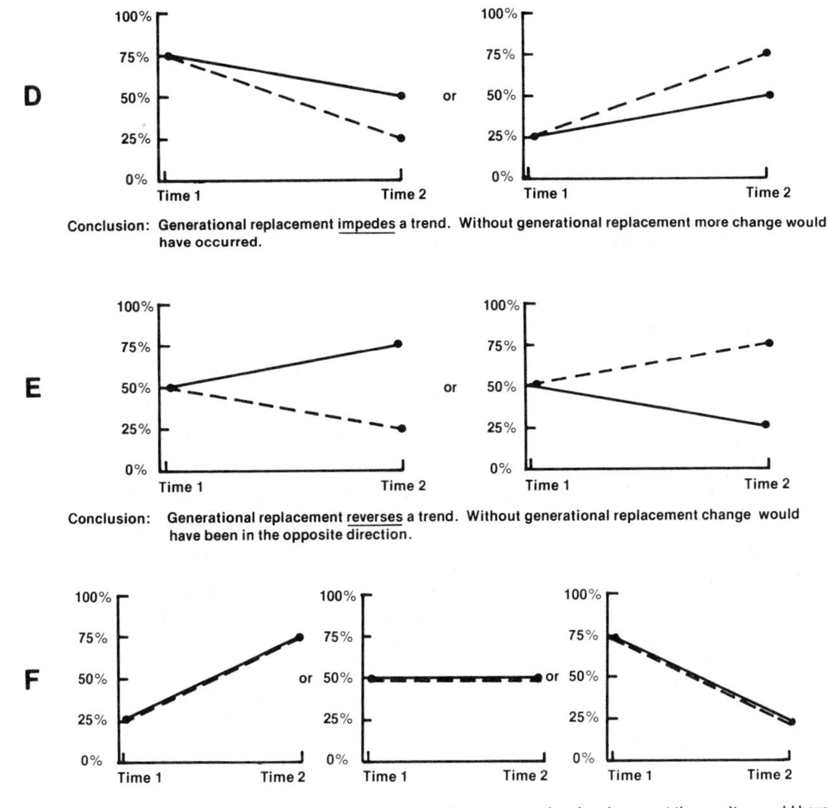

torate. The solid line shows the actual change (whether the line goes up or down is simply a matter of definition; for example, we could talk about the declining percentage of Americans who had not graduated from high school). When the effects of generational replacement are removed, there is no change in the percentage of the electorate who hold a given attitude (or the percentage who share some attribute). In such a case, we can say that generational replacement *creates* a trend. Without replacement, change would not have occurred.

Case B shows the same amount of actual change in the electorate as we observed in Case A. But in Case B there is also change when we remove the effects of generational replacement. However, when the effects of replacement are removed, change is reduced (in this hypothetical example, it is halved).

While there would have been some change even if no generational replacement had occurred, the change would have been less than the amount that actually took place. We can thus say that generational replacement *contributes* to a trend.

Case C shows yet another possibility. There is no actual change among the electorate. But once we remove the effects of generational replacement, there is an increase (or a decrease) in the percentage of the electorate with a given attitude. Generational replacement led to the absence of change among the electorate. We can say that replacement *prevents* a trend. It may seem strange that population change can contribute to stability, but such a result not only is a logical possibility, but actually occurs when we examine some political attitudes.

In Case D, we can see that there is change among the electorate. But once we remove the effects of generational replacement, change actually increases. In such a case, replacement has had yet another effect: it has slowed down the actual rate of change. We can thus say that replacement *impedes* a trend. Without generational replacement, change would have been greater than the change that actually occurred.

In Case E, there is also change among the electorate. But once the effects of generational replacement are removed, the trend moves in the opposite direction. In this case, we can see that replacement *reverses* a trend.

Lastly, we should remember that generational replacement may have no effect on the distribution of an attitude among the electorate. Removing the effects of replacement yields the same results as the actual change (or lack of change) that actually occurred. Case F provides examples of this result. Without generational replacement, the results would have been the same as the actual results among the electorate—an electorate that has experienced replacement, as all electorates must.

Conclusions

Generational replacement is an ongoing process that occurs among all electorates. Data from the U.S. Bureau of the Census reveal that, during the postwar years, about half the white electorate has been renewed every two decades, while replacement has been somewhat faster among blacks.

While census data can be used to calculate the speed of replacement, they cannot be used to measure its impact on political attitudes. To study the effects of replacement, we must turn to surveys of political attitudes conducted during the postwar years. The Michigan SRC data provide the best source for such estimates, for they often allow us to track political attitudes for nearly three decades. Surveys conducted over a lengthy period must register the impact of replacement. To determine what that impact was, we must algebraically remove the effects of replacement. By comparing the actual results with the imaginary results in which the effects of replacement have been removed, we can determine what the impact of replacement was. A concrete illustration of the effects of replacement on changing levels of education among the electorate provides an excellent example of replacement creating a trend.

In fact, there are six basic possibilities, as Figure 4.2 reveals. As we shall see, all these possibilities are found in the real world of American politics. During the remainder of this book, we find real-world examples of generational replacement creating a trend, contributing to a trend, preventing a trend, impeding a trend, and reversing a trend. And we find a case where replacement had no effect whatever. However, we shall always be sensitve to the need to examine the potential effects of replacement, since it is a process that always occurs when we examine electorates over time and since it is a process that *may* affect the way political attitudes change.

II

Continuity and Change in Party Loyalties

[CHAPTER 5]

The Concept of Party Identification

No field of political science has been studied more extensively than the way people vote, and the study of voting behavior focuses on the choices people make between political parties. Of course, individuals run for office, and the importance of individual candidates may be crucial to the voter in any single election. But an election is more than a contest between individuals: it is also a struggle between political parties, that is to say, between competing organized attempts to gain governmental office. Moreover, it can be argued that democratic government is impossible without the organized contest between political parties.

In the United States, the struggle between the Jacksonian Democrats and the anti-Jackson Whigs led to the rapid expansion of the right to vote of all adult white males in the 1830s. In Britain, too, the party struggle between the Conservatives and the Liberals contributed to the gradual extension of the suffrage between the Reform Act of 1832 and the Reform Act of 1884. That parties were associated with democratic reforms in the past does not guarantee that parties today contribute to democracy. Still, parties do provide voters with three basic opportunities:

1. Parties may provide a meaningful choice about the issues. We cannot expect that each candidate will successfully communicate his or her ideas to the electorate, for the average voter will invest too few resources to learn the issue positions of most candidates. But over time the electorate can judge the broad issue positions of the political parties.

2. It is through political parties that voters have an opportunity to choose the executives who will direct the government. For example, without orga-

nized political parties, most Americans would have little choice in selecting the president. To win the presidency, a candidate needs the majority of the electoral votes. If no candidate receives a majority, the final choice (among the three candidates with the most electoral votes) is made by the House of Representatives, with each state delegation casting a single vote. Yet the House procedure has not been used since 1824, for political parties, which organize for a presidential contest in every election, provide all voters in every state (or nearly every state) the choice of a single slate of candidates, greatly increasing the probability that a single candidate will earn a majority of the electoral vote. In Britain, too, the parties play a major role in helping the voter to choose a prime minister, for voters know that if their candidate for parliament wins and if their party gains a majority of the seats in the House of Commons, their votes will be transformed, in effect, into a vote for the leader of their party to serve as prime minister.

3. Parties provide voters with a mechanism for punishing incumbents. Even if the actual incumbent does not run for reelection, voters may still punish the "ins" and reward the "outs" by voting for the party out of power. Thus, voters who were dissatisfied with Lyndon Johnson in 1968 could not vote against him, but could reject Hubert Humphrey, the Democratic candidate. Likewise, voters could no longer punish Richard Nixon in 1976, but some may have voted Democratic to punish the Republican party.

While parties can perform these three basic functions, there is no guarantee that they will. The two major parties may not provide clear choices about the issues, and some voters may feel best represented by small, third parties that have no chance of winning office. In some cases, parties may not provide an acceptable choice between heads of government, and many voters may feel that they have, at best, a choice between two evils. Moreover, the parties may not serve well in punishing incumbents. To effectively punish the incumbent party, voters must support the out party or parties, and, if these parties are unacceptable, their protest is limited to abstaining. While parties do not necessarily perform these three basic functions, it is difficult for any of the functions to be performed without political parties.

Of course, the American party system has its faults. Yet it is hard to imagine a meaningful representative government, at least on a national scale, without political parties. This is perhaps best expressed by Burnham, who has studied the broad historical questions of partisan change (1970, p. 133):

> [P]olitical parties, with all their well-known human and structural shortcomings, are the only devices thus far invented by the wit of Western man which with some effectiveness can generate countervailing collective power on behalf of the many individually powerless against the relatively few who are individually—or organizationally—powerful.

Party Identification Defined

Many studies have been devoted to the structure and organization of political parties (e.g., Schlesinger, 1965, 1975; Sorauf, 1980), but the emphasis of this book is on the way parties influence political behavior among the electorate. This leads to a study of individual attachments to the political parties, which have come to be labeled "party identification." Party identification is an attitudinal variable that measures an individual's sense of attachment to a political reference group. It is not a measure of behavior. Party identifiers do not have to belong to a party in any formal sense; they do not need to pay dues or attend meetings; and, even in those states where individuals register to vote by party, identifiers may or may not be registered. A Democrat may vote Republican and remain a Democrat, just as a Republican may vote Democratic and remain a Republican.

The nature of party identification may best be understood if we examine the questions used to measure it. Since 1952, the Michigan SRC has asked the same basic questions:

> "Generally speaking, do you usually think of yourself as a Republican, a Democrat, an Independent, or what?"
>
> Persons who call themselves Republicans or Democrats are then asked: "Would you call yourself a strong (Republican, Democrat) or a not very strong (Republican, Democrat)?"
>
> Persons who call themselves Independents, answer "no preference," or name another party are asked: "Do you think of yourself as closer to the Republican or to the Democratic party?"[1]

As can be seen, respondents are not asked anything about their political behavior, only how they relate to the two major parties.

The responses to these questions allow researchers to classify respondents into one of seven basic categories: strong Democrats, weak Democrats, Independents who lean Democratic, Independents with no partisan leanings, Independents who lean Republican, weak Republicans, and strong Republicans.[2] (If the researcher is interested in strength of partisanship, not in its direction, four basic categories emerge: strong partisans, weak partisans, Independents who lean toward a party, and Independents with no party leaning.) A small number of persons favor a minor party, but this figure seldom reaches even

[1] In 1980, this question was modified slightly to read, "Do you think of yourself as closer to the Republican Party or to the Democratic Party?"

[2] The SRC party-identification index does not distinguish between respondents who originally call themselves Independents and those who answer "no preference." Very few respondents support minor parties, but those who feel closer to the Republican or Democratic party are classified as Independent leaners.

1%. A somewhat larger number, especially before 1964, could give no response to the questions used to measure party identification; they were classified as being apolitical.

There is no reason why respondents necessarily should feel a sense of attachment to political parties, but most Americans willingly classify themselves as either Republicans or Democrats. During the period between 1952 and 1958, when *The American Voter* data were collected, about three out of four respondents were either Republicans or Democrats.

The American Voter View

Although party identification has declined in importance since *The American Voter* was written (1960) we begin our discussion of this concept with the claims made by Campbell and his colleagues.[3] We look at these claims in general terms, examine them more closely, and then see how later research may force us to modify the conclusions of Campbell et al.

Campbell, Converse, Miller, and Stokes see party identification as a key political concept and consider the high proportion of Americans who willingly identify with one of the major parties as a central political fact (1960, p. 121):

> Few factors are of greater importance for our national elections than the lasting attachment of tens of millions of Americans to one of the parties. These loyalties establish a basic division of electoral strength within which the competition of particular campaigns takes place. And they are an important factor in assuring the stability of the party system itself.

My reading of *The American Voter* suggests that Campbell and his colleagues advanced four major claims about the functions performed by party identification:

1. Party identification contributes to opinion formation.
2. Party identification influences voting behavior.
3. Party identification enhances psychological involvement in politics.
4. High levels of party identification among the electorate provide a check against new party movements and contribute to the established party system.

Let us examine each of these claims in more detail.

Forming opinions

Citizens receive many political messages, but most people spend little time analyzing them. However, each message is not received on a blank slate, for most adults have developed some framework for sorting, evaluating, and interpreting new information. Few citizens have a highly structured ideology that

[3]This concept was first introduced by Belknap and Campbell (1951–1952). For another valuable introduction, see Campbell, Gurin, and Miller (1954, pp. 88–111).

enables them to interpret new information, but party loyalties may help them evaluate new political situations.

Campbell and his colleagues contend: "In the competition of voices reaching the individual the political party is an opinion-forming agency of great importance" (p. 128). The authors claim that party identification "raises a perceptual screen through which the individual tends to see what is favorable to his partisan orientation. The stronger the party bond, the more exaggerated the process of selection and perceptual distortion will be" (p. 133). While Campbell and his associates could not prove that party loyalties "screen" political information, they present some indirect evidence to support their view. "We are convinced that the relationships in our data reflect primarily the role of enduring partisan commitments in shaping attitudes toward political objects" (p. 135).

Influencing voting behavior

"[P]arty identification," Campbell and his colleagues write, "has a profound impact on behavior" (p. 137). They conclude that party identification, along with general orientations toward the parties, are the most important determinants of the way people vote. Today many political scientists would accept this conclusion as common knowledge, but in 1960, when *The American Voter* appeared, it flew in the face of two well-known facts. More people considered themselves Democrats than Republicans, yet the Republicans had scored landslide victories in the two major presidential elections studied by Campbell, 1952 and 1956. If one predicted these elections purely on the basis of party identification, Stevenson, not Eisenhower, would have won.

Although knowledge about party identification would not have led to predicting Eisenhower's victory, it could explain the way many individuals voted, for party identification was strongly related to electoral choice. In both 1952 and 1956, 99% of the strong Republicans voted for Eisenhower. Among strong Democrats in 1952, only 16% voted for Eisenhower; and in 1956, only 15% did.[4] Put differently, in both these elections, strong Republicans were six times as likely to vote for Eisenhower as strong Democrats were.

Enhancing psychological involvement

Persons who are party identifiers are more interested in politics, more concerned about who wins the election, and more likely to vote. Campbell et al. did not know whether party loyalties cause political interest or whether interest in politics causes people to develop stronger party ties. Perhaps both processes are at work. Still, they conclude that "the fact of association is clear enough: the stronger the individual's sense of attachment to one of the political parties, the greater his psychological involvement in political affairs" (p. 143).

[4]These results are based directly on data presented by Campbell et al (1960, p. 139). For a fuller report, see Table 5.1 of this chapter.

These findings led to a thorough reassessment of the Independent. Whereas the civics textbooks could portray Independents as virtuous citizens who base their vote on issues and candidates, not on party labels, the actual picture that emerges from *The American Voter* is far from complimentary (p. 143):

> Far from being more attentive, interested, and informed, Independents tend as a group to be somewhat less involved in politics. They have somewhat poorer knowledge of the issues, their image of the candidates is fainter, their interest in the campaign is less, their concern over the outcome is relatively slight, and their choice between competing candidates, although it is indeed made later in the campaign, seems much less to spring from discoverable evaluations of the elements of national politics.

Contributing to electoral stability

At times, many voters become dissatisfied with the established parties, and minor parties or new parties may develop attractive appeals. But voters who have strong loyalties to the established parties may resist the appeals of new parties and of leaders outside the traditional party system. To the extent that large numbers of citizens have strong party loyalties, the established party system may be at least temporarily protected.

As we have seen, Campbell and his colleagues claim that party loyalties "are an important factor in assuring the stability of the party system itself" (p. 121). While we would not expect voters to retain their loyalties indefinitely if the established parties failed to respond to social and political needs, high levels of partisanship among the electorate provide some breathing space for established parties to develop new policies. As Campbell et al. write: "There is reason to believe that in a system of long-standing parties it is the rare exception that any large proportion of the public departs from the existing parties in search of new policy positions" (p. 365). In part, this is because at least one of the established parties is likely to respond to new popular demands.

The American Voter Reevaluated

New data and new analyses now force us to reevaluate the Campbell et al. arguments. Although party identification is still important to understanding American political behavior, its importance has declined. In fact, even if all the relationships observed by Campbell and his colleagues still held today, the importance of party identification for explaining political behavior would have declined for one simple reason: a smaller proportion of Americans identify as partisans today than when *The American Voter* was written.

During the 1950s, about 35% of the American electorate were strong party identifiers; in the Michigan SRC–CPS survey held in late 1980, only 26% were.[5] In the 1950s, 74% identified as strong or weak partisans; in 1980, 63%

[5]The 1950s data are based on Campbell et al (1960, p. 124). The 1980 data are based on the CPS preelection survey. Virtually identical results obtain if the postelection survey is used.

did. Back in the 1950s, only 6% were Independents with no party leanings; but by 1980, 13% were. Only the decline of "apoliticals" shows a strengthening of partisanship, and this shift occurs mainly among Southern blacks.

The decline of partisan strength affects all the conclusions reached by Campbell and his colleagues. Even if party identification still served as a powerful "perceptual screen," fewer voters would have strong screening mechanisms. Even if party loyalties were as powerful as earlier in contributing to voting choices, the reduced proportion of strong partisans (who are most strongly influenced by their party loyalties) would mean that a larger proportion of the electorate would be susceptible to short-term political forces, such as the appeals of candidates or the issues of the day. If party loyalties were still equally important in contributing to psychological involvement in politics, there are proportionately fewer partisans in the electorate to be influenced by those loyalties. And if party loyalties still contribute to electoral stability, we must now conclude that the prospects for instability have increased. However, even apart from the weakening of party identifications, we must still reassess each of *The American Voter* arguments in light of new evidence.

Forming opinions

The argument that parties serve to form opinions is based largely on indirect evidence and on knowledge about the sequence in which party identification and opinions on the issues develop. Most respondents have the same partisanship as their parents, and most hold the same party loyalties throughout their lives. Moreover, socialization research, summarized by Hyman, suggests that most persons develop party loyalties before they develop positions on the issues (1959, pp. 74–81). As Hyman points out, many new issues emerge after a person develops party loyalties, and socialization into a party could provide an "organizing principle for handling the new issues" (p. 75). *The American Voter* data provides additional evidence that partisan loyalties affect political perceptions, for party loyalties are strongly related to evaluations of the parties as managers of government and were also related to evaluations of Eisenhower and Stevenson (pp. 128–131).

However, all this evidence is rather indirect and does not tell us about the processes through which partisanship may shape the opinions of individuals. Especially in an era when television has made information about the issues more accessible and when overall increases in education among the electorate have enhanced the ability of voters to form issue positions without partisan cues, the importance of partisanship in forming new issue positions may have diminished.

The main challenge to the thesis that parties help form opinions on issues has been raised by Searing, Schwartz, and Lind (1973). They reason that, if party identification structures political learning, there should be a strong relationship between party identification and the positions on issues held by individuals. Using both the 1968 Michigan SRC survey and a 1969 stratified probability survey conducted by the University of North Carolina Regional Survey, they find that such relationships are weak. However, such findings are neither surprising nor new.[6] In fact, *The American Voter* authors find that party identification is weakly related to most issue positions (pp. 168–187).

Campbell and his colleagues were discussing a long-term process through which party identification helps shape opinions over time, and such processes may be difficult to identify through surveys conducted at one point in time or even through panel surveys that cover a mere four-year period. Interestingly, Searing et al. find that the strongest relationships between party identification and issue positions are with the two issues that have long divided the two major parties: government aid for health care, and government guarantees for a good standard of living.

On balance, it seems reasonable to conclude that party loyalties do help structure an individual's view of political events, candidates, and, over the long term, issues.[7] On the other hand, continuing dissatisfaction with a party's position on the issues can lead voters to weaken their party loyalties, especially when issue positions are strongly felt. The movement of white Southerners away from the Democratic party between 1964 and 1968, a period when the national party leadership was strongly identified with black demands, clearly demonstrates that party loyalties can change and that issues are important in changing those loyalties (Beck, 1977; B. Campbell, 1980). Moreover, among individuals who change their party loyalties, we can no longer assume that partisanship precedes the formation of issue positions (Helm, 1979).

Influencing voting behavior

Party loyalties are still important in influencing the way people vote, but the impact of party identification has declined. This decline is apparent when we examine the data in Table 5.1, which show the percentage of white voters of each partisan group who voted for the Democratic presidential candidate between 1952 and 1980.[8] (Because these figures show the percentage voting

[6]For a perceptive criticism of the Searing et al. article, see Sears (1975).

[7]In his excellent review of the political-socialization literature, Sears concludes: "[O]ne might have thought it by now obvious that political trust, party identification, racial prejudice, and other such presumed residues of early socialization are central in determining the average citizen's reactions to political events and choices" (1975, p. 137). Sears presents abundant evidence to support this conclusion, but I would still emphasize that we do not know a great deal about the processes through which partisan loyalties affect attitudinal development.

[8]As with all my analyses of change over time, I examine whites and blacks separately. Including blacks in an analysis of relationship between party identification and presidential vote complicates our analyses because the trend among blacks has been more dramatic than that among whites and because blacks begin voting in much larger numbers after 1960. The correlation between party identification and presidential vote among blacks has always been substantially lower than the relationship among whites, but the relationship drops sharply after 1960. The tau-c relationships for the past eight elections are: 1952, .43; 1956, .56; 1960, .56; 1964, no relationship because all blacks voted Democratic; 1968, .10; 1972, .23; 1976, .08; 1980, .05.

Table 5.1 Percentage of White Major-Party Voters Who Voted Democratic for President, by Party Identification: 1952–1980

Party identification	1952	1956	1960	1964	1968	1972	1976	1980
Strong Democrat	82	85	91	94	89	66	88	87
Weak Democrat	61	63	70	81	66	44	72	59
Independent, leans Democratic	60	65	89	89	62	58	73	57
Independent, no partisan leanings	18	15	50	75	28	26	41	23
Independent, leans Republican	7	6	13	25	5	11	15	13
Weak Republican	4	7	11	40	10	9	22	5
Strong Republican	2	†	2	9	3	2	3	4
Relationship between party identification and direction of presidential vote[a]	.71	.75	.78	.64	.73	.48	.68	.69

Note: To approximate the numbers on which these percentages are based, see Table 7.2. Actual *N*s are smaller, since respondents who did not vote (or who voted for a minor party) have been excluded from these calculations. Numbers will also be lower since the presidential voting report is provided in the postelection interviews, which usually contain about 10% fewer respondents than do the preelection interview in which party identification was measured.

[a]Kendall's tau-c relationship between a sevenfold ordinal measure of party identification as listed above and a twofold ordinal measure of presidential vote.

†Less than 1%.

Democratic among major-party voters, the percentage voting Republican is simply the percentage who voted Democratic subtracted from 100). Table 5.2 supplements our analysis by presenting the vote for the three major candidates in 1968 and 1980.

Because of the problems in classifying Wallace voters in 1968 and Anderson voters in 1980, it is difficult to establish a clear trend; but it seems reasonable to conclude that the relationship between party identification and presidential vote declined sharply in 1964 and declined further in 1968 and 1972. The relationship rose somewhat in 1976, although not back to the pre-1964 levels. In 1976, there were sizable defections from Ford among weak Republicans. If Anderson voters are included in our calculations, the relationship between party identification and presidential vote was weak in 1980. In 1980, there were sizable defections from Carter among both weak Democrats and Independents who lean Democratic.

The impact of party identification on congressional voting choices has also declined since the early 1960s. Table 5.3 presents the percentage of whites who voted Democratic in all 15 congressional elections between 1952 and

Table 5.2 How Whites Voted for President Among Three Major Candidates, by Party Identification: 1968 and 1980

Party identification	1968					1980				
	Humphrey	Wallace	Nixon	Total %	Total *N*	Carter	Anderson	Reagan	Total %	Total *N*
Strong Democrat	80%	10	10	100%	(164)	84%	3	12	99%	(129)
Weak Democrat	55%	17	28	100%	(212)	54%	9	38	101%	(173)
Independent, leans Democratic	51%	18	31	100%	(89)	44%	23	33	100%	(93)
Independent, no partisan leaning	23%	20	57	100%	(84)	20%	13	67	100%	(79)
Independent, leans Republican	4%	14	82	100%	(101)	11%	10	78	99%	(106)
Weak Republican	9%	8	83	100%	(163)	5%	9	87	101%	(151)
Strong Republican	3%	2	96	101%	(117)	4%	4	93	101%	(110)
Relationship between party identification and direction of presidential vote[a]		.58						.53		

[a]Kendall's tau-c relationship between a sevenfold ordinal measure of party identification as listed above and a threefold ordinal measure of presidential vote, with Wallace voters classified in an intermediate position between Humphrey and Nixon voters and with Anderson voters classified in an intermediate position between Carter and Reagan voters.

Table 5.3 Percentage of White Major-Party Voters Who Voted Democratic for Congress, by Party Identification: 1952–1980

Party identification	1952	1954[a]	1956	1958	1960	1962	1964	1966	1968	1970	1972	1974	1976	1978	1980
Strong Democrat	90	97	94	96	92	96	92	92	88	91	91	89	86	83	82
Weak Democrat	76	77	86	88	85	83	84	81	72	76	79	81	76	79	66
Independent, leans Democratic	63	70	82	75	86	74	78	54	60	74	78	87	76	60	69
Independent, no partisan leaning	25	41	35	46	52	61	70	49	48	48	54	54	55	56	57
Independent, leans Republican	18	6	17	26	26	28	28	31	18	35	27	38	32	36	32
Weak Republican	10	6	11	22	14	14	34	22	21	17	24	31	28	34	26
Strong Republican	5	5	5	6	8	6	8	12	8	4	15	14	15	19	22
Relationship between party identification and direction of congressional vote[b]	.77	.85	.83	.79	.78	.81	.67	.70	.66	.72	.64	.62	.59	.51	.49

Note: To approximate the numbers on which these percentages are based, see Table 7.2. Actual *N*s are smaller, since respondents who did not vote (or who voted for a minor party) have been excluded from these calculations. Numbers will also be lower for the presidential election years since the voting report is provided in the postelection interviews, which usually contain about 10% fewer respondents than do the preelection interviews in which party identification was measured. Except for 1954, in which there was only a preelection interview, the off year election surveys are based only on a postelection interview.

[a]The 1954 survey measured voting intention shortly before the election.

[b]Kendall's tau-c relationship between a sevenfold ordinal measure of party identification as listed above and a twofold ordinal measure of congressional vote.

1980.[9] (The percentage who voted Republican is simply the percentage who voted Democratic subtracted from 100.)

The relationship between party identification and congressional vote dropped between 1962 and 1964, and it never regained its pre-1964 level. Moreover, the relationship has been especially low in the five most recent elections, reaching its lowest level in 1980. The decline in the relationship between party identification and congressional vote is due, in part, to the increasing advantages conferred on congressional incumbents (Ferejohn, 1977; Fiorina, 1977a, 1977b), and many voters vote against their party loyalties to support their incumbent congressman—a pattern that provides a net benefit for the Democrats (see Abramson, Aldrich, and Rohde, 1982, pp. 218–219; Cover, 1977). Despite these changes, Republicans are still much more likely to vote for Republican congressional candidates than Democrats are.

A careful reader of Table 5.1 will note that, in most of the eight presidential elections, Independents who leaned Democratic were as likely as, or more likely than, weak Democrats to vote Democratic. Likewise, in most of these elections, Independents who leaned Republican were as likely as, or more likely than, weak Republicans to vote Republican. Such findings have led some political scientists to question whether "leaning Independents" are not "disguised partisans."[10] However, there is another possibility. Leaning Independents may be true Independents, but when pressed to say which party they feel "closer" to, they define that closeness according to the way they plan to vote for president.[11] There is at least some evidence, based on panel analyses, that supports this interpretation (Shively, 1980). Moreover, for congressional voting, weak partisans usually have been more likely to support their party than Independent leaners were (see Table 5.3).

The meaning of Independence has been a subject of growing interest, and the 1980 CPS election study will ultimately provide far greater insight into the meaning of the party-identification measure. In 1980, largely as a result of suggestions by scholars throughout the political science community, the CPS introduced a wide range of questions designed to better elucidate the

[9]The correlation between party identification and congressional vote among blacks has always been substantially lower than that among whites; and, as with black presidential voting, the correlation drops sharply after 1960. The tau-c relationships for the congressional elections are as follows: 1952, .14; 1954, .61; 1956, .53; 1958, .59; 1960, .50; 1962, .28; 1964, .14; 1966, .09; 1968, .02; 1970, .00; 1972, .10; 1974, .06; 1976, .04; 1978, .15; 1980, .00.

[10]For suggestions along these lines, see W. Miller and Levitin (1976, p. 210). In their analysis of the 1976 CPS election survey, Arthur Miller and Warren Miller (1977) classify Independents who lean toward a party as partisans rather than Independents for most of their analyses. See also Keith et al (1977).

[11]For all the data used to construct Tables 5.1 and 5.2, partisan identification was measured in a survey conducted shortly before the presidential election, and the way respondents voted was measured in an interview conducted shortly after the election. For all the midterm congressional elections (except 1954), both party identification and congressional vote were measured shortly after the election.

meaning of partisanship. For example, respondents were asked what they meant when they said they were "strong" or "not very strong" partisans and what they meant if they said they felt "closer" to one of the parties. They were asked, "In your own mind, do you think of yourself as a supporter of one of the political parties, or not?" as well as "Do you ever think of yourself as a political independent, or not?"

Analyses of the CPS study conducted in January–February 1980 suggest that weak partisans may be more partisan than Independent leaners. A full 86% of the strong party identifiers thought of themselves as party supporters, 52% of the weak partisans, 17% of the Independent leaners, and only 4% of the Independents with no partisan leanings. Only 22% of the strong partisans ever thought of themselves as Independents, 46% of the weak partisans, 73% of the Independent leaners, and 51% of the Independents with no party leanings (Dennis, 1981; Weisberg, 1980). Far more extensive analyses of these data will be necessary to shed greater light on the meaning of Independence,[12] but for the moment it seems reasonable to consider leaning Independents to be more partisan than Independents with no partisan leanings, but to be less partisan than weak identifiers. It seems best to treat the Independent category with caution, and in my analyses I avoid lumping leaning Independents with those who have no partisan leanings.

Enhancing psychological involvement

The basic thesis that party identification contributes to political involvement still appears to be valid, but it is now clear that Independents who lean toward a party are as politically involved as weak partisans. My own analysis of the relationship of strength of party identification to electoral participation, for example, shows that, in all eight presidential elections between 1952 and 1980 and in all six off year congressional elections between 1958 and 1978, strong partisans were more likely to vote than any other group. For six of the eight presidential elections and for all six off year congressional elections, Independents with no partisan leanings were the least likely to vote. But there were no consistent differences in turnout between weak partisans and Independents who leaned toward a party (see Chapter 16).

An analysis of white non-Southerners by Keith and his colleagues (1977) shows that Independent leaners were as likely as, or more likely than, weak partisans to be "very much interested" in the current election campaign in every presidential election from 1952 through 1972. (In all six elections, strong partisans were the most interested; pure Independents, the least.) An analysis by Petrocik (1974), pooling the results of seven SRC–CPS surveys conducted between 1952 and 1972, shows that, on most measures of participation and involvement, Independent leaners were somewhat more involved

[12]Dennis (1981) has presented the most comprehensive analyses of these new items.

than weak partisans. Petrocik built a six-item index of political participation that stressed campaign activity. Strong partisans scored 98 on this index, weak partisans 53, Independent leaners 63, and pure Independents 46. An analysis by Valentine and Van Wingen (1980), comparing weak partisans with Independent leaners in the seven presidential election surveys between 1952 and 1976, found that, on most measures, Independent leaners were somewhat more likely to participate than weak partisans were.

There are, however, many factors that contribute to participation in politics; among these, level of education is usually the most important. Independent leaners have higher educational levels than do weak partisans, and, once these educational differences are taken into account, some of the participatory advantages of Independent leaners are eliminated (Petrocik, 1974, p. 38). Moreover, while strong Democrats tend to have relatively low levels of education,[13] they have high levels of participation and involvement (although somewhat lower levels than strong Republicans). That strong Democrats have high levels of political involvement, despite their relatively low levels of education, reinforces the basic conclusion that *strong* party loyalties contribute to political involvement.

Contributing to electoral stability

The argument that high levels of partisan identification contribute to electoral stability seems fairly sound, and may have been strengthened through a series of cross-national comparisons by one of *The American Voter* authors, Philip Converse. Converse, along with Dupeux (Converse and Dupeux, 1962), compared the political attitudes of Americans and Frenchmen and discovered that Americans (in 1958) had higher levels of partisanship than Frenchmen did. America also had high levels of electoral stability, whereas in France new parties often sprung up suddenly, gained substantial support for a few elections, and then faded from the political scene. A classic French example, and the most recent at the time of the Converse and Dupeux article, was that of the Poujadists. The Poujadists (the Union for the Defense of Shopkeepers and Artisans) were an overtly anti-Semitic, antiparliamentary movement that appealed mainly to small businessmen. The movement was established in 1953, and, in 1956, it launched a party that gained 12% of the vote and won enough parliamentary seats in the National Assembly to prove a disruptive political force. In 1958, with the end of the Fourth Republic, the Poujadists collapsed as a national political force. Converse and Dupeux conclude that the absence of party loyalties among a large number of Frenchmen contributed to the ability of new parties to gain sudden, if fleeting, electoral success.

These arguments are developed further by Converse in his analysis of party

[13] Petrocik was examining the entire electorate, but the tendency for strong Democrats to have lower levels of formal education obtains even among the white electorate.

loyalties in the United States, Britain, West Germany, Italy, and Mexico (1969).[14] He argues that, when a new party system is established, it tends to become stronger during the course of each generation, stabilizing at a high level of partisan support by the third generation. The United States and Britain, Converse writes, had mature party systems; Germany, Italy, and Mexico did not. High levels of partisan support, Converse predicts, would very likely contribute to the continued maintenance of the party systems in both Britain and the United States.

Converse has most recently advanced these arguments in his analysis of the 1968 American presidential election, in which George Wallace, running as the candidate of the American Independent Party, received 14% of the vote. In his article with Miller, Rusk, and Wolfe, Converse (1969) first makes a historical comparison with voting behavior in the Weimar Republic, the Germany democracy that lasted between 1919 (after the German Empire collapsed), and 1933, when Hitler came to power. The collapse of the Weimar Republic is especially significant, because it is the major example of a democratic political system that died as a result of electoral support for antidemocratic parties. As Converse and his colleagues write: "[R]econstructions of the fall of the Weimar Republic have always suggested that voters for the Nazi party in its culminating surge were very disproportionately drawn from the youngest cohorts of the German electorate" (p. 1104).

Converse draws a parallel between the Nazi success among young Germans and George Wallace's support among young Americans. Wallace, like Hitler, challenged the established parties, and, like Hitler, he fared better among younger voters. Yet Wallace had no special appeal to the young, and one might have expected older and more conservative voters to support him. Converse and his colleagues argue that Wallace fared better among young voters because they had weaker party identifications than did their elders. Older voters may have been more attracted to Wallace than younger voters were, but older voters were restrained from voting for him by their stronger party loyalties. Thus, party loyalties among the electorate helped thwart a new party movement and helped preserve the electoral dominance of the Republican and Democratic parties. By the time of the next election, the American Independent Party had passed from the scene as a major political force. It should be noted that, in 1980, Anderson did better among young voters, at least partly because they had weaker party loyalties than did their elders.

While Converse's arguments have strengthened the original *American Voter* thesis, the electoral-stability thesis can be challenged. The most important evidence to support the thesis comes from the demise of the Weimar Republic, but Shively (1972) uses electoral statistics to suggest that new voters did not

[14]Converse's analysis employs *The Civic Culture* data collected in 1959 in Britain, West Germany, Italy, and Mexico, and in 1960 in the United States. For the original discussion of this study, see Almond and Verba (1963).

provide disproportionate support for the Nazis. However, it is difficult to make inferences, from electoral statistics, about the way individuals vote, and it seems reasonable to conclude that we will never be able to reach definitive conclusions about the role of new voters (with weak party loyalties) in the Nazi electoral victories. Converse's analysis of the 1968 Wallace vote did rely on survey data, and thus he was able to examine individual-level voting behavior. But while Converse's analysis provides some support for the electoral-stability thesis, we should remember that the 1968 SRC survey turned up only 116 Wallace voters. As Converse's analysis involves controls for age, region, and strength of party identification, his conclusions rest on a small number of cases.

To test the electoral-stability thesis, we must wait to see whether new party movements can challenge established parties, and then use survey data to determine whether strong partisans are more likely to resist their appeals. The thesis can be tested through cross-national analysis, although we may face problems with such tests because the very questions used to measure party identification may have different behavioral implications in non-American settings.[15] Given the successes of the newly formed Social Democratic party, two-party electoral dominance has been threatened in Britain. Party loyalties have become weaker in Britain (Crewe, 1981), and it may provide a setting in which to test the thesis. In the American setting, we must wait to see whether new parties can successfully challenge the dominance of the Republican and Democratic parties. Clearly, Anderson's candidacy failed to provide a successful challenge, despite the weak party loyalties of the electorate.[16]

It seems reasonable to speculate that political leaders may be more successful in challenging established parties if support for those parties is weak. Yet the success of new parties depends on many factors other than the overall strength of partisan loyalties among the electorate. The skill of counterelites, the availability of attractive candidates, and the importance of new issues may all affect the future success of new parties. We explore the implications of the current low levels of partisan strength further in Chapters 7 and 16, after we examine the causes of low levels of partisanship among the electorate.

Conclusions

We have seen that party identification is among the most widely studied variables in American politics, and that, according to the authors of *The Amer-*

[15]For a discussion of the differences in the meaning of the questions used to measure party identification in Britain and the United States, see Butler and Stokes (1974). For a discussion of the utility of the concept of party identification in a wide variety of European settings and in Canada, see several of the essays in Budge, Crewe, and Farlie (1976).

[16]For a discussion of the Anderson candidacy, see Abramson, Aldrich, and Rohde (1982, pp. 172–184).

ican Voter, it is one of the most important. Campbell and his colleagues conclude that party identification performs four basic functions. They argue that partisan loyalties (1) contribute to opinion formation, (2) influence voting behavior, (3) enhance psychological involvement in politics, and (4) contribute to electoral stability.

We saw that the decline of party identification among the electorate affects all four of these functions and that Campbell's conclusions also need to be modified in light of more recent data and analysis:

1. Party loyalties do appear to contribute to opinion formation, but we now have a clearer recognition that opinions can alter partisan loyalties.
2. Party loyalties continue to influence voting behavior, but the relationship between party identification and electoral choice has declined since 1964.
3. Party loyalties do enhance psychological involvement in politics, but we now recognize that Independents who lean toward a party are as involved as weak partisans.
4. We now have considerably more evidence to support the electoral-stability thesis, but we also have a greater understanding of the difficulties in testing the thesis.

Even after this evaluation, it is clear that party identification is a key attitudinal variable for understanding political behavior. As we have also seen, assumptions about the age at which party identification is learned play an important role in *The American Voter* formulation. In the next chapter, we examine more closely the way individuals learn partisan attachments.

[CHAPTER 6]

How Party Identification Forms

One of the earliest findings of political-socialization research is that most Americans learn their parents' party loyalties and that these loyalties are learned early in life. Hyman (1959), in his review of adult surveys, including studies conducted by the University of Michigan Survey Research Center, finds a strong relationship between the party loyalties of adults and those of their parents, as reported by those adults. Because these findings are based on reports that respondents provide about their parents' partisanship, Hyman interprets them with caution. Still, he is able to derive interesting theoretical insights about such relationships. As we saw in Chapter 5, Hyman reasons that most people acquire party loyalties before they acquire much information about politics. Party loyalties provide a frame of reference that helps individuals interpret new political information. "Socialization into party," Hyman reasons, "provides another organizing principle for handling the new issues, on which specific socialization had not been possible" (p. 75).

Two pioneering studies of the political socialization process demonstrate that children acquire party loyalties at a very early age. In his study of 659 fourth through eighth graders in New Haven, Connecticut, conducted in 1958, Greenstein asked, "If you were 21 now, whom would you vote for most of the time? . . . mostly Republicans . . . mostly Democrats . . . don't know" (1965, p. 178). Greenstein finds that six out of ten fourth graders prefer either the Republicans or the Democrats, although only a third could name a party leader and only one in six could name a leader of both major parties. Knowledge about political leaders increases from grade four through grade eight, as does the percentage who volunteer that they are Independents. While Greenstein's results are based on a single city, he does compare children of higher and lower socioeconomic status and finds few differences between them, although children from higher-status homes are more likely to name party leaders and are more likely to volunteer that they are Independents.

The socialization study conducted by Easton and Hess (reported in Hess and Torney, 1965) also provides evidence that partisanship is learned early in life. Their survey is based on 12,000 white children in grades two through eight, conducted in late 1961 and early 1962. (The children attended public schools in eight major metropolitan areas.) Children were asked, "If you could vote would you be? . . . A Republican . . . A Democrat . . . Sometimes a Democrat and sometimes a Republican . . . I don't know which I would be . . . I don't know what *Democrat* and *Republican* mean." Hess, along with Torney, reports that, even among second graders, over a third have a party preference. By fifth grade, over half the children are either Republicans or Democrats, but the percentage choosing the two major parties levels off through the eighth grade, while the percentage choosing the category "Sometimes a Democrat and sometimes a Republican" increases (Hess and Torney, 1965, pp. 44–45). The Easton and Hess study, like Greenstein's, finds that children from higher-status backgrounds are more likely to be Independents.

Both the Greenstein study and the Easton and Hess study suggest that children often acquire their partisanship from their parents. Greenstein asked children about their parents' party loyalties and reports that "only a handful" of children have party preferences different from those of their parents (p. 72). While Easton and Hess did not ask children about their parents' partisanship, they provide indirect evidence that the family is important in teaching party loyalties. Because they had a very large sample, Easton and Hess are able to identify a large number of siblings. In his analysis with Torney, Hess (Hess and Torney, 1967, pp. 98–99) is able to identify 205 sibling pairs. Hess finds that siblings usually do not have similar political attitudes, but they did have highly similar attitudes on a question that asked how they felt when they learned that John F. Kennedy had been elected president. "This sibling similarity," Hess and Torney conclude, "supplements other evidence that many children identify with their parents' party" (p. 99).

All this indirect evidence could not provide a reliable guide about the proportion of children and parents that have similar partisanship, and it could provide few clues about the processes through which parents transmit partisanship to their children. Better evidence requires studies that directly measure the partisanship of parents and of preadults. Fortunately, the student–parent study conducted by the Survey Research Center of the University of Michigan provides precisely this type of evidence.

The SRC Student–Parent Study

The Michigan student–parent study is based on a national sample of over 1500 high school seniors, conducted in the spring of 1965.[1] The study has three features that are highly unusual in studies of preadults. First, it is based on a national probability sample, although it is more precise to say that it is based on a sample of schools, not of school children. Second, in addition to these students, the researchers also directly interviewed their parents (in some cases, the father; in some, the mother; and in some, both). Lastly, the Michigan researchers conducted a follow-up survey eight years later, in which both the offspring and their parents were reinterviewed. The key advantage of this survey, for our purposes, is that it allows us to compare the attitudes of students with those of their parents. Before turning to such comparisons, three qualifications are in order:

1. If we discover that parents and children have similar attitudes, this does not directly tell us about the processes through which children learn their political attitudes. Since children and parents share the same general social and cultural setting, we would expect some similarity of partisanship between children and their parents even if there were no political communication within the family. Indeed, the Michigan student–parent study demonstrates that there is some similarity between the partisanship of students and their parents even in households where students do not know their parents' partisanship or where politics is never discussed (Jennings and Niemi, 1974, pp. 48–49).
2. The student–parent comparisons are based on data collected at only one point in time, and such studies may have special properties that could lead to atypical results. From the standpoint of studying partisanship, the most obvious special characteristic of 1965 is that it was shortly after Lyndon Johnson's landslide victory over Barry Goldwater. As the data presented in Table 5.1 showed, this was an election in which many Republicans voted Democratic for president and many even voted for Democratic congressional candidates (see Table 5.3). On the other hand, Goldwater carried five states from the deep South: Georgia, which had never before voted Republican; Alabama, Mississippi, and South Carolina, which had not voted Republican since Reconstruction; and Louisiana, which had voted Republican only once (1956) in the 21 presidential elections between 1880 and 1960. The spring of 1965 may have had some other special characteristics that are less obvious. It may have preceded by only a few months the period during which partisan loyalties among the American electorate began to decline. Moreover, the spring of 1965 shortly followed the rapid politicization of Southern blacks, resulting

[1] Adolescents who are not enrolled in school are not included in the survey. According to census estimates, about 15% of the 16- to 17-year-olds were not enrolled in school back in 1965, and nonenrollment was somewhat higher among blacks than among whites. For more information about these estimates, see Coleman et al. (1966, pp. 444–459).

from the civil rights movement, Johnson's explicit appeals to blacks, and Goldwater's candidacy as the Republican standard-bearer. For all these reasons, somewhat different results might have been obtained if the student–parent survey had been conducted several years earlier or even a few months later.

3. It is helpful to rely on a variety of statistical measures in interpreting the relationship of parental attitudes to student attitudes. Weissberg and Joslyn (1977), in their critique of Jennings and Niemi's (1968, 1974) major analyses of the Michigan survey, argue that Jennings and Niemi's procedures may tend to underestimate the similarity of parental and student attitudes, especially when attitudes are highly skewed in one direction. In fact, Jennings and Niemi are usually quite careful in interpreting their results, and realize that their analyses might tend to underestimate the similarity of student and parental attitudes. Nonetheless, it is often helpful to look closely at the actual distribution of responses in comparing parental and student attitudes, and we should not rely only on summary measures of association.

With these cautions in mind, we may turn to Table 6.1, which shows the distribution of student party identification according to the party identification of their parents. As with all such comparisons in this book, results are reported separately for whites and for blacks.

The data for whites show a striking correspondence between the partisanship of students and their parents. While students tend to have weaker partisanship than their parents, they usually have the same basic partisanship. While only one student in three has a party identification and strength that is identical to that of his or her parent, nearly six out of ten have the same partisanship (if Independent leaners are classified as Independents) and over two out of three have the same basic partisanship (if Independents who lean toward a party are classified as partisans). Moreover, only a small percentage cross from the Democratic orientations of their parents to become Republicans (8% if Independent leaners are excluded from these calculations, 12% if Independent leaners are classified as partisans), although, not surprisingly given the timing of the survey, a slightly larger percentage of children of Republican parents identify as Democrats (10% if Independent leaners are excluded, 20% if Independent leaners are classified as partisans).

Among blacks, however, there is virtually no relationship between parental and student party identification. The low statistical association reflects the failure of the small number of black Republican parents to transmit their partisanship to their children; but since there are only 18 black Republican parents, these results should be treated with caution. However, because both black parents and black students are overwhelmingly Democratic, the overall percentage of black students who have the same partisanship as their parents is somewhat higher than among white students. In a sense, parental partisanship has been rendered almost superfluous, since the subcultural norms of the

Table 6.1 Party Identification of High School Seniors, by Parent's Party Identification and Student's Race: 1965

Part A Student's Race: White

	Parent's party identification						
Student's party identification	Strong Democrat	Weak Democrat	Independent leans Democratic	Independent, no partisan leaning	Independent, leans Republican	Weak Republican	Strong Republican
Strong Democrat	38%	21%	18%	10%	1%	1%	0%
Weak Democrat	33	37	23	14	11	12	7
Independent, leans Democratic	14	18	21	17	13	11	7
Independent, no partisan leaning	8	10	18	29	20	15	6
Independent, leans Republican	2	3	9	13	19	13	21
Weak Republican	4	7	8	10	26	34	29
Strong Republican	2	3	2	6	10	13	30
Total %	101%	99%	99%	99%	100%	99%	100%
Weighted *N*	(360)	(408)	(160)	(170)	(88)	(268)	(211)

tau-b = .48 gamma = .56

Percentage with same party identification and strength = 33%.

Percentage with same party identification (Independent leaners classified as Independents) = 58%.

Percentage with same basic party identification (Independent leaners classified as partisans) = 69%.

Part B Student's Race: Black

Student's party identification	Parent's party identification: Strong Democrat	Weak Democrat	Independent, leans Democratic	Independent, no partisan leaning	Independent, leans Republican	Weak Republican	Strong Republican
Strong Democrat	45%	42%	14%	24%	31%	20%	44%
Weak Democrat	29	30	23	49	0	67	41
Independent, leans Democratic	15	12	38	22	69	0	0
Independent, no partisan leaning	4	13	22	6	0	0	15
Independent, leans Republican	2	2	0	0	0	0	0
Weak Republican	3	1	0	0	0	0	0
Strong Republican	1	0	4	0	0	13	0
Total %	99%	100%	101%	101%	100%	100%	100%
Weighted *N*	(92)	(46)	(11)	(10)	(3)	(8)	(7)

tau-b = .10 gamma = .14

Percentage with same party identification and strength = 34%.

Percentage with same party identification (Independent leaners classified as Independents) = 64%.

Percentage with same basic party identification (Independent leaners classified as partisans) = 74%.

black community are powerful enough to instill loyalty to the Democratic party, even when parental partisanship runs counter to those subcultural norms. There is, however, one similarity between white students and black students: both tend to have weaker party loyalties than do their parents.

A variety of forces could contribute to the relatively weak party loyalties of the students. The school itself may play a role by stressing the virtues of independence. Students may be taught, in civics courses, courses in the problems of American democracy, or even in American history courses, that one should vote "for the candidate, not the party." While we have little compelling evidence that children learn the political values taught in the school, some children may learn, if only temporarily, to have weak party ties or to declare that they are Independents.

The weak partisanship of high school seniors might also result from their youth and political inexperience—in other words, from their position in the life cycle. Perhaps they have not yet learned to develop stronger party loyalties, but would develop stronger ties as they gain opportunities to reinforce their partisanship through political behavior. Even self-professed Independents might have to make partisan political choices, and through these early choices a sense of partisan commitment might emerge. Indeed, Jennings and Niemi (1974) clearly accept this interpretation. "This greater independence of students is clearly a result of the development of partisanship over the life cycle. . . . Since we know from adult studies that partisanship increases steadily over the adult years, it appears that the maximum proportion of Independents is reached some time during the adolescent years" (p. 40). Jennings and Niemi clearly expected that the students would develop stronger party ties as they aged, although, as we shall see, this expectation was not fulfilled.

It is also possible that the weak partisanship of these seniors results from distinctive formative socialization experiences. They may have learned their initial party ties during a period of weakened partisanship, while their parents learned their party loyalties in a more partisan era. Indeed, as we shall see, there is considerable evidence to suggest that the weak partisanship of young Americans results from what may be called a generational explanation. It would be interesting to know what the partisan loyalties of the parents were when they were in their late teens, but, of course, no such data exist. We also have no earlier nationwide sample of teenagers with which to compare these students.

Jennings and Niemi realized that they could not satisfactorily explain the reasons that students have weaker party loyalties than their parents, but they provide an extensive discussion of the conditions that may lead students to acquire different party loyalties from their parents. A basic conclusion is that children from less politicized homes are less likely to learn their parents' loyalties than those who come from more politicized households. Thus, the similarity in parental and student partisanship is lowest where family members have little interest in public affairs. The greater the level of political conversation between the parents, the higher the level of student–parent partisan correspondence. Children from less politicized homes are less likely to perceive correctly their parents' partisanship, and Jennings and Niemi conclude that "variations in family transmission patterns are in large part due to declining accuracy of perceptions among less politicized families" (p. 49).

The ability of either parent to transmit his or her partisanship to the child is reduced when one parent supports a party and the other is an Independent, and is substantially reduced when parents support different political parties. When parents do not have similar partisanship, the mother is slightly more successful in transmitting her partisanship than the father is, perhaps because children often have closer affective ties with their mothers than with their fathers. But while parental differences weaken the intergenerational transmission of partisan loyalties, such differences are rare. In those cases where both parents are interviewed, both have similar basic partisanship in 72% of the cases, and they support different parties in only 12% of the cases.[2]

Students are also less likely to follow their parents' partisanship when their friends support the opposite party. However, only a third of the students perceive a difference between their parents' and their friends' partisan loyalties. Where there is a difference between parents and friends, there is a substantial tendency for parent–student correspondence to be reduced. However, Jennings and Niemi (1974, pp. 51–53) conclude that the overall effect of friends' partisanship is small and that it more often serves to reinforce the impact of parental partisanship than to reduce it.

Another force that affects the transmission of parental partisanship is the actual political behavior of parents (Jennings and Niemi, pp. 49–51). Although most parents voted according to their party loyalties, a substantial percentage of weak Republicans deserted Goldwater (a finding consistent with the nationwide sample of the electorate reported in Table 5.1), while some Democrats voted for him. I have examined the partisan identification of white high school seniors according to their parents' vote for president among all seven subsets of parental partisan identification. Within each of the seven partisan subsets, parents who voted for Johnson were more likely to have Democratic children than those who voted for Goldwater.

That children often derive their cues about appropriate partisanship from such immediate acts as the way their parents vote may have important consequences for the way party realignments occur. Converse (1975), for example, notes that national samples of adults conducted in the 1950s and 1960s reveal apparent discrepancies when adults report their parents' partisan loyalties. Many respondents who were in their teens during the early 1930s report

[2]Based on results reported in Jennings and Langton (1969, p. 358). In this analysis, Jennings and Langton classify parents who are Independent leaners as partisans.

that their parents were Democrats, although there is substantial indirect evidence (based on older cohorts sampled during the 1950s and 1960s) to suggest that many of these parents were probably Republicans. However, many of these Republican parents may have defected to Roosevelt in the 1932 and 1936 elections and then returned to the Republican fold in subsequent elections. As teenagers during this period may have learned their parents' partisanship from the way their parents voted and as they were no longer living with their parents when their parents again began to vote Republican, they never learned their parents' "correct" partisanship.

Partisan transmission, Converse concludes, "while demonstrably effective, rests in many cases on amazingly superficial cues—mainly the most salient parental vote preference for the most visible office in the land, without any nuances of contradictory political philosophy or general partisan dispositions" (p. 144). The Jennings and Niemi evidence about the influence of parental partisanship "lends strong support to the surmise that many children of Roosevelt Republican parents in the later 1930s and 1940s suffered no sense of repudiation of family tradition as they began to establish their own personal voting histories of Democratic predilection" (p. 144).

The successful transmission of party identifications across generations can impede partisan change among the electorate. If there were perfect transmission of partisanship from generation to generation, the relative strength of parties over time would be largely a function of differential birth rates of Democrats and Republicans. The looseness of the process and the way in which intergenerational transmission of party loyalties may be affected by short-term political forces demonstrate that the intergenerational transmission process allows for change as well as continuity.

More Recent Evidence

Although the Michigan student–parent survey is the best single data set with which to examine the parental transmission of partisan loyalties, the special circumstances of the spring of 1965 may have affected the results. A more recent study by Tedin (1974) examines the influence of parental political attitudes in a special-purpose survey conducted between June and September of 1972. Tedin's survey, like the Michigan student–parent survey, was also conducted in an atypical period—but one that had the opposite attributes of the earlier study. While the Michigan study was conducted shortly after a Democratic landslide, Tedin's study was conducted shortly before Richard Nixon's landslide over George McGovern. Whereas the Michigan study was conducted shortly before partisanship among the electorate began to erode, Tedin's survey was conducted during a period of weak partisan loyalties.

Tedin's sample is smaller than the Michigan study, consisting of only 183 recent high school graduates and 322 of their parents. As it is based on white, mainly middle-class teenagers in Iowa City, one cannot generalize from his results to all American teenagers. However, Tedin clearly recognizes the limits of his survey, and observes the appropriate cautions in reporting his results. His research task is to establish the basic correlations between the political attitudes of parents and those of their children and then to determine the conditions that increase or decrease those relationships.

Tedin measures the attitudes of parents and their children toward racial integration, policy toward China, and marijuana laws. He also includes a measure of party identification, using the same basic seven-point party-identification index employed by the Michigan SRC and used in the Michigan student–parent survey. Tedin presents his results using a Pearson's *r*, which assumes interval-level measurement (see p. 47 above). The relationship between parental and adolescent party identification (.48) is higher than the relationship of parent and adolescent attitudes on the three policy issues. Parent–child correspondence among whites in the Michigan survey yields a Pearson's *r* of .60. Although Tedin's study shows a smaller parent–adolescent correspondence than does the Michigan survey, these correlations should be compared with caution, as Tedin's survey does not represent the universe of white high school graduates. Still, as we shall see, there is some evidence to suggest that the relationship between parental partisanship and the partisanship of their children may be lower today than it was in the mid-1960s, and Tedin's study provides an important clue that helps explain why that relationship may have eroded.

Tedin hypothesizes that the successful transmission of political attitudes partly depends on the salience of the issue to the parent, and partisan salience is measured by the strength of party identification. Parents with strong party identifications are particularly successful in transmitting their partisanship. Among parents who are strong partisans, student–adolescent correspondence is .68; among parents who are weak partisans, the relationship is .31; among parents who are Independents, correspondence is .28.

My reanalysis of the Michigan student–parent data yields results similar to those reported by Tedin. Partisan strength is an important factor in the successful transmission of partisan loyalties. This may be seen by recalculating the data presented in Table 6.1. Among white parents who are strong partisans, 67% have children with the same partisanship, a figure that rises to 83% if Independent leaners are included. Among white parents who are weak partisans, 54% have children with the same partisanship, or 69% if Independent leaners are included. Independents who lean toward a party are the least likely to transmit their partisanship: only 39% have children who identify with the party toward which the parents lean, although this figure rises to 60% if children who lean toward a party are included.

I replicated Tedin's calculations with the Michigan student–parent data and found similar results when the data were presented in correlational terms.

Among white parents who are strong party identifiers, the student–parent correspondence is .74 (using a Pearson's *r* to obtain a result comparable to Tedin's); among parents who are weak partisans, it is .54; among Independents,[3] it falls to .32.[4] (These results, it should be noted, lend support to my conclusion that weak partisans have stronger partisan commitment than do Independents who lean toward a party.)

The clear tendency of strong partisans to be more likely to transmit their partisanship to their children may help to explain why the relationship of parent–adolescent partisanship is weaker in the Tedin study than in the Michigan student–parent sample. The Iowa City parents have substantially weaker partisan loyalties than does the national sample conducted some seven years earlier. While Tedin's study cannot be used to estimate the partisan loyalties of parents in the nation as a whole, it is clear that the parents of high school seniors today would have weaker party ties than the parents of high school seniors in the mid-1960s. Using the data in the following chapter (see Table 7.3), we can estimate that, in 1964, about one third of the parents of high school seniors were strong party identifiers (as Jennings and Niemi found); by 1980, this figure was probably one in four. Assuming that partisan strength is still important for the successful transmission of party loyalties, the parent–student correspondence in party identifications would almost certainly be lower today than when the Michigan student–parent sample was conducted.

In addition to Tedin's study, a major cross-national study provides important evidence on the transmission of partisan loyalties. In 1974, a survey of political attitudes was conducted using probability samples of the American, Dutch, British, West German, and Austrian electorates. (The American sample was conducted between June and September.) The major results of this study are presented by Barnes, Kaase, and their colleagues (1979). The resulting national samples ranged from 1200 to 2300, with a sample of 1700 adults in the United States. In each household in which there was a 16- to 20-year-old residing, the researchers attempted to interview both the youth and one of the youth's parents. The number of parent–offspring pairs ranged from 173 to 257, with 244 parent–offspring pairs in the United States.

The number of pairs in the American sample is much smaller than that in the 1965 Michigan student–parent survey, so the chance for sampling error is far greater. In addition, since many youths of this age do not live at home—especially in the United States—the resulting parent–offspring pairs are not fully representative of the actual population of parents and children.[5] More-

[3]Based on a threefold division of Independents who lean Democratic, Independents with no partisan leaning, and Independents who lean Republican. If pure Independents are excluded, correspondence is .41.

[4]Given the negligible number of black Republican parents, a similar comparison of black parents and students is not feasible.

[5]For a discussion, see Jennings, Allerbeck, and Rosenmayr (1979, pp. 451, 484).

over, the American study was conducted during a very atypical period, at the height of the Watergate crisis. Despite these limitations, this study provides the only cross-national data that allow us to actually compare the political attitudes of parents with those of their children.

In the United States, respondents were asked the standard SRC question on party identification, although the follow-up question on partisan strength was modified to three responses ("very close," "fairly close," and "not very close"). In the other four countries, respondents were asked, "Which party do you usually feel closest to?" and those who felt closest to a party were asked whether they felt "very close," "fairly close," or "not very close." In their analysis of these data, Jennings, Allerbeck, and Rosenmayr (1979) reported that 88% of the American parents express a party preference, while only 77% of their offspring do.[6] In the other four countries, parents are much more likely to express attachment to a party than their offspring are. The difference between the United States and the other countries could have resulted from cross-national differences in the political-socialization process, but it might also have resulted from the different question that was used to measure partisan attachment in the United States.

Direct parent–offspring comparisons show that, in all five countries, parents have stronger partisan attachments than do their children, and in all five there is only a weak tendency for parents and their children to share the same level of partisan attachment. A direct comparison of parents and offspring in the United States yields a tau-b of only .15. The correlation is somewhat lower in the Netherlands (.08), which has a complex multiparty system, while it is slightly higher in Britain (.24), Germany (.21), and Austria (.23).

Jennings and his colleagues also studied the extent to which parents and their offspring have the same basic party loyalties. In order to attain cross-national comparability, they divide partisans in each country into supporters of leftist parties and supporters of rightist parties and then directly compare the partisanship of parents and their offspring. In the United States, parent–offspring correspondence yields a tau-b of .55, a higher level of correspondence than for any other political variable measured in the American sample. Parent offspring correspondence is at the same high level in Germany (.53), higher in Britain (.65), and highest by far in Austria (.81), which has a highly polarized two-party system. Correspondence is lowest in the Netherlands (.38), which has a party system that cannot be classified easily along a left–right continuum.[7]

[6]The national SRC–CPS survey conducted in 1974 shows that, among 18- to 24-year-olds (actual *N* of 154), only 52% identify with a party, which suggests that the sampling procedures used to identify youths in the cross-national survey may tend to overestimate the percentage of identifiers in the United States.

[7]For further evidence on Britain, see Dowse and Hughes (1971). For a recent discussion of the parental transmission of partisan values in France, see Percheron and Jennings (1981).

Jennings and his colleagues conclude that parent–offspring similarity is high, even in Holland. "In the other countries it reaches a level seldom found in this or any other investigations of the political socialization process. . . . Thus there is strong presumptive evidence for the transmission and maintenance of party cleavages within the family circle" (p. 463).

Conclusions

Our review of extant political-socialization research provides considerable insight about the way partisan loyalties are learned, but it also reveals substantial gaps in our knowledge. We have strong clues that the process of partisan transmission is largely a haphazard affair, depending on immediate behavioral cues, and not on a conscious process of political indoctrination. But we know very little about how these cues are transmitted. Direct data on the transmission of parental partisanship have been collected only during fairly atypical periods, and we cannot say how parental transmission works in electoral periods when a larger percentage of adults vote according to their partisan identifications. Nor can we judge the way partisan loyalties are transmitted during periods of partisan realignments, although Converse has provided some interesting speculation about how those processes may operate.

Most important, we are at a loss to say how the process of early partisan learning may have changed. Studies below the high school years are all based on nonrepresentative surveys, which often utilize differing measures and differing modes of data presentation. And although the Michigan student–parent sample provides an excellent baseline for studying adolescent political learning, it cannot be used to calculate the extent to which parental transmission of party loyalties may have changed over time unless a comparable national sample of high school seniors and their parents is conducted. Despite these gaps in our knowledge, we do have considerable reason to speculate that the influence of parental partisanship may have decreased, if only because parental partisan loyalties are weaker today than they were in the mid-1960s.

[CHAPTER 7]

How Party Identification Changes

Partisan loyalties are more stable over time than any other political attitude. This is best demonstrated through panel studies, in which the same individuals are studied more than once. The Michigan SRC has conducted two major national panel surveys: one studied change between 1956, 1958, and 1960; the other, between 1972, 1974, and 1976. Both studies show that the white electorate has highly stable partisan attachments and that there is less partisan stability among blacks.

Between 1956 and 1958, the over-time correlation of party identification among individual whites is .75 (tau-b); between 1958 and 1960 it is .75; and during the four-year period between 1956 and 1960, it is .71. Although party identification is substantially weaker among whites in the 1970s, the overall individual-level stability of party identification is only marginally lower than during the late 1950s. Between 1972 and 1974, the overall individual-level correlation of party identification among whites is .70; between 1974 and 1976, it is .74; and during the four-year period between 1972 and 1976, it is .68.[1]

The high level of stability indicated by these summary statistics may be better understood in percentage terms, and as an example I have presented the partisan loyalties of whites and of blacks in 1976 according to the partisan loyalties of these same individuals some four years earlier (see Table 7.1). The table shows, for example, that, among the 130 whites who are strong Democrats in 1972, 62% are strong Democrats four years later; among the

[1] Among blacks, individual-level stability is lower throughout all these time periods. Between 1956 and 1958, it is .39; between 1958 and 1960, .59; and between 1956 and 1960, .41. Between 1972 and 1974, it was .37; between 1974 and 1976, .57; and between 1972 and 1976, .41.

Table 7.1 Party Identification in 1976, by Party Identification in 1972, by Race

Part A Race: White

	1972						
1976	Strong Democrat	Weak Democrat	Independent, leans Democratic	Independent, no partisan leaning	Independent, leans Republican	Weak Republican	Strong Republican
Strong Democrat	62%	18%	12%	4%	3%	1%	2%
Weak Democrat	26	54	30	7	3	4	3
Independent, leans Democratic	7	12	39	15	8	1	1
Independent, no partisan leaning	3	8	7	44	22	6	2
Independent, leans Republican	1	2	9	21	42	19	6
Weak Republican	1	4	2	8	16	52	34
Strong Republican	1	1	1	1	5	17	52
Total %	101%	99%	100%	100%	99%	100%	100%
Total *N*	(130)	(280)	(138)	(131)	(143)	(178)	(155)

tau-b = .68   gamma = .78

Percentage with same party identification and strength = 50%.
Percentage with same party identification (Independent leaners classified as Independents) = 74%.
Percentage with same basic party identification (Independent leaners classified as partisans) = 80%.

Part B Race: Black

	1972						
1976	Strong Democrat	Weak Democrat	Independent, leans Democratic	Independent, no partisan leaning	Independent, leans Republican	Weak Republican	Strong Republican
Strong Democrat	72%	38%	38%	25%	75%	0%	17%
Weak Democrat	26	41	50	25	0	33	17
Independent, leans Democratic	2	16	12	17	0	0	17
Independent, no partisan leaning	0	3	0	25	25	0	0
Independent, leans Republican	0	3	0	0	0	33	17
Weak Republican	0	0	0	8	0	33	0
Strong Republican	0	0	0	0	0	0	33
Total %	100%	101%	100%	100%	100%	99%	101%
Total *N*	(46)	(32)	(8)	(12)	(4)	(3)	(6)

tau-b = .41 gamma = .56

Percentage with same party identification and strength = 48%.

Percentage with same party identification (Independent leaners classified as Independents) = 72%.

Percentage with same basic party identification (Independent leaners classified as partisans) = 83%.

155 whites who are strong Republicans in 1972, 52% are strong Republicans four years later. By recalculating the percentages presented in Table 7.1, we would see that 50% of the whites sampled in 1972 have the same party identification and strength four years later, 74% have the same partisanship (if Independent leaners are classified as Independents), and 80% have the same basic partisanship (if Independents who lean toward a party are classified as partisans). Viewed in these percentage terms, blacks, too, have fairly high over-time consistency.

Panel analysts recognize that not all the change measured among individuals between two points in time is real change. Some change reflects measurement error. There are several procedures that attempt to account for such measurement error and to calculate the "true" over-time statistics. Depending on the correlation used and the assumptions one uses to correct for measurement unreliability, the "true" over-time correlation of party identification during the 1956–1960 period may range from .72 to .93 (Asher, 1974).[2] Given the goals of this book, I do not attempt to correct for unreliability. However, there is one point to remember: the real over-time stability of political attitudes is almost always higher than the simple over-time correlation.

Almost certainly, some of the instability in party identification among individuals over time results from measurement error. Some scholars (Dreyer, 1973) argue that virtually all of the over-time change in party identification among individuals can be explained as a random process. Other scholars have argued more convincingly that at least some of the change in party identification results from disaffection with policies. Brody (1977) argues that the movement away from the Republican party in the late 1950s often reflected dissatisfaction with the economy during the late Eisenhower years, whereas some movement away from the Republicans in the mid-1970s resulted from Watergate. Markus (1979) demonstrates that disaffection with racial policies led to partisan conversions between 1965 and 1973. And an analysis of partisan change by Fiorina (1981, pp. 108–120) suggests that individual-level changes in party identification in both the late 1950s and the mid-1970s were affected by both personal economic experiences and perceptions of economic conditions.

Although there may be some controversy about the role of issues in leading to partisan change, one fact seems clearly supported by panel data: young adults are more likely to change their partisanship than older adults are. My analyses of the Michigan panel data from 1956 to 1960 and from 1972 to 1976

[2] Achen (1975) argues that, although party identification is more stable over time than other political attitudes, this over-time stability results from better measurement of party identification. Once differences in measurement unreliability are taken into account, he argues, the true over-time correlation of party identification is no higher than other variables. However, several scholars have challenged Achen's assumptions (Converse and Markus, 1979; Hunter and Coggin, 1976; Niemi and Weisberg, 1976), and it seems reasonable to conclude that Achen has overcorrected for measurement error in his estimates of the "true" over-time correlation of political attitudes.

demonstrate that the cohort between the ages of 21 and 29 consistently has lower levels of over-time stability than do their elders, whether one examines change over two-year periods or over the broader, four-year periods. There are even lower levels of over-time stability among the 18-, 19-, and 20-year-olds sampled during the 1972–1974–1976 panel, but they make up only a small subset of the sample.

Unfortunately, once one divides the electorate by age, the size of the subsets becomes rather small. For the 1956–1958–1960 period, there are only about 200 21- to 29-year-olds; and for the 1972–1974–1976 period, there are only about 300. It is therefore useful to turn to the Michigan student–parent data. Among the 1700 youths sampled in the spring of 1965, some 1300 were reinterviewed in the spring of 1973; and among the 1900 parents interviewed in 1965, some 1100 were reinterviewed. While the student–parent panel is less representative than the two national electorate panels, it provides us with an opportunity to study a much larger number of young adults and enables us to examine attitude change among black youths and their parents.

The student–parent panel corroborates the results obtained with the two more representative panel studies of the electorate. M. Kent Jennings has kindly provided me with the tables to compare change in partisanship over this eight-year period among whites and among blacks.[3] There is far more partisan change among young adults than among their parents. As with the two national electorate panels, party identification is more stable among whites than among blacks. The reason for this greater stability is to be found in the high level of partisan instability among black Republicans, which suppresses the basic statistics used to measure the association between partisanship over time. In fact, most blacks are Democrats, and most remain Democrats. Even so, black parents have somewhat more stable partisan loyalties than do black youths.

Among both white and black parents and among black youths, there is very little change in the basic direction of partisanship between 1965 and 1973. Among white youths, however, there is considerable partisan change. If we classify Independents who lean toward a party as Independents, only 57% have the same basic party identifications in 1973 as they had eight years earlier; if we classify Independents who lean toward a party as partisans, 61% do.

Why were white youths more likely to change their partisanship than any other group? Blacks, young or old, had few reasons to defect from their basic Democratic loyalties between 1965 and 1973; for even if they were dissatisfied with the Democrats, the Republicans offered no attractive alternatives. Whites were buffeted by stronger forces for partisan change. Some may have sup-

[3]Unless otherwise indicated, throughout this book my reports of results from the student–parent panel are based on information supplied by Jennings. These data are now available to the social science community through the Inter-University Consortium for Political and Social Research.

ported Johnson because of his moderate Vietnam policies, only to be disillusioned when the war escalated; some Southerners may have been dissatisfied with Johnson's support for the civil rights demands of blacks; many Democrats were disaffected when McGovern became the Democratic standard-bearer; by early 1973, the beginnings of Watergate may have led to doubts about the Republicans.

Yet change occurred mainly among the young, and at least two reasons may account for their relative partisan fluidity. First, young adults have not developed a habitual pattern of partisan voting. They have not yet had many political experiences, and will not have had the chance to reinforce their partisanship through political behaviors. Older adults may have solidified their partisan preferences through prior behavior, so that short-term disaffection is less likely to lead to a change in their partisan commitments.[4]

Second, young adults are more likely than their elders to experience social changes that may contribute to partisan change. For example, most young adults marry, and for some this may lead to pressures to alter their partisan loyalties. Few Americans choose their mates for political reasons, yet the tendency to marry persons of the same race, region, social class, and religion leads to partisan homogeneity among most couples. Beck and Jennings (1975) analyze the parent sample in the Michigan student–parent survey to estimate the effects of marriage on partisan conversion and find that wives are often influenced by the partisanship of their husbands, while husbands are less often influenced by the partisanship of their wives. Beck and Jennings conclude: "Traditional views of masculine rule are upheld here" (p. 91). Of course, the greater impact of the husband may result not from a conscious process of conversion, but because a family's social and economic position is more often determined by the husband's occupation and income than by the wife's. It would be interesting to know whether the influence of husbands has declined in recent years, when women have exhibited somewhat greater autonomy.

Geographic mobility may also have some influence on partisan conversions. Admittedly, most early studies of geographic mobility find that movement from region to region or from cities to suburbs has little influence on changing partisan loyalties (Campbell et al., 1960, pp. 441–472; Converse, 1966; Greenstein and Wolfinger, 1958–1959; Rubin, 1976, pp. 19–23). While the effects of geographic mobility are probably small, there is some evidence that such movement may cause partisan change, especially among young adults. In a recent study that relies on a secondary analysis of the 1970 Michigan SRC–CPS congressional election survey, Brown (1981) classifies migrations according to movements to and from congressional districts with differing

[4]For an interesting attempt to study the effects of voting defections on changes in party identification, see Howell (1980), who also provides interesting insights about the meaning of Independence.

levels of partisan competition. Such movements do lead to changes in congressional voting, with respondents often shifting to support the predominant party of their new district. Migrations less often lead to changes in party identification, but they are more likely to lead to partisan change among young adults than among their elders.

Lastly, social mobility up and down the occupational hierarchy is most likely to occur during young adulthood. Intergenerational social mobility (social mobility between children and their parents) is a potential source of partisan change. Many young men and women rise to a higher occupational position than their fathers held, and many also move down the occupational hierarchy. The extent of social mobility depends on the occupational categories employed, but analyses of the Michigan SRC data by Barber (1970) suggest that nearly four out of ten respondents are upwardly mobile, while one out of ten is downwardly mobile.

Given that the middle class (nonmanually employed workers and their dependents) is more Republican than the working class (manually employed workers and their dependents), there is at least some tendency for upwardly mobile Democrats to become Republicans, and some tendency for downwardly mobile Republicans to become Democrats. However, social mobility often fails to lead to partisan change. First, although there is a tendency for social class to be related to partisan change, the relationship of class to direction of party identification has been fairly weak throughout the postwar era (Abramson, 1975, pp. 51–52; 1978a). That about half the white middle-class party identifiers support the Democratic party reduces the pressures on the upwardly mobile to learn Republican loyalties. Second, early socialization often retards partisan change. Even in Britain, where social class is strongly related to partisan preferences, both the upwardly and the downwardly mobile often retain their parents' partisan loyalties (Abramson, 1972; Butler and Stokes, 1974, pp. 95–102). However, as Barber's analysis of American data shows, mobility sometimes leads respondents to change their partisan preferences; and, since intergenerational social mobility is most common during young adulthood, there is additional pressure on young adults to modify their partisan identification.

Partisan Strength Through the Life Cycle

Up to this point, we have focused on the acquisition of partisan identification and asked how persons learn to become Democrats, Republicans, or Independents. We now examine the way partisan strength changes over time. (For an important attempt to distinguish between the acquisition of partisanship and the processes through which those loyalties become more intense, see Claggett, 1981.) Before attempting to analyze partisan change through the life cycle, we first examine change in partisanship for the white electorate as a whole. Table 7.2 presents the party loyalties of whites between 1952 and 1980.

A large and growing proportion of Americans claims to be neither Republican nor Democratic. Regardless of how we define attachment to a party, the proportion of identifiers has declined markedly since 1964. Through 1964, the proportion of strong party identifiers never falls below 35%. In 1966, there is a sudden drop to 27%, and since then there has been a gradual decline. In 1978, only 21% of the white electorate are strong party identifiers, although this figure rises marginally to 23% in 1980. Through 1964, about three out of four whites are identifiers, but this proportion declines in each subsequent survey between 1966 and 1974, and has leveled off since then; in 1980, only 62% of the white electorate identify with the two major parties. Between 1964 and 1980, the percentage of pure Independents rises from 8% to 14%. Moreover, two separate measures of mean partisan strength also show a sizable decline in party loyalties of the white electorate.[5]

One of the most well-documented findings of political-attitude research is that young adults have weaker party identification than have their elders. This is clearly documented in Table 7.3, which shows the percentage of whites who are strong party identifiers between 1952 and 1980. The data are presented according to birth cohorts, using the basic cohort matrix presented in Table 4.1. In all fourteen surveys, young adults are less likely to have strong partisan ties than are their elders. A similar relationship between age and partisan strength also obtains when one examines a similar cohort matrix showing the percentage of strong and weak party identifiers or the two measures of mean partisan strength. Moreover, in all nine surveys since 1964, young adults have been more likely to be Independents with no partisan leanings.

The weak party identification of the young may affect future political behavior, for, as we have seen, there has been a sizable decline in partisan strength among the white electorate. Will this trend continue? We cannot answer this question with certainty, but we can gain greater confidence about the future of a trend by studying age-group differences. "It is the inevitable fact of life," Hyman writes, "that the young will replace the old and will determine the future course of any trend. Thus if the young differ from the old, and were to continue to do so despite their own aging, some prediction can be ventured"

[5]Both measures are described in Table 7.2. The basic measure assumes that weak partisans are more partisan than Independent leaners, while the alternative measure assumes that they have equal levels of partisan strength. The basic measure was developed independently by Converse and by me (Abramson, 1976; Converse, 1976). However, neither Converse nor I would argue that the scoring truly reflects the differing levels of partisanship of the four basic partisan subgroups. In a recent paper, Markus and Converse (1980) develop another mean partisan-strength measure that scores strong partisans as 10, weak partisans as 5, Independent leaners as 4, and pure Independents as 1. Translated on a 0 to 3 metric, their procedures would score strong partisans as 3, weak partisans as 1.33, Independent leaners as 1, and pure Independents as 0. Their new measure therefore yields results very similar to my alternative partisan-strength measure.

Table 7.2 Party Identification Among Whites: 1952–1980

Party identification	1952	1954	1956	1958	1960	1962	1964	1966	1968	1970	1972	1974	1976	1978	1980
Strong Democrat	21%	22%	20%	26%	20%	22%	24%	17%	16%	17%	12%	15%	13%	12%	14%
Weak Democrat	25	25	23	22	25	23	25	27	25	22	25	20	23	24	23
Independent, leans Democratic	10	9	6	7	6	8	9	9	10	11	12	13	11	14	12
Independent, no partisan leaning	6	7	9	8	9	8	8	12	11	13	13	15	15	14	14
Independent, leans Republican	7	6	9	5	7	7	6	8	10	9	11	9	11	11	11
Weak Republican	14	15	14	17	14	17	14	16	16	16	14	15	16	14	16
Strong Republican	14	13	16	12	17	13	12	11	11	10	11	9	10	9	9
Other party	†	0	†	†	1	†	1	†	†	†	†	†	†	†	†
Apolitical	2	2	2	3	1	3	1	1	1	1	1	3	1	3	2
Total %	99%	99%	99%	100%	101%	101%	100%	101%	100%	99%	99%	99%	100%	101%	101%
Total *N*	(1615)	(1015)	(1610)	(1638)[c]	(1739)[c]	(1168)	(1394)	(1131)	(1387)	(1395)	(2397)	(2246)[c]	(2490)[c]	(2006)	(1405)
Strong party identifiers	35%	35%	36%	38%	36%	35%	36%	27%	27%	27%	24%	24%	23%	21%	23%
Strong and weak party identifiers	75%	75%	73%	77%	76%	75%	75%	71%	68%	66%	62%	60%	61%	59%	62%
Mean partisan strength (basic measure)[a]	2.03	2.01	1.97	2.05	2.03	1.99	2.04	1.85	1.82	1.79	1.72	1.67	1.68	1.63	1.70
Mean partisan strength (alternative measure)[b]	1.92	1.88	1.86	1.92	1.89	1.86	1.92	1.71	1.71	1.70	1.64	1.60	1.60	1.57	1.62

[a]Mean partisan strength with strong partisans scored as 3, weak partisans as 2, Independents who lean toward a party as 1, and pure Independents and apoliticals as 0. Persons who supported minor parties have been excluded from these calculations.

[b]Mean partisan strength with strong partisans scored as 3, weak partisans and Independents who lean toward a party as 1.5, and pure Independents and apoliticals as 0. Persons who supported minor parties have been excluded from these calculations.

[c]Weighted *N*s. †Less than 1%.

Table 7.3 Percentage of Whites Who Are Strong Party Identifiers, by Years of Birth: 1952–1980

Years of birth	1952	1956	1958	1960	1962	1964	1966	1968	1970	1972	1974	1976	1978	1980
1956–1962											*	11	8	11
1948–1955									*	*	16	12	13	17
1940–1947					*	*	*	11	21	14	17	15	15	16
1932–1939		*	*	34	21	28	19	22	19	15	19	21	17	27
1924–1931	30	27	32	34	30	32	23	26	23	24	25	25	23	24
1916–1923	24	32	35	28	30	33	25	19	31	27	26	30	26	29
1908–1915	32	35	34	40	36	37	31	34	35	35	32	26	38	39
1900–1907	34	36	40	35	55	49	36	41	32	34	37	42	**	**
1892–1899	46	43	47	42	37	47	37	45	**	**	**	**	**	**
1884–1891	43	53	47	48	**	**	**	**	**	**	**	**	**	**
1876–1883	49	**	**	**	**	**	**	**	**	**	**	**	**	**
All whites	35%	36%	38%	36%	35%	36%	27%	27%	27%	24%	24%	23%	21%	23%

Note: For the numbers on which these percentages are based, see Table 4.2. Actual *N*s are slightly smaller, since persons for whom party identification was not ascertained have been excluded from these analyses.

*Not included because the full eight-year cohort had not yet entered the electorate.

**Not included because the advanced age of the cohort makes it nonrepresentative for comparisons across time or because there are too few cases remaining.

(1972b, p. 243). The problem is to explain why young adults have weaker partisanship than their elders. Since I am using data originally analyzed by Campbell and his colleagues, their discussion is my point of departure.

The American Voter authors demonstrate clearly that young adults have weaker party attachments than do their elders (Campbell et al., 1960, p. 162). Combined data collected in seven surveys between 1952 and 1957 show that the percentage of strong party identifiers increases steadily with age; the percentage of Independents (including Independents leaning toward either major party) decreases. But Campbell and his colleagues not only present their findings, but also advance alternative explanations for these findings and attempt to test these explanations.

Age differences may result from generational effects, for "age may mark an historical epoch in which the person has matured or undergone some special variety of experience that has left an imprint on his attitudes and behaviors." "[T]he historical interpretation of our data," they reason, "would suggest that partisan feeling was more intense several decades ago than now. If older persons have more intense party loyalties than younger, it is a reflection of the politics of an earlier American period" (p. 161). On the other hand, age differences may result from the differing position of people in the life cycle, for "age may serve as an index of the length of time that the individual has lived in a specified state or engaged in a specified behavior" (p. 161).

In attempting to discriminate between these explanations, Campbell and his colleagues rely mainly on an indirect test that compares the partisan loyalties of persons of the same age who have held their loyalties for differing lengths of time. Despite the indirect nature of their test, Campbell and his colleagues reach strong conclusions that support a life-cycle formulation, and their conclusions were widely accepted.

The life-cycle explanation, as formulated in *The American Voter*, has importance that goes far beyond a discussion of social-psychological mechanisms. It could explain a process through which partisan strength among the electorate can be held in equilibrium (see also Converse, 1969). Even though older voters with strong party ties are dying and being replaced continuously by younger voters with weak party loyalties, the dynamics that increase partisan strength with age can prevent the erosion of partisanship among the electorate. As party loyalties are held to contribute to electoral stability (see the discussion in Chapter 5), the life-cycle explanation, if valid, has major implications for the political system.

Today we have far better data with which to test the life-cycle thesis. In fact, the 1956–1958–1960 and the 1972–1974–1976 national panel surveys do not prove very helpful, since, as we shall see, the predicted gains in partisan strength with age are so small that they would be difficult to detect during a mere four-year period. But we now have a series of cross-sectional surveys (surveys conducted at one point in time) that allow us to track the partisan loyalties of birth cohorts for nearly three decades, and these surveys have become the main source of data with which to test between a life-cycle and a generational explanation.

Let us begin by examining the relationship between age and partisan strength in 1952. As can be seen in Table 7.3, the percentage of strong identifiers is lowest among persons born between 1916 and 1923 (ages 29–36) and next lowest among those born between 1924 and 1931 (ages 21–29). Alternative measures of partisanship show similar results, and, of all the measures of partisanship, only the percentage of pure Independents is unrelated to age. As Campbell's discussion suggests, there are two plausible explanations for the weakness of party loyalties among these young adults. A life-cycle explanation suggests that their weak party loyalties result from political inexperience, whereas a generational explanation suggests that there are differences between their formative socialization and that of their elders.

If a life-cycle explanation for the weak party loyalties of the young were valid, we would expect their feelings of party identification to grow stronger with age. The cohort born between 1916 and 1923, which has the largest percentage of weak partisans, should develop stronger partisan attachments as it ages. So, too, the cohort born between 1924 and 1931 should develop stronger partisanship as persons in that age group gain more experience and have more opportunities to grow attached to the party of their choice. Thus, the percentage of strong partisans should grow as these cohorts move through the life cycle.

We might also expect other changes in partisanship. Perhaps Independents who lean toward a party might develop partisan attachments. Even some pure Independents might develop partisan attachments, and we might expect the percentage of pure Independents to decrease as a birth cohort aged. But changes among Independents might be more problematic. Claggett (1981), for example, argues that *The American Voter* thesis does not predict that Independents will become more partisan, since the life-cycle thesis does not predict that persons will *acquire* partisanship as they age. Other scholars have argued that Independence may constitute a commitment of its own (Dennis, 1981; Valentine and Van Wingen, 1980; Weisberg, 1980). Regardless of our expectations concerning Independents, both measures of mean partisan strength should increase as the two younger cohorts gain more political experience and have more time to become attached to their party. Indeed, given *The American Voter* thesis, partisanship should increase among all birth cohorts.

A generational explanation is based on different assumptions and predicts different relationships. It assumes that there is a formative period during which fairly enduring attitudes are learned; after that, attitudes tend to become relatively stable. While such assumptions are not valid for all political attitudes (as we shall see in our analysis of feelings of political efficacy and trust), they may be valid for party identification. As we have seen, even before they enter the electorate, many persons have already learned party loyalties, although these loyalties are likely to be weak. And as we saw, partisan change among individuals more frequently occurs among young adults than among their elders. We also saw that the most important experiences in changing a person's party loyalties probably occur between the time that person first enters the work force and the first few elections in which he or she participates. In addition, although many persons have party loyalties even before they vote, they have had few opportunities to reinforce those loyalties through political behavior. If social and political conditions contribute to the formation of strong party loyalties during early adulthood, the relative level of party identification among the cohort continues to be high. But if conditions during this formative period contribute to the development of weak party loyalties, party loyalties are likely to remain weak.

Of course, the millions of adults who enter the electorate have a wide range of experience. However, a generational explanation maintains that the political conditions of the time may tend to create a common set of experiences for young adults. A political generation is "a group of human beings who have undergone the same historical experiences during their formative years" (Rintala, 1979, p. 8). If the generational explanation is correct, most persons in the 1916–1923 cohort experienced formative socialization in the late 1930s and during World War II, and by 1952 would be relatively resistant to partisan change; party identification among this cohort might well remain low as its members age. Persons born between 1924 and 1931 experienced formative socialization during or after World War II, and in 1952 would still be relatively open to partisan change. A generational explanation would not necessarily predict either a rise or a decline in their partisan strength, but, given the political and social conditions following 1952, their party loyalties might remain low.

Many scholars have discussed the weakening of parties and party leadership during the postwar years. Eisenhower provided little leadership for the Republicans; and Johnson, Nixon, and Carter all developed personal campaign organizations that bypassed formal party structures. (For a discussion of party leadership during the postwar years, see Broder, 1972; Burnham, 1969; Ladd, 1978.) The division of responsibility between the president and Congress for much of this period may have dampened the development of strong party ties. Candidates often played down their party and ran highly individualized campaigns. By stressing candidates at the expense of parties, television may have further weakened party loyalties. Television made the dissemination of political information less costly, so that the political party may have declined in importance as a means of reducing information costs. And although there was rapid social change—massive migration from the farms to the cities, the mass mobilization of blacks, the growth of higher education—neither party seemed able to capitalize on these changes by offering programs to reinforce party loyalties. Given these conditions, in spite of the predictions generated by the life-cycle explanation, party loyalties might fail to become stronger among the young as they gain political experience.

These explanations can be tested by a time-series cohort analysis. In the absence of panel data covering a lengthy period, one cannot compare the same respondents sampled at different times; but birth cohorts sampled in 1952 can be compared with persons born during the same years sampled in subsequent surveys. A life-cycle explanation predicts that strength of party identification will increase among the 1916–1923 and 1924–1931 cohorts as they age; a generational explanation predicts that the strength of party identification among these cohorts will remain low. To the extent that the youngest cohorts still have relatively flexible partisan loyalties, their level of party identification might, indeed, decline.

Before attempting to discover whether partisan strength increases, however, we should determine how much we would *expect* it to increase if the life-cycle explanation were valid. According to data presented by Campbell and his colleagues (1960, p. 162), 24% of the 21- to 24-year-olds are strong party identifiers, and 53% of the 70- to 75-year-olds are. Thus, one might expect an increase of .58 percentage points per year as cohorts age (Shively, 1979c). (Using similar logic, one can predict per annum gains for other measures of partisanship.[6]) Obviously, .58 percentage points per year is only a small gain, and, given that sampling error is far greater than half a percent, it would be impossible to detect such a gain unless we could observe a birth cohort for many years. But over 28 years, the cumulative gain in the percentage of strong partisans would be some 16 percentage points.

Reading across the rows of Table 7.3 reveals no instance where gains of this magnitude are recorded. Between 1952 and 1980, the 1916–1923 cohort registers a gain of 5 percentage points, far less than that predicted by the life-cycle explanation. The 1924–1931 cohort registers a 6-point drop. Between 1960 and 1980, the 1932–1939 cohort registers a 7-point drop in the percentage of strong partisans. Only the 1940–1947 cohort, if tracked between 1968 and 1980, registers anything close to the "expected" gain in partisan strength, rising some 5 percentage points, whereas a life-cycle explanation predicts a 7-point gain during a 12-year period.

This comparison of "endpoints" wastes a large amount of data.[7] The data

[6]Shively predicts that the combined percentage of strong and weak partisans would increase .34 percentage points per year. Using the basic measure, Converse (1976) makes a careful estimate of the "expected" gains in mean partisan strength and argues that partisan strength should increase .0082 points per year for the entire electorate, but some .0108 points per year for respondents below the age of 53. A similar procedure would lead us to predict that mean partisan strength (using the alternative measure) would increase .0080 points per year.

[7]Another danger of such endpoint comparisons is that they may place too much emphasis on the very youngest cohort when first sampled. Converse argues that there is a systematic tendency for standard sampling procedures to lead to *overestimates* of the partisan strength of cohorts below the age of 25. Readers may choose to ignore the earliest entry for the younger cohorts.

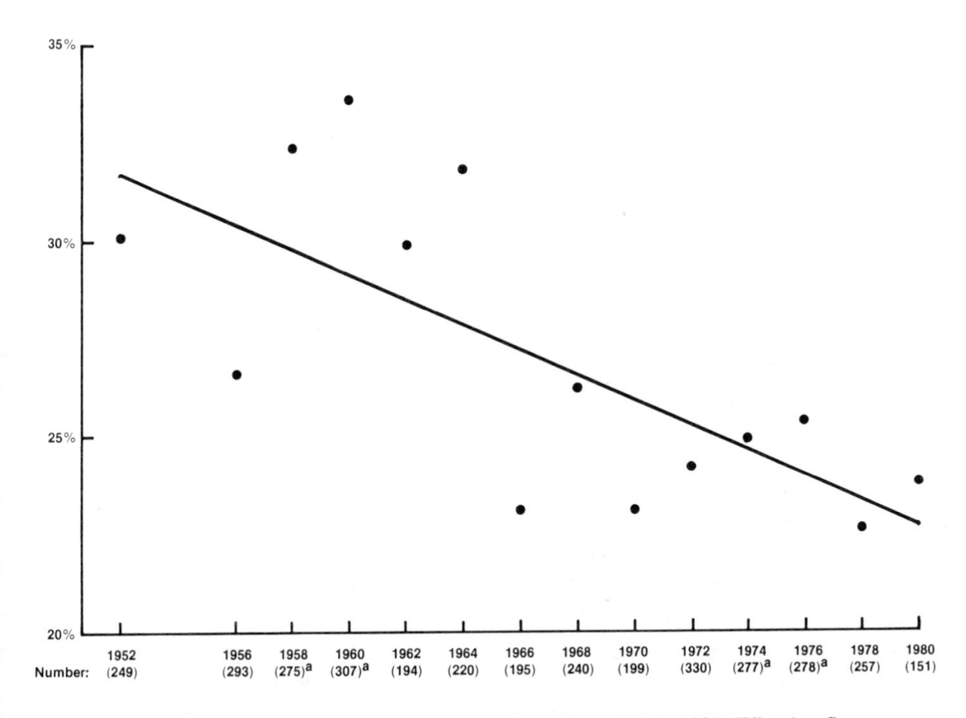

Figure 7.1 Percentage of Whites, Among Cohort Born 1924–1931, Who Are Strong Party Identifiers: 1952–1980.
([a]Weighted *N*s.)

displayed in Table 7.3 present results from fourteen separate surveys, but the verbal discussion focuses mainly on two of them. However, as our discussion in Chapter 3 indicates, there are methods that allow us to estimate the change over many data points. For purposes of illustration, we may transform the data in the row presenting partisanship among the 1924–1931 cohort into a simple scatter plot (Figure 7.1). The method of least squares shows that the line that best fits all these points *declines* at a rate of .32 percentage points per year of age.[8] Clearly, for this cohort, the percentage of strong partisans has not increased with age, but has registered a slight decline. The generational explanation would predict a trendline very close to zero, so the data appear to fit a generational explanation far better than a life-cycle interpretation.

In fact, none of the seven birth cohorts that can be tracked over a period of ten or more years registers the gains in partisan strength predicted by the life-cycle explanation, and six of these cohorts show a slight decline in the percentage of strong partisans. Converse (1976, p. 56) has suggested that the

[8]The ideal way to calculate the slope estimate is to use the individual-level observations rather than the overall level of partisanship for each cohort. Using the individual-level observations yields similar slope estimates, but provides a more efficient estimate of the standard error of the estimate (Johnston, 1972, pp. 228–238).

best single summary measure of the way partisan strength changes with age is the mean of the separate slope estimates for each of the cohorts. The mean slope for the seven basic cohorts displayed in Table 7.3 is −.14 percentage points per year. Rather than increasing with age, partisan strength registers a slight decline. The overall slope is thus in the wrong direction, given the predictions based on the life-cycle explanation, and is close to the slope of zero predicted by the generational explanation. Moreover, the bottom-line estimates for the other measures of partisan strength all yield slope estimates in the opposite direction from that predicted by a life-cycle explanation.[9]

In addition to the data collected through these SRC–CPS election surveys, two other data sets provide evidence that runs counter to the life-cycle explanation. Gallup surveys can be used to test the explanation, although, since they do not distinguish between strong and weak partisans or between Independents who lean toward a party and those who do not, they do not measure partisan *strength* as well as do the Michigan surveys. Still, if the life-cycle explanation were correct, one might predict the percentage of Independents to decline as a birth cohort ages.

Glenn has analyzed Gallup data collected from 1945 through 1971 (Glenn, 1972; Glenn, 1977, pp. 55–57; Glenn and Hefner, 1972). Glenn finds that the total percentage of Independents in the electorate rose during this 26-year period, from 20% in 1945 to 29% in 1971. Tracking birth cohorts over time, Glenn finds virtually no evidence that birth cohorts become less Independent as they age. Given the differences between the oldest and the youngest cohorts sampled in 1945, one might expect the percentage of Independents to *decline* by .20 percentage points per year of age (Glenn, 1977, p. 56). A least-squares regression analysis, similar to the technique suggested by Converse, shows that the average per annum change in Independence among birth cohorts is an *increase* of .20 percentage points.[10] Glenn concludes that "the widely cited finding of Campbell, Converse, Miller, and Stokes that older people have stronger party identification on average than young adults reflects, largely or entirely, an intercohort rather than a life-stage difference" (Glenn and Hefner, 1972, p. 44).

The Michigan student–parent data provide further evidence that young adults do not become more partisan as they age. Between 1965 and 1973, party identification becomes substantially weaker among both young whites and young blacks. In 1965, 24% of the white students are strong party iden-

[9]Per annum change for the combined percentage of strong and weak partisans is −.04, per annum change in mean partisan strength (using the basic measure) is −.0024, while per annum change (using the alternative measure) is −.0029. On the other hand, the percentage of Independents with no partisan leanings increases slightly (.09 points per year), while a life-cycle explanation might predict that it should decline.

[10]These are my calculations based on data presented by Glenn (1972, pp. 500–501) and by Glenn and Hefner (1972, pp. 36–37).

tifiers; in 1973, only 14% are. In 1965, 63% are strong or weak party identifiers, but this figure falls to 51% eight years later. The percentage of pure Independents rose only slightly, from 14% to 16%. Both measures of mean partisan strength also show a decline, falling from 1.72 to 1.49 on the standard measure and from 1.65 to 1.47 on the alternative measure. Furthermore, while young blacks have stronger party loyalties than do young whites, their party loyalties also erode over this period.[11] The decline of partisanship among young adults, Jennings and Niemi (1981) conclude, is "startling." Because a life-cycle explanation would lead one to expect the proportion of identifiers to rise among a cohort maturing from its late teens into its mid-20s, the decline of party identification "provides a compelling argument for a generation effects interpretation" (p. 154).

A direct comparison of individual-level change also demonstrates that party loyalties weakened among these young adults. For example, among white youths who are strong Democrats in 1965, only 20% are strong Democrats eight years later and 1% have become strong Republicans. Among those who are strong Republicans in 1965, only 33% are strong Republicans eight years later, and 7% have become strong Democrats. But very few youths with weak party loyalties have become strong partisans. Among white youths who are weak partisans in 1965, only 11% are strong partisans in 1973; among those who are Independent leaners, only 9% have become strong partisans; and among those who begin as Independents with no partisan leanings, only 5% have become strong partisans. A similar movement in the direction of weaker partisan ties is found among young blacks, although there are too few black Republicans for us to make meaningful comparisons.

Since over an eight-year period we would expect less than a 5-point gain in the percentage of strong partisans, the Michigan student–parent data must be used with caution. However, the net direction of individual-level change among young adults is toward *weaker* partisan ties. At the very least, these data clearly provide no support for a life-cycle formulation.

The SRC–CPS election surveys, the Gallup data analyzed by Glenn, and the Michigan student–parent panel all provide compelling evidence that partisan strength has not increased with age. But these data do not provide definitive evidence that *The American Voter* formulation is wrong. The social-psychological processes discussed by Campbell and his colleagues might be operating, but historical experiences could have prevented partisan strength from increasing. As birth cohorts age, they are subjected not only to the effects of formative socialization and of aging, but also to the social and political events of each period during which they are surveyed. Let us suppose that

[11] Among black youths, strong partisanship falls from 38% to 25%, the combined percentage of strong and weak partisans falls from 69% to 56%, and the percentage of pure Independents rises from 6% to 13%. Mean partisan strength among young blacks falls from 2.01 to 1.67 on the standard measure and from 1.98 to 1.67 on the alternative measure.

party loyalties do tend to increase with age and with duration of attachment to a party, but that the events of the postwar years have suppressed this development. A life-cycle explanation for the relationship between age and partisan strength might be valid, but no absolute age–strength gains could be detected. Several scholars have developed techniques that attempt to "control" for the effects of history, but all such techniques rely on assumptions that can be questioned.[12]

Converse (1976), in an elegant defense of the life-cycle formulation, relies on no statistical techniques to control for historical effects. He employs a more straightforward technique, similar to the least-squares regression methods employed above (which were borrowed from Converse), but argues that it is unreasonable to expect partisan strength to increase with age after 1964. Converse labels the years between 1952 and 1964 as the "steady-state period," whereas the years after 1964 are called the "era of political crisis." Converse demonstrates that there are gains in partisan strength with age between 1952 and 1964. Although life-cycle processes may have operated after 1964, partisan gains with age do not emerge in any absolute strength because such gains, though present, are canceled out by historical forces.

As I demonstrate elsewhere (Abramson, 1979b), Converse overestimates gains in partisan strength, especially among the young, by failing to examine whites and blacks separately (see Converse, 1979, for his reply). Even so, there is certainly some evidence for life-cycle effects—if one focuses on the years through 1964 and ignores the evidence collected after 1964. This would render the Michigan student–parent panel irrelevant for testing between a life-cycle and a generational explanation, since those data were collected during the "era of political crisis." And it requires that the data in Table 7.3 be truncated after 1964. (Only the data presented by Glenn for 1945 through 1961 could be used.)

Given enough imagination, one can even demonstrate partisan gains with age even during the years after 1964, and it seems reasonable to predict that controversies over the life-cycle and the generational explanation will continue. However, Converse now appears to have largely abandoned his support for the life-cycle thesis. In a recent paper with Markus (Markus and Converse, 1980), Converse implicitly abandons his earlier position. Using complex autoregressive models applied to the SRC voting studies conducted from 1952 through 1978, Converse finds distinct generational effects in the development of partisan strength. As Markus and Converse conclude: "[T]races of the

[12]See, for example, Knoke and Hout (1974) and Shively (1979a; 1979c). However, in his more recent work, Knoke (1976, pp. 133–137) emphatically rejects the life-cycle thesis. I discuss problems with Shively's procedures in Abramson (1979a); for his reply, see Shively (1979b). In addition, three studies directly use my previously published cohort matrices to develop tests between life-cycle, generational, and period effects (Claggett, 1981; Kritzer, 1979; Williams, 1980).

original inter-cohort distinctions are retained well into middle age, although, according to the model, initial differences become progressively diluted in the stream of common historical experiences shared by cohorts whose life spans overlap appreciably" (p. 21).

While Converse now concedes that there are generational effects, he has not directly repudiated his earlier position. Let us suppose that the life-cycle thesis can be salvaged, at least for the "steady-state period." Salvaging the explanation is costly. The life-cycle thesis, as reformulated by Converse (1976), argues that such gains can be expected only during "normal" periods, that is, periods when "shocks" to the electorate do not impede partisan growth. This is a far more restrictive thesis than that advanced by Campbell et al. (1960), which seems to predict absolute increases in partisan strength with age—not increases that can be offset by other forces. Moreover, as I argued earlier, the life-cycle formulation, as advanced in *The American Voter,* has major implications for the stability of democratic political systems, for it could explain a process through which partisan strength among the electorate is held in equilibrium over time. It is now apparent that life-cycle forces, if they exist, prevent partisan decay only under special, though still unspecified, conditions. We cannot be confident that the normal processes of aging will maintain party loyalties among the electorate. In fact, rather than leading to an equilibrium in partisan strength, the ongoing processes of generational replacement have led to a dramatic erosion of partisan loyalties.

As we saw in Chapter 4, the continuous processes of generational replacement can contribute to change among the electorate. The decline of partisan loyalties represents one of the clearest examples of the way replacement can create a trend. Figure 7.2 allows us to estimate the importance of replacement among the white electorate. The solid line presents the actual percentage of strong partisans among the white electorate, whereas the bottom line shows what the percentage would have been with no generational replacement. (For our procedures in making such estimates, see Chapter 4.) As Figure 7.2 shows, the percentage of strong partisans drops 12 percentage points between 1952 and 1980. If no new cohorts had entered the electorate, and if we took differential death rates into account by immortalizing the elderly,[13] the percentage of strong partisans would have been the same in 1980 as it was in 1952.

A closer examination of Figure 7.2 reveals that other processes may also have been at work. If there had been no generational replacement between 1952 and 1964, the overall percentage of strong partisans would have risen 5

[13]The percentage of strong partisans for each cohort is presented in Table 7.3. For cohorts that have too few cases to be included in this matrix, I assign a percentage based on all surviving respondents, plus the oldest cohort still in the matrix. As cohorts that left the electorate through death have a high percentage of strong partisans, using data from the oldest surviving cohort to estimate their partisanship probably tends to lower our estimate of the percentage of strong partisans and may underestimate the impact of replacement processes.

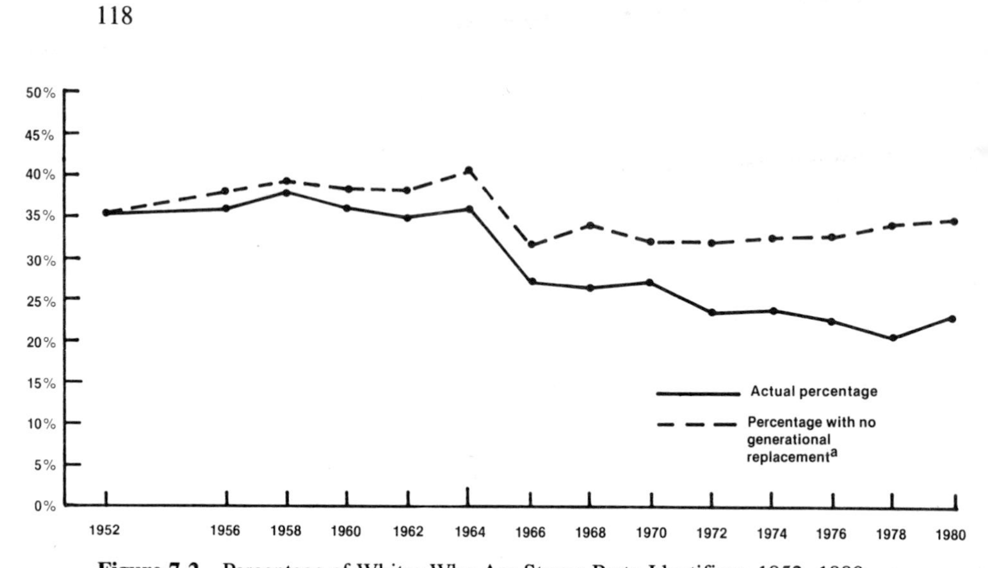

Figure 7.2 Percentage of Whites Who Are Strong Party Identifiers: 1952–1980. (*Note:* For the numbers on which the percentages for the solid line are based, see Table 7.2. For the numbers on which the percentages for the broken line are based, see Table 4.2. Actual *N*s are marginally smaller, since respondents for whom party identification was not ascertained have been excluded from the analysis. [a]Assuming that no persons born after 1931 entered the electorate and that older cohorts did not diminish through death.)

percentage points, mainly because of increases in partisan strength among birth cohorts that entered the electorate before or during World War II (born before 1924). During this period, generational replacement may have prevented a trend toward increasing partisan strength by holding these levels in a state of equilibrium. Between 1964 and 1966, there is a sharp drop in partisan strength, which results almost solely from the impact of historical forces. (For a detailed discussion of the decline during these two years, see Converse, 1976, pp. 69–80.) But if no generational replacement had occurred, the percentage of strong partisans would have been fairly stable from 1966 on, whereas the actual percentage of strong partisans continues to decline. (For similar calculations using the standard measure of mean partisan strength, see Abramson, 1978b.)

Other data sets also suggest that generational replacement plays an important role in contributing to the erosion of partisan loyalties. Glenn's analyses of Gallup data show that, among persons born before 1925, 20% are Independents in 1945. This percentage is virtually unchanged (21%) 26 years later. The overall percentage of Independents grew by 9%, entirely because of the entry of new birth cohorts into the electorate and the continuous diminution of older birth cohorts through death. The Michigan student–parent data cannot be used to calculate the effects of generational replacement on overall levels of partisan strength, but these data show only a small decline in the partisanship of the parental generation. As there is a sizable decline in partisan strength among the electorate between early 1965 and 1973, these data, too, suggest that generational replacement contributes to the erosion of partisanship among the electorate. The small decline in partisanship among the middle-aged cohorts could not have accounted for the substantial decline of partisanship among the electorate as a whole.

On balance, the ongoing processes of generational replacement are the major dynamic that contributes to the erosion of party loyalties. While an analysis of change among birth cohorts does not tell us *why* younger cohorts develop weaker partisanship than do their elders, it highlights a basic process through which the political attitudes of mass electorates may be gradually transformed.

Republicanism Through the Life Cycle

Campbell and his colleagues not only document the weak partisan loyalties of young adults, but also show that young adults are less likely to identify with the Republican party. Their data show that, among adults below the age of 45, only one out of three party identifiers is a Republican (Campbell et al., 1960, p. 162); among respondents between the ages of 45 and 54, four out of ten are. Among older respondents, the percentage of Republicans rises slightly; and among persons 65 years and older, nearly half of the party identifiers are Republican.

While such findings could mean that more persons become Republicans as they age, they could also result from the effects of the New Deal realignment. Most persons who were in their late 40s during *The American Voter* surveys entered the electorate before the Hoover–Smith election of 1928 (when, according to some scholars, the earliest phase of the Democratic realignment began). They all entered the electorate before the Roosevelt victories of 1932 and 1936, when the Democratic party dominance was established. They were first eligible to vote when the Republican party was dominant, and therefore may have been socialized to Republican party loyalties that, ultimately, servived the Democratic landslides of the 1930s. Persons below the age of 45 entered the electorate during a period of Democratic dominance, and may have been more likely to learn Democratic party loyalties.

Campbell and his colleagues clearly recognize these alternative explanations for the Republicanism of the elderly. "If party identification is typically a life-long commitment, changed on the national scale only by major social cataclysms, it would be reasonable to conclude that the present age division in party identification is the consequence of the Depression and the New Deal" (p. 166). If this interpretation were correct, they reason, "the present Republican following must inevitably decrease as time replaces the older age groups with the young groups in which people of Democratic commitment are more numerous" (p. 166).

But Campbell et al. also recognize that the Republicanism of the elderly may also be a life-cycle phenomenon. Republicanism, because of its "air of respectability, conservatism, and social status" (p. 166) may have a greater appeal to the middle-aged and the elderly. Therefore, one could hypothesize that "the two parties have different appeals to people of different ages, and although the Democratic Party may have an advantage in its appeal to young people, this advantage may be gradually dissipated as these young Democrats grow older and respond differently to political stimuli" (p. 166). While Campbell and his colleagues clearly favor a generational interpretation, they make no attempt to test between these alternative explanations.

As we shall see, Campbell and his colleagues are correct in favoring a generational interpretation, but wrong in suggesting that generational replacement would lead to a continued decline of Republicanism. While there has been a substantial decline in the percentage of the electorate that identifies as Republican, there has also been a decline in the percentage that identifies as Democratic (Table 7.2). If we compare the ratio of Democrats to Republicans from 1952 through 1980, we see very little change among the white electorate. Throughout the last quarter of a century, there have been about three Democrats for every two Republicans.[14]

Surveys conducted early in Reagan's presidency record a surge in Republican strength that has eroded this Democratic advantage. For example, a CBS News/*New York Times* poll conducted in April 1981 shows that the Democratic lead among the entire electorate has slipped to a five to four margin and finds that, among whites, the Democratic margin has been eliminated altogether (Clymer, 1981). However, the overall evidence is mixed, and it would be premature to conclude that a long-term shift toward the Republicans has occurred.[15] In any event, the SRC–CPS data, generally considered the best data source for monitoring changes in partisanship, do not reflect these Republican gains. The postelection CPS survey conducted in November and December of 1980 records only a negligible shift toward the Republican party.[16]

[14]The Republicans did notably worse in 1964, when just over one in three party identifiers was a Republican.

[15]For an excellent summary of surveys conducted through late 1981, see *Public Opinion*, 4 (December/January 1982), 38–39.

[16]Among white party identifiers in the postelection interview, 43% are Republicans; and if Independents who lean toward a party are included, 47% are. Part of the growth in Republicanism results from the fact that preelection Republicans are more likely to be in the postelection interview than preelection Democrats are. Once this is taken into account, we find no net shift to the Republican party among party identifiers; when Independent leaners are included, there is a net shift of 2 percentage points.

The thesis that Republicanism increases with age has received little support in subsequent surveys. Crittenden (1962), through an analysis of Gallup data, claims that Republicanism increases with age; but a subsequent reanalysis of his data by Neal Cutler (1969–1970) suggests that there is no absolute increase in Republicanism. Only a "correction for trend" procedure of dubious validity allows Crittenden to reach his conclusions. A more recent analysis by Knoke and Hout (1974), based on a secondary analysis of SRC–CPS data, employs a complicated procedure that allows one to simultaneously estimate the impact of generational, life-cycle, and period (historical) effects; this procedure finds some evidence that Republicanism increases with age. However, Converse (1976, pp. 122–130) carefully examines the Knoke and Hout analysis and suggests that their results may have been distorted by focusing only on presidential election years. But Converse does not present a systematic analysis of his own data to test between a life-cycle and a generational explanation.

Fortunately, the techniques Converse developed to examine the relationship between age and partisan strength can also be employed to study the relationship between age and Republicanism. Table 7.4 presents the basic cohort table that shows the percentage of Republicans among all white party identifiers between 1952 and 1980.[17] While my analysis concentrates on the percentage of identifiers who are Republican, other measures of Republicanism yield similar results.

The data presented for 1952 and 1956 represent part of the data reported in *The American Voter,* so the results are similar to those reported by Campbell. There is an increase in Republicanism as one moves above the age of 45, and, of course, the same basic generational division emerges. Persons who entered the electorate after 1928 (born after 1907) are much less Republican than those who entered the electorate earlier (Campbell et al., 1960, p. 154). If a life-cycle explanation for the low level of Republicanism of young adults were valid, we would expect Republicanism to increase with age. A generational explanation, on the other hand, predicts that the low levels of Republicanism of respondents born after 1907 will persist even as they move through the life cycle.

Before examining change with age over the next quarter of a century, we should first estimate how much of an increase in Republicanism we would expect if a life-cycle explanation were valid. If we use *The American Voter* data as a guide, we find that, among respondents between the ages of 21 and

[17]As Republicans tend to live slightly longer than Democrats, an old birth cohort might become more Republican as it ages simply because Republicans outlive Democrats. We suspect that differential death rates are not too important in affecting our results (Segal, Felson, and Segal, 1973), although they would become more important if we attempted to track a cohort over its old age. To the extent that differential death rates do affect our estimates, they work to strengthen support for a life-cycle explanation.

Table 7.4 Percentage of White Party Identifiers Who Are Republicans, by Years of Birth: 1952–1980

Years of birth	1952	1956	1958	1960	1962	1964	1966	1968	1970	1972	1974	1976	1978	1980
1956–1962											*	34	38	45
1948–1955									*	*	27	38	35	40
1940–1947					*	*	*	37	40	40	34	43	40	39
1932–1939		*	*	42	41	33	37	41	44	45	54	45	44	47
1924–1931	32	36	35	33	29	33	35	34	34	43	41	43	33	45
1916–1923	30	36	30	36	37	38	40	40	44	35	34	31	39	30
1908–1915	34	41	37	40	32	27	35	42	35	40	51	49	32	35
1900–1907	46	44	41	36	44	34	39	40	42	41	46	40	**	**
1892–1899	42	54	46	55	45	50	46	44	**	**	**	**	**	**
1884–1891	46	44	44	47	**	**	**	**	**	**	**	**	**	**
1876–1883	42	**	**	**	**	**	**	**	**	**	**	**	**	**
All whites	38%	41%	37%	41%	40%	35%	38%	40%	41%	41%	40%	42%	38%	41%

Note: To approximate the numbers on which these percentages are based, see Table 4.2. Actual *N*s are smaller, since these data are based only on Republican and Democratic identifiers.

*Not included because the full eight-year cohort had not yet entered the electorate.

**Not included because the advanced age of the cohort makes it nonrepresentative for comparisons across time or because there are too few cases remaining.

24, only 30% of the party identifiers are Republican; while among those between the ages of 70 and 75, 48% are.[18] We might thus expect Republicanism to increase at an annual rate of .36 percentage points, and, over the course of 28 years, there would be a 10-point gain in Republicanism as a cohort aged. On the other hand, proponents of a life-cycle thesis might not expect a gradual increase in Republicanism with age. They might predict that there should be a jump in Republicanism as members of a birth cohort pass the age of 45.

In fact, regardless of how we examine these data, we see only small increases in Republicanism with age. If we compare endpoints, only members of the 1924–1931 cohort register the predicted gain. There is also little evidence that cohorts register gains in Republicanism as they reach their late 40s.

As we know, however, endpoint comparisons do not fully capitalize on all 14 available data points, and we can turn to least-squares regression analysis to fit a trendline to the data for each birth cohort. When we examine the seven basic cohorts in Table 7.4, we find that only two cohorts (1924–1931 and 1932–1939) register the increase in Republicanism predicted by the life-cycle explanation. But a bottom-line estimate shows that the mean change for all seven cohorts is an increase of only .16 percentage points per year, less than half the increase a life-cycle explanation would lead us to expect. Moreover, other measures of Republicanism all show smaller increases with age than a life-cycle explanation would lead us to predict.[19]

Gallup data also lead us to question the thesis that Republicanism increases with age. Using Gallup data to systematically track changes in party identification with age, Glenn finds no increases in Republicanism and concludes that "the thesis that cohorts experience an absolute increase in Republicanism as a consequence of aging receives no support from our data" (Glenn and Hefner, 1972, p. 35). Rather, "the positive association of Republicanism with age, consistently revealed by cross-sectional data gathered at various times

[18] A least-squares regression analysis of the relationship of Republicanism to age predicts a nearly identical gain of .39 percentage points per annum. As the data in *The American Voter* combine all three types of Independents, we cannot use those data to calculate "expected" gains in Republicanism using alternative measures. My analyses, based on the 1952 and 1956 SRC data, suggest that the percentage of Republicans (classifying Independent leaners as partisans) should increase .27 percentage points per annum. In addition, I develop two mean-score measures of Republicanism. The basic measure scores strong Republicans as 6; weak Republicans as 5; Independents who lean Republican as 4; pure Independents, apoliticals, and supporters of minor parties as 3; Independents who lean Democratic as 2; weak Democrats as 1; and strong Democrats as 0. The alternative measure is similar to the basic measure, but scores weak Republicans and Independents who lean Republican as 4.5 and weak Democrats and Independents who lean Democratic as 1.5. According to my analyses, mean Republicanism (using the basic measure) should increase .0100 points per annum, while mean Republicanism (using the alternative measure) should increase at .0084 points per annum.

[19] When Independent leaners are classified as partisans, Republicanism increases only .14 percentage points per year of age, the mean level of Republicanism (using the basic measure) shows an increase of .0063 points per year, while the alternative measure shows an increase of .0059 points per year.

during the past 30 years or so, reflects intercohort (or 'generational') differences rather than the effects of aging" (p. 35). According to my recalculations based on Glenn's data, one might expect Republicanism to increase about .38 percentage points per year of age if the life-cycle explanation were valid. A least-squares regression analysis reveals that Republicanism does increase slightly with age, but only at a rate of .038 percentage points per year, only one-tenth as fast as a life-cycle explanation predicts.

The Michigan student–parent panel data do show a slight increase in Republicanism among white parents (from 39.5% in 1965 to 43.3% in 1973). During this same period, however, white students show almost no change in Republicanism (from 38.8% to 38.1%), while both black parents and black students show marginal movement away from the Republican party.

On balance, we find substantial support for *The American Voter* conclusion that the Democratic propensities of the young result from generational experiences and are not a result of youth per se. Yet the ratio of Republicans to Democrats in the white electorate has not declined during the last quarter century. Why, given the failure of young adults to become more Republican, does the proportion of Republicans remain fairly constant?

The failure of Republicanism to decline seems all the more perplexing because there is evidence that generational replacement helped to make the Democrats the dominant party. Some analyses suggest that, in the 1930s, and perhaps through Eisenhower's first election, generational replacement eroded Republican loyalties. Andersen (1979, pp. 53–72), in an ingenious attempt to estimate party identification before 1952, suggests that Republican strength declines fairly consistently from 1920 through 1952 and that in large part generational replacement accounts for that decline.[20]

Andersen's analyses are consistent with Beck's (1974) arguments about the way different political-socialization experiences can contribute to party realignments. During a party realignment, Beck argues, the new majority party cannot capture the loyalties of the established supporters of the losing party, but it is likely to capture the loyalties of new entrants into the electorate. As Beck notes, when one examines the relationship of party identification to age, the biggest increase in Democratic strength is found among those who were in their 20s when the Depression of 1929 struck, as compared with those who were in their 30s at that "critical watershed." As Beck writes: "This change in the distribution of partisanship is both sharp and durable, preordaining the emergence of a new Democratic majority as the process of population replacement worked its inexorable magic" (p. 204).

[20] Andersen relies heavily on recall data about previous partisan loyalties, and both the reliability of such data and the proper inferences that can be made from such recall data have been seriously questioned (Niemi, Katz, and Newman, 1980; Reiter, 1980). A recent analysis by Erikson and Tedin (1981) also suggests that generational replacement may be less important than Andersen claims.

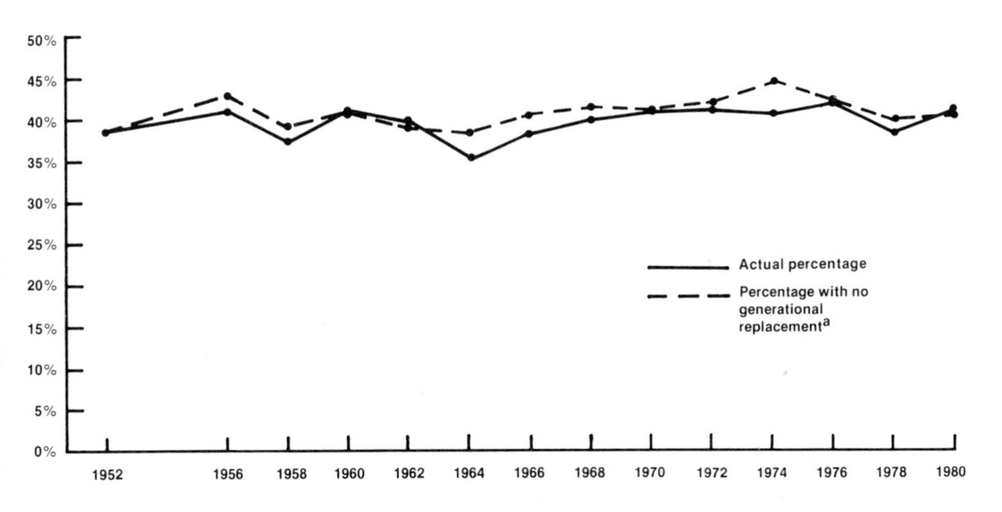

Figure 7.3 Percentage of White Party Identifiers Who Are Republicans: 1952–1980. (*Note:* For the numbers on which the percentages for the solid line are based, see Table 7.2. For the numbers on which the percentages for the broken line are based, see Table 4.2. Actual *N*s are smaller, since these calculations are based only on strong and weak party identifiers. [a]Assuming that no persons born after 1931 entered the electorate and that older cohorts did not diminish through death.)

By the 1950s, however, the magic had run its course. This is clearly demonstrated by Figure 7.3, which shows the actual percentage of Republicans among white party identifiers (the solid line) between 1952 and 1980 and the percentage that would have been Republican if no generational replacement had occurred (the broken line).[21] There is very little difference between the actual level of Republicanism and the estimates removing the effects of replacement.

Three factors prevented continued generational replacement from weakening the Republican party:

1. Much of the replacement that weakened the Republicans had already occurred by 1952. By the 1950s, predominantly Republican cohorts made up only a small proportion of the electorate.
2. The cohorts that entered the electorate after the 1950s have usually been as Republican as the electorate as a whole. In fact, from 1968 on, there has been only a very weak relationship between Republicanism and age; and in the two most recent surveys, there is actually a negative relationship.
3. Even though actual increases in Republicanism as cohorts move through

[21]The estimates in Figure 7.3 are based on the cohorts presented in Table 7.4. For cohorts that are too old to be included in this table, I base the estimates about levels of Republicanism on the last two entries for the cohort. As there is no reason to suspect that Republicanism decreases with age, it would be misleading to make estimates based on the oldest surviving cohort.

the life cycle are small, these increases help prevent overall levels of Republicanism from declining.

Examining Republicanism over time underscores two points about attitude change among the electorate. First, it demonstrates that, in making predictions based on the analyses of age-group differences, we must be especially cautious unless we have some basis for predicting the attitudes of birth cohorts that are too young to be sampled. While we know the size of birth cohorts below the age of 18 and we can make some guesses about the size of cohorts yet unborn from our knowledge of the number of women of childbearing age, we do not necessarily know anything about the political attitudes of these age groups. Campbell and his colleagues seem to have made inferences about the partisanship of cohorts that had not yet entered the electorate, and their projections are not fully supported.

Second, the data in Table 7.4 and Figure 7.3 demonstrate that generational replacement will not contribute very much to a trend unless both the entering and the departing cohorts contribute to the same change. Entering cohorts had levels of Republicanism equivalent to the overall levels of Republicanism among the electorate. As the more heavily Republican cohorts had largely left the electorate by 1952, further generational replacement did little to affect the overall ratio of Republicans to Democrats. By contrast, when we examine changes in partisan strength (Table 7.3 and Figure 7.2), we find that the entering cohorts have weak partisan loyalties, while the cohorts dying out of the electorate have strong partisan ties. Under these conditions, both the entering and the departing cohorts contribute to the same trend, and generational replacement leads to the decline of partisan loyalties among the white electorate.

Partisan Change Among Blacks

Table 7.5 presents the party identification of blacks between 1952 and 1980. Among blacks, as among whites, partisan loyalties have been declining in recent years, for there has been a substantial drop in the percentage of strong Democrats since 1968. In 1980, there is a surge in partisan strength among blacks, due mainly to a jump in the percentage of strong Democrats. When we examine the partisanship of blacks over the last quarter century, we find other sudden changes.

Through 1962, about one black in seven is classified as an "apolitical," that is to say, someone who could not relate to the questions used to measure party identification. In 1964, as a result of the controversies surrounding the Civil Rights Act, as well as efforts by civil rights leaders to mobilize Southern Blacks, the proportion of apoliticals falls to less than one in twenty and remains less than one in twenty in all subsequent surveys. Through 1962, the proportion of black party identifiers who are Republican ranges from one in four to

Table 7.5 Party Identification Among Blacks: 1952–1980

Party identification	1952	1954	1956	1958	1960	1962	1964[a]	1966	1968[a]	1970[a]	1972	1974	1976	1978	1980
Strong Democrat	30%	24%	27%	32%	25%	35%	54%	30%	55%	46%	36%	40%	34%	37%	45%
Weak Democrat	22	29	23	19	19	25	24	31	28	28	31	26	36	29	27
Independent, leans Democratic	10	6	5	7	7	4	6	11	6	6	8	15	14	15	9
Independent, no partisan leaning	4	5	7	4	16	6	6	14	4	11	12	12	8	9	7
Independent, leans Republican	4	6	1	4	4	2	1	2	†	1	3	†	1	2	3
Weak Republican	8	5	12	11	9	7	3	7	2	3	4	†	2	3	2
Strong Republican	5	11	7	7	7	6	2	2	1	1	4	3	2	3	3
Other party	1	0	1	0	0	1	0	0	0	0	†	0	†	1	0
Apolitical	17	15	18	16	14	15	4	3	3	2	2	4	1	2	4
Total %	101%	101%	101%	100%	101%	101%	100%	100%	99%	98%	100%	100%	99%	101%	100%
Total *N*	(171)	(101)	(146)	(161)[d]	(171)[d]	(110)	(415)	(132)	(283)[d]	(280)[d]	(267)	(224)[d]	(290)[d]	(230)	(187)
Strong party identifiers	35%	35%	34%	39%	32%	41%	56%	32%	56%	48%	40%	42%	36%	39%	48%
Strong and weak party identifiers	65%	75%	68%	69%	59%	73%	83%	70%	86%	79%	75%	69%	75%	71%	77%
Mean partisan strength (basic measure)[b]	1.80	1.83	1.78	1.88	1.61	1.92	2.30	1.84	2.35	2.14	2.02	1.95	2.03	2.01	2.14
Mean partisan strength (alternative measure)[c]	1.72	1.72	1.63	1.78	1.53	1.80	2.20	1.72	2.23	2.02	1.90	1.90	1.91	1.94	2.06

[a]Includes black supplement sample.

[b]Mean partisan strength with strong partisans scored as 3, weak partisans as 2, Independents who lean toward a party as 1, and pure Independents and apoliticals as 0. Persons who supported minor parties have been excluded from these calculations.

[c]Mean partisan strength with strong partisans scored as 3, weak partisans and Independents who lean toward a party as 1.5, and pure Independents and apoliticals as 0. Persons who supported minor parties have been excluded from these calculations.

[d]Weighted *N*s. †Less than 1%.

one in six; in 1964, less than one black party identifier in sixteen is a Republican, and this proportion remains low in all subsequent surveys.

Partisan change among blacks is sudden and dramatic, compared with change among whites. Figure 7.4 shows the percentage of whites and of blacks who are strong party identifiers from 1952 through 1980, while Figure 7.5 presents the percentage of party identifiers who identify as Republican. Figure 7.4 shows a sharp gain in black partisanship between 1960 and 1964. If the percentage of strong partisans is used as a guide, blacks have levels of partisanship comparable to whites through 1960, somewhat higher levels in 1962, but substantially higher levels in all but one survey since 1964. Actually, if we rely on measures of mean partisan strength (which are more sensitive to the elimination of apoliticals), differences are even more dramatic. Blacks have weaker partisan strength than whites between 1952 and 1960, comparable levels in 1962, but substantially higher levels in all but one survey since 1964 (compare Tables 7.2 and 7.5). As Figure 7.5 reveals, blacks have been less Republican than whites throughout the postwar years, but these differences increase greatly between 1960 and 1964, and sharp partisan differences persist in all subsequent surveys.

As I demonstrate elsewhere (Abramson, 1975, pp. 65–68), these sudden shifts among blacks do not result from generational replacement, but are caused by political conditions that affect blacks of all ages. For example, before 1964, blacks who reached voting age before the Roosevelt era are more Republican

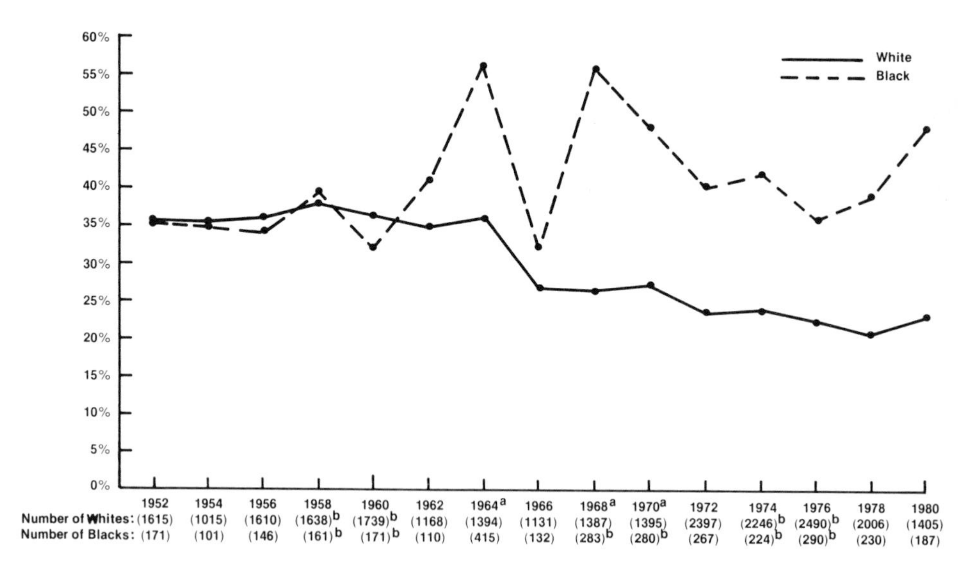

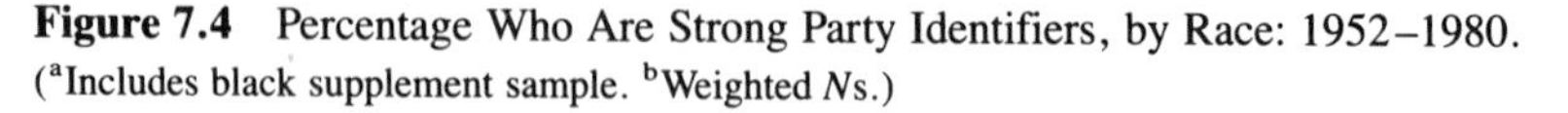

Figure 7.4 Percentage Who Are Strong Party Identifiers, by Race: 1952–1980. ([a]Includes black supplement sample. [b]Weighted *N*s.)

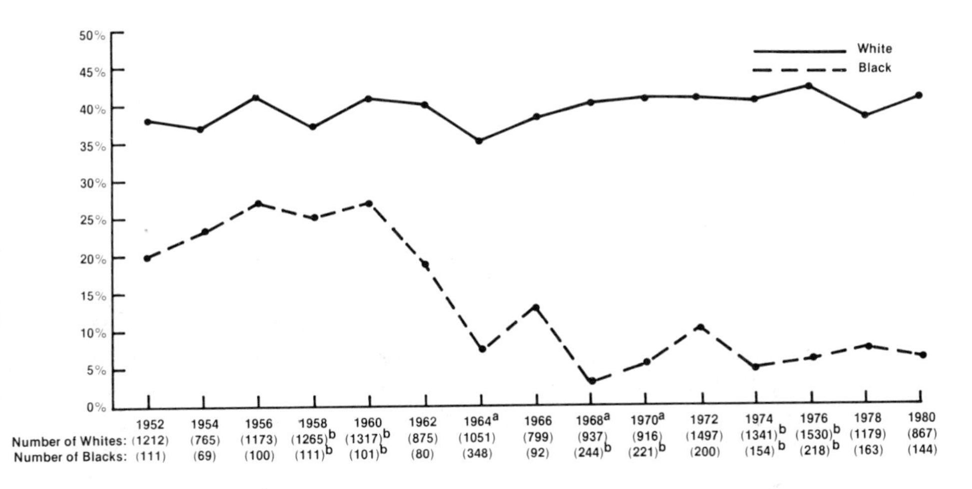

Figure 7.5 Percentage of Party Identifiers Who Are Republicans, by Race: 1952–1980.
([a]Includes black supplement sample. [b]Weighted *N*s.)

than younger blacks. This age difference reflects the residual Republican loyalties that developed before the New Deal, although, even among older blacks, there are roughly three Democratic identifiers for every one Republican identifier. But in 1964, the Republicanism among older blacks is virtually eliminated, and, in most subsequent surveys, older blacks are no more likely to be Republican than younger blacks are. Likewise, the proportion of apoliticals declines among blacks of all ages, and, by 1966, older blacks are no more likely to be apoliticals than are younger blacks.

The rapid change in party identification among older blacks demonstrates that even mature adults may discard established party loyalties. However, it must be borne in mind that blacks were atypical because their party loyalties were seldom reinforced by political behavior. In the South, blacks were often disfranchised and thus had no opportunity to reinforce party loyalties through political behavior; even in the North, blacks participated less often than whites. Black Republicans, in particular, were unlikely to participate, and panel surveys still show that black Republicans have highly unstable partisan loyalties. Thus, while the partisan malleability of blacks demonstrates that rapid partisan change can occur, it also suggests that such change is likely to occur under special conditions that may not be found among most electorates.

Conclusions

Party identification is the most stable political attitude that political scientists have identified. While there is some change in the partisan loyalties of adults, such change is most prevalent among young adults, who are the most likely group to experience changing social conditions, such as marriage, migration, and occupational mobility. While few adults actually convert from one party to another, there is considerable flux in partisan strength over time. When birth cohorts are tracked over time, there is virtually no increase in partisan strength as cohorts age, although there is some support for the life-cycle thesis if we restrict the analysis to the years between 1952 and 1964. There is little support for the thesis that persons become Republicans as they age.

The individual-level stability of party identification can contribute to change among the electorate as a whole. Precisely because young adults do not become more strongly partisan as they age, the continuous generational replacement during the postwar years has created a dramatic erosion of party loyalties among the electorate. During the past quarter century, generational replacement has done little to affect the ratio of Republicans to Democrats, although replacement may have eroded that ratio during the 1930s and 1940s.

Given the trends so clearly identified in this chapter, it is tempting to speculate about the future of partisan loyalties. Such speculations must be tempered because we have no data on cohorts born after 1962. It seems reasonable to speculate that persons born after 1962 have weak partisan loyalties, for we know that their parents have relatively weak partisan ties. We also have no reason to speculate that future events will restore political parties as attractive institutions that can forge strong loyalties. Yet new events could shape stronger partisan loyalties among future cohorts. Moreover, projections about the future of partisan loyalties depend in part on the assumptions one makes about life-cycle effects. If one assumes that life-cycle forces will increase partisan strength among cohorts in future decades, then the erosion of party loyalties may be halted—even though previous levels of partisan strength will not be restored (Converse, 1976, pp. 112–115).

Prospects for the Republicans are more difficult to predict. As we saw, during the past three decades, generational replacement has not eroded the strength of the Republican party relative to that of the Democrats. Yet until recently, commentators have portrayed gloomy prospects for the Republicans by focusing on the absolute percentage of Republicans, noting, for example, that the number of Republicans is smaller than the number of Independents. But our analysis clearly shows that, in the last three decades, the ratio of Republicans to Democrats remains fairly constant. Moreover, the very weakness of partisan loyalties helps the Republicans to compete, for only strong partisans are highly resistant to attractive appeals from the opposite party, and only one American in six is a strong Democrat. The recent surge in Republican identification is not revealed in the SRC–CPS data, but these data do show that the Republicans have more support among the young than among the elderly. If these cohort differences persist, future generational replacement will aid the Republican party.

The future of the Republican party depends far more on the ability, and luck, of Reagan and other Republican leaders than on the inexorable processes of generational replacement. The weakness of partisan loyalties, especially among the young, may provide an opportunity for these leaders to forge a new party alignment, but only the future will determine whether these opportunities are realized.[22]

[22]For a discussion of Republican prospects in light of Reagan's victory and his policy reforms, see Abramson, Aldrich, and Rohde (1982, pp. 231–234).

III

Continuity and Change in Feelings of Political Efficacy

[CHAPTER 8]

The Concept of Political Efficacy

Next to party identification, no political attitude has been studied more extensively than feelings of political effectiveness. We now have data to measure such feelings among adults for a period of 28 years, and can thus study attitude change through the life cycle and the impact of generational replacement. We can assess over-time stability of these feelings with both the 1956–1960 and the 1972–1974–1976 Michigan SRC panels and with the 1965–1973 student–parent panel. These feelings have been studied extensively among preadults as well. And, like party identification, feelings of political effectiveness have important behavioral consequences.

Although many scholars have developed measures to assess whether citizens feel they can influence political leaders, the measure was first introduced by the University of Michigan Survey Research Center. Campbell, Gurin, and Miller (1954, pp. 187–194) used responses to several questions to measure "the feeling that individual political action does have, or can have, an impact upon the political process, i.e., that it is worth while to perform one's civic duties" (p. 187). Four of their items have been used in all presidential election surveys since 1952 and in all off-year congressional surveys since 1966:[1]

1. Sometimes politics and government seem so complicated that a person like me can't really understand what's going on.
2. Voting is the only way that people like me can have any say about how the government runs things.

[1] A fifth question, "The way people vote is the main thing that decides how things are run in this country," was employed in 1952 and was used in the sense-of-political-efficacy scale developed by Campbell, Gurin, and Miller. It was dropped after 1952.

3. I don't think public officials care much what people like me think.
4. People like me don't have any say about what the government does.

For all four of these items, a "disagree" response is scored as efficacious.[2]

Campbell, Gurin, and Miller demonstrate that responses to these questions are highly related to each other and argue that they could be combined to form a scale. Feelings of political efficacy are highly related to participation in the 1952 presidential election. Although persons who score high on the political-efficacy scale have substantially higher levels of education than those who score low, feelings of political efficacy contribute to political participation even when controls for level of education are introduced. Campbell et al. (1954) conclude (p. 194):

> In summary, it is reasonable to conclude that citizens who feel that public officials are responsive and responsible to the electorate, who think that individual political activity is worth while and capable of influencing public policy, and who see that the private citizen's channels of access to governmental decision-makers are not confined to the ballot box, are much more likely to be politically active than those citizens who feel largely overwhelmed by the political process.

Campbell continues to use the sense-of-political-efficacy measure in *The American Voter.* As Campbell and his colleagues (1960) write: "To some people politics is a distant and complex realm that is beyond the power of the common citizen to affect, whereas to others the affairs of government can be understood and influenced by individual citizens" (p. 104). They demonstrate that feelings of political effectiveness are strongly related to turnout in the 1956 presidential election. Indeed, such feelings are consistently related to turnout in all subsequent presidential elections (Table 16.2) and in all four off-year elections for which the relationship can be assessed.

Since the concept of sense of political effectiveness was introduced, many social scientists have used similar concepts, using such labels as "sense of effectiveness in public affairs" (Douvan and Walker, 1956), "political potency" (Agger, Goldstein, and Pearl, 1961), "subjective political competence" (Almond and Verba, 1963), and "subjective civic competence" (Matthews and Prothro, 1966). Other scholars have focused on feelings of political ineffectiveness, using such terms as "political futility feelings" (Kornhauser, Sheppard, and Mayer, 1956), "political anomie" (Farris, 1960), "political futility" (McClosky and Schaar, 1965), and "political incapability" (Olsen, 1969).

[2]This wording raises the possibility that some respondents are scored as inefficacious because they tend to agree with questions posed by interviewers. In 1968, the SRC also includes some forced-choice questions to measure feelings of political efficacy. A careful analysis of the data by Wright (1975) suggests that acquiescence "response set" biases are not an important problem with the SRC data, but that such biases may be a problem when less skillful interviewers are used.

Of all these studies, that by Almond and Verba provides the greatest scope through the comparative study of political attitudes in the United States, Britain, West Germany, Italy, and Mexico. As their study was conducted for the United States in 1960 and for the other four countries in 1959, similar results might not obtain today, but their feelings are of great theoretical significance. Almond and Verba developed a five-item measure, labeled "subjective political competence," designed to assess the extent to which respondents believe they can influence local-level political decisions.

Almond and Verba find that, in all five countries, persons who feel they are politically competent are more likely to be politically active. For example, such persons are more likely to follow politics regularly, to pay attention to election campaigns, and to discuss politics. Persons who feel politically competent are more likely to express satisfaction with voting and to believe that local government activities have beneficial effects. Moreover, in all five countries, persons who score high on subjective political competence are more likely to endorse democratic norms. For example, they are more likely to believe that elections are necessary and that the ordinary person should be active in the community. Like the SRC sense-of-political-efficacy measure, feelings of subjective political competence are strongly related to education, but, in all five nations, the relationship between feelings of subjective political competence and these behaviors and attitudes persist even after controls for level of education are introduced.

The five-item subjective-political-competence scale became the key dependent variable in the Almond and Verba study, which attempts to discover how such factors as organizational membership and socialization experiences contribute to feelings of competence. Almond and Verba argue that the political-competence scale provides a handle that enables them to study a wide range of political attitudes (1963, p. 257):

> In many ways, then, the belief in one's competence is a key political attitude. The self-confident citizen appears to be the democratic citizen. Not only does he think he can participate, he thinks others ought to participate as well. Furthermore, he does not merely think he can take part in politics; he is likely to *be* more active. And, perhaps most significant of all, the self-confident citizen is also likely to be the more satisfied and loyal citizen.

The Easton–Dennis Formulation

Almond and Verba's discussion suggests that the study of feelings of political effectiveness may provide a key to understanding more general attitudes toward the political system. Easton and Dennis (1967) also raise this possibility in their seminal study of feelings of political effectiveness among American school children. We examine their study carefully, for it has greatly influenced subsequent studies of political efficacy among preadults. Moreover, discussing their article provides an opportunity to examine Easton's important distinction between three objects of support—a distinction that becomes crucial in our subsequent discussion of political trust.

Easton and Dennis (1969) define *support* as "feelings of trust, confidence, or affection, and their opposites, that persons may direct to some object" (p. 57). Easton and Dennis maintain that support may be "specific" if it is provided in return for satisfactory outputs, but they argue that few children support the political system for such specific reasons. They are interested in the development of "diffuse" support, by which they mean "the generalized trust and confidence that members invest in various objects of the system as ends in themselves" (pp. 62–63). "The peculiar quality of this kind of attachment to an object," they write, "is that it is not contingent on any *quid pro quo;* it is offered unconditionally" (p. 63). High levels of diffuse support may help a system persist over time. "Diffuse support forms a reservoir upon which a system typically draws in times of crises, such as depressions, wars, and internecine conflicts, when perceived benefits may recede to their lowest ebb" (p. 63).

Easton develops an important distinction between three different objects of support. (For a complete discussion, see Easton, 1965, pp. 171–219; see also Easton, 1975.) According to Easton and Dennis (1969), the *political community* is "that aspect of a political system that we can identify as a collection of persons who share a division of political labor" (p. 58). The *regime* is the "constitutional order in the very broadest sense of the term. It refers to the underlying goals that the members of the system pursue, the norms or rules of the game through which they conduct their political business, and the formal and informal structures of authority that arrange who is to do what in the system" (p. 59). Lastly, the *authorities* are "those members of a system in whom the primary responsibility is lodged for taking care of the daily routines of a political system. In a democratic system we describe them as the elected representatives and other public officials, such as civil servants" (p. 60).

What would high levels of support look like? Let us imagine what support for the political system would have been in the United States in the mid-1950s. Certainly, support for the political community would have been high. Few Americans wanted to fundamentally restructure the components of the political system. A hundred years earlier, during the 1850s, support would have been low, with many Southern whites wanting to break away from the basic political community. But, with the exception of Puerto Rican nationalists, the vast majority of Americans in the 1950s valued their membership in the United States of America. Alaskans and Hawaiians were seeking full-fledged membership in the community through statehood.

There was probably also a high level of support for the basic "rules of the game," such as those spelled out in the U.S. Constitution. Such basic rules as the separation of powers between the branches of the federal government and the division of powers between the federal government and the states were widely supported, at least among the politically knowledgeable. But there were some controversies. Supporters of states' rights questioned the growing role of the federal government, opponents of school integration sometimes questioned the authority of the Supreme Court, and urban interests favored redistricting legislatures according to population. But these controversies were fought out within a broad framework of agreement, at least among political elites.

Support for the political authorities was also probably high, but perhaps not as high as support for the community and the regime. For example, although Eisenhower was the most popular of all postwar presidents, his presidential approval ratings dropped during the late 1950s. Americans may have harbored suspicion toward politicians and bureaucrats (Mitchell, 1959), but actual empirical measures suggest that trust in government officials was relatively high (see Chapter 13).

Easton's empirical study of the origins of support among American preadults was conducted in the early 1960s, which was probably also a period of high support (although studies of adults show that Kennedy's popularity fell late in his presidency). Easton, along with Hess, conducted a nonrepresentative survey of 12,000 white children in the second through eighth grades in eight major metropolitan areas in late 1961 and early 1962. Their study of political effectiveness focuses on children in grades three through eight.

In their study of feelings of political efficacy, Easton and Hess modified some of the SRC sense-of-political-efficacy questions to make them more suitable for school children. They ultimately employed five basic questions (Easton and Dennis, 1967; Hess and Torney, 1967, pp. 256–257), which have been widely used in subsequent studies of American preadults:[3]

1. What happens in the government will happen no matter what people do. It is like the weather, there is nothing people can do about it.
2. There are some big, powerful men in the government who are running the whole thing and they do not care about us ordinary people.
3. My family doesn't have any say about what the government does.
4. I don't think people in the government care much what people like my family think.
5. Citizens don't have a chance to say what they think about running the government.

Responses to these five items are highly related to each other, and the pattern of responses suggests that a meaningful measure could be developed, even for third graders. "[B]y grade 3," Easton and Dennis (1967) claim,

[3]As with the SRC efficacy questions, a "disagree" response is always scored as efficacious, an "agree" response as inefficacious. Easton and Dennis acknowledge this problem.

"children have already begun to form an attitude . . . which we could call a sense of political efficacy. This basic orientation is likely to become crystallized early in the life of the individual and to be maintained through these grades" (p. 31). Third graders do not have high feelings of political effectiveness, but, even among third graders, three out of four can be assigned a sense-of-political-efficacy score.

Easton and Dennis claim that their scale measures support for a basic regime norm. They argue that the "norm of political efficacy . . . embodies the expectation in democracies that members will feel able to act effectively in politics" (p. 26). Among adults, Easton and Dennis argue, the efficacy questions may be tapping a "disposition" to be effective, but children, they claim, cannot distinguish between the way the political system operates and the way it should operate. As they write: "We could not expect to find many children . . . who could make the intellectual distinction between the expectation that people should be able to master their political environment and a judgment as to whether people do in fact feel they are politically potent" (p. 26). To Easton and Dennis, therefore, high scores on their political-efficacy scale indicate that children support the "regime norm" that people should be able to influence the political system.

Feelings of political efficacy increase with grade level. Among third graders, only 16% score high on the political-efficacy scale. This percentage is 18% among fourth graders, jumps to 36% among fifth graders, is 44% among sixth graders, 48% among seventh graders, and 54% among eighth graders. Levels of political effectiveness are strongly related to measured intelligence, with high-IQ children scoring as more efficacious than those with medium IQ, and medium-IQ children scoring as more efficacious than those with low IQ scores. In addition, children from high socioeconomic backgrounds (as measured by the child's report of his or her father's occupation) score higher than those from medium socioeconomic backgrounds, and those from medium backgrounds score higher than those from low socioeconomic backgrounds. On the other hand, there are only negligible differences between boys and girls.

Easton and Dennis claim that the growing support for the regime norm of political efficacy has important substantive implications for the American political system (p. 38):

> This early acquisition of the norm [of political efficacy] may operate as a potent and critical force in offsetting later adult experiences which, in a modern, rationally organized mass society, undermine the political importance of the ordinary member. But for the inculcation of this norm at an early and impressionable age, later adult political frustrations in modern mass societies might be less easily contained; disillusionment with this norm of democracy might well find more favorable conditions for growth.

Easton and Dennis's pioneering efforts merit our careful attention, but two of their basic assumptions can be questioned. First, it is questionable whether their scale measures attitudes toward the regime. At least two of the questions, "big, powerful men" (question 2) and "people in the government" (question 4), seem to focus on specific political authorities; and only the last question, "citizens don't have a chance," does not partly call for an evaluation of political incumbents. It may be difficult to build empirical measures of support that avoid tapping attitudes toward the authorities—a problem Sears (1975) raises in his critique of the Easton objects-of-support categories.

It is also questionable whether efficacious responses demonstrate support for the regime norm that citizens in a democracy should be effective. This conclusion rests on the assumption that children cannot distinguish between what is and what ought to be. However, some children may feel that ordinary people or that their family cannot influence the government, but may also accept the norm that citizens in a democracy should be able to influence political leaders. In my view, the items developed by Easton and Dennis and by Hess and Torney do not measure merely support for the regime norm about how political leaders should respond, but actual beliefs about citizen effectiveness and government responsiveness. In any event, Easton and Dennis conclude that studies of sense of political efficacy among adults do measure actual feelings of political effectiveness.

Internal and External Political Efficacy

Political scientists have often followed the lead of Campbell et al. (1960) and used the four standard sense-of-political-efficacy questions to form a single measure. Political-socialization researchers have often employed the same five items developed by Easton and Dennis, and many simply cite these authors as proof that the items can be used to form a single measure—even though the interrelationship of these items should be demonstrated separately for each survey for which they are employed.

The concept of sense of political efficacy may incorporate two basic attitudes, however, as Lane's (1959) imaginative discussion suggests. Lane interprets feelings of political efficacy to be a conviction that the polity is democratic and that the government is responsive to the people. Lane's conception has two components: the image of oneself as effective, and the image that the government is responsive. However, Lane believes that these two components are related to each other; the concept of political efficacy "contains the tacit implication that an image of the self as effective is intimately related to the image of democratic government as responsive to the people" (p. 149).

Lane's insightful discussion at first had little impact on the way political scientists measured feelings of political efficacy. However, events have changed the way people respond to the political-efficacy questions, forcing political scientists to rethink the concept. For example, Converse (1972) demonstrates that three of the standard political-efficacy items register a slight increase between 1952 and 1960, but a decline after that. However, the percentage of respondents who disagree that voting is "the only way that people like me can have any say about how the government runs things" rises consistently between 1952 and 1966, then shoots up markedly between 1966 and 1968. (For a distribution of responses for all four questions from 1952 through 1980, see Table 10.2.)

The changing responses to these questions appear to have resulted from the political events of the mid-1960s. As Converse argues, changing responses to the "voting is the only way" item are not surprising. "Developments of the 1960's were marked by a great expansion of forms of political participation associated primarily with the civil rights movement and resistance to the Vietnam War. Sit-ins, demonstrations, marches, and various more or less violent disruptions came to be a common recourse for dissent, as a means of exerting grass-roots influence on government beyond voting alone" (p. 328). Adding credence to his interpretation, Converse finds that the greatest increases in feelings of effectiveness on this item are among college graduates. Given that many of the new forms of participation developed on college campuses, persons most aware of events on these campuses would be more likely to recognize new strategies for influencing the government.

The changes observed by Converse are substantively important, for they suggest that feelings of political efficacy may be altered by events; we pursue the implications of this finding in Chapter 10. But Converse also recognizes that these changes have implications for the way feelings of political efficacy should be measured. "This is an interesting case," Converse writes, "of a scale deemed unidimensional by Guttman criteria in 1952, one component of which has pulled out of line rather markedly in response to . . . events in a subsequent period. Our analysis of these trends would have been greatly muddied if we had proceeded with the composite scale taken as a whole" (p. 329).

Clearly, time-series analyses of changes in feelings of political effectiveness may be misleading if they proceed with the original measure developed in *The Voter Decides* and utilized (with only minor changes) in *The American Voter.* Several strategies are possible. In 1968, new sense-of-political-efficacy items were introduced to supplement the original four, and these questions can be used along with the standard questions to create new measures (Iyengar, 1980a; A. Miller, Goldenberg, and Erbring, 1979; W. Miller, 1979; W. Miller and Levitin, 1976; W. Miller, A. Miller, and Schneider, 1980). But that strategy impedes our ability to study change over time and also makes it more difficult to examine change over the life cycle, since these new items have not been used to study preadult political attitudes. Another strategy is to drop the "voting is the only way" item and use the remaining three to form an attenuated index. In his careful analysis of the correlates of political efficacy and political trust, Wright (1976) uses the four-item sense-of-political-efficacy index for much of his analysis, but relies on a three-item measure that excludes the "voting is the only way" item in his analyses of change over time.

In our view, the best procedure is to return to Lane's original insight that the concept of sense of political efficacy incorporates two different components. A compelling empirical analysis by Balch (1974), based mainly on a sample of 1100 university students and conducted in the summer of 1968, provides considerable justification for developing two separate measures. Balch demonstrates that responses to two of the standard sense-of-political-efficacy items, "voting is the only way" and "politics . . . seem so complicated," relate to measures of political interest, political knowledge, propensity toward conventional political participation, and propensity toward nonconventional political participation in different ways than do responses to the two remaining items, "public officials care" and "don't have any say."

The strongest and most interesting results obtain when these four items are correlated with measures of political trust. Persons who score as efficacious on the "public officials care" and "don't have any say" items consistently score as more trusting than those who score as inefficacious. But responses to the two remaining questions, "voting is the only way" and "politics . . . seem so complicated," are not consistently related to political trust. In many cases, the relationships, though weak, are in the opposite direction: persons who score as efficacious on these items are less trusting than those who feel efficacious.

Balch's analysis strongly suggests that it would be useful to consider the sense-of-political-efficacy concept as containing two separate components. Two items, "voting is the only way" and "politics . . . seem so complicated," Balch argues, seem best suited to measure feelings of personal political effectiveness, which Balch labels "internal" political efficacy. The remaining two items, "public officials care" and "don't have any say," measure beliefs about government responsiveness, or "external" political efficacy. As Balch writes: " 'Internal efficacy' is the individual's belief that means of influence are available to him. 'External efficacy' is the belief that the authorities or regime is responsive to influence attempts" (p. 24).

Other analyses based on national samples also suggest that the four standard political-efficacy items may measure two components. A careful analysis of the 1972 SRC–CPS election survey by Craig (1979) shows that responses to the "voting is the only way" and "politics . . . seem so complicated" questions are only weakly related to feelings of political trust and to a measure of "government attention to the people/responsiveness." Responses to the "public officials care" and "don't have any say" questions are strongly related to feelings of trust and feelings that the government is responsive. Craig argues that the concept of political efficacy contains separate "input" and "output" dimensions—a classification that corresponds with Balch's basic distinction. Moreover, a factor analysis that Finifter and I conducted with the 1978 SRC–CPS survey shows that persons who score as efficacious on the two "external" political-efficacy items are more trusting on a political-trust dimension that contains nine political-trust items, whereas responses to the two "internal" political-efficacy items are not related to this overall political-trust dimension (Abramson and Finifter, 1980). Marsh's (1977) analysis of a national sample of 1800 Britons conducted in late 1973 and early 1974 (part of the Barnes and Kaase study) also demonstrates the same basic division.

Our analyses of feelings of political efficacy are guided by Balch's distinction.[4] We make this distinction mainly because the burden of evidence points to this position. But we are also guided by practical considerations, since the Michigan student–parent study, which is of great utility in our subsequent discussion, measures only feelings of "internal" political efficacy in its 1965 survey of high school seniors.

Conclusions

Feelings of political effectiveness have been studied for nearly three decades. The approach developed by Campbell and his colleagues has had the most continuing impact on the way these feelings are studied. Easton and Hess modified the SRC questions to study preadults, and, since many scholars have followed their lead, the Michigan questions play a major role in the study of preadult political socialization.

It now appears that feelings of political efficacy have two distinct dimensions. Feelings of personal political effectiveness can be labeled "internal" political efficacy, while beliefs about government responsiveness can be called "external" political efficacy. As we shall see, these two attitudes have followed very different trends during the postwar years. The decline of "external" political efficacy, as we shall demonstrate, plays a major role in accounting for the decline of turnout. If we do not carefully distinguish between the two basic dimensions of sense of political efficacy, we cannot recognize the importance of this attitude change on political behavior.

While our own analyses distinguish between "internal" and "external" efficacy, we cannot afford to ignore the extensive research literature that does

[4]One of the original authors of *The American Voter,* Warren Miller, now uses separate "internal" and "external" political-efficacy indices, but includes the "don't have any say" question in his "internal" efficacy measure (W. Miller and Levitin, 1976, p. 175; W. Miller, 1979; W. Miller, 1980). Miller includes the "don't have any say" question in the "internal" political-efficacy measure presented in the *American National Election Studies Sourcebook* (W. Miller, A. Miller, and Schneider, 1980, p. 273). But neither Warren nor Arthur Miller has ever presented any justification for this combination of items.

not make this distinction. Especially when we examine the way feelings of political efficacy develop among preadults, we are forced to rely on a wide variety of studies that utilize numerous measures and analytical techniques. To focus only on the handful of studies that carefully examine the dimensions of this concept would prevent us from drawing on a vast research literature.

[CHAPTER 9]

How Feelings of Political Efficacy Form

Students of preadult political learning have investigated feelings of political efficacy more extensively than any other political attitude. In part, this emphasis results from political-socialization researchers replicating measures used by prior researchers. But it also flows from a theoretical interest in this basic attitude. Feelings of political efficacy contribute to political participation among adults. Since preadults have few opportunities to participate in politics, political-socialization researchers have studied an attitude that contributes to participation.

As a result of the large number of studies that measure feelings of political efficacy among preadults, we now have many "findings," but there have been few attempts to evaluate these findings to improve our understanding of the political learning process. This chapter attempts to bring these findings together to assess explanations about the way feelings of political efficacy develop. We begin by assessing the limited evidence on the transmission of these feelings from parents to their children. Most of this chapter attempts to integrate the many studies that compare the sense of political efficacy of whites and of blacks, as well as several studies that compare whites with Hispanics. We evaluate explanations that may account for the subcultural differences.

Parental Transmission

In studying the way party identification is learned, we find a very high level of intergenerational transmission, and we attempt to specify the conditions under which transmission fails. But when we examine parental transmission of feelings of political effectiveness, we find little evidence of intergenerational learning.

My reanalysis of the Michigan student–parent survey shows that both white and black students feel more efficacious than their elders.[1] There is one intergenerational similarity, however. White parents feel substantially more efficacious than black parents, and white students feel substantially more efficacious than black students. Table 9.1 directly compares feelings of personal political effectiveness ("internal" political efficacy) among parents and their teenage children, examining whites and blacks separately. As we can see, individual-level comparisons show little evidence of intergenerational transmission. For both whites and blacks, there is only a fairly weak tendency for parents who score high on feelings of "internal" political efficacy to have more politically efficacious children than do parents with low feelings of political efficacy.

These conclusions are very similar to those of Jennings and Niemi (1974), even though the latter compare overall feelings of political efficacy among parents with feelings of "internal" political efficacy among students.[2] Should we accept their conclusion that "parental efficacy is but a weak predictor of student efficacy" (p. 128)? As I mentioned earlier (p. 89), Weissberg and Joslyn (1977) argue that Jennings and Niemi's procedures tend to deflate levels of parent–child correspondence. Jennings and Niemi recognize that they may somewhat underestimate the impact of parental socialization. Moreover, a recent analysis by Dalton (1980), reanalyzing the Michigan student–parent data, suggests that the relationship of parental efficacy to student efficacy rises (from a Pearson's r of .14 to .49) if one takes problems of measurement error into account. But even when one controls for measurement error, parents are far less important in transmitting feelings of political efficacy than in transmitting partisan loyalties.

Although Jennings and Niemi's analysis might have been clearer if they had focused on the transmission of "internal" political efficacy, their basic conclusions are sound, and their analysis of the conditions under which the parental transmission of feelings of efficacy does occur is extremely valuable.

[1] In this analysis, I used the sense-of-political-efficacy scale developed by Jennings and his colleagues to measure feelings of political efficacy among high school seniors, and I used similar scoring procedures to build this measure among the parental sample. The data are based on the combined responses to the "voting is the only way" and "politics . . . seem so complicated" items. (The "voting is the only way" question was worded differently for students than for their parents.) The sense-of-political-efficacy scale is skewed more in the direction of high efficacy responses than the simple additive index I employ when analyzing the SRC–CPS election studies. In analyzing the over-time stability of feelings of "internal" political efficacy, Jennings uses a simple additive index.

[2] However, Jennings and Niemi do compare parental responses to each individual efficacy item with the similar item used for students.

Table 9.1 "Internal" Political Efficacy of High School Seniors, by Parent's "Internal" Political Efficacy and Student's Race: 1965

Part A Student's Race: White

	Parent's political efficacy		
Student's political efficacy	Low	Medium	High
Low	25%	19%	17%
Medium	37	41	36
High	38	41	47
Total %	100%	101%	100%
Weighted *N*	(619)	(580)	(512)

tau-b = .08 gamma = .12 Percentage with same political-efficacy score = 37%.

Part B Student's Race: Black

	Parent's political efficacy		
Student's political efficacy	Low	Medium	High
Low	44%	23%	38%
Medium	24	32	15
High	32	45	47
Total %	100%	100%	100%
Weighted *N*	(133)	(19)	(30)

tau-b = .11 gamma = .21 Percentage with same political-efficacy score = 43%.

Note: Based on two-item sense-of-political-efficacy scale developed by Langton and Jennings (1968).

Their main finding is that parent–child correspondence increases when both parents have similar feelings of political effectiveness. Parental transmission seems especially important when both parents feel highly efficacious. But even though there may be some subsets of parents who successfully transmit their feelings of political effectiveness, most children do not appear to learn feelings of political effectiveness from their parents.

Several other studies also suggest that American parents are unlikely to transmit feelings of effectiveness to their children. Dennis (1969), for example, conducted a probability sample of Milwaukee households in the summer of 1967 in which both parents and children were interviewed. Dennis develops two measures of political efficacy, one of which clearly focuses on beliefs about government responsiveness ("external" political efficacy). At all three grade levels studied (fifth, eighth, and eleventh), he finds only a low level of correspondence between the feelings of efficacy of parents and those of their children. He concludes that his findings "would appear to confirm the hypothesis that parents only to a low extent reproduce their basic political attitudes in their children" (p. 30).

The cross-national participation study conducted by Barnes, Kaase, and their colleagues provides additional evidence. (For a description of this study, see pp. 96–97.) In their analysis of parent–offspring correspondence, Jennings and his colleagues developed one measure that focused mainly on feelings of "internal" political efficacy, which they label "political efficacy," and another that focused on "external" political efficacy, which they label "system responsiveness."[3]

In the United States (using 244 parent–offspring pairs that compare parents with their 16- to 20-year-old children), there is only a weak relationship between feelings of "political efficacy" among parents and their children (tau-b of .13). Parent–offspring correspondence is even lower in Britain (.06) and Austria (.08) and only somewhat higher in the Netherlands (.20) and West Germany (.24) (Allerbeck, Jennings, and Rosenmayr, 1979, p. 489). In America, parent–offspring correspondence is very low when "system responsiveness" is measured (.06), although correspondence is higher in the other four countries: Netherlands (.21), Britain (.25), West Germany (.28), and Austria (.14) (Jennings, Allerbeck, and Rosenmayr, 1979, p. 482). The basic finding is that the transmission of feelings of both "internal" and "external" political efficacy is a weak process in all five of these Western democracies. (For further evidence on Britain, see Dowse and Hughes, 1971.) As we saw earlier (Chapter 6), in all five countries, there is fairly strong evidence that parents transmit their party loyalties to their children.

It is hardly surprising that parents succeed in transmitting partisan loyalties, but fail to transmit feelings of political effectiveness. Party loyalties have real-world referents—organized political parties that compete for votes. Adults have many ways of overtly revealing their partisan ties: by telling their children how they plan to vote, by commenting on a political campaign, or even by openly participating in partisan activities. Parents are unlikely to be aware of their feelings of personal political effectiveness or their beliefs about government responsiveness. Even though they may have such feelings, there are few concrete ways to communicate them. Whatever the reasons for the relative weakness of the parental transmission of feelings of political effectiveness may be, one conclusion seems clear. The dynamics of learning feelings of political effectiveness among preadults must be substantially different from the dynamics of learning party loyalties.

[3]The political-efficacy index includes the two standard "internal" efficacy items, as well as the "don't have any say" item, although Jennings and his colleagues note that only two of these items measure "internal" political efficacy. The "system responsiveness" index includes the "public officials care" question plus two of the newer efficacy items.

Racial and Subcultural Differences

Though we cannot readily explain the source of feelings of political effectiveness among preadults, Easton and Dennis's (1967) study strongly suggests that such feelings exist among young children. Since their survey, numerous studies of preadults have measured feelings of political effectiveness, including the Michigan student–parent survey. These studies have focused on a wide number of sociological variables, which have been measured in different ways from survey to survey. But one variable has been used in many preadult studies, that of race.

In an earlier book (Abramson, 1977), I present an extensive survey of racial differences in feelings of political effectiveness among preadults. My book discusses thirty surveys that report on feelings of political effectiveness among both black and white preadults. Of these, twenty show clearly that blacks feel less politically efficacious than whites, while five find that blacks feel less efficacious on some measures, but equally efficacious on others. One study reveals no overall pattern. Only four studies find that blacks feel marginally more efficacious than whites, and three of these are based on atypical samples, while the remaining survey is based on a very small sample. I conclude that, on balance, there is considerable evidence that black children feel less politically efficacious than white children.

Since my book appeared, nine additional studies of racial differences have come to my attention. Two studies of the St. Louis metropolitan area conducted by Ruth Jones (one in September 1971, another in May 1972) show that blacks feel less politically efficacious than whites,[4] while a study of North Carolina school children conducted in early 1973 by German and Hoffman (1978) shows that blacks feel less politically efficacious on a three-item index that measures feelings of effectiveness toward the police. Moreover, nationwide probability samples conducted by the National Assessment of Educational Progress in 1969 and in 1975–1976 show that blacks score as less efficacious on a question asking whether or not they could influence local-government decisions (see R. Jones, 1979; for an additional analysis of the 1975–1976 survey, see Scott, 1981).

On the other hand, surveys conducted among national samples of high school seniors in 1976, 1977, 1978, and 1979 by the University of Michigan Survey Research Center show that blacks feel somewhat more efficacious than whites. Unfortunately for our purposes, these surveys focus mainly on drug and alcohol use, asking only two questions about feelings of political efficacy, both of which are substantially different from those used in the Michigan SRC student–parent study. In all four surveys, blacks are more likely to agree with the statements: "The way people vote has a major impact on how things are

[4] See R. Jones (1976) for a report of these studies. Data about racial differences in feelings of political efficacy were provided through a personal communication from Ruth Jones.

run in this country" and "People who get together in citizen action groups to influence government policies can have a real effect."[5] Further analysis is necessary, however, to determine whether these items are valid measures of sense of political efficacy.

In addition to these nine surveys, in March 1981 I conducted my own survey of a representative sample of tenth graders in Saginaw, Michigan. I used this survey to develop two measures of sense of political efficacy: one focuses on beliefs about government responsiveness; the other, on the respondent's perception of his or her ability to influence local government.[6] Preliminary analysis of these data shows no significant differences between blacks and whites.

These more recent surveys do not lead me to alter my conclusion that black preadults feel less politically efficacious than whites, for the bulk of the findings still point toward this generalization. However, these recent surveys should make us especially cautious of the ways differences in wording may affect racial differences.[7]

Unfortunately, there have been few studies of subcultural differences for other groups.[8] The major published study of Hispanics, however, shows them to have lower feelings of political efficacy than do Anglos. Garcia (1973) conducted a survey of 683 Hispanics and 544 Anglos in the third through ninth grade in the spring of 1970 and in January 1971. The schools are located in both urban and rural areas of California. Garcia employs a measure of sense of political efficacy similar to that used by Easton and Dennis. While 39% of the Anglos score high on sense of political efficacy, only 22% of the Hispanics do.

[5]These surveys were based on 16,000 to 18,000 for each year, but not all questions were asked of all students. Five different questionnaire formats were used, and the political-efficacy questions were asked on only one form. Results are thus based on between 2500 and 2900 whites and between 300 and 500 blacks for each year. Questions about interest in the government were asked on four forms, and thus are based on four times as many cases. Questions that measure feelings of self-confidence were asked on a single questionnaire format. For a question-by-question report of these results, see Bachman, Johnston, and O'Malley (1980a, 1980b) and Johnston, Bachman, and O'Malley (1980a, 1980b). For all four books, the efficacy results are reported on page 39.

[6]The Saginaw Socialization Study was a pilot study designed to develop measures to test for racial differences in feelings of political efficacy and trust. It was based on a representative sample of tenth-grade students enrolled in public schools in Saginaw, Michigan, and surveyed 158 whites and 185 blacks. The survey was conducted on March 17 and 19, 1981. As of this writing, only preliminary analyses of these data have been conducted.

[7]For most surveys, "disagree" responses are scored as efficacious. For the 1976 through 1979 Michigan SRC surveys, "agree" responses are scored as efficacious; whereas the Saginaw Socialization Study relies on a forced-choice format. More research is needed to understand better how differences in item construction may affect the responses of different subcultural groups.

[8]My discussion of blacks is based on an extensive review of both published and unpublished research. I have not attempted a similar systematic review of unpublished research on other subcultural groups. My review rests mainly on published material, although in some instances I located unpublished material on Hispanics in my review of research on black political socialization.

Several additional studies also show Hispanics to have lower levels of sense of political efficacy than do Anglos. A study of schools in the Chicago area, conducted by Krause (1972) in the spring of 1968, finds that Hispanics feel significantly less efficacious toward the mayor than do white suburban children, but finds no significant differences in feelings toward the president or the police. Button's (1974) study of Austin, Texas, students (conducted in late 1971 and early 1972) shows Hispanics to score lower than Anglos on a variety of measures of political effectiveness, most of which are based on the Easton–Dennis items. And Lamare's (1974) study of El Paso elementary school children (conducted in April 1972), shows Hispanics to have lower levels of sense of political efficacy (using some of the Easton–Dennis questions) than do Anglos. On the other hand, Hirsch and Gutierrez's (1977) study of Crystal City, Texas, conducted in the early 1970s, finds no consistent differences on items measuring feelings of political efficacy among students who identify as Chicanos, Mexican-Americans, or Anglos.[9]

Explanations for Differences

Using racial differences as a point of departure, I attempt to evaluate explanations that might account for differential feelings of political effectiveness. I argue that racial differences in these attitudes could have resulted from differences in political education within American schools (the political-education explanation), from social-structural conditions that contribute to low feelings of self-confidence among blacks (the social-deprivation explanation), from differences in intelligence (the intelligence explanation), and/or from differences in the political environment in which blacks and whites live (the political-reality explanation). As I point out, advancing an explanation does not mean it is valid. Second, I note that these explanations are not mutually exclusive, since more than one of them could constitute a valid partial explanation for the low feelings of political effectiveness (and trust) among black preadults.

There is no reason in principle that these explanations need account only for racial differences between black and white Americans. They might also account for other subcultural differences in the way feelings of political effectiveness develop. Indeed, these explanations need not be restricted to the United States, and both the political-reality and the social-deprivation expla-

[9]Hirsch (1971, pp. 146–147) conducted a survey of Appalachian school children in Knox County, Kentucky, in early 1967 and compares his results with those of the Easton and Hess survey conducted in early 1962. Hirsch reports that Knox County school children are less likely to have low feelings of political efficacy than the children surveyed by Easton and Hess. However, it is questionable whether such a comparison can be used to assess relative levels of political efficacy among Appalachian school children with whites living outside of Appalachia, since both surveys are nonrepresentative.

nation have been tested in non-American settings—among adolescents in the state of Andhra Pradesh, India (Iyengar, 1978a, 1980b) and among West Indian adolescents in London and Birmingham, England (Phizakalea, 1975). The social-deprivation explanation has also been tested among adolescents in the states of Punjab and Dehli, India (Malik, 1979). Having evaluated these explanations extensively elsewhere, I discuss them only briefly here, with the aim of seeing how they may account for a wider range of subcultural differences.

The political-education explanation

The first explanation suggests that subcultural differences in feelings of political efficacy result from differences in political education within American schools. American schools explicitly teach political values through the formal content of the curriculum. But teachers may also implicitly stress political values. Black children, and the children of other subcultural groups, are not explicitly taught that they have little ability to influence political leaders, but they may be implicitly taught not to participate actively in politics.

Two assumptions constitute the political-education explanation:

Assumption A.1. Students learn the political values taught in the schools. In other words, schools are effective agents of political socialization.

Assumption A.2. Teachers are less likely to stress norms of political participation when teaching black children (or children of other disadvantaged subcultural groups) than when teaching white children (or children of advantaged groups).

In my view, there is little evidence to support Assumption A.1. While American schools attempt to teach political values, we have little compelling evidence that children learn them. Unlike mathematics or physics, which are learned almost exclusively in school, children learn about politics from many sources. Thus, the effectiveness of the school as a socializing agent is weakened. In fact, most of the arguments about the impact of the school as an agent of political socialization rest on indirect evidence that the family fails to transmit political attitudes, not on direct evidence that students learn the political values taught in the classroom.

While I am skeptical about the role of American schools in teaching political values, it is possible that schools can play a major role in the political-socialization process. Clearly, schools do transmit political information, and they can be used to attempt to instill feelings of loyalty and patriotism. In modern industrial societies, most schools are under state control, and the school can be used to transform political values. In the late nineteenth and early twentieth century, when large numbers of immigrants were entering America, schools may have performed an important role in the Americanization process. But there is little compelling evidence that American schools succeed in teaching such attitudes as feelings of political effectiveness.

Even if we accept Assumption A.1, that schools are effective agents of political socialization, the political-education explanation cannot be valid unless blacks and whites (or disadvantaged and advantaged groups) are taught different political values (Assumption A.2). Are teachers less likely to stress norms of political participation when teaching blacks (or other disadvantaged groups) than when teaching whites (or advantaged groups)? Although there may be sound reasons for expecting this to be the case, there is simply little evidence to support this assumption.

There is very little evidence on differences in the implicit values taught in American schools or on differences in "educational climates" within schools. (For a discussion of this concept, see Levin 1961; Merelman, 1971.) Surely, there is variation from school to school and sometimes from classroom to classroom within the same school. But the extent to which such differences are systematically related to race, ethnicity, or other subcultural differences is simply not known.

While there is little evidence that would lead us to accept the two basic assumptions of the political-education explanation, we do not have data that would allow us to reject them. By provisionally accepting these assumptions, we can predict an additional relationship that could be tested if empirical data were available. I call such predicted relationships additional empirical consequences. The political-education explanation leads to one such consequence.

Empirical Consequence A.1. Black children (and children of other disadvantaged subcultural groups) should be less likely to have a participatory view of the polity and their role within the polity than white children (and children of advantaged groups) have.

If schools contribute to low feelings of political efficacy through teaching nonparticipatory norms, we would expect black children, as well as children from other disadvantaged groups, to have a nonparticipatory view of the political system. While the evidence is not altogether consistent, my earlier review of available research supports this consequence, at least for blacks. But recent research has not supported it. The 1975–1976 survey conducted by the National Assessment of Educational Progress finds that blacks are somewhat more likely to say they are interested in learning about government (National Assessment of Educational Progress, 1976, p. 19). The Michigan SRC surveys conducted from 1976 through 1979 find blacks to be less interested in government and current events than are whites, but these differences are small, averaging only 4 percentage points over the sixteen times the question was asked.[10] And my preliminary analysis of the Saginaw Socialization Study

[10]Bachman, Johnston, and O'Malley (1980a, pp. 96, 136, 152, 177); Johnston, Bachman, and O'Malley (1980a, pp. 96, 135, 153, 179); Bachman, Johnston, and O'Malley (1980b, pp. 96, 134, 153, 179); Johnston, Bachman, and O'Malley (1980b, pp. 97, 136, 154, 180).

shows that blacks were as interested in the 1980 presidential elections as were whites and that blacks and whites differ little in their conception of good citizenship. Unfortunately, there are very few systematic data that would allow us to analyze participatory orientations among other subcultural groups.

On balance, there now appears to be less support for Empirical Consequence A.1 than I earlier concluded, further weakening support for the political-education explanation.

The social-deprivation explanation

A second explanation that may account for racial and other subcultural differences in feelings of political effectiveness holds that social deprivation contributes to low feelings of self-confidence and, in particular, to feelings that one cannot control his or her environment. Feelings of personal self-confidence contribute to feelings of political effectiveness (and to feelings of political trust). Blacks (and other disadvantaged subcultural groups) are socially deprived, and their feelings of self-confidence are low. This low self-confidence contributes to low levels of sense of political efficacy (and to low feelings of political trust). Five assumptions constitute the social-deprivation explanation:

Assumption B.1. Persons deprived of opportunity and denied respect tend to have low levels of self-confidence and, in particular, to feel that they cannot control their social environment.

Assumption B.2. Persons who have low levels of self-confidence tend to have low feelings of political effectiveness.

Assumption B.3. This assumption pertains to trust and is discussed in Chapter 12.

Assumption B.4. Black children (and children of other disadvantaged subcultural groups) are deprived of opportunity and denied respect.

Assumption B.5. Black children (and children of other disadvantaged subcultural groups) have lower levels of self-confidence than have white children (and children of advantaged groups) and, in particular, are less likely to feel they can control their social environment.

The social-deprivation explanation is a social-psychologically based attempt to account for low feelings of political effectiveness, and hinges on the assumption (B.1) that persons who are deprived of opportunity develop low feelings of self-confidence. Impressive data document the assumption that persons with restricted opportunities tend to have lower levels of self-confidence, but the findings often depend on the measures of self-confidence used. Some psychologists, such as Rosenberg (1965), have focused on feelings of personal worthiness, and such feelings are only weakly related to social factors. Other scholars, such as Rotter (1966, 1971), have focused on feelings of environmental control. In Rotter's terminology, persons who feel they can control their environment are labeled "internals"; those who believe that rewards and punishments are not related to their own efforts are "externals."

My earlier review of available evidence suggests that there is considerable support for Assumptions B.1, B.4, and B.5. More recent evidence, provided in Phares' (1976) extensive review, lends additional support for Assumptions B.1 and B.5 and also provides some evidence that Spanish-speaking Americans are more likely to score as "internals" than Anglos are. The Michigan SRC surveys conducted between 1976 and 1979 asked numerous questions to measure self-confidence. While extensive analyses are necessary to develop valid measures, an item-by-item analysis suggests that blacks are as likely as, or more likely than, whites to have high feelings of personal self-worth, but that they are more likely to emphasize the role of luck and to deemphasize the role of planning.[11] The Saginaw Socialization Study also shows that blacks score significantly lower on a measure of the respondent's perceived ability to control his or her environment.

There are also sound reasons for accepting Assumption B.2. Persons who believe they can control their social environment should be more likely to believe that they can control their political environment. As Lane (1959) writes: "Men who have feelings of mastery and are endowed with ego strength tend to generalize these sentiments and to feel that their votes are important, politicians respect them, and elections are, therefore, meaningful processes" (p. 149). There is also considerable empirical support for Assumption B.2, especially when we examine research in which political scientists have used measures of feelings of environmental control.

On balance, there is support for all four of these basic assumptions. Moreover, there is also some support for two additional empirical consequences that can be derived from the social-deprivation explanation.

Empirical Consequence B.1. In social settings where blacks (and other disadvantaged subcultural groups) have higher levels of social opportunity, they should have higher feelings of political effectiveness (and political trust). Controlling for social opportunity should reduce or eliminate racial (and other subcultural) differences in these attitudes.

Most studies of preadult feelings of political effectiveness that allow us to test the relationship between deprivation and efficacy among blacks support this consequence, but support is indirect because measures seldom directly tap the extent to which black preadults are deprived. Moreover, none of the

[11] Bachman, Johnston, and O'Malley (1980a, pp. 183–184); Johnston, Bachman, and O'Malley (1980a, pp. 185–188); Bachman, Johnston, and O'Malley (1980b, pp. 185–188); Johnston, Bachman, and O'Malley (1980b, pp. 186–189).

available studies allows us to determine whether controls for social background would reduce or eliminate racial differences in feelings of political effectiveness.

Unfortunately, there is little evidence on the effects of deprivation among other subcultural groups, and the two studies of Hispanics that allow us to examine these relationships yield mixed results. Garcia's (1973, p. 126) study shows no consistent differences in feelings of political effectiveness between middle-class and lower-class Hispanics (using parental occupation to measure social class) and finds that middle-class Hispanics have much lower feelings of political effectiveness than do Anglos. On the other hand, Lamare (1974) demonstrates that Hispanics from English-speaking linguistic backgrounds have somewhat higher feelings of political effectiveness than do those from mixed linguistic or Spanish-speaking backgrounds. If one concludes, as Lamare seems to, that children from Spanish-speaking backgrounds are relatively deprived, his study provides some support for Empirical Consequence B.1.

Empirical Consequence B.2. Black children (and children from other disadvantaged subcultural groups) with high feelings of self-confidence should feel more politically efficacious (and more trusting) than those with low feelings of self-confidence. Controlling for feelings of self-confidence should reduce or eliminate racial (and other subcultural) differences in these attitudes.

This consequence can be tested more directly, and most extant studies of blacks support it, although they do not allow us to determine the extent to which controls for feelings of self-confidence reduce racial differences. On the other hand, self-esteem is not related to feelings of political efficacy among Appalachian school children (Hirsch, 1971, p. 151). To the best of my knowledge, we have no studies that test this consequence for other subcultural groups.

The social-deprivation explanation receives some support and provides a partial explanation for subcultural differences in the preadult development of feelings of political efficacy. It is, however, a complicated explanation that depends on a social-psychological variable to link deprivation to political attitudes. While the relationships predicted by this explanation have usually been present, they have often been weak. Thus, it seems unlikely that this explanation could, by itself, account for all of the racial (and other subcultural) differences in political attitudes. Several studies of sense of political efficacy have attempted to test this explanation directly (Iyengar, 1978a; Long, 1975, 1976, 1978; Malik, 1979; Phizakalea, 1975, Rodgers, 1974). An extensive analysis of the Michigan student–parent data by Friedrich (1977) directly tests the social-deprivation explanation, but finds little evidence that feelings of "ego strength" contribute to feelings of political efficacy among younger blacks, although a strong sense of "ego strength" is associated with high levels of "external" political efficacy among black parents. Some tests of the social-deprivation explanation have provided support, although most scholars who have attempted such tests conclude that there is relatively little support for the explanation.

The intelligence explanation

We may briefly raise the possibility that racial and other subcultural differences in feelings of political efficacy result from differences in intelligence. This possibility is raised because of the strong relationship between intelligence and feelings of political efficacy revealed in the pioneering work of Easton and Hess. There are abundant data showing that black children, as well as children from other disadvantaged subcultural groups, have lower measured intelligence than do white children and children from advantaged groups.

Two assumptions constitute the intelligence explanation:

Assumption C.1. Low levels of intelligence contribute to low feelings of political effectiveness.

Assumption C.2. Blacks (and members of other disadvantaged subcultural groups) tend to be less intelligent than whites (and members of advantaged groups).

The logical status of the intelligence explanation depends on the reason members of disadvantaged subcultural groups have lower measured intelligence, so we discuss Assumption C.2 first. There are many studies that show blacks to have lower average scores on intelligence tests than have whites. Although other subcultural groups have been less extensively studied, research shows Chicanos, Puerto Ricans, and American Indians to have lower measured intelligence than whites. Moreover, among both whites and members of minority groups, persons of lower socioeconomic backgrounds tend to have lower measured intelligence than do persons with higher backgrounds. (For an extensive summary of the evidence, see Loehlin, Lindzey, and Spuhler, 1975.)

Despite these documented results, the subcultural differences may result partly from cultural biases in intelligence tests. Moreover, to a very large extent, subcultural differences in intelligence probably result from social deprivation. To the extent that intelligence differences are environmentally produced, the intelligence explanation can be incorporated into the social-deprivation explanation, with intelligence becoming an intervening variable between social deprivation and low feelings of political effectiveness.

But we need to use intelligence as an intervening variable in the social-deprivation explanation only if we accept Assumption C.1, which states that low feelings of intelligence contribute to low feelings of political efficacy. Why should cognitive abilities contribute to feelings of political effectiveness? Persons with very limited intelligence cannot understand their political environment and have little or no idea about the methods of influencing political leaders. But once we go beyond a minimum (though admittedly unspecified) threshold, there remains little theoretical reason for expecting intelligence to contribute to feelings of political effectiveness.

It is also possible that the relationship between intelligence and feelings of political effectiveness discovered by Easton and Hess exists only during periods of political tranquillity. A study of 398 high school students in Honolulu, conducted in the spring of 1967 by Harvey and Harvey (1970), finds measured intelligence to be only weakly related to feelings of political effectiveness, and this relationship is eliminated when controls for socioeconomic status are introduced.

As the Harvey and Harvey study is among adolescents who are older than the children surveyed by Easton and Hess and as they employ a different measure of political efficacy, their results are not comparable with the earlier study. Nonetheless, Harvey and Harvey raise the interesting possibility that changing political events might have eliminated the relationship between intelligence and feelings of political effectiveness (pp. 583–584):

> [T]he radical differences in results might be attributed to the significant differences in national political climate, before, and then during, the War in Vietnam and the mid-1960s period of civil and racial conflict. While in the early 1960's the intelligent *child* may have felt efficacious, the conflict and strife of the mid-1960's may have made the intelligent *adolescent* (more observant and more fully aware of the complexity of the political situation) feel less able to present his views or have an impact on the political system.

In summary, there is little theoretical evidence and only limited empirical support for Assumption C.1. Nonetheless, if we did accept these assumptions, we would generate one additional empirical consequence.

Empirical Consequence C.1. Among black children (and children of other disadvantaged subcultural groups), those with high intelligence scores should feel more politically efficacious than those with low intelligence scores. Controlling for intelligence should reduce or eliminate racial (and other subcultural) differences in sense of political effectiveness.

I do not argue that such a relationship exists, only that it would exist if the intelligence explanation were valid. But even if high intelligence contributes to feelings of political effectiveness among whites, it would not necessarily contribute to a high sense of efficacy among disadvantaged subcultural groups. If blacks, for example, are deprived of political power, intelligent blacks might be more likely to recognize this powerlessness than less intelligent blacks, and thus might have lower feelings of political effectiveness.

Unfortunately, there are scant data with which to test this empirical consequence. There are only two studies that allow us to assess the relationships among blacks, and they yield contradictory results. I know of no data that allow us to assess the relationship between measured intelligence and feelings of political efficacy among other disadvantaged subcultural groups.[12] Given the scanty evidence available, we cannot adequately test this empirical consequence.

On balance, the intelligence explanation has only weak theoretical and limited empirical support. It makes somewhat more sense if we view feelings of political effectiveness as a regime norm that intelligent preadults are more likely to learn, but the dominant norm in America today may be feelings of political powerlessness. While the Harvey and Harvey conclusions about the weak relationship between intelligence and feelings of political effectiveness may be highly speculative, they raise the possibility that political conditions may be more important for developing feelings of political effectiveness than are social or psychological attributes. This leads us directly to the political-reality explanation.

The political-reality explanation

Political scientists have usually considered feelings of political effectiveness to be largely a function of social or psychological attributes. They have less often considered ways such attitudes might be affected by actual political power arrangements. Yet we can argue that blacks (and members of other disadvantaged subcultural groups) have less political power than do whites (and members of advantaged groups) and, as a result, feel politically inefficacious. Feelings of political ineffectiveness, even among preadults, may result from the realities that deprive groups of political power. The following assumptions constitute the political-reality explanation:

Assumption D.1. Blacks (and members of other disadvantaged subcultural groups) have less capacity to influence political leaders than whites (and members of advantaged groups) have.

Assumption D.2. This assumption pertains to trust and is discussed in Chapter 12.

Assumption D.3. Black children (and children of other disadvantaged subcultural groups) know these facts, or they are indirectly influenced by adults who know these facts, or both.

Assumption D.1 may seem like a truism, but it is hard to measure political influence. Although few political leaders are black and although there are few political leaders from other disadvantaged subcultural groups, blacks and the

[12] Intelligence is significantly related to feelings of political efficacy (using the four standard SRC items, plus two newly constructed items) among a small sample of young Italian-American men in Boston ($N = 64$), and intelligence is also related (though not significantly) to feelings of political efficacy among young men in Rome ($N = 83$) and Palermo, Italy ($N = 76$) (see Ferguson, 1981, p. 210). While Italian-Americans do form a separate subculture, these youths are not part of a socially disadvantaged subculture.

members of these groups may effectively influence white political leaders. Some political rules, however, tend to minimize black political influence. Dahl (1956, pp. 116–118) demonstrates that the rule that each state have two senators benefits certain groups, such as cotton farmers and silver miners, but weakens the influence of coal miners, wage earners, and blacks. The congressional seniority system tended to deprive blacks of political power. On the other hand, the rules through which presidents are elected may benefit blacks, since many live in pivotal states with large numbers of electoral votes (Polsby and Wildavsky, 1980, p. 172). Few political scientists have speculated about the political power of Hispanics, but they may gain some political leverage in electing presidents through their concentration in California and Texas.

Despite our difficulty in documenting Assumption D.1, the political-reality explanation is compelling. The main problem is that we are attempting to explain differing feelings of political effectiveness among preadults. Let us assume that blacks and other disadvantaged subcultural groups are deprived of political power. Do black children, and children of these other groups, know this fact, or are they influenced by adults who know it?

Few children have a sophisticated understanding of political rules or an understanding of the complexity of political power. We have little reason to believe that black children are particularly sophisticated in such matters. The Michigan student–parent survey finds black high school seniors to be less politically knowledgeable than whites (Jennings and Niemi, 1974, pp. 194–195), and most other socialization studies yield similar results. In addition to those studies that I previously reviewed, national surveys by the National Assessment of Educational Progress show that blacks have less political knowledge than whites (National Assessment of Educational Progress, 1976, 1978). The Saginaw Socialization Study asked a total of nineteen factual questions about politics, seven of which focus on knowledge about blacks. Whites are somewhat more likely to answer the twelve questions that do not pertain to blacks, but blacks score somewhat higher on questions about the number of black elected officials, how blacks voted, and the identity of black political leaders.

Three separate studies suggest that Hispanics have less political knowledge than do Anglos (Button, 1974, pp. 178–182; Garcia, 1973, pp. 26–31; Lamare, 1974, pp. 72–75), but only Lamare's study finds substantial differences.

It is possible that black children and children of other disadvantaged subcultural groups are politically knowledgeable, but that their knowledge cannot be measured through standard questionnaires. Coles (1975) uses highly impressionistic open-ended techniques and argues that black children may be politically sophisticated. As he writes: "The black children I have known in our South, or in our northern ghettos, sound—at six, eight, nine, or ten—like certain articulate, politically conscious middle-class white college students. As these children grow older, they tend to become much less candid, though they do not change their opinions" (p. 24). Coles's conclusion is consistent with the political-reality explanation, but his insights are based on methods that cannot be replicated easily.

It is possible that black children (and children of other disadvantaged subcultural groups) do not know the facts about their lack of political power, but that they are influenced by black adults (or adults from their subcultural group) who do know these facts. As we see in Chapter 10, national probability samples of the American electorate consistently show that black adults feel less politically efficacious than white adults. (The number of Hispanics and members of other disadvantaged subcultural groups sampled is too small to permit such comparisons.) However, we have no direct evidence that black children learn political attitudes from black adults. As the data presented in Table 9.1 reveal, there is little evidence that black children share their parents' feelings of political effectiveness. Dennis's (1969) study of Milwaukee children shows that black children are less likely to share their parents' feelings of political effectiveness than white children are. (We have no data on the transmission of parental feelings of political efficacy for other subcultural groups.)

It is also possible that black children and children of other disadvantaged subcultural groups could learn about political realities from adults other than their parents. For example, Orum and Cohen (1973) argue that the political attitudes of black adults are transmitted to black children through a subcultural socialization process, and Prestage (1969) argues that blacks have a separate political subculture. Unfortunately, we have no data about the communication processes through which such a subcultural socialization process takes place.

Even though we cannot spell out the processes through which children may learn about political realities, the political-reality explanation leads to a series of empirical consequences that are supported by extant political-socialization research.

Empirical Consequence D.1. Feelings of political effectiveness (and political trust) should be lower among blacks (and members of other disadvantaged subcultural groups) who understand political realities than among those who do not.

Most empirical tests of the political-reality explanation have focused on documenting this relationship. Rodgers (1974), and Long (1976) have examined this predicted relationship, and both claim that their results support the political-reality explanation. Rodgers and Long conducted useful tests that do add support for the explanation, although neither actually developed measures of knowledge about the facts that deprive blacks of political power. To the best of my knowledge, this empirical consequence has not been tested with preadult data from other disadvantaged subcultural groups in the United States, although it has been tested by Phizakalea in a comparison of West Indian and working-class English adolescents in London and Birmingham. Phizakalea's study also provides support for the political-reality explanation, although her measure of political knowledge, like those developed by Rodgers and Long, does not assess information about the political conditions that deprive subcultural groups of political power.

A second empirical consequence bearing on political efficacy can also be derived from the political-reality explanation.

Empirical Consequence D.2. Racial (and other subcultural) differences in feelings of political effectiveness should be reduced or reversed in settings where blacks (or other disadvantaged subcultural groups) have political power.

One of the earliest studies of black political socialization, conducted by James Jones (1965) in Gary, Indiana, in 1963, provides some support for this consequence. He finds that whites are more likely than blacks to agree with the statement: "People like me and my parents don't have any say about what the government of our city does." Jones's explanation is consistent with the political-reality explanation: "The whites of Gary are outnumbered by Negroes, Negroes are very active politically, [and] there is a larger percentage of whites who are Republicans in a city dominated by the Democratic party" (p. 166).

However, we have no reason to believe that the blacks are politically advantaged in the three other settings where they score as marginally more efficacious than whites: Pontiac, Michigan; Edgecombe County, North Carolina; and inner-city schools in St. Louis. But Rodgers (1974) argues that the whites in his North Carolina sample have reason to feel politically inefficacious. "[W]e suspect," he writes, "that civil rights activities have embittered many whites who resent any progress in racial equality, and substantial numbers of blacks who feel that too little progress has been made" (p. 265).

At least one study of Hispanics supports this consequence. Hirsch and Gutierrez (1977, p. 39) find that Hispanics in Crystal City, Texas, are more likely than Anglos to believe that the city council would respond to neighborhood complaints—a result they attribute to "the achieving of power by the Chicanos" in Crystal City.

Before attempting to summarize our knowledge about the way feelings of political effectiveness are learned, we should note that several other studies of political effectiveness have attempted to test the political-reality explanation with preadult data.

Iyengar's (1978a) study of adolescents in Andhra Pradesh, India, relies mainly on panel data and finds that feelings of political effectiveness change in response to political events. The first wave of his study was conducted between July and November of 1973, when Indira Gandhi's Congress party was in power, although opposition parties were free to compete. The second wave was conducted two years later, between June and August of 1975, during the "emergency" period, when civil liberties were restricted and many opposition political leaders were imprisoned. During this second period, adolescents who support opposition political parties develop lower feelings of political effectiveness, while supporters of the Congress party and nonpartisans feel more efficacious. Change in feelings of political effectiveness is also systematically related to political attitudes.

A third wave of Iyengar's panel was conducted two years later, between June and August of 1977, after the general election in which Gandhi and the Congress party were defeated by the newly formed Janata party. By examining attitude change between 1975 and 1977, Iyengar (1980b) finds further support for the political-reality explanation. Between 1975 and 1977, adolescents who moved from the opposition parties to the Janata party register very large increases in feelings of political efficacy, as do nonpartisans who moved to the Janata party. But respondents who supported the Congress party in both 1975 and 1977 experience a substantial decline in their feelings of political effectiveness.

Lastly, we should mention Friedrich's (1977) extensive analysis of the Michigan student–parent study, which contains explicit tests of the political-reality explanation. Her findings cannot be summarized in detail, but they are based on a comparison of both the student and parent data and use the 1965 and 1973 panel to study change over time. She concludes: "Both in comparison with the [other] models tested [including the social-deprivation explanation] and by absolute standards, the 'political reality' explanation of the patterns of political attitudes and behavior found among the two generations of blacks has the greatest credibility" (p. 238).

Conclusions

Despite the extensive study of feelings of political efficacy among American preadults, we have surprisingly few data that allow us to assess how differing feelings of political effectiveness develop. Partly, this is because political-socialization research has been largely atheoretical. Although political-socialization researchers have used theoretical arguments about the political attitudes that contribute to the maintenance of democratic political systems, they have seldom explored theories about the differential development of political attitudes.

We can hope that future studies will attempt to develop and test explanations for subcultural differences and that more data will be collected on subcultural groups other than blacks. Such studies should examine the components of political efficacy, so that we gain a better understanding of the ways in which both feelings of personal political effectiveness and beliefs about government responsiveness develop.

Another basic question has seldom been raised in most studies of preadult political attitudes. To what extent do these early feelings of political effectiveness persist over time? It has usually been assumed that preadult feelings of political effectiveness had later significance for adult-level attitudes and behaviors. The very strong statement by Easton and Dennis, quoted on page 140, is not atypical. While the long-term consequences of early feelings of political effectiveness or political powerlessness are difficult to assess, we should at least attempt to determine how these feelings change among adults. We turn to this task in the next chapter.

[CHAPTER 10]

How Feelings of Political Efficacy Change

When we examine changes in partisanship among individuals over time, two central facts emerge: first, party identification is highly stable over time; second, party identification is considerably more changeable among young adults than among their elders. Panel analyses show that feelings of political effectiveness are far more changeable, and evidence about age differences is mixed.

Panel studies of the American electorate allow only one comparison between 1956 and 1960, but comparisons can be made with all three waves of the 1972–1974–1976 panel. During the four-year period between 1956 and 1960, the over-time correlation for feelings of personal political effectiveness, that is, feelings of "internal" political efficacy,[1] among whites is .44 (tau-b). During the two-year period between 1972 and 1974, the over-time correlation among whites is .47; and between 1974 and 1976, it is .44. During the four-year period between 1972 and 1976, it is .41. For all but one of these periods, over-time stability is lower among blacks than among whites.[2]

[1]Scores on this index are based on responses to two questions: "Sometimes politics and government seem so complicated that a person like me can't really understand what's going on" and "Voting is the only way that people like me can have any say about how the government runs things." Respondents who disagree with both statements are scored as highly efficacious; those who disagree with one, but agree with the other, are scored as medium; those who agree with both are scored as low. Respondents with ambiguous responses on one of these questions are scored as high or low according to their response to the remaining question, and those with ambiguous responses to both questions are excluded from the analysis.

[2]During the four years between 1956 and 1960, over-time stability for blacks is .28. During the two years between 1972 and 1974, it is .19; between 1974 and 1976, .45; and for the four years between 1972 and 1976, .25.

One might expect feelings of personal political effectiveness to be more stable than beliefs about government responsiveness, since "internal" political efficacy is tied to self-evaluations, whereas beliefs about government responsiveness are more abstract and impersonal. But feelings of "external" political efficacy[3] are about as stable as feelings of "internal" efficacy. Between 1956 and 1960, the over-time correlation among whites for the "external" political-efficacy index is .39. During the two-year period between 1972 and 1974, the over-time correlation is .46; and between 1974 and 1976, it is .42. During the four-year period between 1972 and 1976, it is .43. For all these periods, stability among blacks is lower than among whites.[4]

Over-time stability can also be examined with percentages, and Table 10.1 compares levels of efficacy in 1976 with those held in 1972. The data are presented separately for whites and for blacks. The table suggests a fairly high level of over-time stability for both "internal" and "external" feelings of political efficacy. For example, among whites who score low on "internal" political efficacy in 1972, 63% score low in 1976; but among those who score high in 1972, only 14% score low four years later. Among whites who score low on "external" political efficacy in 1972, 60% score low in 1976; but among those who score high in 1972, only 11% score low four years later. Similar levels of stability are found for the 1956–1960 comparisons. Moreover, for all these comparisons, the majority of whites have the same score for both surveys. For the most part, percentage comparisons lead to the same conclusions about racial differences that we attain by comparing correlations: feelings of political efficacy are less stable among blacks than among whites.[5]

Not all the observed change among individuals between two points in time reflects real attitude change, for some change results from measurement error. I have not attempted to assess the "true" over-time correlation for sense of political efficacy, but we should remember that the real over-time correlation is almost always higher than the observed over-time correlation.[6]

[3]Scores on this index are based on responses to two questions: "I don't think public officials care much what people like me think" and "People like me don't have any say about what the government does." Scoring procedures for constructing this index are identical to those used to construct the "internal" political-efficacy index (see footnote 1 above).

[4]During the four years between 1956 and 1960, over-time stability for blacks is .18. During the two years between 1972 and 1974, it is .30; between 1974 and 1976, .32; and for the four years between 1972 and 1976, .32.

[5]There is one exception to this statement. In both the 1956–1960 and the 1972–1974–1976 period, blacks were more likely than whites to have the same "internal" political-efficacy score over time. This is a function of the large percentage of blacks with low scores on this index.

[6]For one attempt along these lines, see McPherson, Welch, and Clark (1977), who use the 1956–1960 panel. Their study is limited, since feelings of political efficacy are measured in only two waves during this period, but their findings have interesting implications. They conclude that the "public officials care" and "don't have any say" items are more reliable than the "politics . . . seem so complicated" and "voting is the only way" items. Their findings may explain why feelings of personal political efficacy are not more stable over time than beliefs about government responsiveness. While we may expect feelings of "internal" efficacy to be more stable, they may simply be less reliably measured than feelings of "external" efficacy.

Table 10.1 Political Efficacy in 1976, by Political Efficacy in 1972, by Race

Part A "Internal" Political Efficacy

	1972					
	White			Black		
1976	Low	Medium	High	Low	Medium	High
Low	63%	29%	14%	76%	50%	60%
Medium	29	48	40	23	38	20
High	8	23	46	1	12	20
Total %	100%	100%	100%	100%	100%	100%
Total *N*	(477)	(404)	(219)	(71)	(24)	(5)

White: tau-b = .41 gamma = .59
Percentage with same political-efficacy score = 54%.

Black: tau-b = .25 gamma = .47
Percentage with same political-efficacy score = 64%.

Part B "External" Political Efficacy

	1972					
	White			Black		
1976	Low	Medium	High	Low	Medium	High
Low	60%	30%	11%	57%	26%	18%
Medium	23	37	25	27	47	36
High	16	33	64	16	26	45
Total %	99%	100%	100%	100%	99%	99%
Total *N*	(270)	(297)	(528)	(44)	(34)	(22)

White: tau-b = .43 gamma = .62
Percentage with same political-efficacy score = 56%.

Black: tau-b = .32 gamma = .47
Percentage with same political-efficacy score = 51%.

Several studies have attempted to determine whether short-term changes in feelings of political effectiveness result from political events. Welch and Clark's (1974, 1975) study is particularly useful because they developed separate measures of both feelings of personal political competence and beliefs about institutional responsiveness. Using the 1956–1960 panel study of the American electorate, they find that situational variables such as political participation and political involvement contribute to systematic changes in feelings of political effectiveness. However, voting for a winner or other political success does not contribute to increased feelings of political effectiveness. Situational variables appear to have a slightly greater impact on beliefs about government responsiveness than on feelings of personal political effectiveness—a result we would expect given that "external" political efficacy measures an assessment of the way political leaders react. On balance, however, Welch and Clark find that situational changes do relatively little to change feelings of political effectiveness.

Welch and Clark also explore the thesis that changes in feelings of political effectiveness are purely random, but find only weak support for the thesis that sense of political efficacy was a "nonattitude." Their bottom-line conclusion is that, for about a third of the sample, feelings of political effectiveness remain stable over time; for about a third, real change occurs; and for the remaining third, change is probably random.[7]

Iyengar (1980a) has presented a useful analysis of changes in feelings of "external" political efficacy during the 1972–1974–1976 period.[8] His major finding is that feelings of "external" political efficacy are very stable over time, which "lends some credence to the assumption that the sense of political efficacy is acquired early and persists more or less unchanged thereafter" (p. 254). Iyengar attempts to relate individual-level changes in feelings of political efficacy to levels of interparty competition within the respondent's congressional district; success in voting for the winning presidential, senatorial, congressional, and gubernatorial candidates; party identification; feelings toward the incumbent president; approval of government policy; and the respondent's perceived level of disagreement with the president's policies. Only two of these variables—voting success and approval of government policy—are significantly related to changes in feelings of political efficacy, but even here the relationships are weak. Iyengar concludes that "the sense of political efficacy does not appear to be closely intertwined with evaluations of the incumbent government" (p. 255).[9]

Analyses by Weissberg (1975) and Wright (1976) attempt to examine short-term changes in feelings of political efficacy as measured before and after the 1968 presidential election. Both find little evidence of systematic change in feelings of political efficacy, although both find that feelings of political efficacy declined among Humphrey supporters and rose among Wallace supporters. Since the 1968 efficacy questions differ in the pre- and postelection inter-

[7]In a more recent study of the 1956–1960 panel, Welch and McPherson (1981) demonstrate that individual-level changes in feelings of political efficacy are not related to issue preferences.

[8]Iyengar relies on the "public officials care" question, along with two of the new efficacy questions introduced in 1968.

[9]Iyengar's results here seem to be directly contradictory to the results of his analysis of Indian adolescents, which we discuss in Chapter 9. It is possible, as Iyengar argues in an earlier version of his article, that feelings of "external" political efficacy are more likely to be linked to evaluations of incumbents in less established democratic political systems.

views, we should be cautious in interpreting these results, especially since neither Weissberg nor Wright reports findings separately for feelings of personal political effectiveness and beliefs about government responsiveness.[10]

These panel analyses together provide useful insights about the way feelings of political efficacy change. Unfortunately, none of these studies actually spans the change of incumbency from one party to another. The entire 1956–1960 panel was conducted while Eisenhower was president, the 1968 survey while Johnson was president, and the 1972–1974–1976 panel during the Nixon and Ford presidencies. This may be a major limitation, for, as we will see, cross-sectional surveys (surveys conducted at essentially one point in time) suggest that these feelings are systematically affected when control of the White House changes from one party to the other.

These major panel studies may ultimately yield more knowledge about the way feelings of political efficacy change. I have not conducted an extensive analysis of the 1956–1960 and the 1972–1974–1976 panels, but I have used these data to assess whether feelings of political effectiveness become more stable with age. My findings stand in sharp contrast to my earlier analysis of the relationship of age to partisan stability. Whereas 21- to 29-year-olds have lower levels of over-time partisan stability than do their elders, they do not differ much from their elders in their feelings of political effectiveness. It is true that the small subset of 18-, 19-, and 20-year-olds sampled during the 1972–1974–1976 period have low over-time stability in their feelings of political effectiveness, but the *N*s are too small to permit reliable inferences.[11]

Fortunately, we can turn to the Michigan student–parent panel to study a larger number of youths. These data, of course, are from a single time period, 1965 to 1973, and are further limited because only questions measuring feelings of "internal" political efficacy were asked among the high school seniors in 1965. Jennings kindly provided me with the basic tables to compare levels of over-time stability in "internal" political efficacy for both the student and the parent generation among both whites and blacks.

The student–parent results differ in several important ways from results using the national electorate panels. First, the 1965–1973 panel shows black

[10]A more recent analysis (Ginsberg and Weissberg, 1978) reports results of the pre- and postelection efficacy questions in 1968, as well as results from some efficacy questions that were used in the pre- and postelection interviews in 1972. Unfortunately, Ginsberg and Weissberg present results only for the percentage of efficacious respondents on individual items who become inefficacious after each election and the percentage of inefficacious respondents who become efficacious. This method of presentation makes it difficult to interpret their results. Moreover, this method of presentation leads to some contradictory findings. Most importantly, Ginsberg and Weissberg claim that Wallace voters become less efficacious after the 1968 election, whereas Weissberg earlier clearly shows that they become more efficacious. Ginsberg and Weissberg do not attempt to reconcile these contradictory conclusions.

[11]The only notable exception is a very high level of over-time stability for "internal" political efficacy between 1974 and 1976. Even with this high over-time correlation, the mean level of over-time stability for these young adults for all three comparisons (1972–1974, 1974–1976, 1972–1976) is lower than for the total white electorate.

students to have higher levels of over-time stability than do white students, and shows black parents to have similar levels of over-time stability as white parents. Both electorate panels show blacks to have less stable feelings of "internal" political efficacy than do whites. Unlike the electorate panels, the student–parent panel finds substantial differences in over-time stability of efficacy among younger and older respondents. Among whites, the students have substantially lower levels of over-time stability than do their parents, while black students have slightly lower levels of over-time stability than do their parents. But these generational differences are smaller than differences between students and parents when we examine over-time stability in partisan loyalties.

The different results discovered by the student–parent panel and the national electorate panels may have occurred because the studies focus on change over somewhat different ages. The students in the student–parent panel were 17- and 18-year-olds when first sampled in 1965 and between the ages of 25 and 26 when they were reinterviewed in 1973. Perhaps these youths should not be compared with respondents between the ages of 21 and 29 sampled over a four-year period. As I mentioned earlier, if we restrict our attention to the small number of 18-, 19-, and 20-year-olds in the 1972–1974–1976 panel, over-time stability in feelings of political efficacy is low. Possibly the greatest changes in feelings of political effectiveness occur just as young adults leave school and begin to become more aware of the actual limits on citizen influence.

Another basic question is also difficult to answer. Do the results of the SRC student–parent panel demonstrate attitudinal stability or instability? Jennings and Niemi (1981, p. 37) present the over-time distribution of these attitudes for the student and parent generations, showing the results for the total electorate. They point out that the period of their panel encompassed major political events that could have altered political attitudes. As they conclude: "Considering the great strains over the period of time, it is perhaps surprising that persistence remained as high as it did" (p. 37).

Jennings and Niemi note an additional result. Stability is greatest among respondents with low feelings of "internal" political efficacy. This pattern is found among both whites and blacks, and among blacks the tendency to retain low feelings of political efficacy is particularly strong. The Jennings and Niemi findings are also supported by my analysis of the 1956–1960 and the 1972–1974–1976 panels. Respondents with low feelings of "internal" political efficacy are the most likely to retain their feelings, and this is particularly true among blacks.

When the national electorate panels are used to examine beliefs about government responsiveness, quite different patterns emerge. For whites during the 1956–1960 period, those who score high on feelings of "external" political efficacy are more likely to retain their levels of efficacy than are those with medium or low scores; during the 1972–1974–1976 period, whites with high scores are only slightly more likely to have similar scores over time than are those with low levels of efficacy. For blacks during the 1956–1960 period, respondents with high "external" efficacy are the most likely to retain their scores; but during the 1972–1974–1976 period, blacks with low scores are the most likely to retain their levels of political efficacy.

These results suggest that the dynamics of change for feelings of "external" political efficacy may have been different during the late 1950s from the dynamics during the mid-1970s. During the 1950s, beliefs about government responsiveness may have been reinforced, while persons who felt the government was unresponsive often changed their attitudes. During the 1970s, when there was much more skepticism about the government, persons who felt the government was responsive were less likely to retain those views. Persons who thought the government was unresponsive may have had their feelings reinforced.

On balance, even though feelings of political effectiveness do change over time, they appear to be among the more stable political attitudes. Both the Michigan student–parent panel and the two national panels suggest that respondents who have weak feelings of personal political effectiveness are likely to retain those feelings over time. On the other hand, feelings of political effectiveness are clearly changeable. While short-term political successes do not appear to greatly affect feelings of political effectiveness, they may be altered by major events that lead people to reevaluate their ability to influence the political system or to change their beliefs about the effectiveness of political leaders. Indeed, as we will now see, overall levels of political effectiveness have changed among the American electorate, and these changes appear to reflect political events that lead people to recognize new ways of influencing the political system and that weaken people's belief that the government is responsive to popular demands.

Changing Levels of Political Efficacy

Since 1960, there has been a steady erosion in feelings that the government is responsive to the people, and this change is among the most important trends in postwar American politics. But feelings of personal political effectiveness have not declined, mainly because voters are now more likely to recognize alternative ways of influencing the government. Since the responses to all four political-efficacy items have not followed the same trend, we begin by examining changing responses to the four items separately.

Table 10.2 presents the percentage of whites and of blacks who give the efficacious response to each of the four political-efficacy items in all the surveys between 1952 and 1980. In all twelve surveys in which these questions were asked, blacks feel less efficacious than whites on all four items.

When we examine changing responses among whites to the two questions that measure feelings about government responsiveness, "public officials care"

Table 10.2 Percentage of Adults Who Feel Politically Efficacious, by Race: 1952–1980

Percentage who disagreed that:		1952	1956	1960	1964[a]	1966	1968[a]	1970[a]	1972	1974	1976	1978	1980
Politics and government seem so complicated													
	White	30	38	42	32	28	30	27	27	27	27	27	30
	Black	17	19	35	30	16	20	23	19	20	22	20	18
Voting is the only way people can have say													
	White	18	26	26	27	28	45	42	39	40	45	42	40
	Black	7	12	12	13	16	20	22	22	17	19	26	29
Public officials don't care what people think													
	White	65	74	74	63	59	57	52	51	48	46	46	45
	Black	39	47	62	46	39	42	29	30	26	30	39	36
People like me don't have any say													
	White	70	74	73	70	62	59	66	60	58	57	54	60
	Black	42	44	60	65	49	48	52	53	53	52	41	53

Note: To approximate the numbers on which these percentages are based, see Figure 10.1 or 10.2.

[a]Includes black supplement sample.

and "don't have any say," we find that both register a fairly consistent decline since 1960. In 1960, about three out of four whites give the efficacious response to these questions. By 1980, less than half believe that public officials care what people think, and three out of five think that people like themselves have a say about what the government does. The percentage that believes that politics and government are not too complicated to understand declines between 1960 and 1966, but remains stable since then.

The responses to the "voting is the only way" item register a different pattern. The percentage that disagrees with this statement jumps markedly between 1966 and 1968 and remains stable since then. As Converse (1972, pp. 328–329) notes, this upswing appears to have resulted from a response to real-world political events, the civil rights movement and the anti-Vietnam War protests, that sensitized the electorate to alternative means of attempting to influence the government. As we have noted, the increase in efficacy for this item is greatest among college graduates.

Throughout the entire 28-year period, respondents always register as more efficacious for the two questions measuring beliefs about government responsiveness than for the two questions measuring feelings of personal political effectiveness. After 1960, however, the gap is reduced, especially among whites.

Given the increases in feelings of political efficacy on the "voting is the only way" question, as well as the relatively small decline in efficacy for the "politics . . . seem so complicated" question, there has been very little overall change in feelings of "internal" political efficacy. Because only a small percentage scores high on this index (i.e., disagrees with *both* items), I present the percentage scoring medium or high on this measure (i.e., the percentage that disagrees with at least one of these questions). Figure 10.1 shows the percentage of whites and of blacks scoring medium or high between 1952 and 1980. Although whites register an increase in "internal" political efficacy between 1952 and 1956, efficacy levels are relatively stable since 1956. Blacks show an increase from the very low levels of the 1950s, with the greatest increases among black Southerners (Hyman, 1972a, pp. 372–373). Since 1960, blacks, like whites, register considerable stability. Racial differences on this measure are smallest in 1964, when there was a surge of civil rights activities in the South, and when Lyndon Johnson (who had overwhelming black support) was on the verge of his electoral landslide over Barry Goldwater. In the remaining eleven surveys, differences between blacks and whites never fall below 14 percentage points.[12] To the best of my knowledge, there is only one national survey that finds blacks to score higher on feelings of

[12] As we shall see, persons with higher levels of education are much more likely to score medium or high on feelings of "internal" political efficacy than are those with lower levels of education, and blacks have substantially lower levels of education than do whites. In most surveys, racial differences on this measure tend to persist, although they are reduced, when controls for levels of education are introduced.

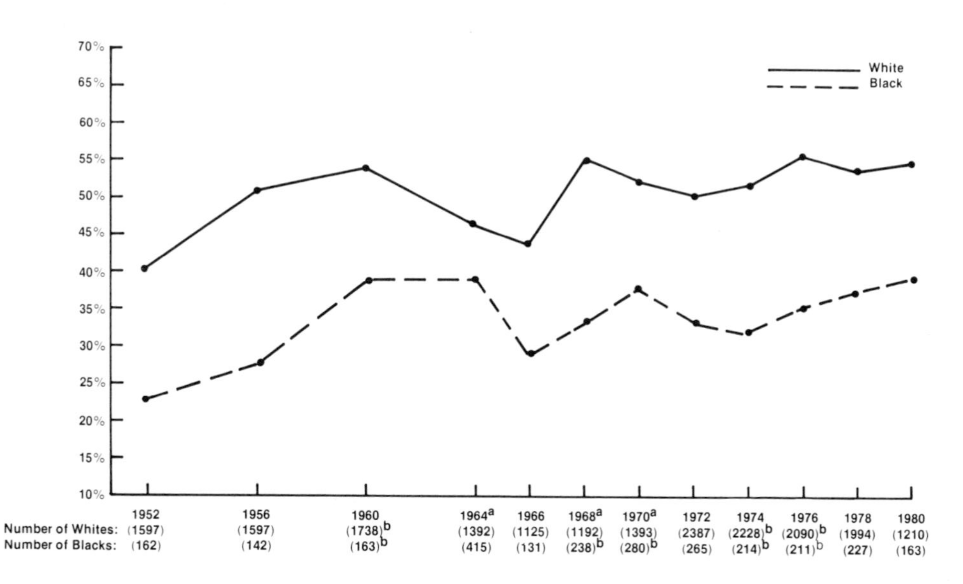

Figure 10.1 Percentage Who Score Medium or High on "Internal" Political Efficacy, by Race: 1952–1980.
([a]Includes the black supplement sample. [b]Weighted *N*s.)

"internal" political efficacy than do whites, but it is based on a totally different measure of this concept.[13]

Beliefs about government responsiveness follow a dramatically different pattern. As Figure 10.2 reveals, feelings of "external" political efficacy are highest among whites in 1956 and 1960, but decline in every survey from 1964 through 1978 and remain low in 1980. Whereas over three out of five whites have high feelings of "external" political efficacy in 1956 and 1960 (i.e., they disagree with both of the items used to build the index), less than two out of five have such feelings in 1978 and 1980. The percentage of blacks scoring high is greatest in 1960, but declines through 1970. Among blacks, the decline in "external" political efficacy stops after 1970, and in the last three surveys these feelings are somewhat higher than in the early 1970s.

Racial differences in feelings of "external" political efficacy are greatest in the 1950s and are low in 1960 and 1964. Racial differences are greater between 1966 and 1974, but never reach the marked differences of the 1950s. In the three most recent surveys, racial differences reach their lowest levels, for "external" political efficacy continues to erode among whites, while reg-

[13]The study (Shingles, 1981) is based on a reanalysis of the National Opinion Research Center survey conducted in 1967 for the Verba and Nie political-participation study (Verba and Nie, 1972). Shingles develops a measure which he labels "internal political efficacy." The questions measure the respondent's self-ranking on a political power "ladder," a question about understanding local government, and the respondent's evaluation of his or her influence over local-government decisions.

Figure 10.2 Percentage Who Score High on "External" Political Efficacy, by Race: 1952–1980.
([a]Includes black supplement sample. [b]Weighted *N*s.)

istering slight gains among blacks.[14] Blacks also score lower than whites on an alternative measure of "external" political efficacy that can be employed from 1968 on.[15]

Given the small number of blacks, it is difficult to examine the efficacy trends among blacks in greater detail, for the number of cases becomes very small once controls for such variables as levels of education or years of birth are introduced. In the broadest of terms, however, we can argue that change among blacks appears to respond to real-world political events. Racial differences are greatest in the 1950s, when Southern blacks were disfranchised and before the civil rights movement began. But we should also recognize that trends among blacks are not perfectly consistent with the political-reality explanation, since the biggest spurt in black political effectiveness (on both indices) is registered between 1956 and 1960, before black enfranchisement and before the height of the civil rights movement.

Lastly, it should be noted that feelings of "external" political efficacy are partly related to changes in presidential incumbency. This is strongly suggested

[14]As we shall see, persons with higher levels of education are much more likely to score high on feelings of "external" political efficacy than are those with lower levels of education. In most surveys, racial differences in feelings of "external" efficacy persist, although they are reduced when controls for levels of education are introduced.

[15]See W. Miller, Miller, and Schneider (1980, p. 279). Their "external" efficacy index includes the "public officials care" item, plus two of the new efficacy items introduced in 1968.

by comparing feelings of "external" efficacy among persons of differing party loyalties. Persons of all partisan groups register a sharp decline between 1960 and 1980, but the pattern of change differs, especially when we study strong partisans.[16] In 1960 (when a Republican held the White House), 55% of the white strong Democrats score high on feelings of "external" political efficacy, while 73% of the white strong Republicans do.[17] By 1964, when feelings of efficacy were next measured, there was a Democratic incumbent. "External" efficacy rises 5 points among strong Democrats, but drops 9 points among strong Republicans. Between 1968 (a Democratic incumbent) and 1970 (a Republican), efficacy drops 6 points among strong Democrats, while it rises 5 points among strong Republicans. And between 1976 (a Republican incumbent) and 1978 (a Democrat), feelings of "external" political efficacy rise 2 points among whites who are strong Democrats, while dropping 9 points among strong Republicans.

The differing pattern of decline between strong Democrats and strong Republicans should not obscure the more basic findings: over the full two decades, feelings of "external" political efficacy drop markedly among white strong Democrats (a total of 11 points) and among Republicans (29 points). There is also a drop in all five other partisan-strength categories. Between 1960 and 1980, the percentage of whites scoring high on "external" political efficacy drops 28 points among weak Democrats, 33 points among Independents who lean Democratic, 23 points among Independents with no partisan leaning, 38 points among Independents who lean Republican, and 28 points among weak Republicans.

Educational Levels and Feelings of Political Efficacy

As Campbell, Gurin, and Miller (1954, p. 191) demonstrated when they first introduced the concept, persons with higher levels of education tend to have higher levels of sense of political efficacy. And, as we saw in Chapter 4, levels of education have risen dramatically during the postwar years as a result of the ongoing processes of generational replacement. Since education appears to contribute to feelings of political efficacy, we might well have

[16] Between 1952 (a Democratic incumbent) and 1956 (a Republican), feelings of "external" efficacy rise for all groups, except for those Independents who lean toward either the Democratic or the Republican party. However, the increase is greater among white strong Republicans (up 13 percentage points) than among white strong Democrats (up 7 points).

[17] Given the strong relationship between feelings of efficacy and levels of education, strong Republicans have always scored as more efficacious than strong Democrats, but the tendency for strong Republicans to score higher is reduced substantially when there is a Democratic president. Examining the percentage of whites scoring high on "external" political efficacy, strong Republicans score an average of 13 percentage points higher than strong Democrats during the six surveys when a Republican is president, but only 5 percentage points higher during the six surveys when there is a Democratic president.

expected feelings of political effectiveness to have risen as well. Yet, as we just saw, feelings of personal political effectiveness have remained fairly stable, while beliefs about governmental responsiveness have declined.

Perhaps this apparent paradox can be explained if we consider the reasons education may contribute to feelings of political effectiveness. One possibility is that the relationship between education and efficacy results from the skills and knowledge one learns through formal education. Persons with higher levels of education may better understand the political world and recognize ways to influence government authorities. A more cynical view is that persons who have higher levels of formal education learn to accept the "norm" that people are effective and that the government is responsive (Wright, 1976). Perhaps the less-educated have a more realistic view of their ability to influence the government and the responsiveness of political leaders than better-educated people do.

But the relationship between education and feelings of political efficacy may have nothing to do with what is "learned" through the educational process. This relationship could be accounted for by the social-deprivation explanation that we examined in the previous chapter. Persons with lower levels of education tend to be socially deprived, and their feelings of self-confidence are low. These low feelings of self-confidence could in turn contribute to their lower feelings of political effectiveness.

If the education–efficacy relationship results from what is learned in school, we might expect higher levels of education to drive levels of efficacy upward. But if education serves mainly as an indirect measure of social opportunity, changing educational levels might have little effect on overall levels of political efficacy.

In a lucid discussion of the relationship between education and political efficacy, Converse (1972) argues that the effects of education on feelings of efficacy may result from the social "pecking order" that education represents. "There is a natural pecking order in societies," Converse speculates, "which arises from a variety of individual traits and determines the ratio of wins to losses, including success at completing an education. The well-educated in modern societies are, on balance, the winners in such transactions, and the poorly-educated are the losers" (p. 326).

The overall educational levels of the society may determine how a given level of education relates to the pecking order. As educational levels rise, the standing of any given level of education within the pecking order changes. For example, several decades ago a bachelor's degree represented a far higher level of success than it does today, and persons who held such degrees had correspondingly greater advantages. Now that a far larger percentage of the population has attained this level, a bachelor's degree no longer represents as much success, and, correspondingly, the advantages of holding such a degree have eroded. If the pecking-order model is correct, Converse argues, "we encompass the static fact that education relates strongly to efficacy, but we do not expect that increasing levels of education lead over time to any particular change in aggregate levels of efficacy" (p. 327).

If education per se contributes to feelings of political efficacy, we would expect overall feelings of political effectiveness to rise. While levels of political efficacy would remain static within each educational level, the percentage of the population with higher levels of education would increase, pushing overall levels of efficacy upward. Converse calls this the "education-driven model," since rising levels of education are expected to drive feelings of political efficacy higher. On the other hand, the pecking-order model predicts that overall levels of efficacy within educational subgroups will decline, so that overall levels of efficacy remain constant, despite the rising educational levels of the electorate. As Converse shows, these competing models lead to fairly precise estimates of the overall changes in levels of political efficacy over time. These predictions, however, assume that all other factors affecting feelings of political efficacy remain constant. In fact, real-world events can contribute to changing feelings of political efficacy, confounding our ability to test these models.

Figure 10.3 presents the percentage of whites among five educational levels who score medium or high on feelings of personal political effectiveness between 1952 and 1980. As we can see, during each of the twelve surveys, persons with higher levels of education score as more efficacious than those with lower levels of education. Despite this static relationship, overall levels of "internal" political efficacy have changed little since 1956, so the education-driven model receives no support. There is somewhat more support for the pecking-order model, although some specific results do not follow from this model. While a college degree represents less relative attainment today than in the 1950s, feelings of personal political effectiveness rise among college graduates. While having some college or only a high school education represents less attainment than in the 1950s, feelings of personal political effectiveness are relatively stable among both subgroups. Among the two lower levels of education, however, feelings of "internal" political efficacy have declined since 1960. Three basic processes appear to have held overall levels of "internal" political efficacy in a state of near equilibrium: the rising levels of personal political effectiveness among the college-educated, the declining levels among the two lower educational groups, and changing educational levels among the electorate.

When we turn to beliefs about government responsiveness, however, neither model is supported. Figure 10.4 presents the percentage of whites among five educational groups who score high on feelings of "external" political efficacy. As feelings of "external" political efficacy actually decline, there can be no support for the education-driven model. Indeed, feelings of "external" political efficacy decline among all five educational groups. Among

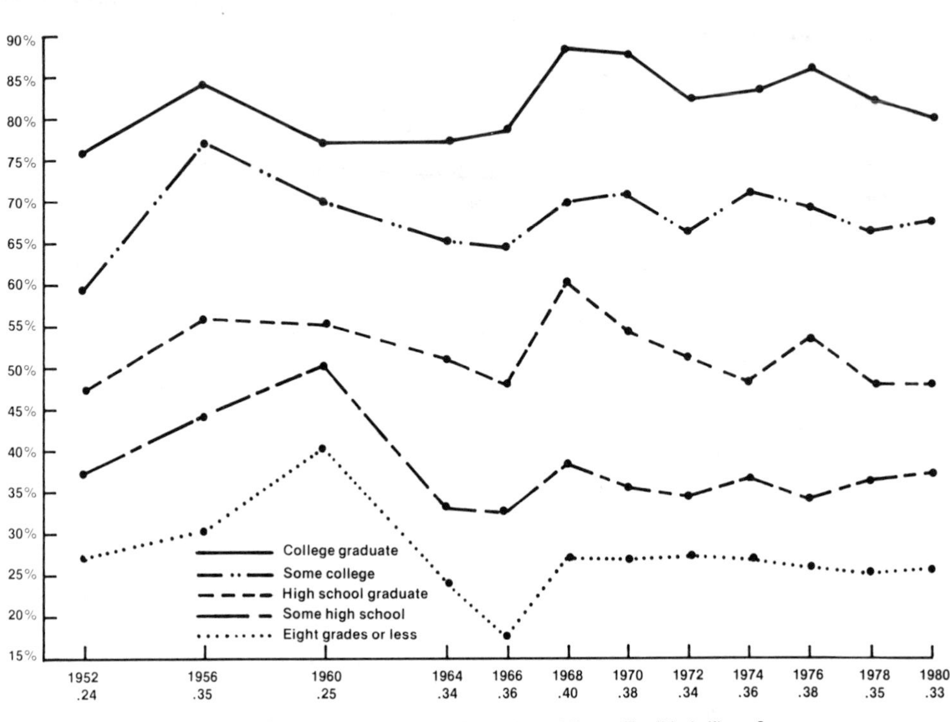

Figure 10.3 Percentage of Whites Who Score Medium or High on "Internal" Political Efficacy, by Level of Education: 1952–1980.

(*Note:* To approximate the numbers on which these percentages are based, see Table 4.3. Actual *N*s are somewhat smaller, since respondents from whom an "internal" political-efficacy score was not ascertained have been excluded from these analyses. *N*s are smaller for 1968, 1976, and 1980, since the political-efficacy questions were employed in the postelection interview. [a]tau-c relationship between a fivefold ordinal measure of education as listed above and a threefold measure of "internal" political efficacy.)

college graduates, there is a sharp decline between 1956 and 1960, but no further decline until 1968. For the other four groups, the decline begins between 1960 and 1964. The decline appears to be occurring at roughly similar rates for all five educational groups, which would be consistent with the pecking-order model if we assume that the relative advantage represented by each educational level declines at the same rate. However, the pecking-order model does not predict an overall *decline* in feelings of political efficacy, since the decline within each educational level should be counterbalanced by increasing educational levels among the electorate as a whole.

For all twelve surveys and with both measures of political efficacy, levels of education are always positively related to feelings of political effectiveness among blacks. Levels of education have risen among blacks, yet their feelings

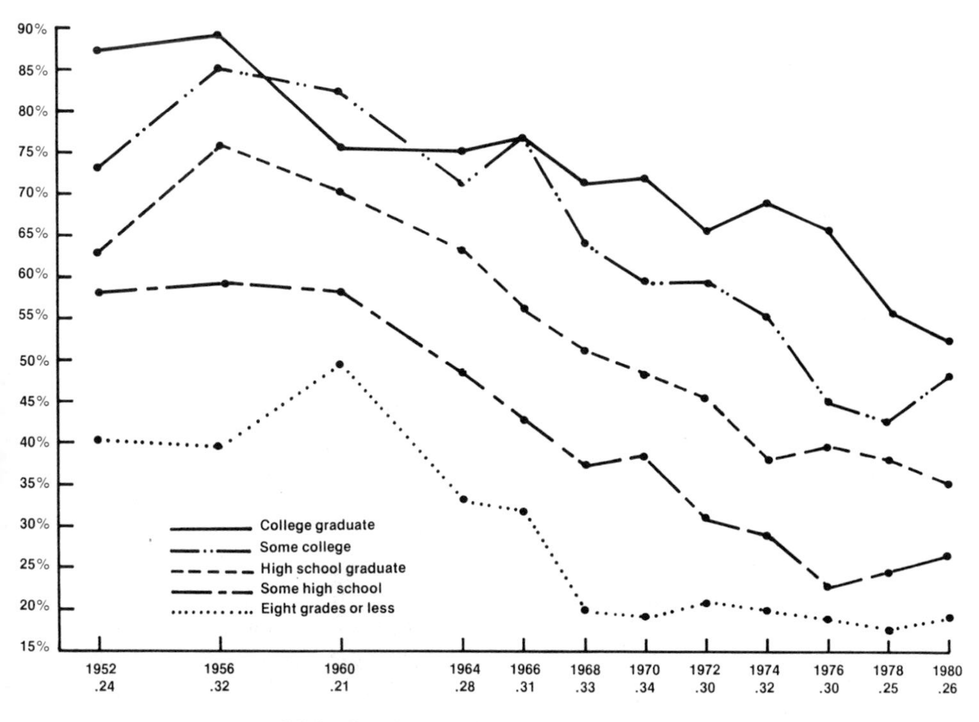

Figure 10.4 Percentage of Whites Who Score High on "External" Political Efficacy, by Level of Education: 1952–1980.

(*Note:* To approximate the numbers on which these percentages are based, see Table 4.3. Actual *N*s are somewhat smaller, since respondents for whom an "external" political-efficacy score was not ascertained have been excluded from these analyses. *N*s are smaller for 1968, 1976, and 1980, since the political-efficacy questions were employed in the postelection interview. [a]tau-c relationship between a fivefold ordinal measure of education as listed above and a threefold measure of "external" political efficacy.)

of "internal" political efficacy have remained static since 1960, while their feelings of "external" political efficacy have declined. The relationship of levels of education to feelings of political efficacy among blacks lends indirect support to the social-deprivation explanation. Blacks who have social opportunities, as indirectly measured by their higher levels of education, tend to feel more politically efficacious.

Why have feelings about government responsiveness declined? Perhaps persons at all educational levels are responding to political events that have caused Americans to question the responsiveness of the government. Disaffection with government policies over race-related issues, policies in Vietnam, the Watergate scandals, and a more generalized feeling that the government has failed to solve social and economic problems may have contributed to the feeling that the government does not respond to the people (Converse, 1972, pp. 329–330; House and Mason, 1975; Wright, 1976, pp. 188–195). These forces appear to have affected whites at all educational levels with about the same impact,[18] although the decline among the college-educated began too early to fit neatly this events-based explanation.

Even though neither of Converse's models receives clear support, his discussion alerts us to an important fact. Although powerful demographic forces may lead to predicting a trend, the trend may not materialize. As Converse acknowledges, most social scientists, if they could not examine the actual relationships beforehand, would have favored the education-driven model and would have expected feelings of political efficacy to rise. The failure of demographic extrapolations to predict the future again becomes apparent when we examine the relationship of age to feelings of political effectiveness.

Feelings of Political Efficacy Through the Life Cycle

The tendency for older adults to have lower feelings of political effectiveness is documented by Campbell, Gurin, and Miller (1954, p. 191) when the concept was first introduced, and many subsequent studies find the same basic relationship (Angello, 1973; N. Cutler and Bengtson, 1974; Jennings and Niemi, 1974, p. 280; Wright, 1976, p. 144). Our analysis shows a consistent tendency for older persons to feel less politically efficacious in all twelve surveys for which this relationship can be assessed. The basic relationship between years of birth and feelings of "internal" political efficacy among whites is presented in Table 10.3, while the relationship for feelings of "external" political efficacy is presented in Table 10.4. These tables follow the same standard cohort matrix presented in Chapter 4.

By reading down each column of Table 10.3, we can see that there has never been a perfectly consistent decline in feelings of "internal" political efficacy with age, but there has always been some erosion, averaging −.49 percentage points per year of age for the twelve surveys.[19] Young adults are not consistently the most efficacious, but the oldest age group has the lowest level of personal political effectiveness in ten of these surveys and among the lowest in the remaining two. A more refined analysis, based on four-year cohort divisions, suggests that there may be a drop in feelings of personal political effectiveness as persons enter their late 60s and early 70s.

By reading down each column of Table 10.4, we can also see that feelings of "external" political efficacy have never declined consistently with age, but there has always been some erosion, averaging −.36 percentage points per

[18] Feelings of "external" political efficacy have also declined among all five educational subgroups among the black electorate.

[19] Based on a least-squares regression analysis calculated down each row.

year of age for the twelve surveys.[20] However, the relationship between "external" efficacy and age is weakest in the three most recent surveys. As with the "internal" efficacy measure, young adults do not consistently have the highest score, but the oldest cohort has the lowest score in ten of the surveys and among the lowest in the remaining two. As with the "internal" efficacy measure, a more refined cohort analysis, based on four-year categories, suggests that beliefs about government responsiveness may decline as cohorts reach their late 60s and early 70s.

It would be reasonable to expect persons to feel less politically efficacious as they reach old age. When they leave the labor force, they become removed from the social and institutional ties that may provide indirect influence on government authorities. Their incomes are often reduced, which may further lower their actual influence, as well as their general feelings of environmental control.[21] The elderly are more dependent on the government to protect them from economic dislocation. Unfortunately, probability samples of the electorate are of limited utility in studying the effects of old age on political attitudes, for the number of elderly people sampled is small, and differential death rates confound attempts to analyze relationships.

Although old age may erode feelings of political effectiveness, there is little reason to expect aging to erode feelings of political efficacy throughout most of the life cycle. Yet there is usually a negative relationship between age and feelings of political effectiveness when the oldest cohort is excluded from consideration. This relationship does not result from aging per se, but from the negative relationship between age and levels of education. As several scholars have demonstrated, the relationship between age and feelings of political effectiveness is greatly reduced when controls for levels of education are introduced (N. Cutler and Bengtson, 1974; Jennings and Niemi, 1974, pp. 280–281; Wright, 1976, p. 146).

It is difficult to advance a plausible thesis that differences between birth cohorts result from different formative socialization experiences. The generational explanation for age-group differences assumes that there is a formative socialization period after which attitudes tend to become relatively stable. But our panel analyses for both the 1956–1960 and the 1972–1974–1976 period find that 21- to 29-year-olds do not have lower levels of over-time stability in their feelings of political effectiveness than do their elders. Nor do older cohorts have highly stable feelings of political effectiveness. Moreover, if the formative experiences of cohorts were strongly different, we would expect different levels of political efficacy to persist among cohorts even after controls

[20]Based on a least-squares regression analysis calculated down each row.

[21]Unfortunately, as Phares (1976, pp. 158–159) points out, there is very little research on the relationship of aging and locus of control, although he speculates that aging should contribute to "external" beliefs.

Table 10.3 Percentage of Whites Who Score Medium or High on "Internal" Political Efficacy, by Years of Birth: 1952–1980

Years of birth	1952	1956	1960	1964	1966	1968	1970	1972	1974	1976	1978	1980
1956–1962									*	45	62	58
1948–1955							*	*	67	64	61	64
1940–1947				*	*	68	61	49	59	56	62	62
1932–1939		*	58	54	56	70	55	60	59	61	55	63
1924–1931	38	60	52	57	54	61	61	62	58	63	55	62
1916–1923	46	52	59	48	49	53	54	49	42	58	47	44
1908–1915	43	49	54	38	40	46	42	43	41	47	35	32
1900–1907	42	52	53	43	24	44	41	33	35	34	**	**
1892–1899	38	51	63	40	26	29	**	**	**	**	**	**
1884–1891	39	43	37	**	**	**	**	**	**	**	**	**
1876–1883	25	**	**	**	**	**	**	**	**	**	**	**
All whites	40%	51%	54%	46%	43%	55%	52%	50%	52%	56%	54%	55%

Note: For the numbers on which these percentages are based, see Table 4.2. Actual *N*s are slightly smaller, since respondents for whom sense of "internal" political efficacy was not ascertained have been excluded from these analyses. *N*s are smaller for 1968, 1976, and 1980, since the sense-of-political-efficacy items were employed in the postelection interview.

*Not included because the full eight-year cohort had not yet entered the electorate.

**Not included because the advanced age of the cohort makes it nonrepresentative for comparisons across time or because there are too few cases remaining.

Table 10.4 Percentage of Whites Who Score High on "External" Political Efficacy, by Years of Birth: 1952–1980

Years of birth	1952	1956	1960	1964	1966	1968	1970	1972	1974	1976	1978	1980
1956–1962									*	39	42	41
1948–1955									46	36	39	37
1940–1947				*	*	55	44	44	48	42	39	40
1932–1939		*	66	62	63	55	53	49	40	49	43	40
1924–1931	58	71	65	59	60	56	54	53	49	49	38	50
1916–1923	57	66	70	59	56	49	49	42	42	41	42	37
1908–1915	65	69	66	56	52	36	43	40	39	40	27	30
1900–1907	61	62	66	52	35	33	40	31	25	28	**	**
1892–1899	52	58	62	40	41	40	**	**	**	**	**	**
1884–1891	46	52	46	**	**	**	**	**	**	**	**	**
1876–1883	39	**	**	**	**	**	**	**	**	**	**	**
All whites	56%	64%	64%	56%	53%	47%	45%	43%	41%	40%	38%	39%

Note: For the numbers on which these percentages are based, see Table 4.2. Actual *N*s are slightly smaller, since respondents for whom sense of "external" political efficacy was not ascertained have been excluded from these analyses. *N*s are smaller for 1968, 1976, and 1980, since the sense-of-political-efficacy items were employed in the postelection interview.

*Not included because the full eight-year cohort had not yet entered the electorate.

**Not included because the advanced age of the cohort makes it nonrepresentative for comparisons across time or because there are too few cases remaining.

for levels of education are introduced, but such controls substantially reduce differences between birth cohorts.

If we track birth cohorts as they age by reading across each row, we find that all birth cohorts born before 1916 register a clear decline in feelings of personal political efficacy, mainly because these feelings drop off as cohorts enter their late 60s. When we track beliefs about government responsiveness among cohorts as they age, we find that all cohorts show a sharp decline, averaging −1.26 percentage points per year of age.[22] This sharp decline is far greater than a life-cycle explanation would predict, since, as we saw above, the average relationship of feelings of "external" efficacy to age for the twelve surveys is a decline of only .36 percentage points.

Our overall conclusions on changing beliefs about government responsiveness are similar to those reached by Neal Cutler and Vern Bengtson (1974) in their analysis of the 1952, 1960, and 1968 SRC surveys: overall change among birth cohorts results from historical forces that reduce feelings of political efficacy among all birth cohorts.[23] Likewise, our conclusions square with those of Searing, Wright, and Rabinowitz (1976), who conducted a cohort analysis using the 1952, 1956, 1960, 1964, and 1968 SRC election surveys. Searing and his colleagues developed a formula that attempts to assess the relative importance of aging effects and period effects (which they call *Zeitgeist* or "spirit of the time" effects). Period effects are more important than aging effects, although the latter are also present.[24] They conclude: "Contemporary events hold more substantial and systematic consequences for political efficacy than do aging factors" (p. 107). All of the cohorts studied register a decline in feelings of political efficacy. "The dramatic declining trend, beginning in 1960, may reflect disenchantment over official pressures toward school desegregation, as well as frustration with a war that leaders seemed unable to bring to an end" (p. 107).

Even though the data do not show generational differences in the formative learning of political effectiveness, generational replacement has had an impact on overall levels of political effectiveness among the electorate. Figure 10.5 shows overall levels of "internal" political efficacy among the white electorate between 1952 and 1980, while Figure 10.6 shows overall levels of "external" political efficacy. For each figure, the solid line shows actual levels of political

[22]Based on a least-squares regression analysis calculated across all seven of the cohorts that can be tracked for at least one decade. The average change is the mean of the change for all seven cohorts.

[23]Cutler and Bengtson conducted a separate analysis for each of three standard sense-of-political-efficacy items: "public officials care," "don't have any say," and "politics . . . seem so complicated."

[24]Searing, Wright, and Rabinowitz conducted a separate analysis for the same three efficacy items analyzed by Cutler and Bengtson.

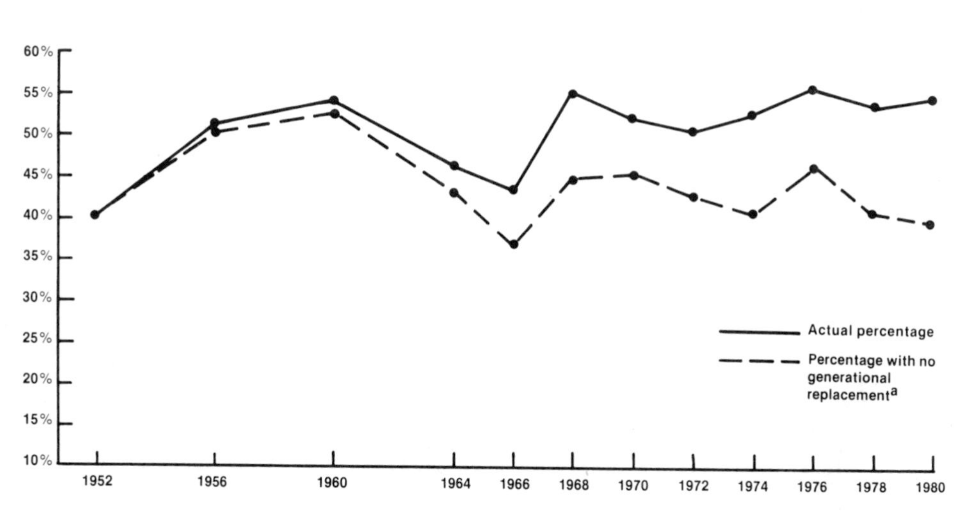

Figure 10.5 Percentage of Whites Who Score Medium or High on "Internal" Political Efficacy: 1952–1980.

(*Note:* For the numbers on which the percentages for the solid line are based, see Figure 10.1. For the numbers on which the percentages for the broken line are based, see Table 4.2. Actual *N*s are somewhat smaller, since respondents for whom an "internal" political-efficacy score was not ascertained have been excluded from the analysis. *N*s are smaller for 1968, 1976, and 1980, since the political-efficacy questions were employed in the postelection interview. [a]Assuming that no persons born after 1931 entered the electorate and that older cohorts did not diminish through death.)

efficacy, while the broken line shows what levels of political efficacy would have been if no generational replacement had occurred.[25]

The results for feelings of personal political effectiveness tell two different stories, depending on when one begins the analysis. If one begins with 1952, one finds that feelings of "internal" political efficacy have increased 15 percentage points; while, in the absence of generational replacement, efficacy would have been virtually the same in 1980 as in 1952. One could conclude that replacement has created a trend, for, in the absence of replacement, feelings of personal political effectiveness would not have increased.

On the other hand, most of the increase in personal political effectiveness actually results from a jump in efficacy between 1952 and 1956, and this sudden increase within four years cannot have resulted from replacement. It would therefore be reasonable to begin the analysis with 1956, in which case the estimates removing the effects of replacement would follow a somewhat different pattern from the broken line in our figure. Between 1956 and 1980,

[25]These calculations are based on the results presented in Tables 10.3 and 10.4. For cohorts too old to be presented in these tables, we estimate levels of efficacy from their surviving members as well as the efficacy among the oldest cohort presented in the basic cohort matrix.

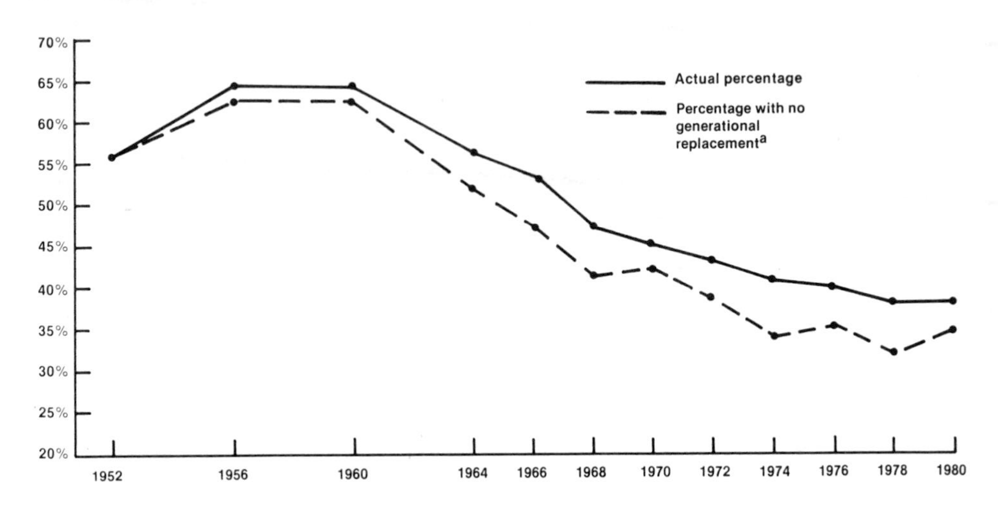

Figure 10.6 Percentage of Whites Who Score High on "External" Political Efficacy: 1952–1980.

(*Note:* For the numbers on which the percentages for the solid line are based, see Figure 10.2. For the numbers on which the percentages for the broken line are based, see Table 4.2. Actual *N*s are somewhat smaller, since respondents for whom an "external" political-efficacy score was not ascertained have been excluded from the analysis. *N*s are smaller for 1968, 1976, and 1980, since the political-efficacy questions were employed in the postelection interview. [a]Assuming that no persons born after 1931 entered the electorate, and that older cohorts did not diminish through death.)

feelings of personal political effectiveness rise 4 percentage points. Without generational replacement, efficacy scores would have dropped 8 points between 1956 and 1980. If one chooses to interpret the 4-point gain as meaningful, one would conclude that replacement has actually reversed a trend. If one concludes that the 4-point shift between 1956 and 1980 should merely be interpreted as stability, replacement would be seen as preventing a trend. The impact of generational replacement on overall levels of "internal" political efficacy is basically a function of the impact of replacement in increasing overall levels of education among the electorate.

Feelings of government responsiveness, on the other hand, have declined during the postwar years. This decline occurred even though younger cohorts with higher levels of "external" efficacy were entering the electorate, while older cohorts with low levels of efficacy were leaving the electorate through death. Between 1952 and 1980, feelings of "external" political efficacy decline 17 percentage points. If no new cohorts had entered the electorate and if older cohorts had not diminished through death, the overall decline would have been 21 points. In other words, assuming other things to be equal, the overall decline in "external" political efficacy would have been about a fifth again as great if generational replacement had not impeded the trend. Similar conclusions would be reached if one begins the analysis with 1956 or 1960, the years when beliefs about government responsiveness are highest.

Conclusions

Political scientists find it difficult to resist the impulse to use their data to predict future relationships, but anyone making projections based on these data should be especially cautious. Yet some speculation may be in order. When we examine feelings of "internal" political efficacy, we see that young adults usually have higher levels of efficacy than do their elders. If these levels are sustained, feelings of personal political effectiveness could rise.

Young adults have not had particularly high feelings of "external" political effectiveness, and in the three most recent surveys, they differ little from the electorate as a whole. Young adults of today score substantially lower in their beliefs about government responsiveness than did young adults of the 1950s or early 1960s. Future generational replacement will not restore beliefs about government responsiveness unless newly entering cohorts have far higher levels of "external" political efficacy. Given the changeability of feelings of political efficacy, however, it is possible that all birth cohorts could register increases in response to future political events.

Unfortunately, feelings that the government is responsive have been declining for almost the entire period during which they have been measured. We know something about the conditions that can erode these feelings, but very little about the conditions that can cause these feelings to increase.

IV

Change in Political Trust

[CHAPTER 11]

The Concept of Political Trust

As we saw in Chapter 1, the decline of political trust is among the most dramatic trends in postwar American politics. Back in 1958 and 1964, about three out of four Americans said the government in Washington could be trusted to do what is right "just about always" or "most of the time," but that percentage has dropped continuously since then, and, by 1980, only one American in four trusted the government to do what is right. Commentators have pointed to this decline, as well as a decline using other measures, as a cause of declining electoral participation.

The President's Commission for a National Agenda for the Eighties, for example, reports: "This widespread public perception that our institutions are not performing well is reflected in an increase in cynicism and a decline in participation in political activity" (1980, p. 2). The Commission also expressed concern about the "distrust of young adult voters" (p. 22).

But while trust has declined, the significance of this decline is a subject of controversy. What does the decline signify? To answer this question, we must deal with a fundamental question of validity. What do the questions used to measure political trust mean? Over the years, many questions have been developed to measure trust in the political system, but the dominant questions have been those introduced by the University of Michigan Survey Research Center in 1958. Since these questions have been used for over two decades, they can be used to study change over the life cycle and to examine the impact of generational replacement. These questions were employed in the Michigan 1972–1974–1976 panel and in the Michigan student–parent panel and thus can be used to study individual-level attitude change over time. Political trust has also played a central role in the study of preadult political attitudes, and, once again, the Michigan SRC questions have been widely used. Because these political-trust questions play such a central role in the controversy over the meaning of political trust, we report them in full:[1]

1. How much of the time do you think you can trust the government in Washington to do what is right—just about always, most of the time, or only some of the time?
2. Do you think the people in the government waste a lot of the money we pay in taxes, waste some of it, or don't waste very much of it?
3. Do you feel that almost all of the people running the government are smart people who usually know what they are doing, or do you think that quite a few of them don't seem to know what they are doing?
4. Do you think that quite a few of the people running the government are a little crooked, not very many are, or do you think that hardly any of them are crooked at all?

In 1964, a fifth question was introduced:[2]

5. Would you say the government is pretty much run by a few big interests looking out for themselves or that it is run for the benefit of all the people?

Considering how often these questions were later used, it is unfortunate that the original researchers never developed an extensive rationale to explain their meaning. The first publication to discuss these questions is a brief chapter by Stokes (1962), one of *The American Voter* authors. Stokes explains that the SRC developed "a series of questions designed to tap basic evaluative orientations toward the national government" (p. 64). As Stokes writes (p. 64):

> The criteria of judgment implicit in these questions were partly ethical, that is, the honesty and other ethical qualities of public officials were part of what the sample was asked to judge. But the criteria extended to other qualities as well, including the ability and efficiency of government officials and the correctness of their policy decisions.

Stokes reports that the responses to these questions are strongly related to each other and that they could be used to form a single attitude scale, which

[1]In order to clarify the questions, in 1974 the CPS modified the "smart people" and "crooked people" questions to read as follows:

"Do you feel that almost all the people running the government are smart people, or do you think that quite a few of them don't seem to know what they are doing?"

"Do you think that quite a few of the people running the government are crooked, not very many are, or do you think hardly any of them are crooked?"

The greatest single change in political-trust scores occurs between 1972 and 1974, but change is greater on the three remaining trust questions than on the two that were modified.

[2]The "few big interests" question was substituted for a question in 1958 that asked, "Do you think that the high-up people in government give everyone a fair break whether they are big shots or just ordinary people, or do you think some of them pay more attention to what the big interests want?"

he labels "orientations toward government." Stokes does not examine the behavioral correlates of these orientations in any detail, but he does find that persons with positive orientations (i.e., those who are more trusting) are more likely to participate regularly in elections. However, these relationships are not strong and are found only among persons with less than a college education.

Despite these modest results, Stokes argues that his scale measures an important political attitude: "[T]hese orientations have far-reaching consequences for a nation's politics. Their composition across social groups, their relation to other psychological orientations to politics, their role in prompting or inhibiting participation—each of these things holds a key to understanding a political system in which public opinion is a principal force" (p. 65). Stokes's major finding is that levels of political trust do not differ much along social-class, ethnic, racial, or other lines.

The political-trust questions were introduced to the preadult political-socialization literature in a major article by Jennings and Niemi (1968), who label them a measure of "political cynicism."[3] "[C]ynicism," they write, "is a basic orientation toward political actors and activity" (p. 177). Jennings and Niemi do not directly examine the behavioral correlates of political cynicism, but they do report that it is found "to be negatively related to political participation" (p. 177). In other words, persons who are politically trusting are more likely to participate in politics. Moreover, Jennings and Niemi claim that political cynicism has strong psychological correlates: "Political cynicism appears to be a manifestation of deep-seated suspicion of others' motives and actions. Thus this attitude comes closer than the rest of our values to tapping a basic psycho-political predisposition" (p. 177).

Unfortunately, neither Stokes nor Jennings and Niemi provides a full discussion of the concept of political trust, an analysis of what the trust questions are supposed to measure, or a discussion of the way political trust relates to behavior. This sketchiness led to problems of interpretation as other scholars began using these measures.

The Miller–Citrin Controversy

Arthur Miller (1974a) presents the first major analysis of the decline of political trust. Miller's main goal is to demonstrate the way attitudes toward political issues correlate with political trust, and we examine some of this evidence later (p. 233). However, in the course of his article, Miller makes sweeping claims about the importance of the decline of political trust. He

[3]In almost all the studies in which these and similar items are used, *cynicism* is merely used as the antonym of *trust*. Sometimes the same researcher uses the same measure and calls it cynicism in one study, trust in another. Such inconsistencies of usage are confusing, but present no serious obstacle. High trust simply equates with low cynicism; high cynicism with low trust.

argues that "a situation of widespread, basic discontent and political alienation exists in the U.S. today" (p. 951). "Such feelings of powerlessness and normlessness," Miller maintains, "are very likely to be accompanied by hostility toward political and social leaders, the institutions of government, and the regime as a whole" (p. 951). The low level of trust among Americans, Miller suggests, could contribute to extralegal political behavior, party realignment, and radical political change (p. 971).

Miller's claims can best be assessed if we recall Easton's distinction among the three objects of support (Chapter 8). According to Easton, the *political community* is "that aspect of a political system that we can identify as a collection of persons who share a division of political labor" (Easton and Dennis, 1969, p. 58). The *regime* is the "constitutional order in the very broadest sense of the term . . . the norms or rules of the game through which they [the members of the system] conduct their political business, and the formal and informal structures of authority that arrange who is to do what in the system" (p. 59). Lastly, the *authorities* "are those members of a system in whom the primary responsibility is lodged for taking care of the daily routines of a political system. In a democratic system we describe them as the elected representatives and other public officials, such as civil servants" (p. 60). Miller's argument strongly suggests that low levels of trust reflect a withdrawal of support not just from the authorities, but from the regime as well.

In an extensive critique of Miller's argument, Citrin (1974) argues that Miller's claims are overstated. Citrin maintains that the decline in political trust probably reflects a withdrawal of support from the political authorities, rather than from the regime or the political community. "[T]he meaning of recent increases in the level of political cynicism," Citrin concludes, "remains ambiguous, and to decisively conclude that there exists widespread support for radical political change or pervasive alienation from the political *system* is premature, if not misleading" (p. 978).

Let us review the evidence Citrin uses to support his conclusion. First, Citrin briefly discusses the "face validity" of the trust questions. What do these five questions seem to be measuring? He argues that they refer mainly to the "people running the government" and that they seem to call for an evaluation of the authorities, not the basic rules of the game. In addition, as Citrin and others (Lodge and Tursky, 1979) point out, the negative assessments elicited by the basic trust questions do not call for a high degree of cynicism. As Citrin writes: "To believe that the government wastes 'a lot' of money, can be trusted to 'do what is right only some of the time,' and includes 'quite a few' people who are 'crooked' or 'don't know that they're doing' need not bespeak a deep-seated hostility toward the political system at the regime or community levels" (p. 975).

Citrin then raises two kinds of arguments about the relationship of responses to the political-trust measure to other political attitudes and behaviors. First, he argues that persons who are politically trusting have favorable attitudes toward the incumbents—thus suggesting that the political-trust index is measuring attitudes toward the authorities. Second, Citrin claims that persons who are politically cynical are not very different from the politically trusting on other measures of political support—thus suggesting that the trust index is not measuring attitudes toward the regime or the community. With both types of arguments, Citrin examines the "construct validity" of the political-trust index. If the political-trust index measures widespread support for the political system, people who are trusting should have predictably different attitudes from those who are cynical.

Citrin presents four examples to demonstrate that the politically trusting are more favorable toward incumbents.

1. Persons who are politically trusting are more likely to approve of the incumbent president's performance. This is not just a function of partisan differences, for in 1968 (when Lyndon B. Johnson was president), the politically trusting were more likely to give Johnson a good job rating than the politically cynical were; while in 1972 (when Richard M. Nixon was the incumbent), the politically trusting were more likely to approve of Nixon's performance as president.

2. The relationship of political trust to direction of party identification varies depending on the incumbent. Citrin analyzes the relationship of trust to party identification between 1964 and 1972, but, if we utilize a four-item political-trust index, we can examine the relationship of party identification to trust in nine separate surveys conducted between 1958 and 1980. These relationships for the white electorate are presented in Table 11.1. (For the procedures we used to construct the political-trust index, see the appendix.[4]) As we can see, there is usually a weak tendency for supporters of the incumbent party to be more trusting than supporters of the party that does not control the White House. Among strong partisans, feelings of political trust appear to respond to changes in presidential incumbency. By tracking our analysis back to 1958 and forward to 1980, we are able to examine three such changes. Figure 11.1 shows the percentage of white strong partisans scoring medium or high on the four-item political-trust index. Between 1958 (a Republican incumbent) and 1964 (a Democrat), trust rises among strong Democrats, while dropping sharply among strong Republicans. Between 1968 (a Democratic

[4] As noted above, the "few big interests" question was not asked in 1958. In order to maximize comparability over time, I usually employ a four-item political-trust index. The standard five-item index is used in my analyses of panel data and in analyzing the Michigan student–parent data. While using all five items creates a more reliable measure, using the four-item index seldom affects the direction of relationships, for the scores of these indices are strongly related to each other. In 1978, for example, scores on these two indices correlate at a tau of .82 and a Pearson's r of .94.

Table 11.1 Percentage of Whites Who Score Medium or High on Political Trust, by Party Identification: 1958–1980

Party identification	1958	1964	1968	1970	1972	1974	1976	1978	1980
Strong Democrat	67	79	72	57	51	44	37	43	37
Weak Democrat	75	75	63	57	58	47	45	45	34
Independent, leans Democratic	66	80	67	59	51	47	39	42	36
Independent, no partisan leaning	75	69	48	52	54	42	42	36	27
Independent, leans Republican	71	62	63	55	65	46	41	37	21
Weak Republican	74	68	70	57	64	49	46	37	31
Strong Republican	79	59	60	62	64	47	49	33	19
Relationship between party identification and political trust[a]	.07	−.15	−.06	.01	.08	.02	.04	−.07	−.08

Note: Based on four-item political-trust index. To approximate the numbers on which these percentages are based, see Table 7.2. Actual *N*s are somewhat smaller than those that can be derived from Table 7.2, since there are some respondents who received no political-trust scores. Numbers will also be lower in 1964, 1968, and 1972, since trust was measured as part of the postelection interviews, which contain about 10% fewer respondents than do the preelection interviews in which party identification was measured.

[a]Kendall's tau-c relationship between a sevenfold ordinal measure of party identification as listed above and a threefold ordinal measure of political trust. A positive relationship indicates that Republicans tend to score higher than Democrats. A negative relationship indicates that Democrats tend to score higher than Republicans.

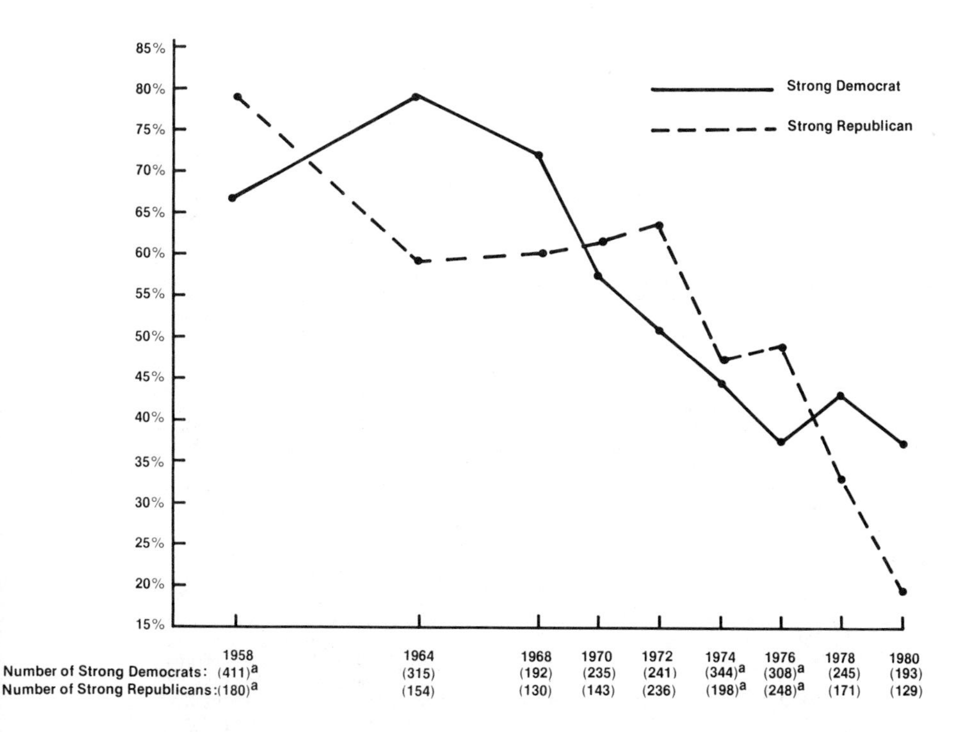

Figure 11.1 Percentage of White Strong Party Identifiers Who Score Medium or High on Political Trust, by Direction of Partisanship: 1958–1980.
(*Note:* Based on four-item political-trust index. [a]Weighted *N*s.)

incumbent) and 1970 (a Republican), trust drops sharply among strong Democrats, while rising slightly among strong Republicans. And between 1976 (a Republican incumbent) and 1978 (a Democrat), trust rises among strong Democrats, while dropping markedly among strong Republicans. These changes are similar to, but sharper than, partisan changes in feelings of "external" political efficacy (see p. 177).

3. There is a strong tendency for persons who are trusting to be more likely to vote for the incumbent party in presidential elections. Once again, we can examine these relationships ourselves, extending the analysis through 1980. As the data in Table 11.2 indicate, whites who score high on political trust are more likely to vote for the incumbent president (or for the candidate of the incumbent party in 1968) than are voters who score low on political trust. Moreover, George C. Wallace, who most clearly represented a challenge to the incumbents, scored substantially better among the politically cynical than among the politically trusting. (John B. Anderson also fared better among the cynical, but differences are too small to be meaningful.) In addition, whites who are politically cynical are somewhat more likely to cast their congressional

Table 11.2 How Whites Voted for President, by Score on Political Trust: 1964–1980

	Low	Medium	High
1964			
Johnson	41%	69%	85%
Goldwater	59	31	15
Total %	100%	100%	100%
Total *N*	(261)	(567)	(182)
1968			
Humphrey	28%	38%	52%
Nixon	49	55	44
Wallace	23	7	4
Total %	100%	100%	100%
Total *N*	(300)	(489)	(105)
1972			
McGovern	37%	27%	16%
Nixon	63	73	84
Total %	100%	100%	100%
Total *N*	(566)	(735)	(122)
1976			
Carter	48%	46%	35%
Ford	52	54	65
Total %	100%	100%	100%
Weighted *N*	(802)	(582)	(66)
1980			
Carter	29%	42%	58%
Reagan	60	50	37
Anderson	10	7	5
Total %	99%	99%	100%
Total *N*	(601)	(218)	(19)

Note: Based on four-item political-trust index. Except for Wallace voters in 1968 and Anderson voters in 1980, supporters of minor-party candidates have been excluded from these calculations.

vote against the party controlling the White House in the 1958, 1974, and 1978 off-year elections, although there is no relationship between trust and the direction of congressional vote in 1970.[5]

[5]In a recent study, Fiorina (1981, pp. 56–61) demonstrates that voters who are politically cynical are more likely to vote according to their "retrospective" evaluations of incumbent performance.

4. Finally, Citrin uses the SRC–CPS "thermometer" questions, which ask respondents to express their feelings toward political leaders by rating them on a thermometer scale ranging from a low of 0° to a high of 100°. Persons who are politically trusting are more likely to have "warm" feelings toward the incumbents. "By contrast," Citrin finds, "the cynics were more likely to view positively politicians who themselves attacked the underlying assumptions of ongoing public policies, whether from the right or left, George Wallace in 1968, George McGovern in 1972" (p. 976).

In addition to showing that persons who are trusting are more likely to be favorable toward incumbents, Citrin presents another set of findings to show that the politically cynical do not differ from the politically trusting on other measures of political support:

1. Citrin argues that even persons who are politically cynical have favorable attitudes toward the American form of government. Citrin's basic results are reproduced in Table 11.3. In interpreting this table, Citrin emphasizes the

Table 11.3 Attitudes Toward American Form of Government, by Score on Political Trust: 1972

	Low	Medium	High
Pride in government			
I am proud of many things about our form of government	74%	92%	98%
I can't find much about our form of government to be proud of	26	8	2
Total %	100%	100%	100%
Total *N*	(419)	(373)	(224)
Change our form of government[a]			
Keep our form of government as it is	43%	63%	81%
Some change needed	32	28	14
Big change needed	25	9	5
Total %	100%	100%	100%
Total *N*	(419)	(373)	(224)

Note: Based on five-item political-trust index developed by Citrin.

[a]The question is worded: "Some people believe that change in our whole form of government is needed to solve the problems facing our country, while others feel that no real change is necessary. Do you think . . . ?"

Source: Based on Citrin (1974, Table 1). Reprinted with permission of the American Political Science Association.

finding that, even among the respondents scoring low on trust, 74% are proud of the American form of government and that only 25% favor a "big change" in our form of government. "This strongly suggests," he concludes, "that many political cynics focus their disaffection on incumbent authorities rather than systemic values and processes" (p. 975).

2. Citrin examines the relationship between feelings of political trust and attitudes toward a variety of protest activities; for example, whether one approved of legal protest marches, of the refusal to obey unjust laws, and of disruptive sit-ins and demonstrations. Citrin notes that, between 1968 and 1972, political cynicism increases while approval of protest activities declines, and he argues that we would not expect approval of protest to decline if cynicism contributed to protest. More importantly, among individuals, there is no consistent tendency for the politically cynical to be more likely to approve of political protest.

3. Lastly, Citrin demonstrates that persons who are politically cynical are as likely to be involved in conventional political activities as persons who are politically trusting. Analyzing relationships for 1964, 1968, 1970, and 1972, Citrin shows that there are few systematic differences between the trusting and the cynical in levels of voting, attention paid to political campaigns, following public affairs, or various forms of campaign activity. (For more recent evidence supporting this conclusion with evidence from 1976 and 1978, see Citrin, 1981, p. 56.) I have not replicated all these relationships, but I can report that there is no relationship between political trust and levels of presidential voting in 1980.[6] Nor is there a tendency for the politically trusting to be more likely to vote in the 1958 off-year congressional elections, although there is a weak relationship in 1974.

After reviewing the evidence, Citrin concludes that the high level of cynicism among the American electorate reflects a largely "ritualistic" response that mirrors the temper of the times. "Thus, the evidence that mistrust of government, as operationalized by Miller, produces neither political apathy nor political activism reinforces the argument that many cynical responses merely record opposition to incumbent officeholders or largely ritualistic expressions of fashionable clichés" (p. 984).

Citrin's critique led to a lengthy rejoinder by Miller (1974b) that provides evidence to support his interpretation of the political-trust measure. For our

[6]For a different interpretation, see Santi (1980). Focusing on the "trust the government" item, he argues that trust is related to turnout and maintains that the decline of turnout between 1964 and 1972 can be attributed to the decline of political trust. Our analyses show that with the most recent SRC survey, conducted in late 1980, there is absolutely no relationship between responses on this item and turnout.

purposes here, Miller's rejoinder is more important than his original article, for in it he probes the meaning of political trust far more thoroughly.

Miller does not directly take issue with Citrin on the question of "face validity," but argues that one cannot judge the meaning of the political-trust scale merely by examining the wording of the five questions used to make up the measure.[7] He argues: "The validity of the trust in government scale as a measure of political disaffection cannot be ascertained simply from the manifest content of the five items used to construct the scale. . . . Questions of validity and focus can only be answered through an examination of the relationship between the trust scale and other political indicators" (p. 990). Miller's reply here is probably an overstatement. Students of attitude measurement agree that tests of meaning based on face validity alone are weak, but a careful reading of the questions that make up a measure may provide some clues about its meaning.

Miller does not deny that feelings of political trust are related to support for incumbents. But he argues that support for candidates is primarily related to "social control" ideology, not to trust. For example, among respondents in 1972 who are primarily to the left on a series of questions about government policies, those who are politically cynical were more likely to vote for McGovern than one would have predicted on the basis of their party identification.[8] Among respondents with "centrist" or "rightist" positions on the issues, there are only weak relationships between cynicism and the way they vote. In fact, among politically conservative voters, the politically cynical voted for Nixon slightly more often than one would have predicted on the basis of their party identification. In the 1972 survey, according to Miller, the "feelings" of whites toward Wallace depended on their ideological position, not on their political trust; among blacks, the trusting felt less cold toward Wallace than did the cynical.

On balance, Miller's evidence does not convincingly refute Citrin's position that the politically trusting are more likely to support incumbents. Miller's own results show that, for the total electorate, the cynical were more likely to vote Democratic for Congress in 1972 than one would have predicted on the basis of their party identification. And even with controls for social-control ideology introduced, cynical whites felt more favorable toward McGovern than trusting whites did; trusting whites, on the other hand, were more likely to feel favorable to the incumbent Nixon than cynical whites did.

[7]Miller notes that his measure was formed through scaling procedures that differ from the additive index procedures that Citrin employs. However, it is doubtful that these differences lead to any substantive differences in their findings.

[8]Miller's measure of ideology is based on responses to "spatial" questions. For examples of these questions, see the third column of Table 15.1.

Miller could have pushed his argument somewhat further, for it seems unreasonable to claim that political-trust measures do not *partly* assess attitudes toward the incumbents. After all, a person who questions the basic rules of the political game or who rejects the political community might very well be expected to distrust the authorities responsible for implementing political decisions. Miller could concede that his political-trust scale partly measures support for incumbents, as long as he could demonstrate that it *also* measures more widespread disaffection.

Miller refutes Citrin's argument directly when he demonstrates that persons who are politically cynical do differ from the trusting on some measures of political support.

1. Miller takes direct issue with Citrin's conclusion that political trust is unrelated to pride in "our form of government" and to beliefs about the need for a "change in our whole form of government." Although Miller does not directly refer to Citrin's own data presentation, he might have done so. Let us return to Table 11.3, where Citrin's own results are presented. One could argue that these very data show that feelings of political trust are related to broader evaluations of the political system. Among persons who score low on political trust, about one-fourth "can't find much about our form of government to be proud of"; while among the politically trusting, only one in fifty is not proud. Among those who score low on political trust, 57% think that either "some change" or "big change" is needed in our form of government; while among the politically trusting, only 19% think change is necessary. Miller does not directly turn to Citrin's own data presentation, but rather argues that these questions about pride in our form of government and about the need to change it are biased measures of support, since persons who are politically conservative are less likely to favor such change than those who are liberal. In fact, Miller claims that the question about the need to change our form of government is strongly related to the political-trust scale. Miller shows that, among both the politically conservative and the politically liberal, the trusting are less likely to favor changing the American form of government.

2. Miller also refutes Citrin's contention that political cynicism is unrelated to support for protest activity. The problem with Citrin's analysis, Miller argues, is that he overlooks the fact that cynicism is highest among persons who are ideologically to the left and right and lowest among persons with centrist political views. Because conservatives are unlikely to endorse protest activity, the relationship between political trust and attitudes toward protest does not clearly emerge until one examines the relationship among subsets of respondents with differing ideological orientations. Miller shows that, among respondents who favor social change to deal with social and political problems, the cynical are more likely to approve of protest activity. The data presented

by Miller support his contention, although even among advocates of social change, differences between the trusting and the cynical are small.

3. Miller examines only briefly the relationship between feelings of political trust and political behavior. He reports that, in 1972, turnout is fairly high among persons who feel both politically efficacious and trusting, while it is low among those who feel both inefficacious and cynical. But this finding does not directly challenge Citrin's contention, and our own findings, that political trust is not related to turnout.

In his rejoinder, Miller presents additional evidence to support his interpretation of the meaning of trust. For example, he finds that political trust is related to feelings of political effectiveness and that this relationship is growing. Persons who are politically trusting are also more likely to believe that political parties help the government pay attention to the people and that Congressmen pay attention to the people who elect them. "To summarize," Miller writes, "political cynicism is related to feelings of political inefficacy, to the belief that government is unresponsive, and to an apparent desire for structural and institutional reform. The trend toward increased distrust, therefore, reflects growing dissatisfaction and discontent with the performance of government in the United States" (p. 992).

In a more recent study, with Goldenberg and Erbring, Miller (1979) again examines the relationship of political trust to feelings of political efficacy, but now concentrates directly on a measure of "external" political effectiveness. The authors find that feelings of political trust and feelings of "external" political efficacy are strongly related: "Cynicism evidently reflects general dissatisfaction with government performance and not simply a lack of support for specific incumbents and is at the same time a direct cause of disillusionment with broader regime norms regarding institutional evaluations" (p. 79).

One additional argument lends support to Miller's interpretation. If political cynicism reflects a rejection of incumbents, one might expect trust to rise when incumbents are changed. But trust has not increased, despite changes of incumbency. Miller et al. note that trust continued to decline even after Ford replaced Nixon. Moreover, as Miller himself has argued, political trust did not increase in the CPS survey conducted in late 1978, although there had been an even more complete change of administration, with the transfer of presidential power from the Republicans to the Democrats. "Given that Carter was widely perceived as an open and honest individual, and that he ran on a platform which promised to restore the citizen's confidence in government, the 1978 data may have been expected to reflect an upsurge in political trust rather than to reveal the lowest level of confidence in government during the past twenty years" (A. Miller, 1979, p. 5). Moreover, as our own analyses show, political trust declined markedly during the last two years of Carter's presidency.

Just what do these widely used political-trust questions actually measure?[9] There seems little doubt that they at least partly tap evaluations of political leaders. In addition to the evidence presented by Citrin, some of which we have updated (see Tables 11.1 and 11.2), analyses I conducted with Finifter also support this interpretation. Finifter and I examine four new questions that the CPS introduced in 1978 that specifically measure trust in President Carter, the Carter administration, and the U.S. Congress. Our analyses clearly show that persons who score high on political trust are more likely to be trusting of Carter, his administration, and the Congress (Abramson and Finifter, 1980, 1981). But even though the political-trust index partly measures attitudes toward incumbents, it might also measure evaluations of the regime and the political community. Moreover, A. Miller (1979) argues that these new questions, especially those about Congress, actually measure support for institutions and that the relationship of the standard trust scale to these new questions supports his interpretation.

There is certainly a need to develop new measures of political trust that more clearly separate evaluations of incumbents from those of the political system more generally. As Finifter and I argue, this effort might use Easton's or some other theoretical definition of the objects of the political system as the starting point and then refer to elements of these definitions in the questions used to measure political trust. Some of the recent work by Muller and his colleagues (Muller and Jukam, 1977; Muller, Jukam, and Seligson, 1982), designed to build measures of political support that more clearly tap evaluations of the regime, may prove of great value in future research. On the other hand, despite the controversy over the meaning of the SRC political-trust items, these questions provide a basis both for evaluating the development of attitudes among preadults and for studying attitude change among adults over time. Thus, it would be foolish to ignore the results based on these standard measures of trust, even though we recognize the need to build better measures.

Trust, Efficacy, and Alienation

Feelings of political trust and feelings of political efficacy are usually correlated. Persons who believe that the government is responsive (i.e., those who score high on "external" political efficacy) are more likely to be politi-

[9]For an interesting exchange over the meaning of recent attitude trends, including the decline of political trust, see the debate between Patrick Caddell, President Carter's chief pollster, and Warren Miller (1979). Caddell argues that "sustained distrust of both the general and specific actors over a long period of time will call into question the viability of the entire constitutional process" (p. 7). Miller, on the other hand, argues that political trust is heavily influenced by partisanship and sees no evidence that the decline of trust has major implications for the American political system. We do not highlight the Caddell–Miller controversy, since neither author systematically evaluates the validity of the SRC political-trust measure with the same thoroughness applied by Citrin in his "Comment" on Arthur Miller or by Miller in his "Rejoinder" to Citrin.

cally trusting, and the relationship between trust and efficacy has been growing in recent years. Some scholars view feelings both of political trust and of efficacy as dimensions of a broader concept: political alienation. Yet they are separate dimensions.[10] Gamson (1968, p. 42) makes this point clearly:

> The efficacy dimension of political alienation refers to people's perception of their ability to influence; the trust dimension refers to their perception of the necessity for influence. Feelings of low efficacy and feelings that the government is not being run in one's interest are, of course, likely to be found together. If one feels he cannot contribute significant inputs he is likely also to feel unhappy with the outputs but this is an empirical hypothesis which might prove false under some conditions (e.g., paternalism, noblesse oblige). In any event, these two aspects of political alienation can be conceptually distinguished and the trust dimension refers to beliefs about the *outputs* of the political system.

Unfortunately, many scholars fail to recognize that alienation has distinct dimensions. Moreover, as Finifter (1972) writes: "So many meanings have been attributed to this concept, many of them vague and mystical, that it verges on losing much of its scientific utility" (p. 3). I attempt to avoid using the term "alienation," but it is impossible to avoid it completely because it is used so frequently by political-attitude researchers.

While feelings of political trust and political efficacy are usually related, it is important to recognize that many people who are politically trusting feel politically powerless. Likewise, there are people who are politically cynical who feel politically effective. Cynical persons who feel politically effective are probably the most threatening to the political order, since they may be more likely to act to remedy what they see as unsatisfactory outputs. Persons who feel both cynical and ineffective may pose a potential threat to the established authorities, but they are probably difficult to mobilize for political action (Finifter, 1970; Wright, 1976). In any event, unlike feelings of political efficacy, which clearly contribute to political participation, feelings of political trust do not appear to contribute directly to participation.

Conclusions

The decline of political trust is among the most dramatic trends in postwar public opinion. Yet, as we have seen, there is considerable controversy about the meaning of this decline. Some scholars argue that the trend signifies widespread rejection of the American political system, while others claim that

[10]For an empirical effort to identify these separate components of political alienation, see Finifter's (1970) analysis of the American data collected as part of *The Civic Culture* study. She empirically identifies two major components of political alienation: "political powerlessness" and "perceived political normlessness." Political powerlessness is clearly the opposite of feelings of political effectiveness, and perceived political normlessness has often been viewed as a measure of political cynicism.

it merely registers dissatisfaction with political incumbents. Examining the controversy between Arthur Miller and Jack Citrin gave us a chance to better understand the meaning of the political-trust measure, as well as to review the process through which political scientists assess the validity of their measures.

In reviewing this debate, we saw that feelings of political trust and feelings of "external" political efficacy are usually related. Persons who are politically trusting are more likely to feel politically efficacious, while those who are cynical are more likely to feel politically powerless. Although these two attitudes are related, they appear to have different behavioral consequences. Persons who score high on "external" political efficacy are more likely to participate in politics, while persons who are politically trusting are no more likely to participate than are those who feel politically cynical.

Just as feelings of political trust and political efficacy may have different behavioral consequences, they may have somewhat different causes. This becomes apparent when we examine the way feelings of political trust are formed. Indeed, as we see in the next chapter, two of the explanations we developed to account for subcultural differences in feelings of political efficacy cannot account for subcultural differences in political trust.

[CHAPTER 12]

How Political Trust Forms

A large number of political-socialization researchers have studied political trust. As with studies of feelings of political efficacy, this emphasis partly results from their tendency to replicate measures used by prior researchers. But, as with studies of efficacy, this emphasis results from theoretical concerns. In a sense, feelings of political trust may be more central to the study of political socialization than are feelings of political efficacy. Feelings of political trust measure, at least indirectly, "support" for the political system, and, according to some socialization researchers, support for the polity must develop fairly early in the lives of its members so that the system will have a reservoir of "diffuse" support to draw on if incumbent authorities fail to provide satisfactory outputs (Easton, 1965, 1975; Easton and Dennis, 1969).

As a result of the large number of studies that measure political trust among preadults, we now have a large number of "findings"; but, as with studies of feelings of political efficacy, there have been few attempts to evaluate these findings to assess our understanding of the political learning process. This chapter attempts to bring these findings together to assess explanations about the way feelings of political trust develop. We begin by assessing the limited evidence on the transmission of political trust from parents to their children. Most of this chapter attempts to integrate the many studies that compare the political trust of whites with that of blacks, as well as several that compare whites with Hispanics. We attempt to evaluate explanations that may account for the subcultural differences that have been discovered by students of preadult political attitudes.

Parental Transmission

In our study of the way feelings of party identification and political efficacy are learned, we turned first to the parental transmission of political attitudes. We found considerable evidence that children learn partisan loyalties from their parents, but little evidence that they learn feelings of political effectiveness from them. Turning to the way political trust is learned, we again find little evidence of intergenerational transmission.

My reanalysis of the Michigan student–parent survey shows that black parents are more trusting than white parents, but there are no racial differences among students.[1] White children are considerably more trusting than their parents, but black children are about as trusting as their parents. Table 12.1 directly compares feelings of political trust among parents and their teenage children. These individual-level comparisons show little evidence of intergenerational transmission. There is only a weak tendency for parents who score high on political trust to be more likely to have children who also score high, although the transmission of political trust appears to be somewhat greater among blacks than among whites.

Once again, our conclusions are very similar to those reached by Jennings and Niemi (1974), although they do not explore racial differences in the transmission of political trust. Weissberg and Joslyn (1977) specifically argue that Jennings and Niemi underestimate the level of parent–child correspondence, ignoring the fact that most students have a trust score that is close to that of their parents. In fact, Jennings and Niemi acknowledge that their procedures may somewhat underestimate the impact of parental socialization. But such underestimates are probably small, for Dalton's (1980) reanalysis of the Michigan student–parent data suggests that, even when problems of measurement unreliability are taken into account, the level of parent–child correspondence for political trust is low (rising from a Pearson's r of .16 to .30).

Jennings and Niemi are somewhat surprised by the low correspondence between parent trust and student trust, since they view trust as a basic attitude that measures "a more pervasive kind of belief system that cuts across particular individuals and objects" (pp. 146–147). Their findings show that "these kinds of general dispositions are subject to heavy undercutting influences outside the family nexus" (p. 147). And in their attempt to discover conditions that might facilitate the parental transmission of political trust, they uncover few relationships. The parental transmission of trust is only slightly greater in households where political conversation is frequent than in those where politics

[1]The political-trust measure employed here is based on the five standard SRC political-trust questions and employs the same scaling procedures used by Jennings and Niemi (1974). The full trust measure ranges from a low of 1 to a high of 6, but Table 12.1 presents three categories: low (1,2), medium (3,4), and high (5,6). In measuring feelings of political trust over time, Jennings and Niemi (1981) employ an additive index.

Table 12.1 Political Trust of High School Seniors, by Parent's Political Trust and Student's Race: 1965

Part A Student's Race: White

	Parent's political trust		
Student's political trust	Low	Medium	High
Low	12%	6%	5%
Medium	52	48	43
High	36	46	52
Total %	100%	99%	100%
Weighted *N*	(527)	(846)	(312)

tau-b (based on 6 × 6 table) = .13 gamma (based on 6 × 6 table) = .16
Percentage with same political-trust score (based on 6 × 6) table = 21%.
Percentage with same political-trust score (based on 3 × 3 table) = 37%.

Part B Student's Race: Black

	Parent's political trust		
Student's political trust	Low	Medium	High
Low	16%	11%	5%
Medium	65	61	57
High	20	28	39
Total %	101%	100%	101%
Weighted *N*	(31)	(93)	(58)

tau-b (based on 6 × 6 table) = .18 gamma (based on 6 × 6 table) = .24
Percentage with same political-trust score (based on 6 × 6 table) = 26%.
Percentage with same political-trust score (based on 3 × 3 table) = 46%.

Note: Based on the five-item political-trust scale developed by Jennings and Niemi (1974).

is not discussed. Students who report that they are close to their parents are more likely to share their parents' levels of trust than those who admit that they are not close, but even this relationship disappears when controls for other variables are introduced. Moreover, mothers and fathers with similar levels of political trust are no more successful in transmitting their levels of trust than are parents with differing political values. In this way, the learning of trust differs from the learning of both party identification and feelings of political efficacy, for, with both of these attitudes, parental transmission is more successful when both parents have similar values.

Several more limited surveys also suggest that American children do not learn feelings of political trust from their parents. A study of junior high school students in Madison, Wisconsin, conducted in the spring and fall of 1966 by Chaffee, McLeod, and Wackman (1973), directly compares parental attitudes with those of their children. Using a political-trust index that measures attitudes about the integrity and honesty of political leaders, Chaffee and his colleagues find only a negligible relationship between parental attitudes and those of their children and conclude that "there seems to be no evidence of value transmission between generations" (p. 361). Dennis's (1969) study of Milwaukee children and their parents, conducted in the summer of 1967, developed a political-trust index that focuses on the honesty of political leaders. Dennis finds a relatively high relationship between parental trust and trust among fifth-grade children (Pearson's r of .33), only a weak relationship among eighth graders (.09), and a relatively high relationship among eleventh graders (.32). However, these relationships are greatly reduced when controls for social-background characteristics are introduced, and Dennis concludes that there is little evidence that children learn basic political attitudes from their parents.

Lastly, we turn to the cross-national parent-offspring data collected in 1974 and analyzed by Jennings and his colleagues (Jennings, Allerbeck, and Rosenmayr, 1979).[2] Using an adaptation of two of the standard SRC–CPS political-trust questions ("few big interests" and "trust the government"), they compare levels of political trust among parents and their 16- through 20-year-old children. Among the American sample, there is only a negligible relationship between parental trust and the trust of their children (a tau-b of .07). Parent–offspring similarity is higher in the other four countries studied: the Netherlands, .30; Britain, .43; West Germany, .27; and Austria, .29. Jennings and his colleagues admit that it is difficult to explain why parent–offspring correspondence is low in the United States, but speculate that these cross-national differences might result from the relatively low relationship between feelings of political trust and support for the incumbent party.

The very low level of parental transmission may be surprising if we view political trust as a fundamental psychopolitical value. It is less surprising if we view the SRC trust measure as largely an evaluation of the authorities. Perhaps such assessments are seldom discussed in American homes, regardless of political conditions. The 1965 SRC student–parent survey was conducted during a quiescent political period, with fairly high levels of political trust. But the 1974 parent–offspring comparisons were made during the height of the Watergate scandal, and parent–offspring correspondence was still very low. Together, these two national samples suggest that the failure of American parents to transmit their feelings of political trust occurs in a variety of political climates.

[2]For a brief description of this study, see Chapter 6.

Racial and Subcultural Differences

Even though we cannot readily explain the source of feelings of political trust among preadults, several studies have demonstrated that preadults have feelings of trust or cynicism toward political leaders. Several scholars have demonstrated that a political-trust dimension can be measured among high school students, and a few have built such measures among elementary school children. Studies of political trust among preadults have focused on a large number of sociological variables, and many have reported on racial differences.

In an earlier book (Abramson, 1977), I analyzed an extensive compilation of surveys on racial differences in feelings of trust among preadults. In that book, I examine thirty-nine surveys that report on feelings of political trust among both black and white preadults. Blacks prove to be as trusting as, or more trusting than, whites in four of the first six studies. However, the summer of 1967 seems to have been a turning point, as Dennis's (1969) Milwaukee study, conducted during that summer, shows blacks to be less trusting than whites. Blacks are less trusting than whites in twenty-four of thirty-three surveys conducted during and after that summer. Four of the remaining studies provide some evidence that blacks are less trusting. Five studies provide no evidence that blacks are less trusting, but three of these are based on atypical samples. Moreover, a major national probability sample of tenth-grade boys, in which the same boys are tracked over time in a panel study, suggests that blacks became less trusting than whites during the late 1960s. In Bachman's (1970) earliest survey, conducted in the fall of 1966, blacks are more trusting than whites; by the spring of 1969, they are less trusting. On balance, I conclude that black preadults are less trusting than whites in most surveys conducted during and after the summer of 1967.

Since my book appeared, eight additional studies of racial differences have come to my attention. Ruth Jones's (1976) studies of school children in the St. Louis metropolitan area (one in September 1971, the other in May 1972) show few racial differences in political trust, although, in the latter study, blacks are less likely than whites to agree that politicians work for the general interest.[3] The six remaining studies show blacks to be less trusting than whites. A study by German and Hoffman (1978) among North Carolina school children, conducted in early 1973, finds that blacks feel more cynical toward the police. Another study of North Carolina students, conducted in early 1974 by Hawley (1976), reports that blacks score higher than whites on a political-cynicism index.

[3]The information about racial differences in these surveys was provided in a personal communication from Ruth Jones.

The national surveys of high school seniors conducted in 1976, 1977, 1978, and 1979 by the University of Michigan Survey Research Center provides valuable information, since all five of the standard SRC trust questions are employed.[4] While blacks are less likely than whites to say that the government wastes tax money, they are less trusting on the four remaining questions and are substantially less trusting than whites on the "smart people" and "trust the government" questions. For example, in 1979, the year that trust differences are smallest, 40% of the whites say the government in Washington can be trusted "almost always" or "often," while only 26% of the blacks do.

In addition to these eight studies, my own survey of a representative sample of tenth graders in Saginaw, Michigan, conducted in mid-March of 1981, led me to develop three measures of political trust, one of which focuses on attitudes toward the federal government, one on President Reagan and his administration, and one on Governor Milliken and his administration. Blacks are significantly less trusting than whites on the trust-in-government index, much less trusting on the trust-in-Reagan measure, and not significantly different from whites on the trust-in-Milliken index.

Unfortunately, there have been only a handful of studies of other subcultural differences, and they yield mixed results.[5] The major published study of the political socialization of Hispanics, conducted by Garcia (1973) in the spring of 1970 and in January of 1971, develops a political-trust index and finds few differences between Hispanics and Anglos. Krause's (1972) study of school children in the Chicago area, conducted in the spring of 1968, finds that suburban white children are the most trusting toward the mayor and the police, but finds no significant differences between Hispanic children and inner-city whites. Button's (1974) study of Austin, Texas, high school students, conducted in late 1971 and early 1972, uses the same five political-trust questions used by Jennings and Niemi and finds Hispanics to be only marginally more cynical than Anglos. On the other hand, a study of elementary school children in San Antonio, Texas, conducted by Barger (1974) in April 1973, finds that Hispanics are more likely than Anglos to disagree that the president and the police are "very honest." A year later, conducting a similar study among San Antonio elementary, middle, and high school students, Barger finds that at all three grade levels Hispanics are more likely to disagree that the president and

[4]Questions about political trust are based on only one of the five questionnaire forms employed, and the results are thus based on between 2500 and 2900 whites for each year and between 300 and 500 blacks. For the results on political trust, see Bachman, Johnston, and O'Malley (1980a, pp. 96–97); Johnston, Bachman, and O'Malley (1980a, pp. 96–97); Bachman, Johnston, and O'Malley (1980b, pp. 96–97); and Johnston, Bachman, and O'Malley (1980b, pp. 97–98).

[5]The reader should remember that my search for differences between blacks and whites is based on an exhaustive search of both published and unpublished research, while my search for other subcultural differences is based mainly on published research literature.

the police are "very honest." And Hirsch and Gutierrez's (1977) study of Crystal City, Texas, students, conducted in the early 1970s, shows that students who identify as Chicanos or Mexican-Americans score higher on an index of political cynicism than do those who identify as Anglos.

Studies of other subcultural groups also appear to yield mixed results. Hirsch's study of Appalachian school children, conducted in Knox County, Kentucky, in May 1967, finds that Appalachian children have far lower levels of political trust than does the SRC sample of high school seniors conducted two years earlier by Jennings and his colleagues (Jaros, Hirsch, and Fleron, 1968). While some of these differences might result from the fact that the Hirsch study was conducted two years after the SRC survey, differences are so great that they probably result at least partly from subcultural forces that erode trust among Knox County children. On the other hand, another subcultural group, the Amish, appear to have very high levels of political trust, at least toward the president (Jaros and Kolson, 1974).

Explanations for Differences

Using racial differences as a point of departure, I attempted to evaluate explanations that might account for racial differences in political trust, but there is no reason in principle that these explanations need account only for differences between black and white Americans. They can also be used to attempt to account for other subcultural differences. There is no reason in principle that these explanations need be restricted to the American political system, and one study of political trust has tested both the social-deprivation and the political-reality explanation among adolescents in the Indian state of Andhra Pradesh (Iyengar, 1978b, 1980b). However, once we go beyond racial differences, there are few documented subcultural differences in feelings of political trust.

Of the four basic explanations that might account for subcultural differences in political attitudes (see Chapter 9), only two bear on political trust—the social-deprivation and the political-reality explanation. While the political-education explanation might in principle account for low feelings of political effectiveness among blacks and members of other disadvantaged subcultural groups, there is no reason to believe that these children are taught to be politically cynical. If blacks and children of other disadvantaged subcultural groups are implicitly taught to be politically passive, we would expect them to be taught to revere—not to distrust—political authorities. The political-education explanation, I conclude, is essentially silent about the conditions that might contribute to political cynicism. Likewise, there is no sound theoretical reason to predict that intelligent persons should be more trusting than those who are less intelligent.

The social-deprivation explanation

While neither the political-education nor the intelligence explanation can explain the way political trust develops, the social-deprivation explanation may help explain racial and other subcultural differences. We have already discussed four of the five assumptions that constitute this explanation (see Chapter 9), and need consider only the one remaining:

Assumption B.3. Persons who have low levels of self-confidence tend to have low feelings of political trust.

There are good reasons for accepting Assumption B.3, although we must admit that the linkages between self-confidence and feelings of political trust are not as direct as those between self-confidence and feelings of political effectiveness. Still, Lane (1959) provides some reason to expect a relationship between self-confidence and political trust. Lane argues that personal trust, self-confidence, and trust in political leaders are all interrelated: "If one cannot trust other people generally, one can certainly not trust those under the temptations of and with the powers which come with public office. Trust in elected officials is seen to be only a more specific instance of trust in mankind. And in the long run, this is probably a projection of attitudes toward the self—self-approval" (p. 164).

Empirical studies of preadults provide some support for this assumption, especially when we focus on research in which political scientists measure feelings of environmental control. On the other hand, the empirical relationships between self-confidence and political trust do not appear to be as strong as the relationships between self-confidence and feelings of political efficacy, and there are more studies where no relationship is found. Support for Assumption B.3 is weaker than support for Assumption B.2 that links feelings of self-confidence to feelings of political effectiveness.

The social-deprivation explanation leads us to predict two additional relationships, which I label empirical consequences, and both receive some support.

Empirical Consequence B.1. In social settings where blacks (and other disadvantaged subcultural groups) have higher levels of social opportunity, they should have higher feelings of (political effectiveness and) political trust. Controlling for social opportunity should reduce or eliminate racial (and other subcultural) differences in political attitudes.

Most studies of preadult feelings of political trust that allow us to test the relationship between deprivation and trust among blacks support this consequence, but support is indirect because measures seldom directly tap the extent to which black preadults are deprived. Moreover, extant studies rarely allow us to determine whether controls for social-background characteristics would reduce or eliminate racial differences in feelings of political trust.

Studies of Hispanics may also provide support for Empirical Consequence B.1. Garcia (1973) finds few differences in levels of political cynicism between Hispanics from middle-class homes and those from lower-class homes (using parental occupation as a measure of social class). He does find that Hispanics who use Spanish in their homes are more politically cynical than those who use English and concludes: "The level of Spanish usage may be the most accurate reflection of the extent of a group's cultural assimilation. Therefore, Chicanos who are least assimilated into the core American culture in terms of economic status and language are most distrustful of the system that has not yet incorporated them" (p. 118).

The presence or absence of a father in the home may be a better measure of deprivation than are crude indicators of parental socioeconomic status. If so, Clarke's (1973) study of black school children in Washington, D.C. (conducted during the summer of 1969), provides support for Empirical Consequence B.1. Clarke directly measures political cynicism through the basic Michigan SRC questions and finds that children whose fathers live at home are more politically trusting than those whose fathers do not. Clarke is not clear as to whether his measure of father absence is an indicator of social deprivation or whether it reveals something about the political effects of the structure of the black family, and he concludes that both factors are probably at work.

Clearly, it is reasonable to speculate that children who do not have fathers living at home are more likely to be deprived than those who do. Yet the one major study that documents this relationship in another subculture discovers the opposite empirical relationship between father absence and trust. Hirsch's study of Appalachian school children finds that children from fatherless homes are more politically trusting (using the same basic measure employed by Clarke) than those who have fathers living at home. Jaros, Hirsch, and Fleron (1968) speculate that the subcultural norms of political cynicism are less likely to be communicated to preadults when the father does not live at home. Hirsch's study leaves us with an anomalous finding. The low overall level of trust among Appalachian school children is certainly consistent with the social-deprivation explanation, for Appalachian children are much more deprived than most American school children. But the findings for father absence do not support this basic empirical consequence.

A second relationship follows from the social-deprivation explanation.

Empirical Consequence B.2. Black children (and children from other disadvantaged subcultural groups) with high feelings of self-confidence should feel more politically (efficacious and) trusting than those with low feelings of self-confidence. Controlling for feelings of self-confidence should reduce or eliminate racial (and other subcultural) differences in political attitudes.

This consequence can be tested more directly, and most extant studies of blacks support it, although they do not allow us to determine the extent to which controls for feelings of self-confidence reduce racial differences. However, the relationships between self-confidence and feelings of political trust do not appear to be as strong as those between self-confidence and feelings of political effectiveness, and there are more studies in which this consequence is not supported. Hirsch's study of Appalachian school children also shows that children with high "self-esteem" have higher levels of political trust than do those with low self-esteem. "Self-esteem," Hirsch (1971) concludes, "would appear to be the most important predictor of political attitudes" (p. 151). However, the actual relationships reported by Hirsch are fairly modest, and it seems unlikely that the high level of political cynicism among Appalachian school children results from low levels of self-esteem. To the best of my knowledge, we have no studies that allow us to examine the relationship of self-confidence to feelings of political trust among other subcultural groups.

While the social-deprivation explanation receives some support and while it may provide a partial explanation for subcultural differences in feelings of political trust, it is a complicated explanation that depends on a social-psychological variable. Although the relationships predicted by the explanation are usually present, they are often weak, and some studies fail to find the predicted relationships. Thus, it seems unlikely that this explanation could, by itself, account for all of the racial differences in political trust.

Several studies of political trust have attempted to test this explanation directly (B. Campbell, 1976; Foster, 1978; Iyengar, 1978b; Long, 1975, 1976, 1978; Rodgers, 1974). An extensive analysis of the Michigan student–parent data conducted by Friedrich (1977) directly tests the social-deprivation explanation and finds little evidence that deprivation leads directly to feelings of political cynicism among blacks. Most importantly, she finds that, among the student generation, blacks who have gone to college are more politically cynical than those who have not; while among the parent generation, blacks with higher levels of education have somewhat lower levels of political cynicism. Among the young, advantaged blacks are more politically cynical than the less advantaged—a finding that runs counter to Empirical Consequence B.1. (For a discussion of the possible contribution of college education to political cynicism among blacks, see Shingles, 1979.)

Some tests of the social-deprivation explanation have found some support for the thesis that low self-confidence may contribute to political cynicism among young blacks, but studies that have evaluated both feelings of political efficacy and feelings of political trust have usually found that the relationships predicted by the social-deprivation explanation are stronger when feelings of political efficacy are examined.

On balance, the social-deprivation explanation seems somewhat weaker when applied to subcultural differences in feelings of trust than it is for explaining differential feelings of political efficacy. The explanation also has a major limitation, since it cannot account for the time-series shift in feelings of political trust. Before the summer of 1967, black preadults were as trusting as whites. Clearly, blacks were socially deprived before that summer. Why, then, were they as trusting as whites, and why have they become less trusting?

The political-reality explanation

The political-reality explanation has considerable potential for explaining subcultural differences in feelings of political trust. We have already discussed two of the three assumptions that constitute this explanation, so we now consider the remaining one:

Assumption D.2. Political leaders are less trustworthy in their dealings with blacks (and members of other disadvantaged subcultural groups) than in their dealings with whites (and members of advantaged groups).

If blacks and other disadvantaged subcultural groups are deprived of political power (Assumption D.1), it is also possible that political leaders are less trustworthy in dealing with them. Leaders are more likely to be trustworthy when they are dealing with persons and groups that have sanctions over them. To the extent that blacks and other disadvantaged subcultural groups are deprived of political power, they may be deprived of the resources necessary to keep political leaders honest.

Nonetheless, it is difficult to provide empirical support for Assumption D.2. Have political leaders broken promises made to blacks and to members of disadvantaged subcultural groups more often than those made to whites and to members of advantaged groups? Have they been more corrupt in their dealings with blacks and other disadvantaged groups? Have they been less competent? It would be difficult to provide empirical evidence to answer any of these questions.

Even if we accept Assumption D.2, we cannot easily demonstrate that black children or children of other disadvantaged groups know these facts or that they are influenced by adults who know these facts (see Assumption D.3). As we saw in Chapter 9, most tests of political knowledge have found black children to be less knowledgeable than white children, and there is some evidence that Hispanic children may be less politically aware than Anglos. It is possible that disadvantaged children are politically sophisticated, but that their sophistication cannot be measured through questionnaires. Coles (1975), as we saw, makes such an argument, but his insights cannot easily be replicated.

It is possible that black children (and children of other disadvantaged subcultural groups) do not directly know about the low trustworthiness of political leaders, but that they are influenced by black adults (or adults from their subcultural group) who do. However, we have little direct evidence that black children learn political attitudes from black adults. As the data in Table 12.1 revealed, there is little evidence that black children share their parents' feelings of political trust. Dennis's (1969) study of Milwaukee children shows that black and white children are equally unlikely to share their parents' feelings of political trust. (We have no adequate data on the transmission of parental feelings of political trust for other subcultural groups.)

Black children (and children of other disadvantaged subcultural groups) could learn about political realities from adults other than their parents. Orum and Cohen (1973) specifically argue that the political cynicism of black school children may result from subcultural socialization processes. However, as I argued earlier, we do not have data about the communication processes through which such subcultural socialization takes place.

The political-reality explanation does have considerable strength, however, even though its basic assumptions are not easily documented. The strength of the explanation comes from the empirical consequences that it generates.

Empirical Consequence D.1. Feelings of political (effectiveness and) trust should be lower among blacks (and members of other disadvantaged subcultural groups) who understand political realities than among those who do not.

One of the very earliest studies of black political socialization finds support for this consequence. Greenberg's (1969) study of Philadelphia school children (conducted in the spring of 1969) finds that blacks who "correctly" perceive that blacks and whites are not treated the same are more politically cynical (on two separate questions) than are blacks who believe that both races are treated the same. More recently, most empirical tests of the political-reality explanation have focused on attempts to document this relationship. Rodgers (1974) and Long (1976) have examined this relationship, and both claim that their results support the political-reality explanation, although neither actually developed measures of knowledge about the facts that deprive blacks of political power. To the best of my knowledge, this empirical consequence has not been tested with preadult data from other disadvantaged subcultural groups.

Empirical Consequence D.2. This consequence focuses on feelings of political efficacy and is discussed in Chapter 9.

Empirical Consequence D.3. Blacks (and other disadvantaged subcultural groups) should be more trusting toward political leaders who depend on black electoral support (or the support of other disadvantaged subcultural groups) than toward leaders who do not rely on black support (or the support of other disadvantaged subcultural groups).

There is considerable support for this consequence when we examine the attitudes of black preadults toward political leaders.

As I argued earlier, the procedures for electing the president give blacks more influence than those for electing most public officials. Democratic presidential candidates in particular have relied heavily on black support. Johnson received about one in seven of his votes from blacks, and both Humphrey and McGovern received about one in five of their votes from blacks. Carter received just over one in seven of his votes from blacks in 1976 and about one in four in 1980. During the postwar years, Republicans have never received more than a small fraction of their votes from blacks (Abramson, Aldrich, and Rohde, 1982, p. 104). In 1980, less than 3% of Reagan's total vote came from black voters.[6] Democratic presidents have been more sympathetic to black demands than have most other elected political leaders. It follows, then, that blacks should support Democratic presidents and that they should not support Republican presidents.

Considerable socialization research supports this consequence. Studies conducted during Johnson's presidency usually show levels of presidential support among blacks to be about the same as that among whites. But once Nixon became president, blacks became far less supportive. Among these studies, a panel analysis by Vaillancourt (1972) is the most interesting, because it tracks the same children over time during the presidential transition from Johnson to Nixon. Her study strongly suggests that black preadults became more negative toward the president as soon as Nixon was inaugurated.

We have few data on preadult attitudes toward Carter, but a study by Maddox and Handberg (1980) of sixth graders in Seminole County, Florida, finds no racial differences in affect toward the president in a study conducted in February 1977, the first full month of Carter's presidency.[7]

My own study of Saginaw tenth graders (conducted in the second full month of Reagan's presidency and before the assassination attempt) reveals sharp racial differences. The basic results are reported in Table 12.2. While blacks are somewhat less trusting of the government than whites are, they are much less trusting of Reagan. While two-thirds of the white students say that President Reagan can be trusted to do what is right just about always or most of the time, only a fourth of the black students trust him. While half of the whites think that the Reagan administration is run for the benefit of all, only a fourth of the black students do. Blacks are also less trusting of William G. Milliken, the Republican governor of Michigan, but there are no racial differences in attitudes toward his administration.

Empirical Consequence D.3 can also be tested by examining the attitudes of blacks toward local-level leaders, and a study by Foster (1978) provides a direct test of the political-reality explanation. In a study conducted in the spring of 1974, Foster examines the attitudes of black children toward the mayor of Peoria, Illinois, and the mayor of East St. Louis, Illinois. Peoria is a predom-

[6]Based on my recalculation of the CBS News/*New York Times* Election Day poll. The SRC–CPS survey suggests that only 1% of Reagan's vote came from blacks.

[7]Presidential affect scores by race were provided in a personal communication from William Maddox.

Table 12.2 Percentage of Tenth Graders Who Trust Government in Washington, President Reagan, and Governor Milliken, by Race: 1981

Percentage who said that:	White	Black
The government in Washington can be trusted to do what is right just about always or most of the time	57	49
President Reagan can be trusted to do what is right just about always or most of the time	69	25
Governor Milliken can be trusted to do what is right just about always or most of the time	76	61
The government is run for the benefit of all	54	41
The Reagan administration is run for the benefit of all	53	27
Governor Milliken's administration is run for the benefit of all	67	65

Note: The numbers on which these percentages are based vary slightly from item to item. The lowest number on which the white percentages are based is 153; the lowest number on which the black percentages are based is 175.

Source: Saginaw Socialization Study, conducted March 17 and 19, 1981.

inantly white city with a white mayor; East St. Louis is a predominantly black city with a black mayor. While 80% of the black children in East St. Louis know the name of their mayor (no white children were surveyed in East St. Louis), only 30% of the black children in Peoria (and only 45% of the white children) know the name of their mayor. In East St. Louis, 67% of the black children say their mayor is doing a good job, while only 45% of the black children in Peoria (and 58% of the white children) think their mayor is doing a good job. Foster argues that his results support the political-reality explanation. "It is plausible that blacks in East St. Louis do have the ability to influence their mayor, or at least believe they do. Thus, they may exhibit more trust in their black mayor. This sense of trust and benevolence is then conveyed from adults to children" (p. 249). Foster concludes that his findings "indicate that political reality structures black attitudes toward political objects" (p. 250).

Before attempting to summarize our knowledge about the way feelings of political trust are learned, we should note that several other studies of political trust have attempted to test the political-reality explanation. As we saw in Chapter 9, Iyengar conducted a panel study of adolescents in Andhra Pradesh, India, and surveyed these youths in three dramatically different political periods. His studies of political trust (Iyengar, 1978b, 1980b) show that trust varies systematically during this time, with supporters of the winning parties gaining in trust, while supporters of the parties that are losing power decline in trust.

Lastly, we should mention Friedrich's (1977) extensive reanalysis of the Michigan student–parent data. Her findings cannot be summarized in detail, but they are based on panel analyses of both the student and the parent generations. Friedrich presents considerable support for the political-reality explanation, arguing that it could explain both attitudes and behavior. She concludes that many of the relationships she uncovers "could be explained by the theory that the political reality of black Americans is based on a perception of the relationship of the black community as a whole to the political system and not just on the impact of individual experience" (p. 239).

The political-reality explanation seems to have considerable potential for explaining differences in political trust. Perhaps the greatest strength of this explanation, when applied to racial differences in the United States, is that it is the only explanation that can begin to account for the changing relationship of race to trust over time. The social-deprivation explanation cannot account for the fact that blacks were as trusting as whites before the summer of 1967. Yet one could argue that the time-series shift in political trust results from changing political conditions.

Between 1954, with the Supreme Court school desegregation decision, and 1965, with the Voting Rights Act of that year, blacks made consistent gains at the national level, and this may have contributed to high trust toward national-level officials. But blacks scored few political gains at the national level after 1965, for when the Vietnam War escalated, Johnson deferred his Great Society reforms. By the summer of 1967, when black children began to manifest low levels of political trust, widespread riots were devastating major American cities. Although it would be difficult to demonstrate that political leaders were less trustworthy toward blacks after the spring of 1967, black perceptions of their trustworthiness clearly seem to have declined. This decline may not stem from any actual lowered "trustworthiness" among political leaders, but may have been affected by the reality of decreasing black political effectiveness at the national level.

It is difficult to judge whether Carter's election increased the effectiveness of blacks. Clearly, Carter relied heavily on black support in 1976 and could not have been elected without it, but black leaders were often dissatisfied with his policies. As we shall see, after Carter assumed office, the political trust of black adults rose slightly, while it continued to erode among whites. The Michigan SRC studies of high school seniors show little consistent change in political trust among blacks between 1976 and 1979, but they suggest that trust declined somewhat among white youths during these years.

Black leaders clearly see Reagan's election as a major political loss, and Reagan's cuts in social spending will fall disproportionately on blacks. We do not yet have adult data on political trust during the Reagan presidency, but the one available study of preadults (the Saginaw Socialization Study) finds blacks to be less trusting than whites.

Conclusions

Despite the extensive study of feelings of political trust among American preadults, we have surprisingly few data to assess the way differing feelings of political trust develop. Partly, this is because political-socialization research has seldom been guided by theories about the differential development of political attitudes.

We can hope that new studies will be conducted to help us better understand the processes through which feelings of political trust develop, and that future studies will gain additional information about subcultural groups other than blacks. Future studies of political trust among preadults should more clearly differentiate among the various objects of support and should strive to develop measures that more clearly differentiate between support for the community, the regime, and the authorities. At the same time, it is important that some studies continue to use the standard measures of political trust, for the resulting pool of information over time may yield greater knowledge about the conditions under which political trust changes and may prove especially valuable in testing the political-reality explanation.

To this stage, we have left a basic question about political trust unanswered. To what extent do early feelings of political trust persist over time? If political trust is actually a basic psychopolitical attitude, as some researchers have claimed, one might expect high levels of persistence over time. While the long-range consequences of the early development of political trust (and cynicism) among preadults may be difficult to assess, we turn, in the next chapter, to adult data to assess the way such feelings change among individuals.

[CHAPTER 13]

How Political Trust Changes

Partisan identification remains a benchmark against which to compare the stability of other political attitudes. When we examine the over-time stability of party identification, two central facts emerge: first, party identification is highly stable over time; second, party identification is considerably more changeable among young adults than among their elders. Feelings of political effectiveness are far more changeable, and the evidence about age differences is mixed. Feelings of political trust closely parallel feelings of political effectiveness, although trust may be somewhat less stable. Although older age groups may have somewhat more stable feelings of political trust than do young adults, age-group differences appear to be small.

Panel studies of the American electorate allow over-time comparisons of political trust only during the 1972–1974–1976 period—years of considerable political turmoil. During the two-year period between 1972 and 1974, the over-time correlation of political-trust scores among whites is .36 (tau-b), while the over-time correlation between 1974 and 1976 is .43.[1] During the four years between 1972 and 1976, the over-time stability of trust among whites is .35. For all these periods, over-time stability is lower among blacks than among whites.[2]

[1]To measure over-time stability, I employ the five-item political-trust index described in the appendix.

[2]Between 1972 and 1974, over-time stability among blacks is .16; between 1974 and 1976, .18; and between 1972 and 1976, only .06.

Over-time stability can also be examined with percentages, and Table 13.1 compares levels of political trust in 1976 with those in 1972. The data are presented separately for whites and for blacks. The table clearly shows some over-time stability among the white electorate. Among whites who score low on political trust in 1972, 81% score low four years later; but among those who score high on political trust in 1972, only 26% score low four years later. While trusting respondents are clearly affected by the overall shift toward cynicism, they tend to move mainly to medium levels of trust, rather than toward low levels. For the white electorate as a whole, 57% have the same levels of trust in 1976 as in 1972. Percentage comparisons also reveal that political-trust scores among blacks are unstable over time. Most blacks are highly cynical in both 1972 and 1976, and the minority of blacks who are trusting in 1972 have become cynical four years later. On the other hand, for the black electorate as a whole, 57% hold similar trust scores in both years—the same percentage attained by whites.

The 1972–1974–1976 panel was conducted during the Watergate crisis, a period in which both a vice-president and a president were forced to resign from office. There was a massive movement toward cynicism among the white electorate between 1972 and 1974. Obviously, many individuals must have become more cynical during this period, but these individual changes would not necessarily lead to low over-time stability in political trust—if all respondents moved an equal number of steps toward greater cynicism (Niemi and Sobieszek, 1977, p. 226). While the atypical events of this period should lead us to treat these results with caution, it does appear that overall stability of political trust may be somewhat lower than the overall stability of feelings of political effectiveness (see Chapter 10).

As we noted earlier, not all the observed changes among individuals between two points in time is real change, for some change results from measurement error. I have not attempted to assess the "true" over-time correlation for political trust, but we should remember that the real over-time correlation is almost always higher than the observed over-time correlation.

No extensive analyses of the 1972–1974–1976 panel have attempted to determine the way short-term changes in political trust may result from reactions to political events. I have not attempted such an analysis, but I have used these data to determine whether feelings of political trust stabilize with age. My analysis shows that 21- to 29-year-olds do not differ much from their elders in the stability of their feelings of political trust. All age groups display a very marked shift toward cynicism between 1972 and 1976, but this movement is not greater for these youths than it is for their elders. It is true that over-time stability is very low among the subset of 18-, 19-, and 20-year-olds, but *N*s are too small for reliable inferences.

Fortunately, we can turn to the Michigan student–parent panel to examine a larger number of youths. Jennings provided me with the basic tables to

Table 13.1 Political Trust in 1976, by Political Trust in 1972, by Race

	1972					
	White			Black		
1976	Low	Medium	High	Low	Medium	High
Low	81%	57%	26%	75%	68%	70%
Medium	17	34	41	21	20	10
High	2	9	32	4	12	20
Total %	100%	101%	99%	100%	100%	100%
Total *N*	(565)	(385)	(205)	(72)	(25)	(10)
	tau-b (based on 11 × 11 table) = .35			tau b (based on 11 × 11 table) = .06		
	gamma (based on 11 × 11 table) = .40			gamma (based on 11 × 11 table) = .07		
	Percentage with same political-trust score (based on 3 × 3 table) = 57%.			Percentage with same political-trust score (based on 3 × 3 table) = 57%.		

Note: Based on five-item political-trust index.

compare over-time stability in political trust for both the student and the parent generation both among whites and among blacks.[3]

The main finding revealed by this panel is the dramatic decline in political trust between the spring of 1965 and the spring of 1973. This decline is especially dramatic among young adults. White high school students have far higher levels of political trust than do their parents in 1965, while black students have levels of trust similar to those of their parents. But trust declines so rapidly among the student generation that, by 1973, young whites equal and young blacks surpass the political cynicism of their parents—in spite of increased cynicism among both white and black parents.

When we examine individual-level change over time using the student–parent panel, we find that white parents have somewhat more stable levels of political trust than do white students, while black parents have far higher levels of over-time stability than black students do. These findings may parallel our findings that the small subset of 18-, 19-, and 20-year-olds have low levels of over-time stability during the 1972–1974–1976 period. It is possible that youths rapidly become more politically cynical after they leave the protective environment of the high school and become more acquainted with political realities.

[3]Jennings employs a simple additive index to measure the over-time stability of political trust. For a description of his measure, see Jennings and Niemi (1981, pp. 415–416). Jennings's scoring procedures are virtually identical to those I employ to build my five-item political-trust measure, although he presents his results according to six levels of trust.

A more basic question to ask is whether the student–parent data demonstrate attitude stability or high levels of change. Clearly, this is a matter of interpretation, and there is some disagreement even among the scholars who have worked most closely with these data. Jennings and Niemi (1981) and Markus (1979) have presented analyses of the over-time stability of political trust among generations, although in neither work do these scholars compare stability for whites and for blacks separately. The conclusions of these scholars seem markedly different.

Jennings and Niemi conclude: "At the individual level the degree of persistence is quite modest for each generation" (p. 64). Noting that there is greater stability for the parent generation, they argue that, even among parents, individual-level stability is low. "[T]he likelihood of changing one's level of trust in the actions and motivations of government officials, though slightly diminished in the middle years, appears to remain substantial over a large portion of the life span" (p. 64).

On the other hand, Markus, who has worked closely with Jennings in analyzing the student–parent panel, reaches different conclusions. Markus (1979) emphasizes that the eight years between 1965 and 1973 were filled with events that eroded political trust and argues that, considering these conditions, over-time stability is high. "[F]or the older cohort," he writes, "the persistence of trust orientations across so tumultuous an eight-year period as the one under study is impressive" (p. 349). And even for the younger cohort, he argues, "a case for individual attitudinal persistence can be made. . . . These patterns provide some important support for assumptions regarding the durability of political orientations, both during the time of passage into adulthood and later in life" (p. 349).

The early learning of political trust may be important if it provides some reservoir of support for the political system when the system fails to respond satisfactorily. At least among whites, students and parents who have high trust in 1965 seldom have low trust eight years later, despite events that substantially eroded trust during this period. The national electorate panel reveals the same pattern (see Table 13.1), and, even among young adults, trusting individuals seldom develop low levels of political trust. High levels of trust appear to provide some protection against the subsequent development of political cynicism.

But this short-term protection cannot prevent the long-term erosion of trust among the electorate. This becomes all too apparent as we turn to examine the steady erosion of trust during the last sixteen years.

The Decline of Political Trust

Before turning to our summary measure of political trust, it is useful to examine the changing distribution of responses to the five basic questions that have been used to measure these feelings. Table 13.2 shows the percentage who give the "trusting" response to the four questions that have been asked since 1958 and to the "few big interests" question that has been asked since 1964. The data are presented according to race.

The most frequently employed question is the one that, on its face, is the most central to the concept of political trust, and the table shows the percentage that think the government in Washington can be trusted "just about always" or "most of the time." In 1958, three out of four whites register the trusting response, and trust rises marginally in 1964. Since 1964, trust on this question has declined almost continually, with the sharpest drop between 1972 and 1974, presumably reflecting the impact of Watergate. But the decline continues in 1976, two years after Watergate, and it continues through Carter's presidency. By the fall of 1980, only one white in four trusts the government just about always or most of the time.

In 1958, blacks have lower levels of trust on this question than do whites and slightly lower levels in 1964, but in 1966 there are virtually no racial differences. In 1968, blacks have slightly lower trust on this question, but the most marked drop in trust among blacks occurs between 1968 and 1970, and from 1970 through 1974, racial differences are marked. After 1974, however, trust rises somewhat among blacks, while continuing to decline among whites, and in both 1978 and 1980, racial differences are eliminated.

Both the "waste tax money" and the "smart people" question register a decline between 1964 and 1968, and both show a decline since then. By 1980, fewer than one out of five whites think the government wastes "not much" or "some" tax money, and only a third say the government is run by "smart people." The decline on the "crooked" question began in 1970, and it has been less marked than the erosion of trust on the remaining four items. Although trust on this question is lowest in 1980, half the whites think that "hardly any" or "not many" government officials are crooked.

Blacks have usually been less likely than whites to say that the government wastes tax money, and only in 1974 do they score as more cynical than whites on this question. For both the "smart people" and the "crooked" question, blacks are more trusting than whites in 1964, as trusting as whites in 1968, but less trusting in all surveys from 1970 through 1978. They are also less trusting in 1980, but differences are small.

The "benefit of all" question was first asked in 1964, and over three out of five whites gave the trusting response. Since then, the percentage has declined continuously, and, by 1980, just under one in five thinks the government is "run for the benefit of all." Blacks are more trusting than whites on this question in 1964, 1966, and 1968, but black trust drops very sharply between 1968 and 1970. In both 1974 and 1976, fewer than one out of five blacks thinks the government is run for the benefit of all. After 1976, black trust rises, and in 1978, for the first time in a decade, blacks are more likely

Table 13.2 Percentage of Adults Who Trust Government, by Race: 1958–1980

Percentage who said that:		1958	1964[a]	1966	1968[a]	1970[a]	1972	1974	1976	1978	1980
Washington can be trusted to do what is right just about always or most of the time											
	White	74	77	65	61	55	56	38	35	29	25
	Black	62	74	64	58	36	31	18	22	29	26
The government wastes not much or only some tax money											
	White	52	49	—	37	29	33	24	22	20	17
	Black	55	69	—	56	40	30	14	28	26	35
People running the government are smart people											
	White	58	68	—	58	53	56	50	45	42	34
	Black	47	71	—	57	37	43	36	30	31	27
Hardly any or not many government officials are crooked											
	White	70	66	—	71	67	62	52	55	56	50
	Black	73	76	—	72	49	33	41	34	45	48
The government is run for the benefit of all											
	White	—	63	52	49	41	39	25	24	23	19
	Black	—	69	64	64	35	24	19	19	31	34

Note: To approximate the numbers on which these percentages are based, see Figure 13.1.

[a] Includes black supplement sample.

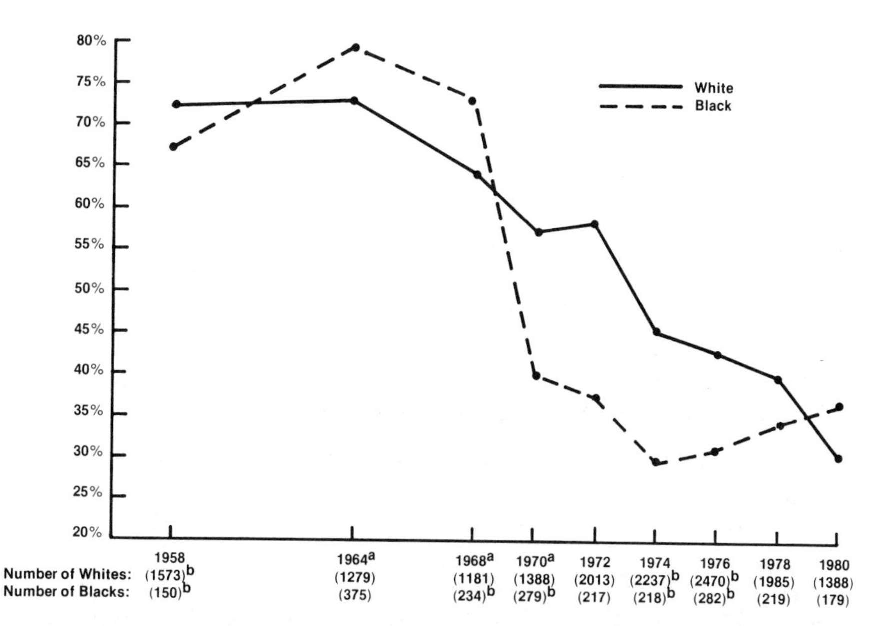

Figure 13.1 Percentage Who Score Medium or High on Political Trust, by Race: 1958–1980.

(*Note:* Based on four-item political-trust index. [a]Includes black supplement sample. [b]Weighted *N*s.)

than whites to be trusting on this item. In 1980, blacks are substantially more likely than whites to say the government is run for the benefit of all the people.

Once we combine these responses to form an index (see the appendix for these procedures), we gain in conciseness, although at some cost. First, in order to examine change over the entire 22-year period, we must use a four-item index. Second, once an index is constructed, we tend to give arbitrary names to the scores, and say that respondents have "high," "medium," or "low" levels of trust. This usage is appropriate, as long as we do not "reify" these labels, that is, regard them as having a concrete meaning.

Figure 13.1 presents the percentage of whites and of blacks who score medium or high on the political-trust index.[4] As we can see, trust among whites is the same in 1958 and 1964, but falls in 1968 and again in 1970. The biggest single drop comes between 1972 and 1974, apparently reflecting the impact of Watergate. After 1974, trust continues to fall, despite changes in incumbents. Even the change from a Republican administration under Ford to a Democratic administration under Carter did not prevent the continued decline

[4]The "high" category has become so infrequent in recent surveys that I do not present this category separately. Back in 1958, 23% of the white electorate score high on this four-item index, and in 1964, 18% do. But by 1980, only 2% of the white electorate score high on this measure.

of trust among whites—evidence that lends some support to Arthur Miller's argument that the erosion of trust has a wider meaning than the rejection of incumbents.

In 1958, blacks are only somewhat less trusting than whites. But black trust rises sharply between 1958 and 1964, and, in both 1964 and 1968, blacks are more trusting than whites. However, black trust drops dramatically between 1968 and 1970. This decline continues through 1974, but, in the three most recent surveys, trust among blacks has increased slightly. Between 1970 and 1976, blacks are much less trusting than whites, but, in 1978, racial differences are small, and, in 1980, blacks are somewhat more trusting than whites.[5]

Educational Levels and Political Trust

As Stokes (1962) reported when the SRC political-trust questions were first used, "the disposition of the individual to take a favorable stance toward government seems to depend somewhat on the extent of his education" (p. 65). Stokes finds that, in 1958, the higher a person's level of formal education, the more likely he or she is to view the government positively, but "the relation is weak enough that education is by no means to be taken as a sovereign factor" (p. 66).

We have examined the relationship between levels of education and political trust among whites and among blacks for all surveys from 1958 through 1980. With the exceptions of 1964 and 1980, white college graduates have been more trusting than whites with lower levels of education, and, in most surveys, whites with an eighth-grade education or less have been the least trusting. What is more striking is the weakness of the relationship between education and feelings of political trust, especially when compared with the strong relationship between education and feelings of political effectiveness (see Figures 10.3 and 10.4).[6]

Given the weak relationship between levels of formal education and political trust, it would be unwarranted to postulate either the "education-driven model," in which increases in educational levels among the electorate push political trust upward, or the "pecking-order model," in which changing educational levels lead to stability in overall levels of trust. (For a discussion of these models as they apply to feelings of political effectiveness, see pp. 178–180.) Given that trust has declined so markedly, we would expect respondents

[5]Given that blacks are more trusting than whites on the "few big interests" item in 1978 and 1980, the five-item index yields somewhat different results. In 1978, racial differences are eliminated if the five-item index is used, and, in 1980, the tendency for blacks to be more trusting is increased. In 1980, 23% of the whites score medium or high on the five-item index, while 33% of the blacks do.

[6]The tau-c correlations between our fivefold measure of education and the political-trust index among whites between 1958 and 1980 are as follows: 1958, .07; 1964, .03; 1968, .07; 1970, .06; 1972, .06; 1974, .15; 1976, .11; 1978, .06; 1980, .00.

at all educational levels to be losing their trust in government. Indeed, this is what has occurred. Trust has declined dramatically at all educational levels.

Among blacks, there has usually been a slight negative relationship between levels of education and feelings of political trust; that is, there is a slight tendency for blacks with higher levels of education to feel *less* politically trusting than blacks with lower levels of education. Moreover, since 1970, blacks who have attended college usually have *lower* levels of trust than those who have not—a finding that runs counter to the thesis that social deprivation contributes to political cynicism. While high levels of education may socialize whites to support the political system, exposure to the college environment may lead blacks to be more skeptical about the competence, honesty, and motives of people in the government (Shingles, 1979).

Reasons for the Decline

Several scholars have speculated at length about the reasons political trust has declined, and some have extensively analyzed the SRC–CPS data. Low levels of trust appear to be most prevalent among persons who are opposed to government policies. For example, Arthur Miller (1974a) shows that political distrust is greatest among respondents who have either a strongly liberal or a strongly conservative position on a wide range of political issues. In 1970, attitudes toward Vietnam are particularly strongly related to trust, with political cynicism being highest among respondents who want an immediate withdrawal of U.S. troops and among those who want a "complete military victory." On the other hand, Wright (1976, pp. 193–194) argues that the trend toward greater cynicism between 1964 and 1970 is of similar magnitude among hawks, doves, and supporters of government policies. Miller's analysis suggests that the movement toward cynicism is somewhat greater among persons who want the United States to withdraw from Vietnam, although the movement is less among those who want to escalate the war effort. Miller's analysis also suggests that the movement toward cynicism is pronounced among persons who oppose racial integration and is especially marked among respondents who think civil rights leaders are moving too slowly.

Jukam (1977) has conducted the most extensive analysis of the relationship of attitudes toward Vietnam and political trust. His analysis suggests that persons who perceive that their own policy positions on Vietnam are similar to the position of incumbents—regardless of their own policy position—have higher levels of political trust than persons who perceive their own policy positions on Vietnam to differ from those of the incumbents.

Available panel data may ultimately be employed to help us understand the reasons political trust declined. Markus (1979) has already conducted an extensive reanalysis of the Michigan student–parent panel in an attempt to determine how opinions on issues contribute to changes in political trust among individuals between 1965 and 1973. Markus examines opinions toward the Vietnam

War and toward race relations, the two issues that dominated this eight-year period, and finds that systematic shifts toward cynicism are related to these opinions. Among both parents and students, respondents who are "doves" on Vietnam in 1973 are more likely to have shifted toward cynicism than are either hawks or persons with a middle position. Among both parents and students, respondents with a pro-black position in 1973 are more likely to have shifted toward cynicism than are those with either an anti-black or a middle position. Markus's analysis suggests that attitudes toward Vietnam are more important in contributing to political cynicism than are attitudes toward racial issues. These panel data are also important because they strongly suggest that, although the decline in political trust and the decline in party identification are roughly parallel trends, these trends are not related to each other (Wattenberg, 1981).

The sharp decline in political trust between 1972 and 1974 almost certainly reflects the impact of the Watergate affair. A more interesting question and one that demands further analysis is to explain why political trust continues to decline after 1974.

Since samples of the black electorate are small, it is difficult to examine the reasons trust fell among blacks, but that decline appears to parallel major political trends in the political fortunes of black Americans. The rise in political trust between 1958 and 1964 may reflect the changes in presidencies from a Republican, Eisenhower, to a Democrat, Johnson, especially as Johnson strongly endorsed programs designed to aid blacks. Even though Johnson largely abandoned further reforms by 1968, black trust in the government dropped only slightly. But once a Republican, Nixon, became president, black trust fell dramatically. Following this logic, we might well have expected a sharp rise in trust after Carter became president. Trust did rise somewhat among blacks, while falling further among whites, but trust among blacks was scarcely restored and was far below the levels when either Eisenhower or Johnson was president.

Political Trust Through the Life Cycle

Several studies have already documented a consistent, if weak, tendency for political trust to be negatively related to age (Jennings and Niemi, 1974, pp. 275–276; A. Miller, 1974a; Wright, 1976, p. 144), and our analyses confirm these previous findings. The basic relationship between years of birth and feelings of political trust among whites is presented in Table 13.3, and this table follows the same standard cohort matrix format that was introduced in Chapter 4.

By reading down each column, we can see that there has never been a perfectly consistent decline in political trust with age, but that there has always been some erosion, averaging −.33 percentage points per year of age for all

Table 13.3 Percentage of Whites Who Score Medium or High on Political Trust, by Years of Birth: 1958–1980

Years of birth	1958	1964	1968	1970	1972	1974	1976	1978	1980
1956–1962						*	52	56	38
1948–1955				*	*	55	47	45	31
1940–1947		*	69	62	66	48	47	41	29
1932–1939	82[a]	79	71	59	64	47	44	41	34
1924–1931	74	76	67	55	59	44	39	35	26
1916–1923	73	73	65	59	57	41	39	36	25
1908–1915	73	68	56	55	49	37	39	29	27
1900–1907	66	69	56	50	51	40	32	**	**
1892–1899	65	64	61	**	**	**	**	**	**
1884–1891	71	**	**	**	**	**	**	**	**
All whites	72%	73%	64%	57%	58%	45%	43%	40%	30%

Note: Based on four-item political-trust index. To approximate the numbers on which these percentages are based, see Table 4.2. Actual *N*s are somewhat smaller since respondents for whom a political-trust score was not ascertained have been excluded from the analysis. *N*s are smaller for 1964, 1968, and 1972, since the political-trust items were employed in the postelection interview.

[a]Based on persons born between 1932 and 1937.

*Not included because the full eight-year cohort had not yet entered the electorate.

**Not included because the advanced age of the cohort makes it nonrepresentative for comparisons across time or because there are too few cases remaining.

nine surveys.[7] Thus, the average relationship between age and feelings of trust appears to be weaker than the relationship between age and feelings of "internal" political efficacy and slightly weaker than the relationship between age and feelings of "external" efficacy.

With both types of political efficacy, there is no consistent tendency for the young to feel the most efficacious, but there is a fairly consistent tendency for the oldest cohort to feel the least efficacious. With trust, however, the opposite pattern obtains. In eight of the nine surveys in which this relationship can be assessed, the youngest cohort has the highest level of political trust, while there is no consistent tendency for the oldest cohort to be the most cynical. The high level of political trust that Jennings and Niemi find among adolescents and that they argue results partly from values taught in the schools appears to have some lasting power into early adulthood. However, these early levels of trust appear to drop off quickly. For example, the 1932–1939 cohort (aged 21 to 26 in 1958) has high levels of trust through 1968, but trust drops

[7]Based on a least-squares regression analysis conducted down each column.

in 1970, when this cohort is between the ages of 31 and 38. Likewise, the cohort born between 1940 and 1947 has high levels of trust in 1968 (when it is between the ages of 21 and 28), but registers one of the sharpest drops of any cohort in 1974, when it is between the ages of 27 and 34. The 1948–1955 cohort has relatively high trust in 1974 (when it is between the ages of 19 and 26), but registers a sharp drop in 1980 (when it is between 25 and 32). (This early dropoff of trust among young adults is revealed even more clearly when more refined four-year cohorts are employed.)

The early decline in trust among young adults is clearly a life-cycle phenomenon, as Jennings and Niemi (1974) argue. But there is little reason to expect other life-cycle effects to shape the development of political trust. While the elderly may have reasons for feeling politically powerless, there is no reason to expect them to become cynical. Yet the negative relationship between trust and age persists in all nine surveys, even if the youngest cohort is excluded from the calculations.

It is difficult to advance a plausible thesis that differences between birth cohorts result from different formative socialization experiences. The generational explanation for age-group differences assumes that there is a formative socialization period after which attitudes tend to become relatively stable. But our analysis of the 1972–1974–1976 panel study of the American electorate provides little support for this assumption. The group of 21- to 29-year-olds does not have lower levels of over-time stability in their feelings of political trust than do their elders. Nor do older age groups have highly stable feelings of political trust.

If we track birth cohorts as they age by reading across each row, we find that all cohorts show a sharp decline in political trust, averaging −2.42 percentage points per year of age.[8] This drop is far greater than a life-cycle explanation would predict, since, as we saw, the average relationship between political trust and age for the nine surveys is a decline of only .33 percentage points per year of age. Moreover, five of the six cohorts that can be tracked for at least a decade register the sharpest single decline between 1972 and 1974, even though the ages of these cohorts vary greatly. Clearly, the main reason for the decline of political trust within each birth cohort cannot be aging, but historical forces that erode trust among persons of all ages.[9]

[8]Based on a least-squares regression analysis calculated across all six of the cohorts that can be tracked for at least one decade. The average decline is based on the mean decline for all six cohorts.

[9]Two earlier cohort analyses of political trust cover a shorter period, and therefore do not capture the impact of historical events that occurred after 1972. A. Miller, Brown, and Raine (1973) examine changes in political trust between 1964 and 1972 and find aging effects among the older cohorts, but also claim to find some potential generational differences among the younger cohorts. Searing, Wright, and Rabinowitz (1976) examine political trust between 1958 and 1968 and find a mixture of aging and period effects for two of the political-trust questions ("crooked" and "trust the government"), but strong period effects for two other questions ("smart people" and "benefit of all").

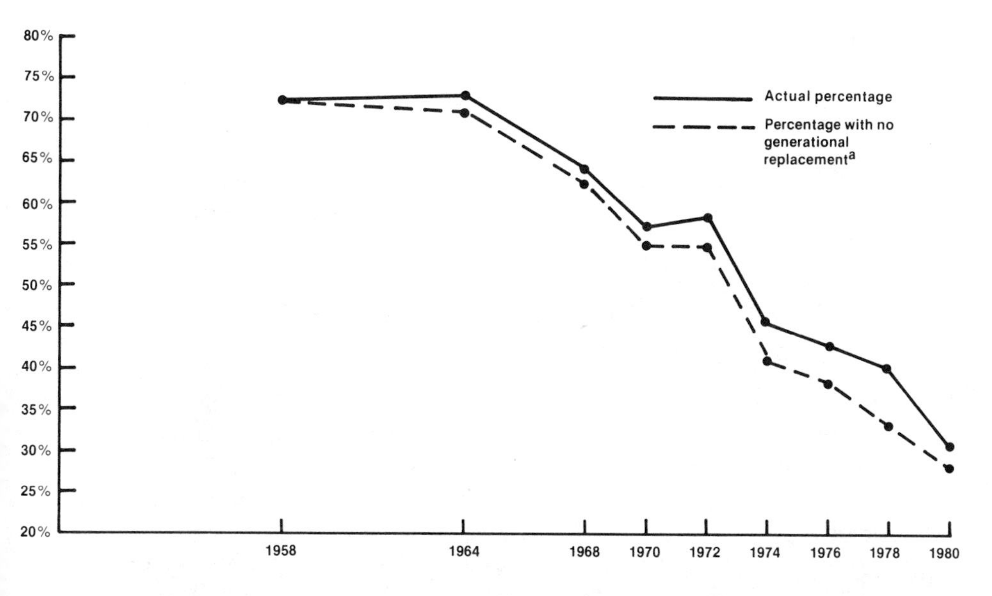

Figure 13.2 Percentage of Whites Who Score Medium or High on Political Trust: 1958–1980.

(*Note:* Based on four-item political-trust index. For the numbers on which the percentages for the solid line are based, see Figure 13.1. For the numbers on which the percentages for the broken line are based, see Table 4.2. Actual *N*s are somewhat smaller, since respondents for whom a political-trust score was not ascertained have been excluded from the analysis. Actual *N*s are smaller for 1964, 1968, and 1972, since the political-trust items were employed in the postelection interview. Also note that the 1932–1939 cohort presented in Table 4.2 includes respondents born in 1938 and 1939 who are not included in these calculations. [a]Assuming that no persons born after 1937 entered the electorate and that older cohorts did not diminish through death.)

Even though the data do not show generational differences in the formative learning of political trust, generational replacement has affected overall levels of political trust among the electorate. Figure 13.2 shows overall levels of political trust among the white electorate between 1958 and 1980. The solid line shows actual levels of political trust, while the broken line shows what political trust would have been if no generational replacement had occurred.[10] While the effects of replacement are small, replacement consistently impedes the decline of trust. Assuming other things to be equal, the decline in political trust would have been somewhat greater if replacement processes had not continuously occurred during these two decades. The effects of replacement result mainly from young cohorts, with relatively high levels of trust, entering the electorate.

[10]This latter calculation is speculative, since cohorts too old to be presented in Table 13.3 have very small *N*s. As with our calculations for strength of party identification and for feelings of political efficacy, we estimate levels of trust for these older cohorts according to the limited information available from the surviving members of these cohorts, as well as from the oldest cohort presented in the basic cohort matrix.

Conclusions

The results presented in this chapter should restrain us from speculating about future levels of political trust. Certainly anyone who extrapolates from the relationship between age and trust at any single point in time would expect trust to rise in future surveys. For example, as of 1980, the youngest cohort has the highest level of political trust (see Table 13.3). But even if young adults sampled in 1980 do not begin to develop lower levels of trust (and they appear to have already begun to decline), the high levels of trust of the late 1950s or early 1960s would not be restored. As the data in Table 13.3 reveal, the youngest cohort sampled in 1980 has far lower levels of political trust than do the most cynical cohorts sampled in 1958 or 1964. Cohorts that enter the electorate in future years would need to have very high levels of trust for future generational replacement to restore earlier levels of trust among the electorate.

Given the changeability of political trust, future events might restore political trust among all age groups. But this possibility is difficult to assess. Unfortunately, feelings of political trust have been declining during almost the entire period that trust has been measured. Therefore, we know something about the conditions that erode political trust, but very little about the conditions that cause such feelings to grow.

V

Change or Continuity: A Study of Trends

[CHAPTER 14]

Change in Tolerance

The three basic attitudes we have studied have been among the most widely and consistently studied in the political science literature, and we have been able to closely study attitude change over time. Feelings of tolerance toward deviant groups have been examined less consistently, yet we now have enough data to demonstrate that tolerance—at least toward Communists, socialists, and atheists—has increased. Whether these changes reflect a basic increase in tolerance or merely a shift of opinion toward specific political groups is a matter of controversy.

The Stouffer Study

Gallup polls have measured attitudes toward Communists as far back as 1937; they found that most Americans favored banning Communist literature and denying Communists the right to hold public office, to hold public meetings, and to speak before student groups (Hyman and Sheatsley, 1953). A Roper survey conducted in 1940 finds that most Americans favor restrictions against Communists. A series of polls conducted by the National Opinion Research Center (NORC) finds that the percentage of Americans that would prohibit a member of the Communist party from speaking on the radio rises steadily from 1943 (when the Soviet Union was our wartime ally) through January 1954 (a few months after the truce that ended the conflict in Korea) (Stouffer, 1955, p. 56).

Do such opinions threaten our heritage of civil liberties? This question was of vital importance in the early 1950s, during the height of Senator Joseph R. McCarthy's efforts to "expose" the domestic "Communist conspiracy." To better understand the nature of public reactions, Stouffer (1955), aided by a grant from the Fund for the Republic, launched a major study to evaluate public opinion toward civil liberties. Two surveys of the American electorate—one conducted by NORC, the other by the American Institute for Public Opinion (Gallup)—were carried out in May, June, and July of 1954. Both survey agencies used probability-sampling techniques,[1] and 4900 Americans were sampled. In addition, both NORC and Gallup conducted a sample of "community leaders" in over 100 small and medium-sized cities, and 1500 leaders were interviewed in the early summer of 1954.

The Stouffer study reveals a high level of intolerance among the mass sample. For example, only 59% think that "a person who favors government ownership of all the railroads and big industries" should be allowed to speak in their community, and only 37% would allow a man to speak "against churches and religion." About 70% would allow a man whose loyalty has been questioned by a congressional committee, but who swears under oath that he has never been a Communist, to speak, but only 27% would extend this right to "an admitted Communist" (Stouffer, 1955, pp. 28–42). On all these questions, community leaders are more tolerant: 84% would allow a socialist to speak, 64% an atheist, 87% a man whose loyalty has been questioned, and 51% an admitted Communist.

According to Stouffer, these questions are designed not merely to measure "transient opinions," but "deeper latent attitudes or dispositions" (p. 13). Whether intolerant respondents would actually seek to restrict the civil liberties of socialists, atheists, or Communists would depend on specific circumstances. Stouffer argues that "we must not take the answers to any specific questions as explicit predictions of action. Rather, we must regard them as indexes of latent tendences" (p. 48). And, as he argues, in measuring such tendencies, it is best to rely on a measure based on many questions.

Most of Stouffer's analysis is based on a scale that combines responses to fifteen questions, most of which are about Communists. These questions, along with the percentage of the mass sample that gives the tolerant response, are reported in Table 14.1. As the table shows, Stouffer categorizes respondents according to their pattern of responses to these questions. About a third of the mass sample is designated as "relatively more tolerant" (Groups 5 and 4), half as "in-between" (Groups 3 and 2), and about a fifth as "relatively less tolerant" (Groups 1 and 0). When the same basic scoring procedures are applied to the community leaders, nearly two-thirds score as "more tolerant" and only one in twenty score as "less tolerant" (Stouffer, 1955, p. 51). Stouffer warns that we should not attach absolute meaning to these labels, but in a relative sense he could demonstrate that community leaders are "more tolerant" than the public as a whole. As Robert Jackman (1972) has subsequently

[1] As we saw in Chapter 2, Gallup more often uses some mix of quota and probability sampling.

shown in a careful reanalysis of Stouffer's data, the greater tolerance of community leaders is largely a function of their higher level of education. (For a further discussion, see R. Jackman, 1977; and St. Peter, Williams, and Johnson, 1977.)

Stouffer clearly recognizes the importance of education in contributing to tolerance among the mass sample. According to my recalculations of data presented by Stouffer, 68% of the college graduates in the mass sample score as "more tolerant," 54% of those with some college, 40% of the high school graduates, 27% of those with some high school, and only 14% of those with an elementary school education. Persons with high levels of education tend to have other social characteristics that are related to tolerance: for example, they tend to be younger, to live in metropolitan areas, to live in the West, and to be male. But even when controls for these other variables are introduced, persons with higher levels of education tend to have higher levels of tolerance.

According to Stouffer, the educational process itself contributes to tolerance. Education teaches people to reject the rigid categorization of people into groups. The ability to make distinctions between differing situations—such as between a Communist working in a defense plant and a Communist making a speech—might contribute to tolerance. In addition, education "tends to encourage respect for dissenting points of view. . . . The farther pupils go up the educational ladder, the more likely they are to learn to respect the right of people to be different from themselves, *even if* and *especially when* they disapprove of such people" (p. 99). While some research has suggested that education may not *directly* contribute to tolerance (Sullivan et al., 1978–1979, 1981), research has consistently shown that persons who are better-educated are more likely to score as tolerant than those with less formal education. Given that the educational levels of the American electorate were certain to rise through the continuing process of generational replacement, Stouffer speculates that tolerance might rise as well. Another major scholar who studied democratic values, McClosky (1964), is optimistic about the future, in part because of "the extraordinary spread of education" (p. 379).

Tolerance Among Preadults

If Stouffer and McClosky's optimism is warranted, one might expect that the younger generation of Americans still in school would have a greater commitment to democratic values than do their elders. But several national surveys of American preadults have revealed a low level of tolerance (R. Jones, 1980; Remmers, 1963; Torney, Oppenheim, and Farnen, 1975). A study of Sacramento, California, school children, conducted in 1968 by Zellman and Sears (1971) concludes that "belief in free expression is taught only as a slogan, not as a generalizable principle, and that children therefore do not learn to apply it to concrete situations" (p. 119). (For a similar conclusion

Table 14.1 Percentage Tolerant on Fifteen Questions Used to Measure Tolerance for Ideological Nonconformists in Stouffer Study (1954) and Nunn, Crockett, and Williams Study (1973) and on Six of These Questions Used in NORC General Social Surveys (1972–1980)

	Stouffer, 1954	Nunn et al., 1973	NORC General Social Surveys					
			1972	1973	1974	1976	1977	1980
Group 5. The most tolerant of all. Give tolerant replies to at least two of these questions:								
Now, I would like to ask you some questions about a man who admits he is a Communist.								
1. Suppose this admitted Communist wants to make a speech in your community. Should he be allowed to speak or not?	27	53	52	60	58	55	55	55
2. Suppose he wrote a book which is in your public library. Somebody in your community suggests the book be removed from the library. Would you favor removing it, or not?	27	54	53	58	59	56	55	57
3. Suppose this admitted Communist is a radio [TV] singer [entertainer]. Should he be fired, or not?	29	52						
Group 4. The next most tolerant. Fail to qualify in Group 5, but give tolerant replies to at least two of these questions:								
4. Should an admitted Communist be put in jail, or not?	34	62						
5. There are always some people whose ideas are considered bad or dangerous by other people. For instance, somebody who is against all churches and religion. If such a person wanted to make a speech in your city (town, community) against churches and religion, should he be allowed to speak, or not?	37	62	65	65	62	64	62	66
6. If some people in your community suggested that a book he wrote against churches and religion should be taken out of your public library, would you favor removing this book, or not?	35	56	61	61	60	60	59	62

Group 3. Fail to qualify for groups 5 and 4, but give tolerant replies to at least two of these questions:					
7. Now suppose the radio or [TV] program he (an admitted Communist) is on advertises a brand of soap. Somebody in your community suggests that you stop buying that soap. Would you stop, or not?	56	69			
8. Or consider a person who favored government ownership of all the railroads and all big industries. If this person wanted to make a speech in your community favoring government ownership of all the railroads and big industries, should he be allowed to speak, or not?	59	72	77	77	76
9. If some people in your community suggested that a book he wrote favoring government ownership should be taken out of your public library, would you favor removing the book, or not?	53	66	68	71	69
Group 2. Fail to qualify for groups 5, 4, or 3, but give tolerant replies to at least two of these questions:					
10. Now I would like you to think of another person. A man whose loyalty has been questioned before a Congressional committee, but who swears under oath that he has never been a Communist. Suppose he is teaching in a college or university. Should he be fired, or not?	69	72			

Note: These percentages are based on the total samples. The Stouffer cross-sectional sample is based on over 4900 respondents; the Nunn, Crockett, and Williams study on over 3500; and the NORC surveys on 1500.

For Group 5, 4, 3, and 2 questions, I show the percentage giving the tolerant reply. "Don't know" responses are, in effect, grouped with the intolerant responses. For Group 1 questions, I show the percentage tolerant plus the percentage giving "don't know" replies.

Source: I am grateful to Clyde Z. Nunn for providing me with the distribution of responses for the Nunn, Crockett, and Williams study. Results for Stouffer study are based on codebook provided by Inter-University Consortium for Political and Social Research. Results for General Social Surveys are based on codebook provided by National Opinion Research Center.

(continued)

Table 14.1 (continued)

	Stouffer, 1954	Nunn et al., 1973	NORC General Social Surveys					
			1972	1973	1974	1976	1977	1980
Group 2 (continued)								
11. Should he be allowed to make a speech in your community, or not?	70	71						
12. Suppose this man is a high school teacher. Should he be fired, or not?	69	68						
Group 1. The next to least tolerant group. Fail to qualify for groups 5, 4, 3, or 2, but give tolerant or *don't know* replies to two of the following questions.[a]								
(with respect to a man whose loyalty has been questioned, but who swears he has never been a Communist)								
13. Suppose he has been working in a defense plant. Should he be fired, or not?	82	80						
14. Suppose he is a clerk in a store. Should he be fired, or not?	89	91						
15. Suppose he wrote a book which is in your public library. Somebody in your community suggests that the book should be removed from the library. Would you favor removing it, or not?	83	85						
Group 0. The least tolerant group. Fail to qualify for any of the groups above.								

[a]Includes "don't know" replies.

about adults, see Prothro and Grigg, 1960.) Zellman and Sears present a penetrating analysis of the conditions that contribute to tolerance for dissent and conclude that self-esteem is a major factor in developing tolerant attitudes (see also Sniderman, 1975, pp. 194–198).

Although these studies suggest that American youths may not be highly tolerant, the University of Michigan student–parent study, conducted in the spring of 1965, suggests that high school seniors may be more tolerant than their parents. For example, 86% of the seniors agree with the statement: "If a person wanted to make a speech in this community against churches and religion, he should be allowed to speak," while 72% of the parents agree. Among the seniors, 36% agree with the statement "If a Communist were legally elected to some public office around here, the people should allow him to take office," while 28% of the parents agree (Jennings and Niemi, 1974, p. 65). While there are only modest differences between students as a group and parents as a group, there is little evidence that children learn these attitudes from their parents, for a direct comparison of the opinions of students with those of their parents yields low correlations.[2]

Jennings and Niemi (1974) did not know whether the greater support for civil liberties among students reflects a life-cycle or a generational difference. "It may be that the newer generation will persist in this edge . . . . Or it may be that when thrust into the adult world of politics, these youthful predilections will erode" (p. 66). As their panel study reveals, differences between the student and parent generations are even more pronounced in 1973. Whereas the percentage of parents that would allow antireligion speeches is almost unchanged, the percentage of students that would allow such a speech increases. While the percentage of parents that would allow a Communist to take office increases, the percentage of students who would do so increases even more (Jennings and Niemi, 1981, pp. 158–159).

A direct individual-level comparison shows considerable stability in responses to the question about a Communist holding office, but somewhat less stability on the question of speaking against religion. Jennings and Niemi (1981) emphasize that the direction of individual-level change is primarily in the direction of greater tolerance. The biggest change is the shift of the younger generation toward allowing antireligion speeches. "[E]xtraordinarily few of those originally supporting such speeches switched their positions, whereas a very large shift occurred among those originally opposed" (p. 58). A similar, though less dramatic, pattern is found in examining changes toward a Communist holding office. "The importance of this observation is that it strongly suggests that individuals were reacting to societal moods rather than simply answering randomly—as would be implied by a 'nonattitudes' interpretation" (p. 58).

[2]Dalton's (1980) reanalysis of the Michigan student–parent data suggests that parent–child correspondence rises from a Pearson's *r* of .14 to .44 when problems of measurement unreliability are taken into account.

Tolerance Through the Life Cycle

One of Stouffer's strongest findings is that young adults are more tolerant than their elders. For example, among the subset of the mass sample that is "more interested" in public affairs, 47% of the 21- to 29-year-olds score as "more tolerant," 43% of the 30- to 39-year-olds, 37% of the 40- to 49-year-olds, 31% of the 50- to 59-year-olds, and only 18% of those 60 years old and over. Stouffer recognizes that these age differences could result from basic cultural differences between young adults and their elders (that is to say, from generational differences) or from the effects of aging. As Stouffer asks: "[D]o these figures reflect mere age change within a static culture, or do they reflect some basic trends in our culture which are working toward increasing tolerance" (p. 90)?

Stouffer could not answer this basic question, but the high levels of education of the young suggest that the young might be relatively tolerant even when they age. But Stouffer argues that there is probably some tendency for aging to reduce tolerance. For example, optimism is related to tolerance, and older persons, quite naturally, are less optimistic about their future than younger persons are. Stouffer reasons: "Physical and social factors which are inevitable accompaniments of aging would tend to combine in the production of increased personal anxiety, would tend to produce increased pessimism, which in turn would tend to produce increased intolerance, at least in some people" (p. 103). But while Stouffer expects persons to become less tolerant as they age, he also predicts newer cohorts to be more tolerant than their parents: "We . . . predict that a person, on the average, is likely to be more tolerant than his own parents. . . . Although he is likely to be more tolerant when he reaches 60 than were his own parents at 60, he may at the same time be less tolerant than he was in his own younger days" (p. 94).

Stouffer's prediction that tolerance would decrease with age can now be tested as a result of one nationwide survey that repeats all of the Stouffer tolerance questions, as well as a series of national surveys that repeats some of them. Unfortunately, there is a gap of nearly two decades between Stouffer's study and the surveys that test his predictions.

The most direct replication of Stouffer's analysis is provided by Nunn, Crockett, and Williams (1978), who, using funds provided by the National Science Foundation, commissioned Response Analysis, Inc., to conduct a national probability sample of 3500 Americans in March, April, and May of 1973. In addition, Nunn and his colleagues commissioned a sample of 650 community leaders, using procedures similar to those employed by Stouffer. Nunn uses all of the basic Stouffer questions with only minor modifications (e.g., changing the word "radio" to "television"). Nunn has provided me with the basic distribution of responses to the fifteen questions used in the "tolerance for ideological nonconformists" scale, and Nunn's 1973 results can be compared directly with Stouffer's 1954 results.

Column 1 of Table 14.1 shows the percentage giving the tolerant reply to each question back in 1954; column 2 shows the percentage giving the tolerant reply nineteen years later. For the first six questions, there are very substantial increases in tolerance, and there are substantial, though less dramatic, increases for the next three questions (7 through 9). For the last six questions (10 through 15), changes are small and inconsistent, but, for these questions, feelings of tolerance are already quite high back in 1954.

Nunn and his colleagues use these questions to directly replicate the Stouffer tolerance scale. Their major finding is that tolerance is substantially higher in 1973 than it was nineteen years earlier. In 1954, 31% of the mass sample score as "more tolerant"; in 1973, 55% do. In 1954, 66% of the community leaders score as "more tolerant"; in 1973, 83% do (p. 51). As with the Stouffer study, community leaders are substantially more tolerant than the mass sample, although Nunn and his colleagues demonstrate that these differences are reduced to nonsignificance when combined controls are introduced for sex, region, exposure to the mass media, city size, occupation, and education (p. 152).

Nunn and his colleagues directly test Stouffer's thesis that aging decreases tolerance. I reproduce their results, with recalculations of my own, in Table 14.2. By reading down each column, we can see that, in both surveys, tolerance decreases with age and that the negative relationship between tolerance and age is stronger in 1973 than in 1954. By reading across each row, we can see that in no case do cohorts become *less* tolerant with age. The older cohorts

Table 14.2 Percentage More Tolerant, by Years of Birth: 1954 and 1973

	Stouffer, 1954		Nunn et al., 1973[a]	
Years of birth	Percent	*N*	Percent	*N*
1944–1952			76	(740)
1934–1943			65	(660)
1925–1933	41	(905)	56	(591)
1915–1924	37	(1174)	48	(552)
1905–1914	31	(1058)	33	
1895–1904	26	(794)	28	(755)
Before 1894	16	(998)		
Total for cross-sectional survey	31%	(4929)	55%	(3298)

*Note: N*s in parentheses are the total number of cases on which percentages are based.

[a]Some approximations were necessary to present the data for 1973.

Source: Based on rearranging results reported in Nunn, Crockett, and Williams (1978, pp. 78, 84).

(to the extent that we can track them over time) become somewhat more tolerant with age, while the two youngest cohorts sampled in 1954 register substantial gains in tolerance. (Cohorts that enter the electorate after 1954 are substantially more tolerant than any of the cohorts already in the electorate at the time of the Stouffer study.) These data, Nunn, Crockett, and Williams conclude, "provide no support for the idea that growing older brings about lowered political tolerance. . . . These trends invite the implication that factors at work during the period of 1954 to 1973 raised the level of political tolerance across the wide range of the adult population being studied here" (p. 85). The most important of these factors was "a whole series of events [that] occurred between 1954 and 1973 that resulted in a diminution in perceived Communist threat" (p. 86).

Two other analyses that replicate the Stouffer study were conducted using data collected in 1972 and 1973 as part of the NORC General Social Survey series. These studies are remarkable, for they were conducted primarily for the use of the social science community, rather than for the aims of the data collectors themselves. (For a discussion of these surveys, see Converse, 1978; S. Cutler, 1978; Glenn, 1978; Hyman, 1978.) As the Stouffer survey has become a classic social scientific study, the NORC includes some of the original Stouffer questions.

One of the major analyses of these data was conducted by Davis (1975), who was at that time director of the NORC. Davis analyzes responses to four questions from the original Stouffer scale (questions 1, 2, 5, and 6), as well as two additional Stouffer questions that were not part of the basic tolerance scale. (The wording of these two additional questions, along with the percentage giving the tolerant reply in 1954 and in the NORC General Social Surveys, is provided in Table 14.3.) Davis's measure uses three questions about Communists, three about atheists. Between 1954 and 1972–1973, there is a substantial shift toward tolerance for all six questions, as can be seen by examining the data in Tables 14.1 and 14.3. Davis concludes that the changes "for the atheist items are about the same as those for the Communists, suggesting that the decline in the Cold War spirit cannot provide a simple explanation for these changes" (p. 506).

Davis constructed a new measure of tolerance using all six questions, and reanalyzes the original Stouffer data with this measure. According to Davis, the average proportion of respondents scoring as "more tolerant" more than doubles between 1954 and the early 1970s.[3]

Davis examines levels of tolerance among four broadly defined cohorts, and his basic results, which I have recalculated from a more detailed table,

[3]Davis reports that the mean proportion "more tolerant" in 1972–1973 is .554. I report a proportion of .536, for this is the result I derive in recalculating Davis's results to present levels of tolerance for each cohort. I report the latter proportion because it leads to more conservative estimates of the effects of generational replacement.

Table 14.3 Percentage Tolerant on Questions About Teaching in Stouffer Study (1954) and NORC General Social Surveys (1972–1980)

Percentage giving tolerant reply	Stouffer, 1954	NORC General Social Surveys					
		1972	1973	1974	1976	1977	1980
There are always some people whose ideas are considered bad or dangerous by other people. For instance, somebody who is against all churches and religion. . . .							
Should such a person be allowed to teach in a college or university, or not?	12	40	41	42	41	39	45
Or consider a person who favored government ownership of all the railroads and big industries. . . .							
Should such a person be allowed to teach in a college or university, or not?	33	56	58	57			
Now, I would like to ask you some questions about a man who admits he is a Communist. . . .							
Suppose he is teaching in a college. Should he be fired, or not?	6	32	39	42	41	39	41

Note: These percentages are based on the total samples. The Stouffer cross-sectional sample is based on over 4900 respondents, and the NORC surveys on 1500 respondents. Percentages show respondents giving the tolerant reply. "Don't know" responses are, in effect, grouped with the intolerant responses.

Source: Results for Stouffer study are based on codebook provided by Inter-University Consortium for Political and Social Research. Results for General Social Survey are based on codebook provided by National Opinion Research Center.

Table 14.4 Mean Proportion More Tolerant, by Years of Birth: 1954 and 1972–1973

	Stouffer, 1954		NORC General Social Surveys, 1972–1973	
Years of birth	Mean	*N*	Mean	*N*
1933–1952			.682	(1218)
1915–1933	.307	(1976)	.498	(1001)
1895–1914	.239	(1761)	.334	(627)
Before 1895	.160	(930)	.262	(48)
Total for cross-sectional survey	.252	(4667)	.536	(2894)

Note: *N*s in parentheses are the total number of cases on which mean proportions are based.
Source: Based on recalculations of results presented in Davis (1975, p. 507).

are presented as Table 14.4. By reading down each column, we can see that, in both the Stouffer survey and the NORC surveys, tolerance decreases with age. As with the Nunn data, the negative relationship between age and tolerance is greater in the 1970s than in 1954. By reading across each column, we can see that in no case do cohorts become *less* tolerant. Instead, tolerance increases and, as with the Nunn data, the greatest gains are among the cohorts that are the youngest in 1954. (As with the Nunn study, persons who enter the electorate after 1954 are more tolerant than those who are already in the electorate when the Stouffer study was conducted.) Davis acknowledges that aging might produce intolerance, but that this intolerance could have been hidden by historical forces that increased tolerance among the entire population. In other words, life-cycle forces could be operating, but could be hidden by historical forces. "But," Davis reasons, "we can argue that if a 'natural' negative effect for age has been offset by a positive period effect, the period effect is really extraordinary" (p. 510).

Steven Cutler and Robert Kaufman (1975) used the 1972 NORC data to test Stouffer's thesis. They developed four tolerance scales, using six items from the original Stouffer scale (1, 2, 5, 6, 8, and 9), plus questions about whether an atheist, a socialist, or a Communist should be allowed to teach in a college or university. (For the distribution of responses to these questions in 1954 and in 1972, see Tables 14.1 and 14.3.) The authors developed three-item scales to measure tolerance toward atheists, socialists, and Communists, plus a nine-item measure of general tolerance toward ideological nonconformity. The authors compare levels of tolerance among five cohorts sampled in 1954 with the same cohorts sampled eighteen years later. Among all five cohorts and with all four measures, tolerance increases, and, as with the Nunn and the Davis analyses, increases are greatest among the younger cohorts. (Unfortunately, Cutler and Kaufman do not present levels of tolerance for cohorts that entered the electorate after 1954.)

Cutler and Kaufman's analysis clearly does not support Stouffer's prediction that tolerance would decrease with age. "Since, in fact, tolerant or liberal attitudes have become more prevalent among all cohorts over the 18-year period, it is clear that growing older is not invariably accompanied by more conservative political attitudes in any absolute sense" (p. 80). On the other hand, because tolerance increases more among the young cohorts than among their elders, one could argue that "in this relative sense . . . growing old would appear to be accompanied by increased conservatism" (p. 80).[4]

While the available data cannot provide definitive answers about the effects of aging on tolerance, the data, as presented by Nunn and by Davis, do allow us to estimate the impact of generational replacement on overall levels of tolerance. On the one hand, we know that this increase cannot result solely from replacement, since all cohorts register gains. On the other hand, we know that the cohorts that entered the electorate since 1954 are more tolerant than cohorts already in the electorate at that time. Furthermore, we know that the greatest diminution through death occurs among the least tolerant cohorts. Simple algebraic calculations (such as those employed in Chapters 4, 7, 10, and 13) allow us to estimate the effects of replacement.

Figure 14.1 presents my recalculations based on the data published by Nunn and his colleagues. As the solid line shows, actual tolerance increases by 24 percentage points between 1954 and 1973. As the broken line shows, if no new cohorts had entered the electorate and if older cohorts had not diminished through death, the increase would have been only 8 percentage points.[5] In other words, my estimates suggest that roughly two-thirds of the total increase results from generational replacement.

Replacement is somewhat less important when the NORC General Social Survey data are employed. Figure 14.2 presents my recalculations based on Davis's analysis of these data. As the solid line shows, there is an actual increase of .284 in the mean proportion scoring as "more tolerant." As the broken line shows, if there had been no generational replacement, the increase would have been .137.[6] According to my calculations, about half of the total

[4]A review of these studies leads Corbett (1982) to conclude: "These results provide strong evidence for the Generational Model" (p. 136). Corbett's study provides an extensive analysis of the 1977 NORC General Social Survey.

[5]The data presented by Nunn and his colleagues are less complete than they should be for estimating tolerance for the older cohorts. In making my estimates, I use conservative procedures that may somewhat underestimate the impact of generational replacement.

[6]To derive these estimates, I was forced to estimate tolerance for the cohort born before 1895 on a small number of these older respondents sampled in 1972–1973. Fortunately, we will be able to supplement my estimates with those made by Davis himself.

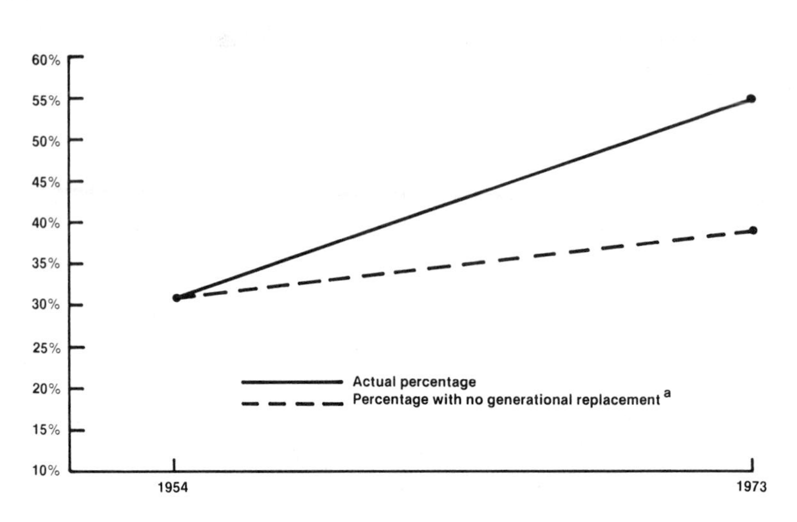

Figure 14.1 Percentage More Tolerant: 1954 and 1973.
(*Note:* For the numbers on which these percentages are based, see Table 14.2. [a]Assuming that no persons born after 1933 entered the electorate and that older cohorts did not diminish through death.) [*Source:* Based on recalculations of results presented in Nunn, Crockett, and Williams (1978, pp. 78, 84).]

increase in tolerance results from replacement. These estimates differ somewhat from Davis's, for he uses a more complex procedure to specify the increase in tolerance resulting from replacement that is unrelated to changing levels of education. His estimates suggest that about a fourth of the total increase in tolerance results from the direct effects of generational replacement, while about one-sixth results from increases in educational levels that result from generational replacement (Davis, 1975, p. 509). Davis's estimates suggest that about two-fifths of the total increase in tolerance results from generational replacement. But while my estimates differ from Davis's in minor ways, both his estimates and mine lead to the same bottom-line conclusion. Much of the increase in tolerance results from across-the-board increases among all birth cohorts, but the overall increase would have been substantially less if generational replacement had not transformed the electorate during these two decades.

Changes in tolerance provide a clear example of generational replacement contributing to a trend. Without replacement, there would have been less change.

Qualifications

Tolerance toward Communists, atheists, and socialists has clearly increased, but some scholars have argued that this change merely reflects the diminished salience of domestic Communism and the easing of Cold War tensions. If

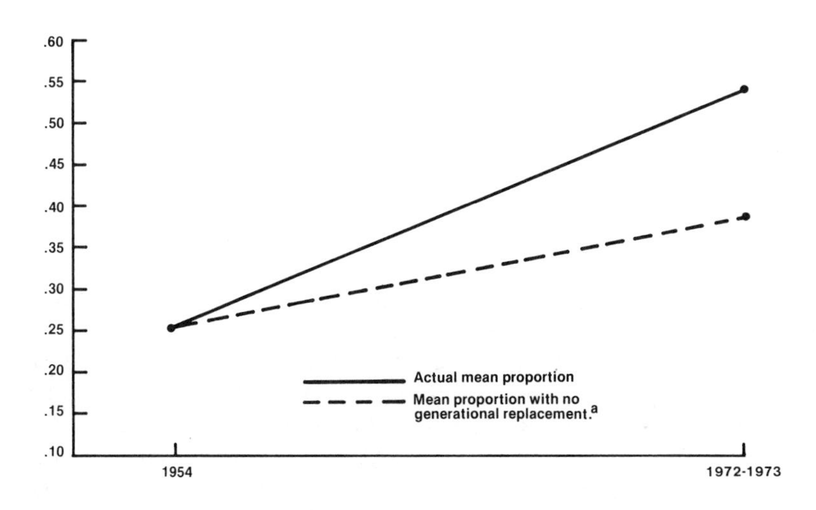

Figure 14.2 Mean Proportion More Tolerant: 1954 and 1972–1973.
(*Note:* For the numbers on which these mean proportions are based, see Table 14.4. [a]Assuming that no persons born after 1933 entered the electorate and that older cohorts did not diminish through death.) [*Source:* Based on recalculations of results presented in Davis (1975, p. 507).]

Americans no longer feel strongly negative toward Communists, they may be less likely to want to deny them their legal rights, but tolerance in a more general sense may not have increased at all.

Several scholars have criticized Stouffer for failing to measure feelings toward Communists, atheists, and socialists. Mary Jackman (1977) argues that Stouffer and many other students of tolerance focus on "action orientations" and merely assume that groups such as Communists are disliked. But some persons may not dislike these groups or may not see them as salient. Jackman argues: "The extremity, salience, and intensity of personal dislike for a group, as well as the nature and strength of prevailing norms of behavior toward the group, may all influence the level of tolerance for that group" (pp. 166–167). Lawrence (1976) has provided an extensive critique of the Stouffer study, as well as of studies by Prothro and Grigg and by McClosky. Lawrence argues that Stouffer simply assumes that Communists, atheists, and socialists are disliked. Most respondents probably do dislike Communists, and, to a lesser extent, atheists and socialists. Lawrence writes: "Failure to determine this more general issue-orientation prevents Stouffer from identifying respondents who do not dislike Communists, atheists, etc., and whose intolerance must therefore clearly be based on other grounds" (p. 83). Moreover, Lawrence argues, Stouffer's work may be out of date, since "the groups investigated are of limited relevance to current problems of civil liberties" (p. 83).

Sullivan, Piereson, and Marcus (1979) provide the most direct challenge to the thesis that tolerance has increased. They concede that tolerance toward

Communists, atheists, and socialists has increased, but argue that general levels of tolerance may not have increased much at all during the past two decades. Tolerance, Sullivan argues, "presumes opposition or disagreement. If there is no reason to oppose, then there is no occasion for one to be tolerant or intolerant. . . . [I]t is pointless to ask people to tolerate a doctrine or practice of which they approve or toward which they are indifferent" (p. 784).

Sullivan and his colleagues argue that increased tolerance toward Communists, atheists, and socialists results largely from the decreased salience of these three groups. They reach this conclusion through factor-analytic techniques that suggest that the public does not differentiate among these groups as sharply as it did in the mid-1950s (Sullivan, Piereson, Marcus, and Feldman, 1979, p. 182). We should be somewhat cautious about accepting this conclusion, since Sullivan does not use a direct measure of salience. Still, the conclusion seems reasonable, because domestic Communism was almost certainly seen as less of a threat in the mid-1970s than it had been two decades earlier, during the height of the McCarthy period.

Sullivan, Piereson, and Marcus make a major methodological contribution to the study of tolerance by developing a measure that controls for group salience. Respondents are provided with a list of groups and asked which they like least and which they like second-least. The list includes socialists, fascists, Communists, the Ku Klux Klan, the John Birch Society, the Black Panthers, the Symbionese Liberation Army, atheists, pro-abortionists, and anti-abortionists (pro-lifers). Respondents are asked questions that measure their tolerance toward the group they like least and the group they like second-least. Sullivan first tested his method with a probability sample of Minneapolis–St. Paul adults in the spring and summer of 1976 (based on a list of adults in the Twin Cities directories). About 200 respondents were asked the tolerance questions about their least-liked group ("content-controlled questions"), while another 200 were asked questions about Communists and atheists drawn from the Stouffer questionnaire. These content-controlled questions were also used in a specially commissioned NORC national sample in 1978, along with some of the original Stouffer questions. Some comparisons were also made with the 1977 NORC General Social Survey.

Once content-controlled measures of tolerance are used, tolerance is often revealed to be very low. Sullivan and his colleagues compare the results of their content-controlled questions with the questions about Communists and atheists borrowed from the Stouffer questionnaire. When one examines levels of tolerance in either the Twin Cities study or the NORC national samples, one finds that respondents are less tolerant toward their least-liked group than they are to either Communists or atheists. Differences are greatest on a question about whether members of these groups should be allowed to teach. Focusing largely on a comparison of questions about teaching, Sullivan and his colleagues conclude: "Certainly this suggests that although tolerance of communists and atheists has increased, the overall extent of tolerance may not have changed much at all" (Sullivan, Piereson, and Marcus, 1979, p. 788).

Sullivan and his colleagues may be overstating their case when they argue that tolerance has not increased much at all during the last two decades. Their case rests mainly on evidence that, as of 1976 and 1977–1978, tolerance is lower with their content-controlled questions than with the Stouffer questions about Communists and atheists. Although their content-controlled measure is quite interesting, it is difficult to attach much substantive meaning to the results. That most Americans would deny civil liberties to the group they like least may or may not pose a threat to civil liberties. As it happens, the targets of intolerance are widely diffused—a condition that Sullivan and his colleagues acknowledge prevents intolerance from threatening civil liberties at the present time.

Assuming that one can meaningfully compare levels of tolerance for specific groups with the content-controlled measures, Sullivan et al. tend to ignore differences in the wording of questions about least-liked groups from the wording of the Stouffer questions about Communists and atheists. In fact, of the six content-controlled questions, only two have any similarity with the Stouffer questions: those about making a speech and those about teaching.

For the freedom-of-speech question, there is actually no difference in the Twin Cities study between the percentage that would allow a Communist to speak and the percentage that would allow a member of their least-liked group to speak, although there are significant differences in the NORC study. The teaching questions are substantially different in their wording. Respondents are asked whether members of their least-liked group "should be allowed to teach in public schools," while they are asked whether a person who is against all churches and religion "should be allowed to teach in a college or university." As for "an admitted Communist," respondents are asked: "Suppose he is teaching in a college. Should he be fired, or not?" A "public school," I suspect, does not conjure up the image of a college or university, but of elementary schools, middle schools, and high schools. Some persons might think that a Communist should not be allowed to teach, but might feel that firing a college teacher is too drastic. I do not know whether such differences in wording have any effect,[7] but Sullivan shows that, in other contexts, seemingly minor differences in question wording can have a dramatic effect on the results (Sullivan and Minns, 1976; Sullivan, Piereson, and Marcus, 1978), so a little more caution here would be in order.

[7]In Sullivan's defense, it should be noted that, in 1954, respondents do not differ much as to whether a person "whose loyalty has been questioned" but who "swears under oath he has never been a Communist" should be fired from a college or a high school. In the Nunn, Crockett, and Williams survey, conducted in 1973, respondents are slightly more tolerant concerning teaching in a college than teaching in a high school (Table 14.1, questions 10 and 12).

If we assume that there is comparability between the content-controlled questions and the Stouffer items (or if we assume that differences of wording can only bias the Stouffer questions to *inflate* tolerance), the very data presented by Sullivan and his colleagues suggest that tolerance may have increased between the mid-1950s and the late 1970s. For example, in his 1954 survey, Stouffer finds that only 27% of his sample would allow a Communist to speak and only 37% would allow an atheist to speak (see Table 14.1). In 1976, 70% of the Twin Cities survey and, in 1978, 50% of the NORC sample would allow a member of their least-liked group to speak. In 1954, only 6% think a Communist should be allowed to teach in a college and only 12% think an atheist should be allowed to teach at a college or university (see Table 14.3). In 1976, 26% of the Twin Cities sample would allow a member of their least-liked group to teach in a public school and, in the 1978 NORC sample, 19% would. Of course, we do not know how many respondents in 1954 would have allowed a member of their least-liked group to speak or to teach. As Communists could hardly have been everyone's least-liked group, tolerance might have been even lower (although it's hard to get below a figure of 6% tolerant). It does appear that respondents were more likely to be tolerant of their least-liked group in the 1970s than they were toward Communists or atheists back in the mid-1950s.

Conclusions

Despite my reservations about their pessimistic conclusions, Sullivan and his colleagues provide us with a clear warning that we should not be complacent about levels of tolerance in America today. Their basic findings clearly show that Americans often express intolerant attitudes. Moreover, even if we look only at the Stouffer questions, we find that a considerable percentage of Americans express intolerant attitudes toward Communists, atheists, and socialists. And, as the continuing NORC General Social Surveys show (see Tables 14.1 and 14.3), tolerance toward Communists and atheists has not increased between the early 1970s and 1980, despite continuous generational replacement during that decade.

Sullivan and his colleagues also clearly remind us that we can document an increase in tolerance only toward left-of-center groups. We could be more confident about changes in tolerance if Stouffer had measured tolerance toward right-wing groups or toward deviant groups that do not clearly fit on a left–right continuum. The Sullivan method of measuring content-controlled tolerance may prove of considerable utility in the future. Additional analyses of the NORC General Social Surveys, which have also measured tolerance toward such groups as militarists and racists, may lead to greater insights. Moreover, we certainly need more studies that examine the conditions under which intolerance—including content-controlled intolerance—may contribute to intolerant political behavior.

The resurgent interest in tolerance may lead to more insight. Meanwhile, we should restrain our criticism of the Stouffer study and other pioneering efforts. Surely, they can be criticized, but they have established a baseline against which we can have at least some understanding of the way feelings of tolerance change over time. Moreover, they have helped greatly to advance the basic arguments that make more penetrating analyses of tolerance possible.

[CHAPTER 15]

Change or Continuity in Conceptual Levels, Issue Consistency, Attitude Stability, and Issue Voting

Many scholars have argued that Americans are more ideological today than they were two decades ago, that they have a more structured view of political issues, and that issues have become more important in determining how they vote. Such changes, if they are real, would have major implications for political behavior. But we face major methodological problems in assessing whether real change has occurred, because in some cases the questions used to measure these attitudes have been changed and because differing analytical techniques have been used to study these attitudes. While some real change has probably occurred, the extent of these changes may well be exaggerated.

Scholars who claim that there has been change are responding mainly to the portrait of the electorate presented by Campbell and his colleagues in *The American Voter* (1960) and by Converse in "The Nature of Belief Systems in Mass Publics" (1964). Since the authors provide the starting point for this research, we again turn to them for their basic formulation.

The American Voter View and Converse Extension

Conceptual levels

Campbell and his colleagues conclude that the American electorate has low levels of ideological conceptualization, does not coherently relate issues to each other, and seldom votes on the basis of the issues. Campbell and his colleagues use eight open-ended questions to measure the way Americans think about politics:

1. Is there anything in particular that you *like* about the Democratic party? [If yes:] What is that? Anything else?

2. Is there anything in particular that you *don't like* about the Democratic party? . . .

3. Is there anything in particular that you *like* about the Republican party? . . .

4. Is there anything in particular that you *don't like* about the Republican party? . . .

5. Is there anything in particular about Stevenson that might make you want to vote *for* him? . . .

6. Is there anything in particular about Stevenson that might make you want to vote *against* him? . . .

7. Is there anything in particular about Eisenhower that might make you want to vote *for* him? . . .

8. Is there anything in particular about Eisenhower that might make you want to vote *against* him? . . .

This battery of questions has been used in every presidential election from 1952 on, with the names of the candidates changed to that of the Democratic and Republican standard-bearers. These questions provide respondents with considerable opportunity to both articulate their political views and use the standard phrases of ideological discourse, such as "liberal," "conservative," "middle-of-the-road," and the like. But only a handful of respondents use such terms. By carefully examining the verbatim responses to these questions as of 1956, Campbell and his colleagues classify the electorate into four basic ideological levels (Campbell et al., 1960, pp. 222–250).

At the highest level (Level A), respondents are called "ideologues" or "near-ideologues." Ideologues respond to these questions with comments that "imply the kinds of conception of politics assumed by ideological interpretations of political behavior and political change" (p. 227). Near-ideologues do not directly use ideological concepts, but employ "concepts of some ideological flavor" (p. 227). Only 3% of the electorate is classified as ideologues (Level A.I), while 10% is classified as near-ideologues (Level A.II).[1]

Some respondents do not use ideological or near-ideological concepts, but view parties and candidates in terms of group benefits. They might like the Democrats for helping "the farmer" or dislike Republicans for aiding "big business." Respondents who see politics in terms of conflicting groups ("perceptions of conflict") make up 15% of the sample, while those who see politics in terms of benefits for a single group make up 18%. Both these groups are classified at Level B.1. Other respondents mention group interests, but provide "low calibre" responses that suggest they are merely repeating slogans and have little knowledge about what they are saying. These respondents are clas-

[1]These percentages are based on all respondents who are classified, and exclude the 4.5% of the electorate who are not classified according to their level of conceptualization.

sified as having a "shallow" perception of group interests (Level B.II) and make up 11% of the sample.

A third group (Level C) express their likes or dislikes according to the "goodness" and "badness" of the times. They simply associate the incumbent administration with war or peace, recession or prosperity. They do not use ideological phrases, nor do they reflect perceptions of group interests. They are not classified in the lowest ideological category because they provide "some reference, however nebulous or fragmentary, to a subject of controversy over public policy" (p. 240). About 25% of the electorate falls into this general category.

Level D represents "absence of issue content." These respondents do not comment on any policy issues and, to the extent that they have any perceptions of the parties, they are "bound up in moralistic themes like mudslinging and chicanery. More often parties are poorly discriminated, and comment is devoted almost entirely to the personal characteristics of the candidates—their popularity, their sincerity, their religious practice, or home life" (p. 244). The remaining 18% of the electorate is classified at Level D.

Campbell and his colleagues provide lengthy verbatim responses that give a good flavor of just what each category includes (see pp. 227–249). It seems fair to say that they are generous in scoring respondents into as high a level of conceptualization as possible. After carefully examining the responses to these open-ended questions, Campbell et al. conclude: "This profile of an electorate is not calculated to increase our confidence in interpretations of elections that presume widespread ideological concerns in the adult population" (p. 249). Rather, "the concepts important to ideological analysis are useful only for that small segment of the population that is equipped to approach political decisions at a rarefied level" (p. 250).

Issue consistency

Perhaps it is unreasonable to judge the electorate according to its ability to use ideological concepts. Ideological terms are not part of the day-to-day discourse of most citizens, nor is the average citizen often called upon to express his or her reasons for liking a particular party or candidate. But Campbell and his colleagues also use responses to closed-ended questions to determine whether voters have structured political views. This approach might identify respondents who do think about politics in a structured way, but who do not use ideological terms in responding to open-ended questions.

By examining the pattern of responses to ten domestic political issues and six foreign policy issues, Campbell et al. conclude that "the data evince a rather slight degree of structure in the attitudes of the mass electorate" (p. 195). Four years later, Converse advanced a major extension of the argument that used two new data sources. In 1958, the SRC conducted a survey not only of the American electorate, but also of congressional candidates. In addition, during 1956, 1958, and 1960, the SRC conducted a panel survey in which the same respondents were interviewed over time. (We use these panel data in Chapters 7 and 10.) As with *The American Voter* analysis of attitude structure, Converse focuses on a set of closed-ended questions. As they have become crucial for a major debate over the attitude structure of the American electorate, the most important of these questions are reproduced in column 1 of Table 15.1, where we also see the distribution of responses for 1956, 1958, and 1960.

A major goal of Converse's analysis is to compare the attitude structure of the mass electorate with that of congressional candidates. Just what would a "structured" set of responses look like? One can begin simply by reading the questions used to measure policy preferences among the electorate. Presumably, a voter who thinks the government should see to it that people find jobs might also favor the government's helping people obtain low hospital costs, might favor federal aid to education, and might not prefer that electrical power be left for private business to handle. One might expect persons who favor government involvement in the economy to be more likely to favor government aid to blacks in finding jobs and housing. And one might expect that persons who are for an active federal government might be more in favor of government involvement overseas. In fact, among the American electorate in 1958, there are few strong relationships on these various issues, and in many cases the relationships are negligible.

When correlations between opinions on different issues are high, Converse argues that there is a high level of "constraint" in the belief systems of individuals. Opinions on issues would then be constrained by opinions on related issues. Given that opinions on these issues are only weakly related to each other, constraint among the electorate is low. For the congressional candidates, there is a substantially higher level of constraint, especially for domestic issues, and thus Converse demonstrates that, among a highly politicized sample, levels of constraint could be substantial. It is important to note, however, that the questions used to measure policy preferences among congressional candidates are different from those used to measure preferences among the electorate.

Given the way differing item construction can affect constraint, we should be cautious about Converse's comparison of the electorate with the candidates. Still, it seems reasonable that a highly politicized sample would answer these questions in a more structured way than would the electorate as a whole. And while relying on closed-ended questions has limitations, especially when compared with the rich analysis that is possible when verbatim responses are studied, Converse is able to demonstrate that the low ideological level of most Americans is probably not just a result of their inability to articulate their political views.

Table 15.1 Distribution of Responses on Public Policy Issues, with Three Types of Question Formats: 1956–1980

Part A Economic Welfare

Likert

"The government in Washington ought to see to it that everybody who wants to work can find a job. Now would you have an opinion on this or not?" [If respondent has an opinion:] "Do you think the government *should* do this?"

	1956	1958	1960
Agree strongly	48.0%	49.0%	52.4%
Agree, but not very strongly	14.7	14.0	12.6
Not sure; depends	7.6	7.8	8.9
Disagree, but not very strongly	11.5	10.6	8.2
Disagree strongly	18.1	18.7	17.9
Total %	99.9%	100.1%	100.0%
Total *N*	(1587)	(1624)[a]	(1737)[a]

Forced-choice

"In general some people feel that the government in Washington should see to it that every person has a job and a good standard of living. Others think the government should just let each person get ahead on his own. Have you been interested enough in this to favor one side over the other?" [If yes:] "Do you think that the government should see to it that every person has a job and a good standard of living *or* should it let each person get ahead on his own?"

	1964	1968
Government should see to it that every person has a job and a good standard of living	36.4%	35.1%
Other, depends	13.0	12.3
Government should let each person get ahead on his own	50.6	52.6
Total %	100.0%	100.0%
Total *N*	(1338)	(1386)

Seven-point scale

"Some people feel that the government in Washington should see to it that every person has a job and a good standard of living. Others think the government should just let each person get ahead on his own. And, of course, other people have opinions somewhere in between." [Card handed to respondent:] Suppose people who believe that the government should see to it that every person has a job and a good standard of living are at one end of this scale—at point number 1. And suppose that the people who believe that the government should let each person get ahead on his own are at the other end—at point number 7. Where would you place yourself on this scale, or haven't you thought much about this?"

	1972	1974*	1976*	1978*	1980*
1 (Government see to job)	14.8%	14.3%	14.0%	8.6%	11.5%
2	6.4	5.6	6.3	4.0	8.1
3	10.3	10.3	9.7	9.0	10.9
4	23.2	24.6	21.7	23.9	20.9
5	14.5	14.8	12.9	18.6	15.9
6	9.3	10.2	13.2	14.8	18.8
7 (Each person on his own)	21.5	20.2	22.1	21.2	13.8
Total %	100.0%	100.0%	99.9%	100.1%	99.9%
Total *N*	(2131)	(2058)[a]	(2272)[a]	(1820)	(1179)

*Reworded to read: "Some people feel that the government in Washington should see to it that every person has a job and a good standard of living. Suppose that these people are at one end of this scale—at point number 1. Others. . ."

Part B Medical Welfare

Likert

"The government ought to help people get doctors and hospital care at low cost. Do you have an opinion on this or not?" [If respondent has an opinion:] "Do you think the government *should* do this?"

	1956	1960
Agree strongly	43.6%	54.1%
Agree, but not very strongly	17.5	11.8
Not sure; depends	9.5	12.6
Disagree, but not very strongly	8.9	6.0
Disagree strongly	20.6	15.6
Total %	100.1%	100.1%
Total *N*	(1554)	(1752)[a]

Forced-choice

"Some say the government in Washington ought to help people get doctors and hospital care at low cost; others say the government should not get into this. Have you been interested enough in this to favor one side over the other?" [If yes:] "What is your position? Should the government in Washington help people get doctors and hospital care at low cost *or* stay out of this?"

	1964	1968
Government should help people get doctors and hospital care at low cost	59.3%	61.7%
Other, depends	7.3	6.7
Government should stay out of this	33.4	31.7
Total %	100.0%	100.1%
Total *N*	(1312)	(1308)

Seven-point scale

"There is much concern about the rapid rise in medical care and hospital costs. Some feel there should be a government insurance plan which would cover all medical and hospital expenses. Others feel that medical expenses should be paid by individuals, and through private insurance like Blue Cross." [Card handed to respondent:] "Where would you place yourself on this scale, or haven't you thought much about this?"

	1970	1972	1976	1978
1 (Government insurance plan)	28.7%	30.8%	27.7%	28.5%
2	8.7	7.2	9.3	9.0
3	7.8	7.6	7.3	7.7
4	14.8	14.4	12.3	13.1
5	6.3	6.6	8.5	9.1
6	9.5	5.8	9.7	10.3
7 (Private insurance plan)	24.2	27.7	25.3	22.4
Total %	100.0%	100.1%	100.1%	100.1%
Total *N*	(1284)	(1112)	(2248)[a]	(1884)

[a] Weighted *N*s.

Source: Based on codebooks provided by Inter-University Consortium for Political and Social Research.

(continued)

Table 15-1 (continued)

Part C Welfare for Blacks

Likert

"If Negroes are not getting fair treatment in jobs and housing, the government should see to it that they do. Do you have an opinion on this or not?" [If respondent has an opinion:] "Do you think the government *should* do this?"

	1956	1958	1960
Agree strongly	49.3%	54.1%	51.8%
Agree, but not very strongly	21.0	18.4	19.7
Not sure; depends	7.5	6.7	8.2
Disagree, but not very strongly	7.5	6.3	5.3
Disagree strongly	14.7	14.5	15.0
Total %	100.0%	100.0%	100.0%
Total *N*	(1522)	(1590)[a]	(1717)[a]

Forced-choice

"Some people feel that if Negroes (colored people) are not getting fair treatment in jobs, the government in Washington ought to see to it that they do. Others feel this is not the federal government's business. Have you had enough interest in this question to favor one side over the other?" [If yes:] "How do you feel? Should the government in Washington: see to it that Negroes get fair treatment in jobs *or* leave these matters to the states and local communities?"

	1964	1968	1972*
Government should see to it that Negroes (colored people) get fair treatment in jobs	45.2%	43.8%	50.2%
Other, depends	8.5	7.3	7.2
Leave these matters to the states and local communities	46.3	48.9	42.6
Total %	100.0%	100.0%	100.0%
Total *N*	(1352)	(1355)	(2235)

*"Negroes" changed to "black people."

Seven-point scale

[Although seven-point scale questions were used from 1970 on to measure attitudes toward blacks and minority groups, these questions were not used to measure changing levels of issue consistency.]

Part D Federal Aid to Schools

Likert

"If cities and towns around the country need help to build more schools, the government in Washington ought to give them the money they need. Do you have an opinion on this or not?" [If respondent has an opinion:] "Do you think the government *should* do this?"

	1956	1958	1960
Agree strongly	52.6%	50.7%	43.0%
Agree, but not very strongly	21.7	19.1	17.7
Not sure; depends	9.4	7.2	11.7
Disagree, but not very strongly	5.8	7.9	8.7
Disagree strongly	10.7	15.1	19.0
Total %	100.0%	100.0%	100.1%
Total *N*	(1593)	(1637)[a]	(1704)[a]

Forced-choice

"Some people think the government in Washington should help towns and cities provide education for grade and high school children; others think that this should be handled by the states and local communities. Have you been interested enough in this to favor one side over the other?" [If yes:] "Which are you in favor of: getting help from the government in Washington *or* handling it at the state and local level?"

	1964	1968
Getting help from government in Washington	38.0%	34.8%
Other; depends	5.7	5.4
Handling it at the state and local level	56.3	59.8
Total %	100.0%	100.0%
Total *N*	(1289)	(1258)

Seven-point scale

[No seven-point scale was introduced to replace the forced-choice questions. The forced-choice question was not used after 1968.]

(continued)

Table 15-1 (continued)

Part E Cold War

Likert

"The United States should keep soldiers overseas where they can help countries that are against communism. Do you have an opinion on this or not? [If respondent has an opinion:] "Do you think the government *should* do this?"

	1956	1958	1960
Agree strongly	49.0%	54.5%	63.3%
Agree, but not very strongly	23.7	24.5	17.4
Not sure; depends	11.1	7.9	7.1
Disagree, but not very strongly	6.5	4.8	3.8
Disagree strongly	9.8	8.4	8.4
Total %	100.1%	100.1%	100.0%
Total *N*	(1405)	(1472)[a]	(1613)[a]

Forced-choice

"Some people think our government should sit down and talk to the leaders of the communist countries and try to settle our differences, while others think we should refuse to have anything to do with them. Have you been interested enough in this to favor one side over the other?" [If yes:] "What do you think? Should we: try to discuss our differences *or* refuse to have anything to do with the leaders of communist countries?"

	1964	1968*
Try to discuss and settle our differences	84.3%	89.6%
Other, depends	4.3	1.1
Refuse to have anything to do with the leaders of communist countries	11.4	9.3
Total %	100.0%	100.0%
Total *N*	(1334)	(1355)

*The question began: "Some people think it is all right for our government to sit . . ."

Seven-point scale

[With regard to Vietnam:] "Some people think we should do everything necessary to win a complete military victory, no matter what results. Some people think we should withdraw completely from Vietnam right now, no matter what results. And, of course, other people have opinions somewhere between these two extreme positions." [Card handed to respondent:] "Suppose the people who support an immediate withdrawal are at one end of this scale—at point number 1. And suppose the people who support a complete military victory are at the other end of the scale—at point number 7. Where would you place yourself on this scale, or haven't you thought much about this?"

	1968	1970	1972
1 (Immediate withdrawal)	13.8%	21.5%	21.2%
2	8.5	8.1	9.8
3	8.1	10.8	13.6
4	30.0	24.4	25.0
5	10.7	9.1	12.1
6	9.2	6.5	6.3
7 (Complete military victory)	19.7	19.6	12.1
Total %	100.0%	100.0%	100.0%
Total *N*	(1242)	(1453)	(2278)

Part F Size of Government

Likert

"The government should leave things like electric power and housing for private businessmen to handle. Do you have an opinion on this or not?" [If respondent has an opinion:] "Do you think the government *should* leave things like this to private business?"

	1956	1958	1960
Agree strongly	43.0%	42.9%	47.2%
Agree, but not very strongly	15.5	16.9	15.9
Not sure; depends	9.6	8.6	7.7
Disagree, but not very strongly	10.6	11.1	9.3
Disagree strongly	21.3	20.4	19.9
Total %	100.0%	99.9%	100.0%
Total *N*	(1249)	(1323)[a]	(1476)[a]

Forced-choice

"Some people are afraid that the government in Washington is getting too powerful for the good of the country and the individual person. Others feel that the government in Washington has not gotten too strong for the good of the country. Have you been interested enough in this to favor one side over the other?" [If yes:] "What is your feeling? Do you think the government is getting too powerful *or* do you think the government has not gotten too strong?"

	1964	1966	1968*	1970	1972*	1976*	1978*	1980*
Government is getting too powerful	43.6%	55.9%	55.2%	44.2%	57.5%	68.8%	73.8%	74.1
Other, depends	4.5	5.2	3.6	8.3	5.1	3.9	2.7	2.8
Government has not gotten too strong	51.8	38.9	41.2	47.5	37.4	27.3	23.5	23.0
Total %	99.9%	100.0%	100.0%	100.0%	100.0%	100.0%	100.0%	99.9%
Total *N*	(1084)	(889)	(1138)	(1051)	(948)	(2046)[a]	(1328)	(920)

*"Has not gotten too strong" changed to "is not getting too strong."

Seven-point scale

[No seven-point scale was introduced to measure attitudes toward government size, but the forced-choice question introduced in 1964 was continued.]

(continued)

Table 15-1 (continued)

Part G School Integration

Likert

"The government in Washington should stay out of the question of whether white and colored children go to the same school. Do you have an opinion on this or not?" [If respondent has an opinion:] "Do you think the government should stay out of this question?"

	1956	1958	1960
Agree strongly	39.7%	39.8%	37.6%
Agree, but not very strongly	9.3	9.2	7.1
Not sure; depends	7.1	5.8	7.7
Disagree, but not very strongly	10.5	7.6	9.3
Disagree strongly	33.4	37.7	38.3
Total %	100.0%	100.1%	100.0%
Total *N*	(1550)	(1625)[a]	(1672)[a]

Forced-choice

"Some people say that the government in Washington should see to it that white and Negro (colored) children are allowed to go to the same schools. Others claim that this is not the government's business. Have you been concerned enough about this question to favor one side over the other?" [If yes:] "Do you think that the government in Washington should: see to it that white and Negro children go to the same school *or* stay out of this area as it is none of its business?"

Seven-point scale

[Although a seven-point scale question measuring attitudes toward school busing was used in 1972, 1974, and 1976, this question was not used to measure changing levels of issue consistency.]

	1964	1966	1968	1970	1972*	1976*	1978*
See to it that white and Negro (colored) children go to the same schools	47.5%	52.8%	43.1%	51.2%	41.9%	33.6%	34.7
Other, depends	8.3	8.5	7.5	11.0	7.7	11.5	13.3
Stay out of this area as it is none of its business	44.2	38.6	49.5	37.8	50.5	54.8	52.0
Total %	100.0%	99.9%	100.1%	100.0%	100.1%	99.9%	100.0%
Total *N*	(1362)	(1124)	(1377)	(780)	(2377)	(2052)[a]	(1777)

*"Negro children" changed to "black children."

Attitude stability

Converse also employs panel data to support his argument. Although he has no panel data for congressional candidates, he argues that the overt behavior of congressmen, such as their votes on congressional roll calls, would almost certainly show them to have fairly stable opinions over time. Among the electorate, however, there is fairly low over-time stability for most political attitudes. Comparing overall stability of political attitudes between 1958 and 1960, Converse argues that only party identification is highly stable, showing a tau-b of .72. For our own estimates of over-time stability during this period, see Chapter 7. Opinions about school integration correlate at .48 between 1958 and 1960, while opinions about government help for jobs, isolationism, and federal aid to education range from .42 down to .36. Opinions about foreign economic and military aid are less stable (about .32), and opinions about federal housing policy show an over-time stability of only .28.

Converse argues that these low over-time correlations demonstrate that, for most of the electorate, opinions "are extremely labile for individuals over time" (p. 241). Moreover, Converse uncovers another interesting relationship. One could predict opinions held in 1960 just as well from opinions measured in 1956 as from opinions measured in 1958. Converse states that "there is no single meaningful process of change shared by all respondents that would generate this configuration of the data" (p. 242). He argues that there probably is a small subset of the electorate that does have stable opinions over time and a much larger subset that responds to issue questions in a largely random way.

Converse recognizes that the low level of over-time stability could result from poor attitude measurement, but maintains that it probably results from the lack of coherent attitudes on the part of most Americans. First, there is a small subset of the electorate that does have stable responses over time. Moreover, respondents who express concern about an issue in an open-ended portion of the interview have substantially more stable responses to closed-ended questions about that issue than do respondents who have not expressed concern. Converse therefore rejects the thesis that low measurement reliability accounts for his results, arguing instead that "large portions of an electorate do not have meaningful beliefs, even on issues that have formed the basis for intense political controversy among elites for substantial periods of time" (p. 245).

Issue voting

Even if voters do not have structured political views, they might be able to translate their issue preferences into an electoral choice by choosing the party and candidate whose policy preferences more closely fit their own. But Campbell and his colleagues argue that, for most voters, issue preferences are not important for making voting choices. They reason that, for a voter to translate his or her preferences into a vote, the voter must fulfill three basic conditions. First, the voter must have an opinion on the issue. Second, he or she must know what the government is doing about the given policy. Third, the voter must perceive differences between the policies of the major parties. In fact, few voters meet all three of these conditions. For domestic policy issues, the percentage that fulfills all three conditions ranges from a high of 35% to a low of 22%; and for the foreign policy issues, from a high of 36% to a low of 18%.

Even those respondents who meet the three basic conditions would not necessarily use their issue preferences as a guide for deciding how to vote. Rather, Campbell and his colleagues claim, "they represent no more than a maximum pool within which the specified issue might have conceivable effect." Campbell et al. conclude: "It seems, then, that the sequence of events that must intervene before bitter partisan controversy dramatized in the press becomes significant for the political response of the man-in-the-street is both lengthy and fallible. Many people fail to appreciate that an issue exists, others are insufficiently involved to pay attention to recognized issues, and still others fail to make connections between issue positions and party policy" (p. 183).

The American Voter View and Converse Extension Reevaluated

A quarter of a century has elapsed since *The American Voter* data were collected, and even the most recent data used by Converse in his "Belief Systems" article are now more than two decades old. To what extent do new data and analyses force us to reevaluate their arguments? Are their findings time-bound, the result of the fairly quiescent period when the data were collected? Are their conclusions correct, even for the period they were studying?

We focus mainly on the question of change and examine the claims of scholars who argue that major change has occurred. We show that in some cases there has been change, while in other cases relatively little has occurred. We also show that in some cases we are unable to demonstrate whether or not any actual change has occurred, because modifications in measurement confound our ability to study change.

Conceptual levels

Campbell and his colleagues recognize that they analyze conceptual levels only for surveys conducted during the single election campaign of 1956 and that their results might partly be a product of the times. After all, "there are periods in which the heat of partisan debate slackens and becomes almost perfunctory, and the positions of the parties become relatively indistinct on basic issues. In times such as these, even the person sensitive to a range of political philosophies may not feel this knowledge to be helpful in an evaluation of current policy, and hence may fail to receive proper assignment in a level of conceptualization" (p. 256). But Campbell and his colleagues argue that the main reason for the low levels of conceptualization is to be found in the cognitive limitations of the electorate. Although levels of conceptualization might vary with events, "we would never expect this change to be of sweeping magnitude, and there is still less reason to believe that the picture of the voting public presented previously was captured at an abnormal moment" (p. 256).

At least five subsequent studies have found substantial increases in levels of conceptualization, but two of these are not comparable to the analyses presented in *The American Voter.* Campbell and his colleagues rely on a careful examination of the verbatim responses to the eight basic questions about political parties and presidential candidates, while two of the later studies rely on the analyses of the coded results. Whether the coded responses can be used to reconstruct the levels-of-conceptualization measure is questionable, and students who have used this procedure have always found a substantially higher percentage of ideologues than have analysts who studied the verbatim responses to these eight open-ended questions.

One study by Field and Anderson (1969) analyzes coded results to compare levels of ideology in 1956, 1960, and 1964. Their estimates of the combined percentage of ideologues and near-ideologues are displayed as the broken line in Figure 15.1. The relatively high level of ideology reached in 1964 could have resulted from Goldwater's presidential candidacy, since he made explicitly ideological appeals designed to provide the voter with "a choice, not an echo." The Field and Anderson study is the first to demonstrate that conceptual

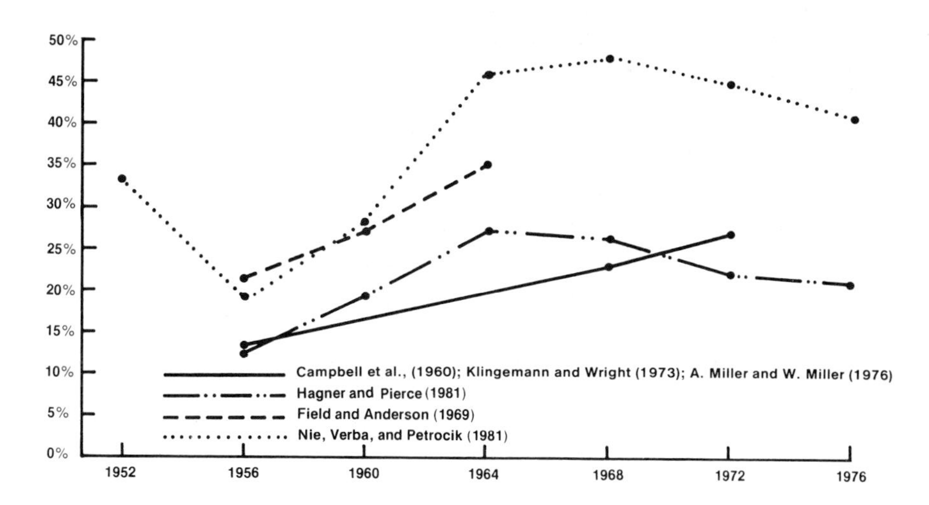

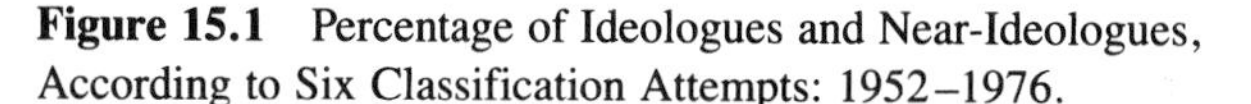

Figure 15.1 Percentage of Ideologues and Near-Ideologues, According to Six Classification Attempts: 1952–1976.

[*Source:* Based on results reported in Campbell et al. (1960), Field and Anderson (1969), Hagner and Pierce (1981), Klingemann and Wright (1973), A. Miller and W. Miller (1976), Nie, Verba, and Petrocik (1981).]

levels could rise, but it also demonstrates that these levels are not high even during an explicitly ideological campaign. Therefore, Field and Anderson conclude, there is some support for Campbell's "cognitive limitations" thesis.

Nie, Verba, and Petrocik, in *The Changing American Voter* (1976), provide the most comprehensive attempt to measure changing levels of conceptualization, for they examine all six presidential elections from 1952 through 1972 and have now studied the 1976 election as well. Like Field and Anderson, they work with the coded version of the data. Their basic results are presented as the dotted line in Figure 15.1.[2]

Nie, Verba, and Petrocik's most important finding is that levels of ideological thinking jumped sharply in 1964, although they have remained fairly stable since then. Nie and his colleagues claim that "the data on levels of conceptualization do support the hypothesis that the way in which citizens conceptualize the political realm is dependent on the political content to which they are exposed" (p. 121). But they also explore the possibility that rising conceptual levels might result from increasing educational levels of the electorate. Levels of conceptualization have risen among all educational groups. My own recalculations, based on data presented by Nie and his colleagues, show that, if educational levels in 1972 had been the same as those in 1956, only 30% of the electorate would have been ideologues, whereas in fact 33% were. Clearly, only a small percentage of the increase in ideological thinking results from the educational upgrading of the electorate. As increasing educational levels among the electorate are almost solely the result of generational replacement (see Chapter 4), it seems reasonable to conclude that the increasing ideological sophistication of the electorate results only in small part from replacement processes.

By dismissing the possibility that increases in levels of conceptualization result from increases in education, Nie and his colleagues are able to strengthen their political interpretation. However, Nie et al. argue that the data also demonstrate the cognitive limitations of the electorate, especially at lower levels of conceptualization. Thus, they write: "Our conclusions must be a middle-of-the-road-one: there has been substantial change in the way the public conceptualizes politics, yet there is evidence for inertia as well" (p. 122).

The analyses by Field and Anderson and by Nie, Verba, and Petrocik are not comparable with those reported in *The American Voter.* But three other analyses have turned to the verbatim responses to the party and candidate questions, and all three suggest that levels of conceptualization have increased. The first of these studies is by Pierce (1970), who has now extended his

[2]The first edition of *The Changing American Voter* contains some minor errors in the basic figures presenting levels of conceptualization. Apparently, in correcting these errors, Nie and his colleagues report drastically incorrect results in the second edition of their book. In a recent communication to the *American Political Science Review* (1981), they report the corrected version of their data, including results for 1976.

analyses to all the presidential surveys conducted between 1956 and 1976 (Hagner and Pierce, 1981). The broken and dotted line in Figure 15.1 represents the combined percentage of ideologues and near-ideologues during all six surveys. The Hagner and Pierce analysis shows that the percentage of ideologues rose between 1960 and 1964, which they attribute to Goldwater's candidacy.

Klingemann and Wright (1973) have presented the most detailed replication of *The American Voter* analyses, although their replication is restricted to 1968. Their analysis shows an increase in ideological levels among the electorate, with 6% rising to Level A.1 (ideologues) and 17% to Level A.II (near-ideologues). The "group-benefit category" declines, but there is little change in the percentage at lower levels of ideology.

Lastly, Arthur Miller and Warren Miller (one of the authors of *The American Voter*) use similar techniques to measure levels of conceptualization in the 1972 CPS survey. According to Miller and Miller, 7% could be classified as ideologues, while 20% are near-ideologues. Miller and Miller do not attempt to classify the electorate into the lower levels of conceptualization, labeling all the remaining respondents as "non-ideologues" (A. Miller and W. Miller, 1976, p. 844). The total percentage classified as ideological or near-ideological by Campbell et al., Klingemann and Wright, and Miller and Miller is represented by the solid line in Figure 15.1.

Converse (1975), who presents and interprets the Klingemann and Wright results, acknowledges that there has been some increase in levels of conceptualization, which he sees as consistent with the rising educational levels among the electorate and "the galvanizing crises of the 1960s" (p. 103). However, as he notes, "all of this limited change turns out to be concentrated within the more sophisticated half of the electorate: the lower half appears to have moved not at all!" Converse's observation would also apply to the more recent results presented by Hagner and Pierce.

The entire thesis of cognitive limitations that prevent the electorate from attaining higher ideological levels is challenged by Eric Smith's (1980) analysis of the 1956–1960 panel data (see also E. Smith, 1981). Smith uses the coded version of the data to replicate both the Field and Anderson and the Nie et al. measures of levels of conceptualization and finds that, with both measures, individual-level over-time stability is low (a tau-b of .24 with the Field and Anderson measure and .31 with the Nie et al. measure). In addition, changing levels of conceptualization are not systematically related to changes in political interest, attention, or activity—a finding, Smith argues, that calls into question the validity of these measures. According to Smith, these procedures do not actually measure the way people think about politics, but only the level of ideological rhetoric among the electorate. However, we should recognize that Smith worked only with the coded version of the data, and we cannot use his results to judge directly the reliability or the validity of measures of conceptualization that use the verbatim responses to these questions. (For a further discussion of problems with Smith's interpretation, see Abramson, 1981.)

Have levels of conceptualization changed? This is a difficult question to answer, because detailed analyses of the verbatim responses to the party and candidate questions have been presented for only two elections: 1956 and 1968. However, as the results summarized in Figure 15.1 show, all students of levels of conceptualization have found some increase in ideological sophistication since 1956. But these results also suggest that the percentage of ideologues has leveled off, and perhaps even declined, since 1964. On balance, we must conclude that there has been an increase in the ideological sophistication of the electorate (or, if Smith is correct, in the use of ideological rhetoric), but that this increase has not been dramatic.

Issue consistency

Until 1974, Converse's thesis that low issue consistency (or "attitude constraint") prevails among the American electorate was widely accepted by political scientists. Then, a series of studies by Nie and his colleagues challenged this thesis by examining the way issue preferences relate to each other in more recent surveys. The basic questions employed by Nie and his collaborators are presented in Table 15.1. Analyzing the SRC data for 1956, 1958, 1960, 1964, 1968, and 1972, as well as the National Opinion Research Center (NORC) surveys conducted in 1971, Nie concludes that levels of issue consistency rose markedly between 1960 and 1964. Moreover, levels of issue consistency remained high through 1973, although, as subsequent studies have shown (Nie, Verba, and Petrocik, 1979, p. 369; Petrocik, 1980, pp. 261–263), they declined somewhat in 1976.

Nie and his colleagues argue that the increase in issue consistency after 1960 demonstrates that the public could respond to political events. When the parties field a more ideological candidate and when issues are presented more clearly by political elites, the public reacts by thinking more coherently about political issues. Nie adds to the plausibility of his argument by examining changes in issue consistency among respondents at higher and lower educational levels. While respondents with at least some college education always have higher levels of issue consistency than those who have not completed high school, these differences are small. Moreover, between 1960 and 1964, levels of issue consistency increased among respondents with higher and lower levels of education. One could infer from these results that overall increases in issue consistency do not result from generational replacement, but this is documented more clearly by examining a time-series cohort analysis conducted by Kirkpatrick.

Kirkpatrick (1976) focuses on attitude constraint for social-welfare issues and shows that there is a tendency for older respondents to have higher attitude constraint than younger respondents have. Consequently, it follows that generational replacement should reduce overall levels of constraint, whereas, as his analysis shows, constraint actually increases. My own calculations, based on the data presented by Kirkpatrick, suggest that, if no generational replacement had occurred between 1956 and 1968, constraint would have increased slightly less than it actually did. Kirkpatrick, like Nie and his colleagues, attributes the increase in constraint mainly to political events.

The findings on issue consistency, especially as reported by Nie and Andersen (1974), had a major impact among political scientists. Prominent scholars, such as Pomper (1975), Converse (1975), and Miller (W. Miller and Levitin, 1976), accepted Nie's conclusion and saw the increase in issue consistency as a major change in the attitude structure of the American electorate.

However, as Nie himself notes, the greatest increase in the intercorrelation of responses to these issue questions corresponds with a change in their wording. Nie argues that the questions used before, during, and after 1964, are "with minor variation in wording and coding, identical" (Nie with Andersen, 1974, p. 546), and he presents a detailed footnote to explain why changes in question wording are unlikely to account for the rise in issue consistency. (Kirkpatrick ignores the problem of wording change, relegating it to an eight-word footnote.) But when the questions are actually laid out side by side and especially when the distributions of the responses to these questions are compared, the differences between the older version of these questions and newer versions often seem quite substantial (see Table 15.1).[3]

As the data in Table 15.1 reveal, responses to these differences in wording are often quite dramatic. In responding to the 1956–1960 version of the economic-welfare question, nearly two-thirds of the electorate give the liberal response, agreeing that the government should see to it that anyone who wants work can find a job, and half agree strongly with this position. But when the question was reworded in 1964 and 1968, half the respondents think that the government "should let each person get ahead on his own." Responding to a seven-point issue scale, used from 1972 through 1980, more respondents side with the conservative position on this issue than with the liberal position. A similar shift of the electorate from a liberal to a conservative position is found in attitudes toward federal aid to education; and, in questions about welfare for blacks, the electorate shifts from a heavily liberal position to a far more evenly divided distribution of opinions. Of course, such shifts could represent real attitude change among the electorate. It is also possible that a shift in the distribution of opinions would not affect the intercorrelations of responses to the various issue positions. Still, these very dramatic shifts in responses should have made political scientists quite cautious in accepting Nie's conclusions.

[3]The idea for presenting the items in this manner came from the presentation of these questions in the May 1978 issue of the *American Journal of Political Science*.

Several studies now demonstrate that the increases in issue consistency may be largely a function of changes in the questions used to measure these attitudes. Several studies have used a split questionnaire method, in which some respondents are asked the older, Likert version of the issue questions, whereas other respondents are asked newer versions. Analyses of a 1973 NORC survey of the electorate by Bishop and his colleagues show that, when the older version of the questions is used, respondents have the same levels of issue consistency as Americans had back in the 1950s (Bishop, Oldendick, and Tuchfarber, 1978; Bishop, Oldendick, Tuchfarber, and Bennett, 1978). An extremely well-crafted and imaginative analysis by Sullivan, Piereson, and Marcus (1978) uses a probability sample of adults in Minneapolis and St. Paul to reach similar conclusions. Several studies of university students also suggest that changes in item wording may greatly affect levels of issue consistency (Brunk, 1978; Petrocik, 1978).

Apparently, the forced-choice questions are more reliable than the Likert questions. Correlations tend to be higher when more reliable questions are used, and, simply as a result of increased reliability, issue consistency is greater when forced-choice questions are employed.

Faced with these analyses, Nie has retreated from his original position. His main defense is the questionable assertion that the pre-1964 questions now yield such skewed distributions that they can no longer be used to measure issue consistency among the American electorate. Whether the skewed distribution precludes estimates of issue consistency involves methodological arguments that need not detain us. The fact remains that the pre-1964 questions are the only items that can be used to compare levels of constraint among Americans today with levels in the 1950s. Given that representative samples of the 1973 electorate, when asked these questions, yield the same levels of constraint that obtained in the 1950s, it would be perfectly reasonable to conclude that no change had occurred. One of *The Changing American Voter* authors now concedes that at least part of the observed change results from changes in measurement (Petrocik, 1978, 1980), and Nie maintains that the SRC–CPS items cannot be used to demonstrate whether or not change occurred (Nie and Rabjohn, 1979, p. 149).

More recently, Nie, Verba, and Petrocik (1979) point to the *decline* in issue consistency in 1976 as support for their position. They argue that the centrist position taken by Carter and Ford, as well as the absence of ideological appeals, should have contributed to a decline in issue consistency. They maintain that there was no change in question wording between 1972 and 1976 and that the decline in issue consistency cannot have resulted from methodological artifacts. "Our substantive explanation," they state, "accounts for the increase and decline in the correlations. The methodological argument explains the increase, but it does not have any provision for the downward trend of 1976" (p. 370). Nie and his colleagues now argue that the electorate responds to the political situation and that levels of issue consistency vary accordingly. They no longer argue that there has been any long-term increase in issue consistency. Their main emphasis is not that the American voter has changed, but that the American voter is changeable.

While research findings about change in issue consistency yield contradictory results, one of Converse's earlier findings has been replicated. Converse, we should recall, finds not only low constraint among the electorate, but relatively high constraint among congressional candidates. A recent analysis by Bishop and Frankovic (1981) compares results of a mail survey of 820 congressional candidates with a national probability sample exit poll of 8700 voters in the 1978 congressional election. (Both these surveys were conducted by CBS News/*New York Times*.) Candidates and voters are asked their opinions on numerous issues, and nine of the questions are "relatively comparable in content" (p. 89). As with Converse's analysis of surveys conducted two decades earlier, candidates have a much higher level of issue consistency than does the mass electorate. Bishop and Frankovic acknowledge that different questions are used for candidates and for voters, but they present results of a test of college students that suggest that these differences in wording do not lead to greater constraint among the candidates. Moreover, as Bishop and Frankovic stress, their test is more conservative than Converse's, for they discover relatively low constraint among the mass sample even though they survey only the more politicized portion of the adult population that actually voted in a low-turnout contest.

Attitude stability

The controversy about levels of conceptualization and issue consistency focuses on whether there has been change since the 1950s. Similar arguments have not yet emerged about whether attitude stability has changed, for the data necessary to address this question became available to the social science community only within the last few years. To determine whether the electorate has more stable attitudes required a new panel study of the American electorate. In 1972, the Michigan SRC–CPS began such a study and reinterviewed a large part of its electorate sample in 1974 and in 1976. These data became available in the summer of 1978, and we use some of these data in earlier chapters (Chapters 7, 10, and 13).

The controversies about attitude stability deal primarily with whether Converse's original conclusions are correct, and several scholars have reanalyzed the 1956–1958–1960 panel data to address this question.

Pierce and Rose (1974) argue that Converse's model of attitude change does not fit the data. As we saw, Converse argues that most Americans do not hold real attitudes, while a smaller subset has coherent attitudes over time. Pierce and Rose posit a probability model that "assumes all respondents have attitudes and all are subject to short-term random forces, which are normally distributed across respondents for any trial" (p. 644), and they claim that the data fit their model better than they fit Converse's. The normative implication of their findings is that citizens have more coherent attitudes than Converse claims. "[T]hese results," Pierce and Rose conclude, "suggest that one of the empirical foundations of the democratic elitist view of the common man—that his opinions on issues of public policy are expressed randomly—needs reformulation" (p. 646).

More recent critiques of Converse argue that he does not use appropriate techniques to control for measurement unreliability. As we have pointed out earlier, some of the change in attitudes among individuals over time results from real attitude change, some from measurement error. There are several techniques, used mainly by experts in psychological attitude measurement, that can be used to "correct" for unreliability and to estimate what correlations would be if measurement were perfect. Achen (1975) argues that, once measurement unreliability is taken into account, the American electorate has far higher levels of attitude stability than Converse claims. Achen states that, while party identification is highly stable when measured among individuals over time, it is no more stable than most attitudes. Party identification, Achen argues, appears to be more stable mainly because it is more reliably measured than most attitudes. Achen cautions that a high level of attitude stability does not necessarily demonstrate that citizens make intelligent decisions.

A more recent analysis of the 1956–1958–1960 panel data by Erikson (1979) yields similar results. Using alternative models to estimate the "true" over-time stability of attitudes, Erikson finds that, with either model, the over-time stability of attitudes is far higher than Converse reports. Erikson's estimates are quite similar to Achen's, regardless of which procedure is employed. Unfortunately, for our purposes, Erikson does not estimate the "true" over-time stability of party identification, even though this measure plays a central role in Converse's original formulation. Erikson further argues that Converse's model of attitude change—in which a small subset of the electorate has coherent attitudes, while most have no real attitudes—cannot be used to account for the seemingly random responses of the electorate.

Erikson's conclusions have implications for the study of attitude formation. If, as he finds, adult attitudes are stable, we must ask where they come from. "Apparently," he concludes, "people do not develop their attitude structures during adulthood, because adults undergo little attitude change. Therefore, adult attitudes must be formed during the mysterious process known as pre-adult political socialization" (p. 113). Erikson clearly rejects the thesis that the mass public does not have coherent political attitudes.

Given this extensive criticism, what should we conclude about Converse's original formulation? Converse (1974) has already provided a detailed critique of Pierce and Rose's analysis, although Achen's and Erikson's critiques of Converse's model seem sounder. Achen and Erikson provide a useful service by attempting to correct for measurement unreliability, but such corrections are tricky. While we know that the over-time correlations of attitudes are artificially low and that such correlations would be higher if we had perfect measures, our measures remain imperfect. Therefore, the estimates by Achen and Erikson are still guesses, and, under different assumptions, the "true" over-time correlations might be lower. Moreover, Converse himself is sensitive to problems of measurement unreliability in his original formulation, and, although he does not apply the type of correction procedures used by Achen and Erikson, he does apply some tests to demonstrate that the low over-time stability of attitudes is not just a function of measurement error.

By turning to the more recent SRC panel, we may attempt to determine whether relative levels of attitude stability among the electorate have changed. Converse, along with Markus (Converse and Markus, 1979), has already presented a preliminary analysis of the 1972–1974–1976 panel, and concludes that there has been little change in the stability of political attitudes. For example, Converse and Markus estimate that, during the 1956–1958–1960 period, the over-time stability of party identification (using a Pearson's *r*) is .84, while during the more recent period it is .81. (Here Converse's results are similar to my own reanalysis of these data, although I rely on ordinal-level statistics in reporting these results in Chapter 7.) Converse and Markus note that, if one takes measurement unreliability into account, the over-time stability of party identification would be even greater, although they do not calculate such "corrected" measures of over-time stability with their other attitude measures.

Converse and Markus present the over-time stability estimates during the 1972–1974–1976 period for evaluations of political leaders and for "moral" issues, such as attitudes toward marijuana and abortion. For these questions, there is substantial over-time stability. There are also a few domestic and foreign policy issues, studied in both the 1956–1968–1960 and the 1972–1974–1976 panel, and for which stability is low during both periods. Converse and Markus conclude that there has been little change in the attitude stability of the American electorate.[4]

Converse may well be correct. Indeed, for those attitudes that we examine in this book, levels of over-time stability are quite similar during both periods, and they are similar both for blacks and for whites. However, the attitudes we examine—party identification, "internal" political efficacy, and "external" political efficacy—were measured with identical questions for both periods. Except for party identification, there is not a single attitude measured by Converse and Markus that was asked and coded in the same way during both

[4]Since Converse and Markus do not employ techniques to correct for measurement unreliability, scholars will almost certainly use these techniques to challenge their conclusions, and one such analysis of the 1972–19741976 panel has already appeared: Judd and Milburn (1980). See Converse (1980) for a reply, and Judd, Krosnick, and Milburn (1981) for a rejoinder.

time periods. Only one question, designed to measure attitudes toward isolationism, is identical in wording, and even for this question the lead-in questions differ and the responses are coded differently. In some cases, Converse and Markus compare the over-time correlations for the Likert questions used during the 1956–1958–1960 period with correlations for the presumably superior seven-point issue scales used during 1972–1974–1976. Given what we now know about the way changes in item construction can affect the correlations between responses to items, we should be cautious about accepting Converse's conclusion that there has been no change between the 1950s and the 1970s.

Issue voting

There is considerable controversy about the best way to measure the effect of issue preferences on voting choices, and the controversy often involves complex methodological issues. This discussion focuses on a limited aspect of the controversy by asking whether the relationship of issue preferences to voting choices has increased since the 1950s.

Our previous discussion of measurement problems in the issue-consistency controversy should lead us to be very cautious in accepting any conclusions about change. The same questions used to measure issue consistency have often been used to measure the extent of issue voting. If issues are related to voting preferences and if the newer questions provide more reliable measures of those preferences, the relationship of issue positions to voting choices would increase simply as a result of improved measurement. Therefore, it is essential that any attempt to study issue voting over time should pay close attention to the way issue preferences are measured.

Before turning to measurement problems, however, it is important to see why we would expect issue voting to have increased. In the first place, the ability of the public to vote according to issues is partly a function of how clearly the issues are drawn by the competing candidates. In an influential treatise, Key (1966) argues that the electorate is more responsive to issues than Campbell and his colleagues claim. Voters who switch their support from one party to another, according to Key, are often motivated by policy concerns. That the public is not more responsive, Key argues, results in large part from the low level of debate advanced by political leaders.

Since the 1950s, there have been several elections—the Johnson–Goldwater contest in 1964, Nixon–Humphrey–Wallace in 1968, and Nixon–McGovern in 1972—in which at least one of the candidates drew the issues more clearly than in the presidential contests of 1952, 1956, and 1960. The 1980 presidential contest also provided relatively clear-cut policy alternatives, although analyses that would allow us to compare issue voting in this contest with the 1952, 1956, and 1960 elections have not yet appeared. In addition to changed political conditions, demographic changes may have increased issue voting.

As a result of generational replacement, the American electorate is much better educated today than it was in the 1950s, and better-educated voters may be better able to translate their issue preferences into voting choices. Moreover, as we have seen, the overall level of party identification is markedly weaker today than in the 1950s, and voters who have weak party ties or no party ties may feel freer to vote according to their policy preferences.

The argument that issues have become more important in recent elections has been widely advanced, even by some of the original authors of *The American Voter.* For example, in their analysis of the 1968 presidential election, Converse, Miller, Rusk, and Wolfe (1969) conclude that Wallace voters were responding largely to issues. All Wallace voters who had cast a previous presidential ballot were party switchers, and their behavior supports Key's basic hypothesis that switchers often vote on the basis of issues. Converse and his colleagues conclude: "The pattern of correlations between issue positions and the vote for these 'changers' would support Key's thesis of a 'rational' and 'responsible' electorate even more impressively than most of the data he found for earlier elections" (p. 1097). However, Converse et al. find that issue preferences do not help predict the vote among major-party voters. Among respondents who voted for either Nixon or Humphrey, party identification was of paramount importance. (For the most extensive analysis of issues and voting in the 1968 presidential election, see Page, 1978.)

Issues may have been more important in shaping voting choices in the 1972 presidential election. As Arthur Miller and his colleagues discover (A. Miller et al., 1976), there were sharp issue differences between voters who supported Nixon and those who supported McGovern. After conducting a detailed analysis of the determinants of the vote in 1972, Miller and his colleagues conclude: "As an explanation of the vote in 1972, issues were at least equally as important as party identification" (p. 770). However, as several critics have pointed out (see especially RePass, 1976), the 1972 SRC–CPS questionnaire employed new methods for measuring issue preferences that located each respondent in an "issue space" ranging from very conservative to very liberal (for examples of these questions, see column 3 in Table 15.1). These measures may be more reliable than the Likert questions used during the 1950s and may thereby inflate the importance of issues compared with similar estimates during *The American Voter* period.

Whether or not there was a real increase in issue voting in 1972 is difficult to determine because of the change in question wording. However, in 1976, many of the "spatial" questions were repeated, so it should be possible to compare issue voting in the Carter–Ford contest with that in the Nixon–McGovern election. In 1976, the importance of party identification in predicting the presidential vote increased (as we saw in Table 5.1), and the impact of issues predicting the vote declined. Arthur Miller's (1978) analyses suggest that issue preferences could explain 34% of the variance in the vote in 1972, but only

18% in 1976. This decline in issue voting seems consistent with the political differences between the two elections. Carter and Ford were more similar to each other in their policy positions than Nixon and McGovern were. It is also possible that, by purposely taking ambiguous positions, Carter was able to diminish the importance of issues and thereby benefit from the favorable ratio of Democrats to Republicans.

Since substantial changes in the wording of closed-ended questions about issue preferences render comparisons over time problematic, several scholars have relied on the open-ended questions about parties and candidates to attempt to measure issue voting (for the wording of these questions, see the beginning of this chapter). Of these studies, the one by Nie, Verba, and Petrocik (1976) has been the most widely cited. In fact, their measurement procedures are relatively crude, since they use the coded responses to count the number of references to issues by each respondent. In 1952, 1956, and 1960, roughly half the respondents mentioned an issue in evaluating the candidates, but over three-fourths mentioned an issue during the 1964 Johnson–Goldwater contest. This figure fell to two-thirds in both 1968 and 1972.

Nie and his colleagues use a simple additive procedure to determine whether each respondent favors the issue position of each of the competing candidates. Among respondents who evaluate the candidates according to issues, the relationship of issue preferences to voting choices changed relatively little between 1952 and 1972. However, since substantially more respondents saw candidates in issue terms in the more recent elections, the overall impact of issues on voting choices was somewhat higher in 1964, 1968, and 1972 than in 1952, 1956, and 1960. While Nie and his colleagues do not report similar relationships for their 1976 update, they do show that the relative contribution of issues on voting choices (compared with the impact of party identification) declined in 1976. They conclude that "the total impact of issues . . . is smaller in 1976 than in any election since 1960" (Nie, Verba, and Petrocik, 1979, p. 374; see also Petrocik, 1980). While a comparable analysis has not yet been reported for the 1980 election, a preliminary analysis by Petrocik, Verba, with Schultz (1981) suggests that the importance of issues on voting choices increased.

Kessel (1980) also turns to the open-ended questions, although his procedures are more complicated. Kessel uses the coded responses to the party and candidate questions to classify answers as either candidate-oriented, party-oriented, or issue-oriented. The importance of these responses in affecting voting choices is measured through a probability procedure known as "probit analysis," which estimates the relative importance of the candidate, party, and issue responses.

According to Kessel, these techniques allow him to predict between 85% and 90% of the individual voting decisions in the seven presidential elections he studies. "There are many areas of life," Kessel writes, "in which attitudes are weak predictors of action, but voting is not one of them" (p. 197). Moreover, attitudes toward the issues consistently prove to be more important in predicting voting choices than attitudes toward the parties and candidates. "There is no support in the present analysis," Kessel concludes, "for the argument that voters were unconcerned with issues in the 1950s. Issues were more salient in 1964 and 1972 than in other years, but the change is on the order of a few percentage points on an already substantial base" (p. 203).

As he clearly recognizes, Kessel's conclusions directly contradict the conventional wisdom among political scientists that issues have grown increasingly important. However, his procedures are substantially different from those of other political scientists, and Kessel may have been overly generous in classifying responses as issue-related. Given the problems of using the coded responses to the open-ended questions about parties and candidates, we should be cautious in accepting his conclusions until his results have been supported by other scholars. We can hope that scholars will also turn to the verbatim responses to these questions to test his conclusions.

Both the Nie et al. and the Kessel analysis have the virtue of using identical measures of issue voting over time. Other analyses have attempted to combine the open-ended questions on parties and candidates with the closed-ended questions about issues and have been snared by the same methodological problems that plague the issue-consistency literature. An article by Schulman and Pomper (1975) provides an example of these problems. In attempting to develop a partisan issue index, they use the open-ended questions about the parties and candidates to determine what issues are the most important during each election they study. Closed-ended questions are then used to measure the respondent's attitudes on those issues. "The selection criterion," Schulman and Pomper claim, "therefore achieves comparability over time, with the issues selected clearly being salient to each election" (p. 5).

Schulman and Pomper develop a causal model to explain the importance of issues in the 1956, 1964, and 1972 presidential elections. They claim that the importance of issues is quite weak in 1956 (a beta weight of .06), but is more sizable in both 1964 (.22) and 1972 (.23). (The relationship between party identification and the vote in these three elections is .45, .36, and .31, respectively.) A research update that replicates the Schulman and Pomper procedures for three additional elections shows that the relationship of issues to the vote is low in 1960 (.11), 1968 (.12), and 1976 (.16) and suggests that the impact of party identification is stronger than that of issues in all three elections, .38, .40, and .34 (Hartwig, Jenkins, and Temchin, 1980). The authors of this update conclude that "issues played a comparatively larger role only in the unusual elections of 1964 and 1972, elections in which an ideological candidate opposed a centrist one" (p. 557).[5]

[5]We should treat these 1968 results with caution, since Wallace voters are excluded from the analysis. Excluding Wallace voters almost certainly reduces the impact of issues while increasing that of party identification.

Schulman and Pomper conducted a time-series cohort analysis to test the thesis that generational replacement may have contributed to the increased importance of issues. The birth cohorts that entered the electorate in 1964 and 1972 do have higher levels of issue voting than do the older cohorts that they replaced. However, Schulman and Pomper argue that generational replacement is not the cause of increased issue voting, for there is an increase in issue voting among all birth cohorts. While Schulman and Pomper do not find generational effects in the development of issue voting, they also conclude that life-cycle effects are not present. They argue that *The American Voter* thesis predicts that the responsiveness of voters to issues should decline as they age. In fact, issue voting increases among birth cohorts as they age. "Maturity," Schulman and Pomper conclude, "does not mean rigidity" (p. 13).

If we can accept Schulman and Pomper's analysis, we will have gained considerable insight about the way political conditions may increase issue voting, as well as knowledge about the way issue voting changes as individuals move through the life cycle. However, we should be quite cautious about their conclusions. First, Schulman and Pomper find that, in all three elections, party identification is more important in determining the vote than issue preferences are (a finding that runs counter to Miller et al.'s analysis of the same 1972 data). Second, while the importance of issues increases, the rise is by no means dramatic. Third, and most importantly, the procedures used to measure issue voting are not comparable over time, as Schulman and Pomper claim. While the open-ended questions used to measure issue salience are unchanged, the closed-ended questions used to measure issue preferences have undergone a substantial change of format (see Table 15.1). If the Likert questions used in 1956 are less reliable than the questions used in 1964 and 1972, we would expect the relationship of issue preferences to voting choices to increase merely as a function of improved measurement.

Most of the arguments about changes in issue voting have largely ignored the basic criteria for transfering issue preferences to voting choices advanced in *The American Voter.* According to Campbell and his colleagues, three conditions must be fulfilled for a voter to translate an issue preference to a voting choice: the voter must (1) have an opinion on the issue, (2) know what the government is doing, and (3) perceive a difference on the issues between the parties. In fact, it is impossible to apply all these tests because, after 1956, the SRC no longer asks respondents whether they know what the government policy is.[6] Despite this problem of noncomparability, several scholars have argued that the voters of today are better able to judge between the parties.

Pomper is the most widely cited proponent of this position and, through a secondary analysis of SRC surveys conducted between 1956 and 1972, he

[6]In 1980, the CPS did add the following question to their seven-point policy scale: "Where would you place what the federal government is doing at the present time?" This may allow for a partial replication of the Campbell et al. procedures.

shows that the electorate is increasingly likely to see the Democrats as the more liberal party on the more important issues. Through a cohort analysis, he demonstrates that the increased issue awareness of the electorate partly results from generational replacement, but that replacement itself is not a sufficient force to account for the increase. Rather, there is an increase in the awareness of issue differences between the parties among all birth cohorts.

Pomper presents a compelling case, especially in his article "From Confusion to Clarity" (1972), although the analysis in his book *Voters' Choice* (1975) suffers by including numerous noncomparable questions introduced by the SRC in 1972. Still, Pomper may have somewhat overdramatized his findings. Pomper presents the percentage of the electorate that sees the Democrats as more liberal on each issue only among respondents who have an opinion on the issue and who see a difference between the parties. But, as Margolis (1977) demonstrates, the percentage of the electorate that sees the Democrats as more liberal on issues has not grown as dramatically if one examines change among the entire electorate, including those who do not have an opinion on a given issue and who do not perceive a difference between the parties. As Margolis also notes, most of the trends analyzed by Pomper cannot be studied after 1968, and those issue positions that could be studied in 1972 do not show a continued increase in issue awareness.

Despite Margolis's reservations, the ability of the electorate to recognize that the Democrats are more liberal on most issues has increased, at least through 1968. In principle, this should increase the ability of the electorate to translate its preferences into votes. For example, voters who are opposed to government aid for medical care can more readily translate this preference into an appropriate vote if they know that the Republicans are more likely to oppose such programs. Likewise, voters who favor government aid for medical care can more readily translate their preferences into an appropriate vote if they know that the Democrats favor such programs. However, we should bear in mind that just because voters are aware of which party is more likely to favor their preferences does not mean that they will choose to vote according to those preferences.[7]

On balance, has issue voting increased? As we have seen, it is difficult to answer this question, because research on issue voting has often been plagued by the same methodological pitfalls caused by changes in question wording that impede the analysis of issue consistency. Moreover, there is no clear

[7]For a discussion of issue voting in the 1972, 1976, and 1980 presidential elections, see Abramson, Aldrich, and Rohde (1982, pp. 128–135). This discussion is guided by the criteria for issue voting advanced in *The American Voter.* Using the spatial questions to measure issue preferences, four new issue-voting criteria are advanced and respondents are tested to determine how many meet them. In addition, a measure of "apparent issue voting" is developed to ascertain the extent to which voters support the candidate closer to their own issue preferences. The analyses strongly suggest that issue voting was more prevalent in 1972 and 1980 than in 1976. However, since the spatial questions were not used extensively before 1970, this analysis cannot be used to address the question of whether issue voting has increased since the 1950s.

evidence of an ongoing trend toward increased issue voting, for several students have concluded that issue voting declined in 1976. There may well have been a modest increase in issue voting, as is suggested by Nie et al.'s analysis, which does use comparable procedures over time, but Nie and his colleagues also found a decline in issue voting in 1976. Moreover, Kessel's analysis, which also uses comparable procedures over time, suggests that there has been little change in issue voting during the entire postwar period. It seems reasonable to conclude that there has been no dramatic change between the electorate of the 1970s and that of the 1950s, and it would be clearly unwarranted to predict that issue voting will increase during the 1980s.

Conclusions

Campbell and his colleagues present a gloomy portrait of the American electorate. Most Americans do not think about politics in ideological terms, do not have structured positions on the issues, do not have stable positions on the issues over time, and do not vote according to the issues.

This portrayal has been subjected to two basic criticisms. Some scholars argue that it is time-bound, reflecting the low level of political discourse of the quiescent 1950s. Others argue that there are methodological problems that mar the portrait even as a description of the 1950s.

Some aspects of the portrait must clearly be redrawn. The electorate does appear to be more ideological today than it was in the 1950s, although this change may reflect a shift in the rhetoric of politics more than a fundamental change in the way voters think about politics. Most analyses show that issues are at least somewhat more important in elections that offer voters clear policy alternatives. There is little evidence that voters have more structured political attitudes or that they have more stable attitudes over time. Perhaps there has been a change in the structure of attitudes, as Nie and his colleagues claim. Perhaps there has been continuity in levels of attitude stability, as Converse and Markus claim. But methodological difficulties caused by changed wording of questions make it difficult to either accept or reject such claims.

The bleak picture of the electorate painted by Campbell and his colleagues may not be correct in all its particulars. For example, analyses that correct for measurement unreliability suggest that the attitudes of the electorate may not be as unstable as Converse claims. But even if we accept the pessimistic portrait of the electorate of the 1950s, that electorate is in one fundamental sense superior to that of today. During the 1952 and 1956 elections, some 62% and 59% of the electorate went to the polls. While this turnout is low compared with that in other industrialized democracies, even the turnout of the dull 1956 Eisenhower–Stevenson rerun is 6 percentage points higher than that registered in 1980. Our next task is to attempt to explain the decline of turnout during the past two decades.

VI

Implications and Conclusions

[CHAPTER 16]

The Decline of Electoral Participation

At the outset of this book, I argued that the trend toward declining turnout is among the most clearly documented and potentially dangerous trends in postwar American politics. It is a trend that is difficult to explain, for many factors should have increased electoral participation. Levels of education are strongly related to turnout, and educational levels have risen dramatically, as we saw in Chapter 4. Yet the steady increase in educational levels has failed to drive turnout upward and even to prevent its decline. The enfranchisement of Southern blacks brought millions of new voters into the electorate, and may have stimulated participation among white Southerners as well (Cassel, 1979). If we assume that turnout should be higher when people expect the results to be close (Aldrich, 1976), we face another paradox. A substantial majority of the electorate thought the 1968, 1976, and 1980 elections would be close, yet turnout declined in all three of these elections. While there may have been some countervailing factors that helped reduce turnout, such as the enfranchisement of 18-, 19-, and 20-year-olds, the decline in turnout may properly be labeled a puzzle (Brody, 1978).

The SRC–CPS data provide an opportunity to examine the way in which attitude trends may have depressed electoral participation. However, like all postelection surveys conducted in the United States, the SRC surveys tend to overestimate turnout. The SRC data tend to overestimate turnout by about 15 percentage points. Can they be used to study electoral participation?

The SRC–CPS Data

There are three reasons that the SRC–CPS data can be used to study the decline of electoral participation. First, although they systematically overreport turnout,[1] the SRC data do closely parallel the real-world trends observed from electoral statistics and the census estimates of the voting-age population. The SRC data, for example, show that turnout peaked in 1960 and record a decline of 8 percentage points between that election and 1980.[2] The correlation between the actual trend from 1952 through 1980 and the trend with the SRC data is .86, the correlation between the two trends from 1960 to 1980 is .98. The SRC data record a decline of 10 percentage points in voting for congressional candidates between 1962 and 1978. The correlation between the actual trend from 1958 through 1978 and the trend observed with the SRC data is .78, the correlation between the two trends from 1962 through 1978 is .79.

Second, we can use the SRC data because, although they always overestimate voting, we have some evidence that such overestimates are not substantially different for the various attitude groups we are studying. In 1964, 1976, 1978, and 1980, the SRC–CPS supplemented its election survey by a check of official voting records to determine whether or not respondents actually voted. Our analysis shows that, in all three presidential surveys, there are only negligible differences in voting overreports among persons with different levels of partisan strength or differing levels of "external" political efficacy. In 1978, there are also few differences in overreporting, although pure Independents were more likely than any other partisan group to falsely report voting.

Third, we can rely on the SRC data because they allow us to analyze the decline of turnout between 1964, 1976, and 1980 with the "validated" results that utilize voting records. These data, too, overestimate turnout, showing a 71.1% turnout rate in 1964, 60.9% in 1976, and 56.6% in 1980 (whereas actual turnout is 61.9%, 54.3%, and 53.2% in these elections), and record a substantially greater decline than do the actual voting statistics. Still, they provide a valuable data set to supplement our analyses, by allowing us to turn to surveys that do not rely on the reports of respondents.

The SRC data set, whatever its limitations, clearly provides the best data source to study the way changes in political attitudes contribute to the decline of turnout, for the SRC has measured important political attitudes over the very period when turnout declined. Indeed, this chapter demonstrates that roughly seven-tenths of the overall decline in turnout among white Americans can be accounted for by the combined effects of weakening party loyalties and declining beliefs about government responsiveness.

Our discussion of the effects of attitude trends on turnout is restricted to the white electorate. As we know, participation trends for blacks have been

[1]For a discussion of the reasons the SRC studies overestimate turnout, see Clausen (1968–1969), Katosh and Traugott (1981), and Traugott and Katosh (1979).

[2]For the sake of comparability with the official election statistics, I report here the SRC trends for the total electorate. However, as we shall see below, the decline of turnout among the white electorate is somewhat greater.

quite different from those for whites. Among blacks, there is a substantial increase in participation between 1960 and 1968. In addition, as we have seen, attitudinal trends among blacks differ from those among whites. The correlates of participation among blacks are an important subject in their own right, and they have been discussed extensively by others (Olsen, 1970; Verba and Nie, 1972; Verba, Nie, and Kim, 1978). However, the increased participation among blacks results from institutional change that made it possible for Southern blacks to vote, not from attitudinal change among the black electorate.

Attitudes That Cannot Explain the Decline

Our main goal is to examine the effects of attitude change on the decline of turnout. But we do not wish to argue that the decline results only from attitude change, for it also results partly from demographic change. Young adults are less likely to vote than their elders, partly because they are more often geographically mobile, have weaker community ties, and have not yet established the social ties that contribute to voting. Because young adults are less likely to vote, the enfranchisement of 18-, 19-, and 20-year-olds in 1971 serves to reduce turnout. While the total voting-age population increased by definition, the total number of actual voters increased by a smaller rate. According to estimates by Wolfinger and Rosenstone (1980, p. 58), the enfranchisement of these young adults decreased turnout by about 1 percentage point between 1968 and 1972.

Even apart from the enfranchisement of young Americans, a change in the age distribution of the electorate helped reduce turnout. As the "baby boom" generation entered the electorate, young adults made up a growing proportion of the voting-age population. Boyd (1981) estimates that about a fourth of the decline in turnout between 1960 and 1976 resulted from this changing age distribution. Boyd's demographic explanation for the decline of turnout serves to remind us that attitude change does not account for all of the decline in electoral participation. And, as we shall see, not all attitudes have contributed to this trend.[3]

First, attitudes that have not changed cannot account for behavioral change. As we saw in Chapter 10, there has been little change in overall feelings of personal political effectiveness, that is, feelings of "internal" political efficacy. Although persons with high feelings of internal efficacy are more likely to vote than those with lower feelings of personal effectiveness, the absence of change in this attitude rules it out as a cause of the erosion of turnout (W. Miller, 1980).

[3]For a useful summary of some of the attitudinal, sociological, and demographic correlates of turnout, see Reiter (1979). For other multivariate analyses, see Ashenfelter and Kelley (1975), Cassel and Hill (1981), and Shaffer (1981). For a discussion of these studies, see Abramson and Aldrich (1981, 1982).

Another attitude that cannot directly account for the decline of turnout is "sense of citizen duty." Campbell and his colleagues developed a measure to determine whether each respondent accepts the norm that citizens have an obligation to vote. It measures "the feeling that oneself and others ought to participate in the political process, regardless of whether such political activity is seen as worth while or efficacious" (Campbell, Gurin, and Miller, 1954, p. 194). Such feelings have not been studied over time with as much regularity as have feelings of political effectiveness, even though *The American Voter* finds a very strong relationship between such feelings and the likelihood of voting. Yet there has been little change in overall levels of citizen duty during the postwar years (W. Miller, Miller, and Schneider, 1980, p. 288), so, once again, we cannot find an explanation for changes in turnout by examining this attitude (Brody, 1978). Likewise, although persons who are interested in politics are more likely to vote, interest in politics has not waned during the past two decades (W. Miller, Miller, and Schneider, 1980, p. 307).

On the other hand, as we saw in Chapter 13, feelings of political trust have declined quite dramatically. Yet the decline of trust cannot directly account for the decline of turnout, because, as we saw in Chapter 11, persons who are politically trusting are no more likely to vote than those who are cynical.

Declining concern with electoral outcomes can partly account for the decline of turnout, for respondents who are concerned are more likely to vote. As Brody (1978) has shown, concern about which party wins the election has declined steadily since 1964. In fact, among the white electorate, this decline began after the 1960 presidential election and has continued fairly steadily through 1980. Ferejohn and Fiorina (1979) argue that the decline in turnout can largely be explained by declining concern over electoral outcomes. They argue that the decline in turnout does not constitute a "puzzle," since "recent fluctuations in turnout in Presidential elections appear to arise from variations in election specific factors" (p. 30). But it is difficult to develop a series of election-specific explanations to account for the continual decline in concern over electoral outcomes. It is easy to see that this decline may have resulted from the erosion of party loyalties, for there is a very strong relationship between strength of party identification and concern about which party wins. In fact, assuming that declining party loyalties contribute to a declining concern with which *party* wins presidential elections, about half of the decline in concern among the white electorate between 1960 and 1980 can be accounted for by the weakening of party identification (Rollenhagen, 1981). Therefore, we turn to the erosion of partisanship to begin our analysis of the decline of turnout.

The Decline of Party Identification

As we saw in Chapter 5, feelings of attachment to political parties contribute to psychological involvement in politics. In all eight presidential elections in which both party identification and voter turnout were measured, as well as in all six congressional elections in which the relationship can be assessed, strong partisans have been more likely to vote than weak partisans, Independent leaners, or Independents with no partisan leanings. Pure Independents have usually been the group least likely to vote for president and have always been the group least likely to vote in off-year congressional elections.

Since the partisan group most likely to vote has declined in size and since the group least likely to vote has grown (see Table 7.2), the overall weakening of party loyalties among the white electorate may partly contribute to the decline in electoral participation. Table 16.1 shows the percentage of whites that say they voted for president in all the elections between 1952 and 1980 and examines participation levels within each partisan-strength category. By reading down each column, we can examine change in turnout among each partisan group. It is clear that there has been little change in turnout among strong partisans. After 1960, the three remaining groups all register a decline.

Two facts should become apparent if we ponder the data presented in Table 16.1. First, there would have been some decline in turnout even without a decline in any of the four columns, simply because the distribution of respondents in the partisan-strength categories had shifted. Second, there would have been a substantial erosion in turnout even if partisanship had not declined,

Table 16.1 Percentage of Whites Who Report Voting for President, by Strength of Party Identification: 1952–1980

Year of election	Strong		Weak		Independent, leans toward a party		Independent, no partisan leaning		All whites[a]	
	Percent	*N*	Percent	*N*	Percent	*N*	Percent	*N*	Percent	*N*
1952	85	(512)	74	(578)	81	(255)	74	(81)	79.5	(1426)
1956	82	(575)	76	(598)	74	(248)	78	(145)	78.2	(1566)
1960[b]	88	(602)	82	(639)	82	(215)	75	(145)	83.3	(1601)
1964	86	(470)	78	(516)	79	(194)	62	(95)	80.0	(1275)
1968	87	(332)	76	(506)	77	(251)	66	(134)	77.9	(1223)
1972	82	(481)	74	(811)	72	(461)	50	(253)	72.5	(2006)
1976[b]	87	(468)	71	(824)	73	(474)	56	(316)	72.8	(2082)
1980	86	(284)	71	(467)	73	(288)	56	(160)	73.1	(1199)

*Note: N*s in parentheses are the total number of cases on which percentages are based.

[a]Based on respondents who were Democrats, Republicans, or Independents. Apoliticals and supporters of minor parties have been excluded from these calculations.

[b]Weighted *N*s.

because no partisan group increased its participation and because three groups register a decline.

We can estimate what turnout would have been from 1960 on if no decline in partisan strength had occurred. As with our estimates of the impact of generational replacement, we use a simple algebraic procedure. Using the distribution of partisans in 1960 as our base, we assume that levels of turnout for each subgroup would have been the same even if no erosion of partisanship had occurred.[4] While this estimation procedure is remarkably simple, more complex procedures yield similar results.[5]

Figure 16.1 presents the results of our algebraic estimates. The solid line presents the percentage of whites who say they voted for president, whereas the broken line shows the percentage that would have reported voting if there had been no change in the relative size of the partisan-strength groups.[6] As there is no erosion of partisanship between 1960 and 1964, the lines follow a virtually identical pattern. But from 1968 on, the estimated turnout with no partisan change is greater than the actual (self-reported) turnout. According to the SRC–CPS data, there is a decline of 10.2 percentage points in turnout

[4]In analyzing the effects of generational replacement on political attitudes, I begin with the first period the attitude being studied is measured. For example, in analyzing the impact of postwar generational replacement on the decline of party identification, Figure 7.2 begins with 1952, for, although the decline in party identification does not begin until after 1964, generational-replacement processes are at work from 1952 on. In analyzing the effects of attitude change on the decline of turnout, I begin with 1960. This is because no decline in levels of the basic attitudes we are studying occurs before 1960. That year not only is the high-water mark for electoral participation, but also marks a high point for one of the two attitude trends we are studying: feelings of "external" political efficacy.

[5]Aldrich and I apply a complex probability procedure called probit analysis to estimate the effects of these attitude changes on turnout. While probit analysis helps to identify the election-to-election impact of these attitude changes, the bottom-line estimates of the effects of these changes are similar to those obtained using our algebraic estimation procedures (Abramson and Aldrich, 1981, 1982).

[6]For example, the 1980 estimates are calculated as follows:

Partisan-strength group	*Size of group (set at 1960 size)*		*Percentage who said they voted*		*Product*
Strong partisans	(602)	×	86%	=	517.72
Weak partisans	(639)	×	71%	=	453.69
Independents, lean toward a party	(215)	×	73%	=	156.95
Independents, no partisan leanings	(145)	×	56%	=	81.20
Total	(1601)				1209.56

The percentage that would have voted with no change in strength of party identification is the sum of the products divided by the size of the white electorate in 1960: 1209.56 ÷ 1601 = 75.6%.

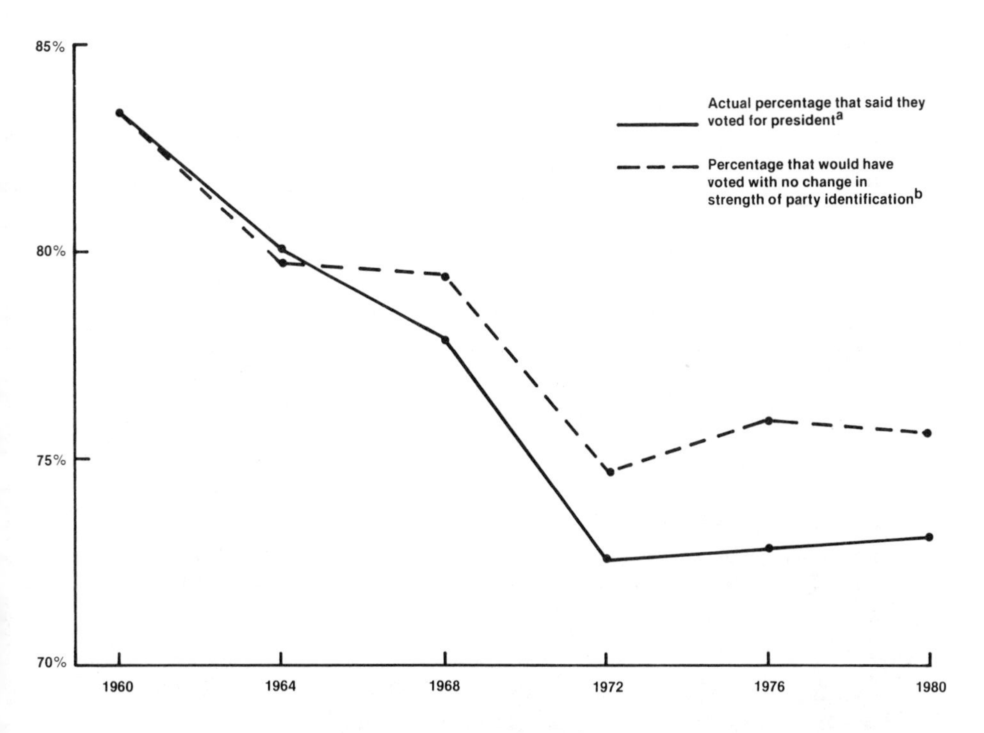

Figure 16.1 Percentage of Whites Who Report Voting for President, Assuming No Change in Strength of Party Identification: 1960–1980.

(*Note:* For the numbers on which these percentages are based, see Table 16.1. [a]Based on respondents who were Democrats, Republicans, or Independents. Apoliticals and supporters of minor parties have been excluded from these calculations. [b]Assuming that the percentage reporting voting in each partisan-strength subgroup was the same as that reported in Table 16.1, but that the overall proportion in each partisan-strength category remained at the 1960 level.)

between 1960 and 1980; if there had been no decline in party loyalties, then (everything else being equal) the decline would have been 7.7 percentage points. Roughly three-fourths of the decline in turnout would have occurred without any erosion of partisanship. Viewed from another perspective, however, about one-fourth of the decline in turnout can be attributed to the erosion of partisan loyalties.[7]

Similar results obtain when we turn to the validated voting records for the 1964 and 1976 surveys, although, given the sharp decline of "validated" turnout in 1980, the impact of partisanship is reduced when we compare 1964 and 1980. According to our estimates, about a fourth of the decline in turnout

[7]Shaffer (1981) uses a similar algebraic correction procedure to estimate the impact of the decline of partisanship on turnout among non-Southerners (including blacks) between 1960 and 1976. He finds that about one-fourth of the decline results from the weakening of partisan loyalties.

Table 16.2 Percentage of Whites Who Report Voting for President, by "External" Political Efficacy: 1952–1980

Year of election	High		Medium		Low		All whites[a]	
	Percent	*N*	Percent	*N*	Percent	*N*	Percent	*N*
1952	84	(805)	76	(372)	66	(260)	78.7	(1437)
1956	83	(1026)	70	(324)	57	(247)	76.6	(1597)
1960[b]	89	(1050)	77	(351)	60	(226)	82.4	(1627)
1964	84	(722)	76	(315)	71	(250)	79.5	(1287)
1968	86	(561)	79	(271)	61	(356)	77.2	(1188)
1972	82	(897)	72	(534)	57	(593)	72.0	(2024)
1976[b]	84	(834)	73	(553)	59	(704)	72.6	(2091)
1980	84	(467)	72	(377)	57	(366)	72.1	(1210)

*Note: N*s in parentheses are the total number of cases on which percentages are based.
[a]Based on respondents who received a score on the "external" political-efficacy index.
[b]Weighted *N*s.

between 1964 and 1976 results from the weakening of party identification, but only a seventh of the decline can be accounted for if we compare 1964 and 1980.

Because data limitations restrict our ability to examine the effects of feelings of political effectiveness, we do not examine the decline of congressional turnout in detail, but this decline also results from the erosion of partisan loyalties. According to our estimates, about a third of the decline in congressional turnout between 1962 and 1978 results from the erosion of partisanship.[8]

The Decline of External Political Efficacy

As we saw in Chapter 8, feelings of political effectiveness contribute to electoral participation. And as we saw in Chapter 10, feelings of "external" political efficacy, that is, feelings that the government is responsive, have declined markedly during the past two decades. In fact, the decline in feelings of political effectiveness closely parallels the decline in turnout: both trends began between 1960 and 1964.

The data in Table 16.2 allow us to examine the relationship between feelings of "external" political efficacy and participation among whites in all eight

[8]If, however, we use 1966 as a starting point for the analysis (since, for purposes of comparability, we cannot study the effects of political efficacy until that date), only about one-fifth of the decline in turnout can be accounted for by the decline in partisan loyalties.

presidential elections between 1952 and 1980.[9] By reading down each column of Table 16.2, we can examine change in turnout among each political-efficacy group. Among whites with high levels of "external" political efficacy, turnout is highest in 1960 and declines since then. Among whites with medium levels, turnout is fairly high in 1960 and somewhat lower in 1972, 1976, and 1980. On the other hand, there has been little consistent change among respondents with low feelings of political efficacy, and turnout is only marginally lower in the three most recent surveys than in 1960.

We can estimate what turnout would have been from 1960 on if no decline in feelings of "external" political efficacy had occurred, by using the distribution of responses in each efficacy category in 1960 as our base and by assuming that levels of turnout for each efficacy subgroup would have been the same even if no erosion in feelings of "external" efficacy had occurred. Figure 16.2 presents the results of these estimates, with the solid line presenting the percentage of whites who say they voted for president, and the broken line the percentage that would have reported voting if there had been no change in the relative size of the three efficacy subgroups.

In every survey from 1964 on, estimated turnout with no change in feelings of political effectiveness is higher than the reported turnout. Figure 10.3 shows a decline of 10.3 percentage points in reported turnout between 1960 and 1980. If there had been no decline in feelings of "external" political efficacy, then (everything else being equal) the decline would have been only 4.7 percentage points. In other words, less than half the decline in turnout would have occurred without any change in beliefs about government responsiveness. At the same time, somewhat over half the decline in turnout can be attributed to the erosion in feelings of "external" political efficacy.[10]

Unfortunately, we are somewhat thwarted in our efforts to estimate the effects of the erosion in feelings of political efficacy on the decline in "validated" turnout, as the first voter-validation study was conducted only in 1964, after the decline in feelings of "external" political efficacy was already under way. Still, the validated results also suggest that the erosion in these feelings contributes to the decline in turnout. According to our estimates, about a third of the decline in turnout between 1964 and 1976 results from the erosion in

[9]In examining these trends over time, we do not present change among each efficacy level with controls for levels of education. Throughout the entire postwar period, whites with higher levels of education score higher in "external" political efficacy, and this relationship has changed little throughout these years (see Figure 10.4). Overall increases in educational levels among the electorate could have been expected to increase both feelings of political effectiveness and levels of electoral participation. Thus, to the extent that the decline in efficacy contributes to the decline of turnout, these effects occur *despite* the overall increases in educational levels among the American electorate.

[10]Shaffer (1981), who uses the same two items we employ to build his measure of political efficacy, estimates that two-thirds of the decline in participation among non-Southerners results from the decline in political efficacy. However, Shaffer may have somewhat overestimated the impact of the decline of efficacy (Abramson and Aldrich, 1981, note 25).

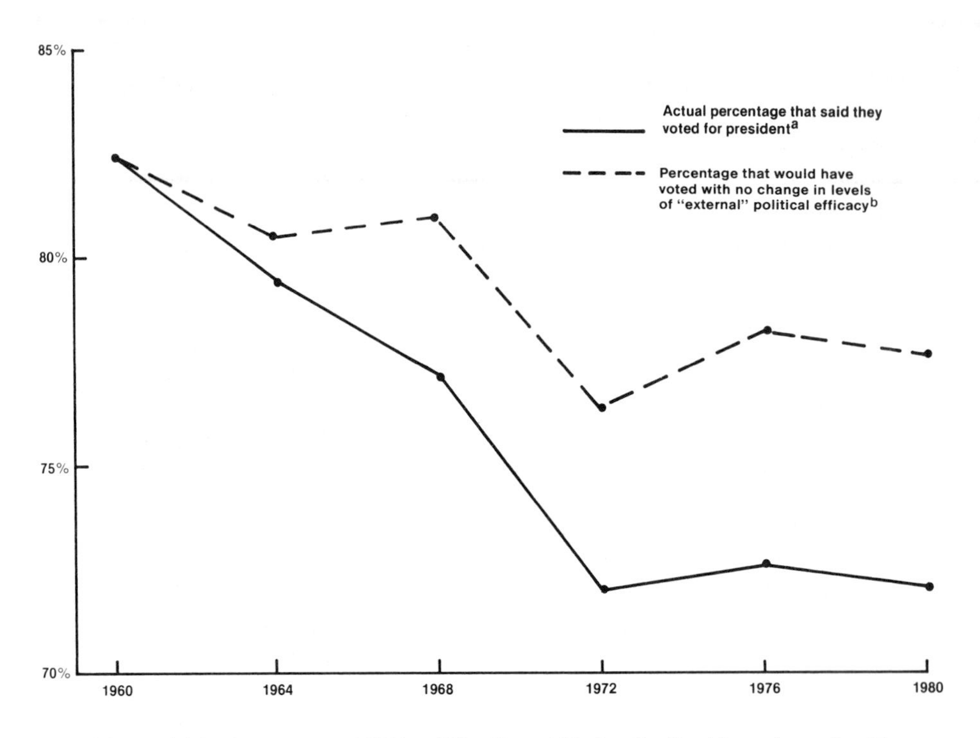

Figure 16.2 Percentage of Whites Who Report Voting for President, Assuming No Change in Levels of "External" Political Efficacy: 1960–1980.

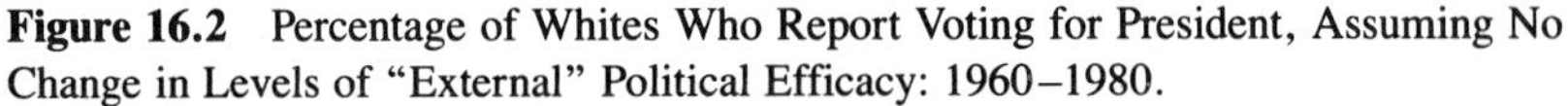

(*Note:* For the numbers on which these percentages are based, see Table 16.2. [a]Based on respondents who received a score on the "external" political-efficacy index. [b]Assuming that the percentage reporting voting in each efficacy category was the same as that reported in Table 16.2, but that the overall proportion in each efficacy category remained at the 1960 level.)

feelings of political efficacy, although, if one examines only the decline between 1964 and 1980, eroding feelings of efficacy account for only a fifth of the decline.

We are also hindered in our efforts to estimate the effects of the erosion in feelings of political effectiveness on the decline in congressional voting, because the first survey that allows us to examine the relationship between these feelings and off-year voting was conducted only in 1966. Nonetheless, our estimates suggest that about one-fifth of the decline in off-year turnout between 1966 and 1978 results from declining beliefs about government responsiveness.

On balance, the decline in feelings of "external" political efficacy appears to provide a partial explanation for the decline in electoral participation and may account for somewhat over half the decline in turnout in presidential elections. Unfortunately, we do not have an appropriate baseline for estimating the effect of this erosion on the decline in turnout in off-year congressional elections. For the presidential voting trend, the decline in beliefs about government responsiveness appears to account for more of the decline in turnout than does the erosion of partisan strength. We may now turn to the next logical question: What is the combined effect of both these attitudinal trends?

The Combined Impact of the Decline of Party Identification and of External Political Efficacy

The combined impact of the two attitudinal trends on the decline in participation depends on how these attitudes are related to each other; the maximum opportunity for the combined trends to have a greater impact on the decline in participation occurs if these attitudes are unrelated to each other.

We have examined the relationship between strength of party identification and feelings of "external" political efficacy for each of the twelve surveys conducted between 1952 and 1980 in which both these attitudes are measured. Strength of party identification and beliefs about government responsiveness are only very weakly related. There are no consistent differences in levels of "external" efficacy among strong partisans, weak partisans, and Independents who lean toward a party.[11] Pure Independents do have the lowest level of "external" political efficacy in ten of the twelve surveys, but differences between pure Independents and the other three partisan-strength groups are often fairly small (Abramson and Aldrich, 1981, Table 5).

When we classify each respondent according to his or her partisan strength and feelings of "external" political efficacy, twelve subgroups emerge. There has been a very substantial shift in the distribution of respondents in these groups. This shift begins in 1964, when feelings of "external" political efficacy decline, and intensifies in 1966, when strength of party identification registers its greatest decline. For example, back in 1960, nearly one-fourth of the white electorate is in the combined category with the highest potential for political participation—strong partisans with high feelings of "external" political efficacy. Since 1972, about one white in ten falls into this category. Change is less dramatic among the category with the lowest potential for participation—pure Independents with low feelings of political efficacy. In 1960, fewer than one white in forty is in this subgroup; by 1976 and 1978, this group has grown to one in sixteen and one in seventeen, respectively. In 1980, one white in twenty falls into this group.

Over the years between 1952 and 1980, the four groups with the highest participation in presidential elections have been strong partisans with high

[11]One might expect strong partisans to feel the most politically efficacious, but, as I note in Chapter 10, the "external" efficacy of strong partisans appears to be affected by which party occupies the White House. As I note, among whites, strong Republicans have always scored higher on the "external" efficacy measure than strong Democrats have, because strong Republicans have higher levels of formal education. But the tendency for strong Republicans to score higher is reduced substantially when there is a Democratic president.

Table 16.3 Percentage of Whites Who Report Voting for President, by Strength of Party Identification and "External" Political Efficacy: 1952–1980

	Strong						Weak					
	High		Medium		Low		High		Medium		Low	
Year of election	Percent	*N*	Percent	*N*	Percent	*N*	Percent	*N*	Percent	*N*	Percent	*N*
1952	89	(292)	83	(130)	75	(87)	79	(311)	74	(151)	63	(112)
1956	88	(377)	75	(110)	67	(84)	82	(378)	70	(126)	58	(90)
1960[b]	93	(384)	85	(128)	65	(89)	86	(416)	73	(143)	78	(74)
1964	90	(288)	81	(105)	81	(75)	82	(269)	78	(138)	67	(109)
1968	95	(155)	90	(69)	72	(99)	87	(225)	77	(104)	59	(154)
1972	91	(232)	85	(121)	63	(126)	82	(356)	71	(207)	64	(245)
1976[b]	91	(204)	90	(138)	75	(123)	84	(333)	69	(214)	59	(270)
1980	93	(124)	88	(90)	73	(66)	83	(177)	68	(153)	60	(136)

Note: *N*s in parentheses are the total number of cases on which percentages are based.

[a]Based on respondents who were Democrats, Republicans, or Independents and who received a score on the "external" political-efficacy index.

[b]Weighted *N*s.

levels of political effectiveness, strong partisans with medium levels, weak partisans with high levels, and Independent leaners with high levels. These four groups make up two-thirds of the white electorate in 1960, but only about two-fifths from 1972 onward. The four attitude subgroups with the lowest participation have been pure Independents with low levels of political effectiveness, weak partisans with low levels, Independent leaners with low levels, and pure Independents with medium levels. Back in 1960, these four subgroups make up only one-tenth of the white electorate; from 1976 on, they make up three-tenths. Clearly, there have been very extensive shifts in the combined distribution of these two basic attitudes, and this shifting distribution creates a potential explanation for the decline of turnout.[12] (For the full report on the combined distribution of these attitudes, see Abramson and Aldrich, 1981, Table 6.)

[12]The four subgroups with the highest average level of off-year turnout are all three subgroups of strong partisans and weak partisans with high levels of "external" political efficacy. These groups make up half the white electorate in 1966, but just over a third in 1978. The four subgroups with the lowest participation are all three subgroups of pure Independents plus weak partisans with low feelings of political efficacy. These four groups grew only slightly, from just under a fourth of the white electorate in 1966 to just over a fourth twelve years later.

Independent, leans toward a party						Independent, no partisan leaning							
High		Medium		Low		High		Medium		Low		All whites[a]	
Percent	*N*	Percent	*N*	Percent	*N*	Percent	*N*	Percent	*N*	Percent	*N*	Percent	*N*
84	(164)	71	(59)	81	(31)	86	(35)	80	(25)	45	(20)	79.4	(1417)
77	(165)	71	(51)	65	(31)	84	(98)	77	(22)	62	(21)	78.4	(1553)
86	(160)	81	(36)	53	(19)	89	(81)	76	(37)	33	(27)	83.6	(1594)
84	(116)	71	(41)	73	(37)	65	(43)	57	(28)	62	(24)	80.0	(1273)
83	(128)	76	(62)	65	(49)	71	(49)	74	(34)	51	(45)	78.0	(1173)
82	(212)	71	(125)	58	(121)	61	(92)	58	(76)	32	(85)	72.6	(1998)
84	(190)	73	(110)	62	(172)	72	(103)	57	(83)	43	(126)	73.1	(2066)
88	(112)	70	(74)	57	(100)	70	(47)	62	(55)	40	(55)	73.3	(1189)

Table 16.3 presents the percentage of whites who say they voted for president in all the elections between 1952 and 1980 among each of the twelve attitude subgroups. By reading down each column of Table 16.3, we can examine change in turnout among each subgroup. Seven of the subgroups register no consistent change in turnout between 1960 and 1980; two groups, weak partisans with medium efficacy levels and Independent leaners with medium efficacy levels, register only a moderate decline (a drop of 1.5 percentage points per four-year period). Three subgroups register a decline of close to 3 percentage points per election: weak partisans with low feelings of political effectiveness, pure Independents with high feelings of political effectiveness, and pure Independents with medium levels of political effectiveness.[13]

To estimate the effects of the combined attitude change on the decline in turnout, we use the distribution of respondents in each attitude subgroup as our base, but we must assume that levels of turnout for each subgroup would have been the same even if there had been no attitude change among the

[13]Based on a least-squares regression analysis of turnout within each attitude subgroup between 1960 and 1980.

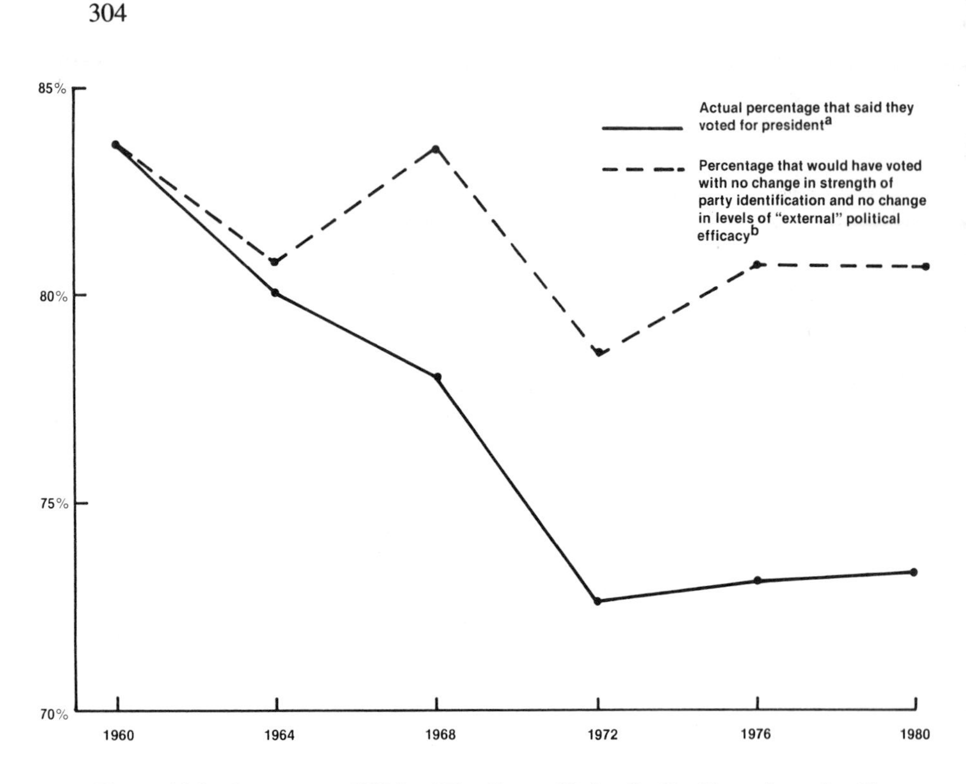

Figure 16.3 Percentage of Whites Who Report Voting for President, Assuming No Change in Strength of Party Identification and Levels of "External" Political Efficacy: 1960–1980.

(*Note:* For the numbers on which these percentages are based, see Table 16.3. [a]Based on respondents who were Democrats, Republicans, or Independents and who received a score on the "external" political-efficacy index. [b]Assuming that the percentage reporting voting for each attitude subgroup was the same as that reported in Table 16.3, but that the overall proportion of respondents in each partisan-strength and efficacy category remained at the 1960 level.)

electorate. Figure 16.3 presents the results of these estimates. The solid line shows the percentage of whites who say they voted for president, while the broken line shows the percentage that would have voted if there had been no change in the relative size of the twelve attitude subgroups.

In every survey from 1964 on, estimated turnout with no attitude change is higher than reported turnout. Figure 16.3 shows a decline in turnout of 10.3 percentage points between 1960 and 1980. If there had been no decline in either partisan strength or feelings of "external" political efficacy, the decline would have been 2.9 percentage points. In other words, just under three-tenths of the decline in turnout would have occurred without any change in the distribution of these attitudes. Conversely, over seven-tenths of the decline in turnout can be attributed to the combined effects of the erosion of partisanship and the decline in feelings of "external" political efficacy.

The "validated" voting results also suggest that the combined impact of declining party loyalties and eroding feelings of "external" political efficacy played a major role in the decline of turnout. According to our estimates, about three-fifths of the decline in presidential turnout between 1964 and 1976 results from the combined impact of these two trends. However, given the sharp decline of validated turnout in 1980, the combined impact of these trends accounts for only a third of the decline in turnout between 1964 and 1980.

The year 1966 presents the first opportunity to examine the joint effect of these attitudes on voting in off-year congressional elections. According to our estimates, about two-fifths of the decline appears to have resulted from the combined impact of these two attitude trends. However, the combined impact of these attitude trends on the decline in off-year turnout might well have been greater if we had been able to measure the combined relationship of these attitudes to turnout in either the 1958 or the 1962 off-year congressional election.

Conclusions

The combined effect of the decline in partisan strength and the decline in beliefs about government responsiveness appears to account for about seven-tenths of the decline in presidential turnout. Although we do not have an appropriate baseline for estimating the effect of attitude change on the decline in congressional turnout, the combined trends appear to account for about two-fifths of the decline even for the limited period that we are able to study.

It should be recognized that the data presented in this chapter do not account for all of the changes in postwar electoral participation. For example, the decline in participation between 1968 and 1972 is greater than one would predict from attitude change alone. And these attitudes do not account for the rise in participation between 1952 and 1960.[14] Clearly, additional analyses should be undertaken. One of the major areas for future attitude research should be the evaluation of the impact of both short-term and long-term forces on the decline in turnout. Analyses of individual-level change, which can be explored through both the 1956–1958–1960 and the 1972–1974–1976 SRC panel studies, may also provide insights about the decline in electoral participation. These panel data may aid in determining the causal direction between attitudes and behavior.

But while further research is needed, the results in this chapter may suggest useful research strategies. At the very least, these results suggest that attitudinal change may contribute to behavioral change. And, given the massive

[14]About a third of the increased participation between 1952 and 1960 can be accounted for by the rise of "external" political efficacy. But these feelings increase between 1952 and 1956, and turnout falls in 1956. Moreover, increased turnout cannot have resulted from changes in partisan loyalty, since partisan strength is stable between 1952 and 1960.

research literature devoted to the two attitudinal variables under scrutiny—party identification and sense of political efficacy—it should be heartening to learn that changes in the distribution of these attitudes may have important behavioral consequences.

From the standpoint of those who wish to increase electoral participation, however, these findings are hardly encouraging. The decline in party identification, as we saw in Chapter 7, is largely the result of generational replacement, and, given the very low level of partisan loyalties among young adults, party loyalties are likely to remain weak for the remainder of this century. On the other hand, feelings of "external" political efficacy are somewhat stronger among young adults than among their elders (see Chapter 10). Whether beliefs in government responsiveness will in fact increase probably depends mainly on the future actions of political leaders. This study cannot predict those actions, but it does suggest that it will be difficult to restore higher levels of electoral participation unless the attitudes of the American electorate toward the political system change.

[CHAPTER 17]

Summary and Conclusions

Our review of political attitudes has examined one of the most extensive research literatures in political science. Clearly, there has been a great deal of cumulative knowledge, although there are still gaps, problematic findings, and contradictory conclusions. Let us briefly summarize what we do know, and then turn to some of these gaps and contradictions.

Political Attitudes Studied

We began by examining feelings of party identification. We reviewed the basic claims for this concept advanced by Campbell and his colleagues. Party loyalties, they argue, contribute to opinion formation, influence voting behavior, enhance psychological involvement in politics, and promote electoral stability. Although the decline of party identification since 1964 affects all these claims, we conclude that the concept of party identification is still crucial for our understanding of political behavior. We discovered that party loyalties are often learned through the family, although the influence of the family has probably declined somewhat during the past two decades. We examined changes in party loyalties during the postwar years and saw that these loyalties are considerably weaker among white Americans than they were in the 1950s or early 1960s.

We turned next to feelings of political effectiveness and found that these feelings would prove of considerable importance to understanding political behavior. However, we conclude that the concept is best seen as having two separate components: beliefs about personal political effectiveness, which can be labeled "internal" political efficacy; and beliefs about government responsiveness, which can be labeled "external" political efficacy. We saw that there is little evidence that these feelings are learned through the family, and we evaluated explanations that might contribute to subcultural differences in these feelings. Both a social-psychologically based social-deprivation explanation and an explanation based on the political realities facing disadvantaged subcultural groups may account for their low feelings of political effectiveness. We saw that feelings of "internal" political efficacy have been relatively stable during the postwar years, but that, since 1960, feelings of "external" political efficacy have declined dramatically among both white and black Americans.

We found that there is considerable controversy about the meaning of political trust, but, through a careful examination of the construct validity of the standard SRC political-trust measure, we concluded that political trust has a very substantial component that measures support for incumbent authorities. We concluded that feelings of political trust are unlikely to be learned through the family, and we evaluated explanations that might account for subcultural differences in these feelings. We found that a simple explanation based on the political realities facing black Americans might be the most powerful explanation for political cynicism among black preadults. We found that there has been a dramatic decline in political trust since 1964, although the timing of the decline has been different for whites than for blacks.

We examined feelings of tolerance and discovered that tolerance, at least for left-of-center political groups, has increased during the postwar years, although there is controversy about whether it has increased in a more general sense. We also examined possible changes in levels of conceptualization, issue consistency, attitude stability, and issue voting. We concluded that the percentage of the electorate that thinks about (or at least talks about) politics in ideological terms has increased, and we found some evidence that the importance of issues in affecting voting choices increases in elections in which political leaders offer relatively clear policy alternatives.

Lastly, we showed that two of the basic attitude trends we studied—the decline in party identification and in feelings of "external" political efficacy—could account for about seven-tenths of the decline in turnout among white Americans. Attitudinal change can contribute to behavioral change.

The Differing Effects of Generational Replacement

One of the major goals of this study has been to demonstrate the importance of generational replacement on attitude change among the electorate. In Chapter 4, I argued that generational replacement is an ongoing process that continuously transforms the electorate. The actual rate of replacement varies according to the age distribution of the population and is affected by birth and death rates. During the postwar years, it has taken just over two decades for half the white electorate to be renewed. Given its higher birth and death rates, the black electorate is transformed somewhat faster, so that half the black electorate has been renewed in less than two decades.

The impact of generational replacement on the total distribution of attitudes among the electorate can vary greatly, and I outlined six basic possibilities (Figure 4.2):

1. Generational replacement can *create a trend;* i.e., there can be conditions in which no change would have occurred without replacement.
2. It can *contribute to a trend;* i.e., without replacement, there would have been change among the electorate, but the change would have been smaller.
3. It can *prevent a trend;* i.e., without replacement, change would have occurred.
4. It can *impede a trend;* i.e., without replacement, change among the electorate would have been greater.
5. It can *reverse a trend;* i.e., without replacement, change would have been in the opposite direction.
6. It may *have no effect* on the distribution of an attitude among the electorate.

We found that all six possibilities were actually realized when we examined attitude change over the past three decades. The decline of partisan strength among the white electorate represents a case where generational replacement *created a trend* (Figure 7.2). Throughout this entire period, young whites with weak party loyalties were entering the electorate, while older cohorts with high levels of partisan loyalty diminished through death. If no replacement had occurred between 1952 and 1980, there would have been no change in the overall strength of partisanship among the electorate. Similar results obtain when alternative measures of partisanship are employed.

A closer examination of these data also reveals that, between 1952 and 1964, generational replacement *prevented a trend.* Without generational replacement, partisan loyalties would have increased, for, during this period, there were gains in partisan strength among the prewar cohorts (born before 1924). Without the continuous process of death among these older age groups and the continuous entry of new cohorts with weak party ties into the electorate, the percentage of strong partisans would have increased somewhat during these years.

Replacement appears to have had *no effect* on the ratio of Republicans to Democrats during the postwar years, although there is some evidence that earlier replacement contributed to the Democratic advantage over the Republicans during the realignment of the 1930s (Andersen, 1979; Beck, 1974). Political scientists clearly expected that replacement would continue to weaken the Republican party. In an absolute sense, replacement has reduced the percentage of whites who identify as Republicans, but it has also reduced the percentage of Democrats. The comparative advantage of the Democrats over the Republicans was virtually unaffected by replacement between 1952 and 1980 (see Figure 7.3).

For blacks, it should be remembered, the trend was quite different, and Republicanism was virtually eliminated among blacks between 1960 and 1964. However, these changes did not result from replacement, but from events that eliminated Republicanism among young and old alike.

Our conclusions about the effects of replacement on feelings of "internal" efficacy depend on when we begin our analysis. If we begin with 1952, we would conclude that replacement had *created a trend*. But since most of the increase in feelings of personal political effectiveness occurred between 1952 and 1956, it would be reasonable to begin the analysis four years later. If we ignore the gain of 4 percentage points in efficacy between 1956 and 1980, we would conclude that replacement had *prevented a trend,* since, in the absence of replacement, these feelings would have declined. If we view this gain as meaningful, we would conclude that replacement had actually *reversed* the direction of a trend (Figure 10.5).

Feelings of "external" political efficacy and "political trust" have declined dramatically, but in both cases the decline would have been somewhat greater if there had been no generational replacement (Figures 10.6 and 13.2). In both cases, replacement *impeded* a trend.

The overall increase in tolerance toward ideological nonconformists results partly from generational replacement. Here I relied on recalculating the data presented by other scholars (Figure 14.1 and 14.2), although independent estimates of the effects of replacement by Davis (1975) yield similar conclusions. Replacement *contributed* to a trend. Even without replacement, tolerance toward Communists, atheists, and socialists would have increased, but this increase would have been substantially smaller without the impact of replacement.

On balance, replacement processes can have a wide variety of effects on the distribution of political attitudes. Obviously, if age is not related to the political attitude under scrutiny, generational replacement will not have any effect. But when there is a tendency for young people to differ from their elders, replacement may have an impact, and the nature of that impact can vary. As we saw, there is evidence to suggest that all six of the theoretically possible effects of replacement have occurred in the real world of postwar American politics.

Gaps and Contradictions

Although we have amassed a great deal of cumulative knowledge about political attitudes, there are still gaps. One of our goals has been to examine attitude change throughout the life cycle, and I purposely focused on political attitudes rather than on behavior in order to facilitate that study. Yet it is apparent that we know little about the attitudes of young children. We know almost nothing about the attitudes of children below the third grade, and we have far less comprehensive knowledge about the attitudes of elementary or middle school children than we have about high school students. The major study of the parental transmission of political attitudes focuses on high school seniors (the Michigan student–parent study), and the only other parent–offspring data based on a national sample is among 16- through 20-year-olds (the Barnes and Kaase study).

What few data we have on younger children suggest that there is little intergenerational transmission of such feelings as political efficacy and political trust, but we lack the more representative surveys that might lead to more reliable conclusions. Moreover, our data about attitudes changing with age among preadults are based almost exclusively on cross-sectional surveys, that is, surveys conducted at a single point in time. Such surveys cannot directly demonstrate that attitude differences among children at different grade levels actually result from aging, and most of these studies are further limited since they are based on nonrepresentative surveys. Moreover, future studies of preadults may be impeded by government regulations under the Freedom of Information Act, which may require parental consent before children can participate in social science surveys.[1]

We also know very little about the political attitudes of the elderly. There are serious obstacles that make it difficult to use national samples of the electorate to assess the effect of old age on political attitudes, partly because such surveys are based on samples of the noninstitutionalized population and partly because differential death rates among the elderly create problems for cohort analysis. As the elderly population grows in numbers, it will become increasingly important to study their attitudes, yet to date there has been no great interest in "political gerontology" (N. Cutler, 1977a).

There is some controversy about whether the study of political attitudes through the life cycle is a worthwhile enterprise and especially whether the study of preadult political attitudes is warranted. In large part, this debate hinges on whether attitudes learned early in life tend to persist over time. Some scholars argue that there is little reason to study the political attitudes of preadults, unless it can be demonstrated that these attitudes persist into

[1] It is difficult to know at this stage what effect federal "informed-consent regulations" will have on research with preadults. One study (Lueptow et al., 1977) suggests that these regulations reduce the response rate among preadults, but do not introduce biases for oversampling preadults with higher levels of measured intelligence or higher grade-point averages. We do not know the extent to which parental refusal to allow students to participate in social science surveys may be related to the political attitudes of parents. In practice, the decision to require parental permission may rest with local school authorities. For example, such permission was not required for my socialization study in Saginaw, Michigan, mainly because I guaranteed anonymity for the respondents.

adulthood. Others argue that, even if such attitudes do not persist, we can gain insights about the political learning process through studying preadults. What little evidence we have on the persistence of preadult political attitudes does not provide a clear answer.

There is some evidence that political attitudes are less stable among young adults than among their elders, although, as we saw, even here the evidence is mixed (witness the differences between my findings with the SRC–CPS national electorate panels and those with the SRC student–parent panel). Moreover, the available data do not provide clear evidence of either persistence or change. While there is some attitude persistence, even among young adults, there is also considerable change. It appears that few young adults actually change their basic partisan loyalties, that those with low feelings of "internal" political efficacy are likely to retain those feelings, and that those with high levels of political trust resist national-level trends toward increased cynicism. But do such patterns demonstrate stability, or do they provide evidence of change?

Most scholars agree that partisan loyalties are stable, but there is controversy about other political attitudes. Panel data do not provide a definite answer because they are subject to a variety of interpretations. Most political scientists have paid very little attention to the way measurement error may seem to lead to attitude change over time, but those who have focused on this problem have generally concluded that attitudes are more stable than they initially appear (Achen, 1975; Erikson, 1979). Erikson has concluded that his analysis suggests that early socialization may be more important in the development of political attitudes than many political scientists believe.

In some cases, we do have clear evidence of change, but face disagreement on the meaning of a trend. The controversy over the meaning of political trust provides a classic example. Clearly, there has been a shift in the distribution of these attitudes. But some claim that there has been a shift from high levels of trust to low levels, while others argue that the shift has been from high levels to moderate levels. Moreover, some scholars argue that the decline in political trust reflects widespread cynicism about the political system as a whole, while others argue that it is focused mainly on political incumbents. Even the extent of the decline of party identification has been questioned. Some emphasize that the proportion of party identifiers has dropped to only six out of ten adults, while others emphasize that most self-professed "Independents" actually lean toward a political party. New research on the meaning of partisanship and the meaning of Independence, which will be facilitated by new questions introduced by the CPS in 1980, will add fuel to such controversies.

Lastly, there is a growing concern among political scientists with the need to improve attitude measurement. Almost all scholars who have worked closely with these questions, especially those measuring sense of political efficacy and political trust, recognize that they can be improved. But while we recognize that there is a need to improve such measures, we also know that modifications of question wording can greatly affect the way people respond. Given unlimited financial resources, it would be possible to retain the old measures currently in use, but to include new measures as well. Even though interviews cannot be extended indefinitely, since the patience and goodwill of respondents would be too sorely tried, one could greatly increase the size of the sample and use the old version of attitude questions for half the sample and use "improved" questions for the remaining half. This would allow for innovation, while guaranteeing continuity. But cost is a limiting factor, and political scientists will have to make choices between continuing old measures and introducing new ones.

If the current nature of the funding for the ongoing CPS election studies continues, there will be considerable input from scholars on ways to improve measures, and considerable pressure to include new questions.[2] My own view is that established questions should generally take precedence, especially when they have been used for a long time and when they have been used extensively in the research literature. By studying measures with comparable questions over time, we may learn more about the effects of political events on attitude change, we may be able to trace attitudes over the life cycle, and we may continue to study the impact of generational replacement. At the same time, however, we also need better measures, especially measures of political trust that more clearly differentiate among the different objects of support.

How discouraged should students be? Every scientific field is filled with controversy, and it is not surprising that the study of human beings has more than its share. Given the nature of disagreements among political scientists, however, it is important for students not to accept uncritically the claims made by scholars, but to look carefully at the evidence they present. This caution applies as well to the conclusions reached in this book!

The Future of Political Attitudes

If we can employ cohort analysis to estimate the past effects of generational replacement, can we also employ it to project the future of political attitudes? Certainly, cohort analysis has been suggested as a tool for social forecasting (Duncan, 1969; Hyman, 1972b), but we should recognize its limitations.

[2] In return for long-term funding from the National Science Foundation, which committed $2,750,000 for the study of elections between 1977 and 1982, the University of Michigan Center for Political Studies incurred obligations to the entire social science community. Under terms of this grant, surveys were to be supervised by a Board of Overseers drawn from social scientists throughout the United States. The board sponsored several conferences on ways to improve the CPS surveys. As a result of these conferences, new questions were introduced in the 1980 CPS election study. While these activities may lead to improvements in our measurement of political attitudes, they are more likely to create pressures for innovation than for continuity. At present, however, prospects for continued long-term funding are apparently small, given the Reagan cutbacks in funding for the NSF Social Science Division.

Perhaps the major limitation is that we have no reliable data on the political attitudes of persons who have not yet entered the electorate. Given that the 1980 CPS survey provides the last data point in our analysis, we have no national survey data with which to estimate the attitudes of the 64 million Americans (as of 1980) who were born after 1962 and who will be joined by millions of Americans each subsequent year. Once we move beyond eighteen years in our projections, we do not even know how many new entrants into the electorate there will be, although we can make some projections based on the number of women of childbearing age. We have even less knowledge about the number of persons who will immigrate to the United States, for these numbers will vary according to political decisions and will be influenced by the effectiveness of controlling illegal immigration.

Clearly, persons born after 1962 will continue to make up a growing portion of the electorate. Not only will their numbers swell, but differential death rates will be higher among persons born before 1963—especially among the older members of this broadly defined cohort. According to my estimates, based on U.S. Bureau of the Census (1977) projections, generational replacement will slow down during the next two decades because the cohorts entering the electorate will be relatively small as a result of lower birth rates. Even so, persons born after 1962 will make up 9% of the white electorate in 1984, 16% in 1988, 23% in 1992, 29% in 1996, and 36% by the year 2000. (Persons born after 1962 will make up 43% of the black electorate by the year 2000.)

We can make guesses about the political attitudes of these youths. One can simply project that they will resemble the cohorts for which we do have data. Another possibility is that known relationships about years of birth and political attitudes will continue among the cohorts born after 1962. (For example, we could assume that persons born after 1962 will have even weaker party loyalties than the cohort born between 1956 and 1962, about which we do have data.) But we could have little confidence about such guesses.

We also do not know how the attitudes of Americans born before 1963 will change during the coming years. Even when the young differ from their elders, they may come to resemble them when they themselves age, and thus even a strong relationship between age and political attitudes does not necessarily portend a trend. For example, if there is a natural tendency for persons to become more partisan with age and if that tendency is reinforced in the future, feelings of party loyalties among the electorate might stabilize and the trend toward eroding party loyalties might be halted or even reversed. If persons become more politically cynical with age, the tendency for young Americans to be more trusting than their elders does not portend the growth of political trust.

In addition to the possibility that life-cycle forces might affect future trends, we must also recognize that age (and years of birth) are not the only, and are sometimes fairly weak, determinants of political attitudes. Political attitudes often respond to real-world political events. Even party loyalties, which are the most stable of the political attitudes we have studied, responded to events that weakened partisanship between 1964 and 1966. Feelings of "internal" political efficacy were affected by political events that sensitized Americans to the possibilities of ways other than voting that might provide citizens with political influence. Clearly, political events were more important than aging in eroding both feelings of "external" political efficacy and political trust. And although young Americans were far more tolerant of ideological nonconformists than were their elders in both the mid-1950s and the early 1970s, the increase in tolerance during those two decades resulted partly from political conditions that reduced the perceived threat of domestic Communism.

Despite these cautions, we can use cohort analysis to make some projections, as long as we recognize that they are highly tentative. While such projections should not be taken as a reliable guide to the future, they do help clarify the dynamics that can contribute to attitude change.

Of all the attitudes we have studied, we have the soundest basis for making projections about the future strength of party identification. Unless we assume that future cohorts will have dramatically different partisanship than the cohorts currently in the electorate, we can safely project that party identification will remain weak through the remainder of the century. If partisan strength grows with age during the next two decades, overall levels of party identification should stabilize. Some assumptions can even lead to projecting a slight increase in partisan loyalties (Converse, 1976, p. 114). But, if life-cycle effects do not assert themselves by way of *absolute* increases in partisan strength as cohorts age, partisan loyalties will continue to decline unless the cohorts yet to enter the electorate have unexpectedly high levels of partisan loyalty.

Such projections assume that the present two-party system will continue through the end of the century. By the year 2000, one or even both of the major parties may no longer exist, or they may exist but share the loyalties of the electorate with new political parties. If a large proportion of the electorate supports new parties, we have no basis for projecting the overall strength of partisan ties. According to the logic advanced by Campbell and his colleagues (1960), support for new parties should be weak, since partisan loyalties presumably become stronger with continued attachment to a political party. But the particular conditions that might favor new parties might also lead to strong commitment to those parties. Given that we have no reliable data on the way partisan strength actually develops during periods of partisan realignment, no reasonable projections are possible if a new party system emerges.

The SRC–CPS data provide no reason for projecting that the ratio of Republicans to Democrats will change. While these data do not register the recent surge in Republican loyalties, they clearly show that the dynamics of replacement that probably weakened the Republicans in the 1930s and 1940s had all but ended by the time Eisenhower was elected in 1952. In fact, during the two most recent CPS surveys, age was negatively related to Republicanism, with the older cohorts being the most Democratic.

The cohort data suggest a possible increase in feelings of "internal" political efficacy, since these feelings are stronger among the young. But even though young Americans have consistently tended to feel more politically effective than their elders, feelings of "internal" efficacy have remained fairly static (or perhaps increased slightly) from 1956 on. As we have seen, such feelings have been held in a state of near-equilibrium by generational replacement, although we could also conclude that replacement had reversed a trend toward declining efficacy.

Feelings of "external" political efficacy have usually been higher among young adults. But these relatively high beliefs in government responsiveness among the young do not provide much basis for predicting that these feelings will be restored among the electorate in the future, for in recent years young adults have had levels of "external" political efficacy below those of the least efficacious cohorts of 1956 or 1960. Likewise, the tendency of the young to be more politically trusting than their elders does not provide much basis for projecting the restoration of political trust. First, from 1974 on, levels of political trust have been far lower among young Americans than among any age groups during the 1958 and 1964 surveys, when trust was first measured. Even if cohorts entering the electorate had the same trust levels as do the young cohorts of today, trust would not be restored to its earlier levels. Moreover, there is at least some evidence that political trust among young adults erodes fairly quickly as they gain political experience.

Cohort comparisons suggest that tolerance may increase. For both periods when tolerance toward left-of-center ideological nonconformists was studied (1954 and 1972–1973), tolerance has been much higher among the young than among the old. Moreover, there is no convincing evidence that persons become less tolerant with age. If levels of tolerance among the youngest cohorts of 1972 and 1973 continue to prevail among cohorts that enter the electorate and if the cohorts in the electorate in 1972–1973 retain their tolerance, tolerance would rise markedly by the end of the century. Lest we reach the optimistic conclusion that support for civil liberties is destined to increase, three qualifications are in order. First, such a trend would be unlikely to continue if domestic Communism again becomes a perceived political threat. Second, there has been no gradual increase in tolerance between 1972–1973 and 1980 (Tables 14.1 and 14.3), despite the generational replacement that occurred during these years. Lastly, even though tolerance toward Communists, atheists, and socialists has increased, there is some evidence that tolerance in a more general sense is still fairly low (Sullivan, Piereson, and Marcus, 1979).

The future of political attitudes will depend far more on future social and political events than on the dynamics of demographic change. We should not forget that political leaders often shape events, and we should be sensitive to the ways that their very knowledge of the political attitudes of the electorate may affect their own behavior. Political leaders may modify their own behavior partly because of knowledge they have obtained through political-attitude research. For example, the very weakness of party loyalties among the electorate may have contributed to elite behavior that further weakened political parties. The low level of political trust among the electorate may prompt leaders to remind the electorate that trust in political institutions has declined. Such strategies may in turn further erode trust among the electorate. Future studies of political attitudes should emphasize the way the knowledge gained by political science research can itself influence political behavior.

Of course, political-attitude research does not mold the actions of political leaders to the same extent that their actions mold political attitudes. The actions of political leaders, as well as social, economic, and political conditions that are often beyond their control, clearly influence the way attitudes change. We should always bear this in mind in the study of political attitudes. In their study of political attitudes, political scientists have drawn heavily from the ideas of psychologists, sociologists, and economists. This is as it should be, for the boundaries between academic disciplines are artificial. But throughout this book, we have been continually reminded that political attitudes can respond to political events. The study of political attitudes can never be divorced from the study of politics itself.

[APPENDIX]

Scoring for the Political-Trust Indices

As indicated below, the value for each item was scored as 2, 1, or 0, ranging from highest trust to lowest trust.

1. How much of the time do you think you can trust the government in Washington to do what is right—*just about always* (2), *most of the time* (1), or *only some of the time* (0)? [The volunteered response "none of the time," which makes up 4% of the responses in 1978 and 1980, and less in previous surveys, was also scored as 0.]
2. Do you think the people in the government waste *a lot* of the money we pay in taxes (0), waste *some* of it (1), or *don't waste very much of it* (2)?
3. Do you feel that almost all of the people running the government are smart people who usually *know what they are doing* (2), or do you think that quite a few of them *don't seem to know what they are doing* (0)? ["Other, depends," was scored as 1.]
4. Do you think that *quite a few* of the people running the government are a little crooked (0), *not very many* are (1), or do you think that *hardly any* of them are crooked at all (2)?
5. Would you say the government is pretty much run by a *few big interests* looking out for themselves (0) or that it is run for the *benefit of all* the people (2)? ["Other, depends," was scored as 1.]

For all five items, "don't know" and "not ascertained" responses were scored as 1, but respondents with more than two such responses were excluded from the analysis.

Scores on the trust indices are the sums of the individual values for each item. Scores ranged from 0 to 10 on the standard five-item index and from 0 to 8 on the four-item index that omits the "few big interests" item. In collapsing the five-item index into three basic categories, I considered scores of 0 through 3 as low, 4 through 6 as medium, and 7 through 10 as high. In constructing the four-item index, I considered scores of 0 through 2 as low, 3 through 5 as medium, and 6 through 8 as high.

References

ABRAMSON, PAUL R.

1972 "Intergenerational Social Mobility and Partisan Choice." *American Political Science Review* 66:1291–1294.

1975 *Generational Change in American Politics*. Lexington, Mass.: Heath.

1976 "Generational Change and the Decline of Party Identification in America: 1952–1974." *American Political Science Review* 70:469–478.

1977 *The Political Socialization of Black Americans: A Critical Evaluation of Research on Efficacy and Trust*. New York: Free Press.

1978a "Class Voting in the 1976 Presidential Election." *Journal of Politics* 40:1066–1072.

1978b "Generational Replacement and Partisan Dealignment in Britain and the United States." *British Journal of Political Science* 8:505–509.

1979a "Comment: On the Relationship Between Age and Party Identification." *Political Methodology* 6:447–455.

1979b "Developing Party Identification: A Further Examination of Life-Cycle, Generational, and Period Effects." *American Journal of Political Science* 23:78–96.

1981 "Comment on Smith." *American Political Science Review* 75:146–149.

ABRAMSON, PAUL R., and JOHN H. ALDRICH.

1981 "The Decline of Electoral Participation in America." Paper presented at the annual meeting of the American Political Science Association, New York.

1982 "The Decline of Electoral Participation in America." *American Political Science Review* 76:502–521.

ABRAMSON, PAUL R., JOHN H. ALDRICH, and DAVID W. ROHDE.
1982 *Change and Continuity in the 1980 Elections*. Washington, D.C.: Congressional Quarterly Press.

ABRAMSON, PAUL R., and ADA W. FINIFTER.
1980 "On the Meaning of 'Political Trust': New Evidence from Items Introduced in 1978." Unpublished manuscript, Michigan State University.
1981 "On the Meaning of Political Trust: New Evidence from Items Introduced in 1978." *American Journal of Political Science* 25:297–307.

ACHEN, CHRISTOPHER H.
1975 "Mass Political Attitudes and the Survey Response." *American Political Science Review* 69:1218–1231.

AGGER, ROBERT E., MARSHALL N. GOLDSTEIN, and STANLEY A. PEARL.
1961 "Political Cynicism: Measurement and Meaning." *Journal of Politics* 23:477–506.

ALDRICH, JOHN H.
1976 "Some Problems in Testing Two Rational Models of Participation." *American Journal of Political Science* 20:713–733.

ALDRICH, JOHN H., and RICHARD D. MCKELVEY.
1977 "A Method of Scaling with Applications to the 1968 and 1972 Presidential Elections." *American Political Science Review* 71:111–130.

ALLERBECK, KLAUS R., M. KENT JENNINGS, and LEOPOLD ROSENMAYR.
1979 "Generations and Families: Political Action." In Samuel H. Barnes, Max Kaase, et al., *Political Action: Mass Participation in Five Western Democracies*. Beverly Hills, Calif.: Sage Publications. Pp. 487–522.

ALLPORT, GORDON W.
1935 "Attitudes." In Carl Murchison, ed., *A Handbook of Social Psychology.* Worcester, Mass.: Clark University Press. Pp. 798–844.

ALMOND, GABRIEL A., and SIDNEY VERBA.
1963 *The Civic Culture: Political Attitudes and Democracy in Five Nations*. Princeton, N.J.: Princeton University Press.

ANDERSEN, KRISTI.
1979 *The Creation of a Democratic Majority, 1928–1936*. Chicago: University of Chicago Press.

ANGELLO, THOMAS J., JR.
1973 "Aging and the Sense of Political Powerlessness." *Public Opinion Quarterly* 37:251–259.

ASHENFELTER, ORLEY, and STANLEY KELLEY, JR.
1975 "Determinants of Participation in Presidential Elections." *Journal of Law and Economics* 18:695–733.

ASHER, HERBERT B.
1974 "Some Consequences of Measurement Error in Survey Data." *American Journal of Political Science* 18:469–485.

BACHMAN, JERALD G.
1970 *Youth in Transition*. Vol. 2: *The Impact of Family Background and Intelligence on Tenth-Grade Boys*. Ann Arbor, Mich.: Institute for Social Research.

BACHMAN, JERALD D., LLOYD D. JOHNSTON, and PATRICK M. O'MALLEY.
1980a *Monitoring the Future: Questionnaire Responses from the Nation's High School Seniors, 1976*. Ann Arbor, Mich.: Institute for Social Research.
1980b *Monitoring the Future: Questionnaire Responses from the Nation's High School Seniors, 1978*. Ann Arbor, Mich.: Institute for Social Research.

BALCH, GEORGE I.
1974 "Multiple Indicators in Survey Research: The Concept 'Sense of Political Efficacy.'" *Political Methodology* 1:1–43.

BARBER, JAMES ALDEN, JR.
1970 *Social Mobility and Voting Behavior.* Chicago: Rand McNally.

BARGER, HAROLD M.
1974 "Images of the President and Policeman among Black, Mexican-American and Anglo School Children: Considerations on Watergate." Paper presented at the annual meeting of the American Political Science Association, Chicago.

BARNES, SAMUEL H., MAX KAASE, et al.
1979 *Political Action: Mass Participation in Five Western Democracies*. Beverly Hills, Calif.: Sage Publications.

BECK, PAUL ALLEN.
1974 "A Socialization Theory of Partisan Realignment." In Richard G. Niemi, ed., *The Politics of Future Citizens: New Dimensions in the Political Socialization of Children*. San Francisco: Jossey-Bass. Pp. 199–219.
1977 "Partisan Dealignment in the Postwar South." *American Political Science Review* 71:477–496.

BECK, PAUL ALLEN, and M. KENT JENNINGS.
1975 "Parents as 'Middlepersons' in Political Socialization." *Journal of Politics* 37:83–107.

BELKNAP, GEORGE, and ANGUS CAMPBELL.
1951–1952 "Political Party Identification and Attitudes Toward Foreign Policy." *Public Opinion Quarterly* 15:601–623.

BERELSON, BERNARD R., PAUL F. LAZARSFELD, and WILLIAM N. MCPHEE.
1954 *Voting: A Study of Opinion Formation in a Presidential Campaign*. Chicago: University of Chicago Press.

BISHOP, GEORGE F., and KATHLEEN A. FRANKOVIC.
1981 "Ideological Consensus and Constraint Among Party Leaders and Followers in the 1978 Election." *Micropolitics* 1:87–111.

BISHOP, GEORGE F., ROBERT W. OLDENDICK, and ALFRED J. TUCHFARBER.
1978 "Effects of Question Wording and Format on Political Attitude Consistency." *Public Opinion Quarterly* 42:81–92.

BISHOP, GEORGE F., ROBERT W. OLDENDICK, ALFRED J. TUCHFARBER, and STEPHEN E. BENNETT.
1978 "The Changing Structure of Mass Belief Systems: Fact or Artifact?" *Journal of Politics* 40:781–787.

BOYD, RICHARD W.
1981 "Decline of U.S. Voter Turnout: Structural Explanations." *American Politics Quarterly* 9:133–159.

BOYD, RICHARD W., with HERBERT H. HYMAN.
1975 "Survey Research." In Fred I. Greenstein and Nelson W. Polsby, eds., *Handbook of Political Science*. Vol. 7: *Strategies of Inquiry*. Reading, Mass.: Addison-Wesley. Pp. 265–350.

BRODER, DAVID S.
1972 *The Party's Over: The Failure of Politics in America*. New York: Harper & Row.

BRODY, RICHARD A.
1977 "Stability and Change in Party Identification: Presidential to Off-Years." Paper presented at the annual meeting of the American Political Science Association, Washington, D.C.
1978 "The Puzzle of Political Participation in America." In Anthony King, ed., *The New American Political System*. Washington, D.C.: American Enterprise Institute. Pp. 287–324.

BRODY, RICHARD A., and BENJAMIN I. PAGE.
1975 "The Impact of Events on Presidential Popularity: The Johnson and Nixon Administrations." In Aaron Wildavsky, ed., *Perspectives on the Presidency*. Boston: Little, Brown. Pp. 136–148.

BROWN, THAD A.
1981 "On Contextual Change and Partisan Attributes." *British Journal of Political Science* 11:427–447.

BRUNK, GREGORY C.
1978 "The 1964 Attitude Consistency Leap Reconsidered." *Political Methodology* 5:347–359.

BUDGE, IAN, IVOR CREWE, and DENNIS FARLIE, eds.
1976 *Party Identification and Beyond: Representations of Voting and Party Competition*. London: Wiley.

BURNHAM, WALTER DEAN.
1969 "The End of American Party Politics." *Trans-action* 7(December): 12–22.
1970 *Critical Elections and the Mainsprings of American Politics*. New York: Norton.
1975 "American Politics in the 1970s: Beyond Party?" In Louis Maisel and Paul M. Sacks, eds., *The Future of Political Parties*. Beverly Hills, Calif.: Sage Publications. Pp. 238–277.
1978 "The 1976 Election: Has the Crisis Been Adjourned?" In Walter Dean Burnham and Martha Wagner Weinberg, eds., *American Politics and Public Policy*. Cambridge, Mass.: M.I.T. Press. Pp. 1–25.
1981 "Shifting Patterns of Congressional Voting Participation in the United States." Paper presented at the annual meeting of the American Political Science Association, New York.

BUTLER, DAVID, and DONALD STOKES.
1974 *Political Change in Britain: The Evolution of Electoral Choice*, 2nd ed. New York: St. Martin's.

BUTTON, CHRISTINE BENNETT.
1974 "Political Education for Minority Groups." In Richard G. Niemi, ed.,

The Politics of Future Citizens: New Dimensions in the Political Socialization of Children. San Francisco: Jossey-Bass. Pp. 167–198.

CADDELL, PATRICK H.

1979 "Trapped in a Downward Spiral." *Public Opinion* 2 (October/November), 2–7, 52–55, 58–60.

CAMPBELL, ANGUS, PHILIP E. CONVERSE, WARREN E. MILLER, and DONALD E. STOKES.

1960 *The American Voter.* New York: Wiley.

CAMPBELL, ANGUS, GERALD GURIN, and WARREN E. MILLER.

1954 *The Voter Decides*. Evanston, Ill.: Row, Peterson.

CAMPBELL, BRUCE A.

1976 "Racial Differences in the Reaction to Watergate: Some Implications for Political Support." *Youth and Society* 7:439–459.

1980 "Realignment, Party Decomposition, and Issue Voting." In Bruce A. Campbell and Richard J. Trilling, eds., *Realignment in American Politics: Toward a Theory.* Austin: University of Texas Press. Pp. 82–109.

CASSEL, CAROL A.

1979 "Change in Electoral Participation in the South." *Journal of Politics* 41:907–917.

CASSEL, CAROL A., and DAVID B. HILL.

1981 "Explanations of Turnout Decline: A Multivariate Test." *American Politics Quarterly* 9:181–195.

CHAFFEE, STEVEN H., JACK M. MCLEOD, and DANIEL B. WACKMAN.

1973 "Family Communication Patterns and Adolescent Political Participation." In Jack Dennis, ed., *Socialization to Politics: A Reader.* New York: Wiley. Pp. 349–364.

CITRIN, JACK.

1974 "Comment: The Political Relevance of Trust in Government." *American Political Science Review* 68:973–988.

1981 "The Changing American Electorate" In Arnold J. Meltsner, ed., *Politics and the Oval Office: Towards Presidential Governance*. San Francisco: Institute for Contemporary Affairs. Pp. 31–61.

CLAGGETT, WILLIAM.

1981 "Partisan Acquisition Versus Partisan Intensity: Life-Cycle, Generation, and Period Effects, 1952–1976." *American Journal of Political Science* 25:193–214.

CLARKE, JAMES W.

1973 "Family Structure and Political Socialization Among Urban Black Children." *American Journal of Political Science* 17:302–315.

CLAUSEN, AAGE R.

1968–1969 "Response Validity: Vote Report." *Public Opinion Quarterly* 32:588–606.

CLYMER, ADAM.

1981 "The G.O.P. Bid for Majority Control." *New York Times Magazine,* June 14, pp. 110–115.

COLEMAN, JAMES S., et al.

1966 *Equality of Educational Opportunity.* Washington, D.C.: U.S. Government Printing Office.

COLES, ROBERT.

1975 "What Children Know About Politics." *New York Review of Books* 22 (February 20), 22–24.

CONVERSE, PHILIP E.

1964 "The Nature of Belief Systems in Mass Publics." In David E. Apter, ed., *Ideology and Discontent*. New York: Free Press. Pp. 206–261.

1966 "On the Possibility of Major Political Realignment in the South." In Angus Campbell, Philip E. Converse, Warren E. Miller, and Donald E. Stokes, eds., *Elections and the Political Order.* New York: Wiley. Pp. 212–242.

1969 "Of Time and Partisan Stability." *Comparative Political Studies* 2:139–171.

1972 "Change in the American Electorate." In Angus Campbell and Philip E. Converse, eds., *The Human Meaning of Social Change*. New York: Russell Sage. Pp. 263–337.

1974 "Comment: The Status of Nonattitudes." *American Political Science Review* 68:650–660.

1975 "Public Opinion and Voting Behavior." In Fred I. Greenstein and Nelson W. Polsby, eds., *Handbook of Political Science*. Vol. 4: *Nongovernmental Politics*. Reading, Mass.: Addison-Wesley. Pp. 75–169.

1976 *The Dynamics of Party Support: Cohort-Analyzing Party Identification*. Beverly Hills, Calif.: Sage Publications.

1978 "Toward More Cumulative Inquiry." *Contemporary Sociology: A Journal of Reviews* 7:535–541.

1979 "Rejoinder to Abramson." *American Journal of Political Science* 23:97–100.

1980 "Comment: Rejoinder to Judd and Milburn." *American Sociological Review* 45:644–646.

CONVERSE, PHILIP E., and GEORGES DUPEUX.

1962 "Politicization of the Electorate in France and the United States." *Public Opinion Quarterly* 26:1–23.

CONVERSE, PHILIP E., and GREGORY B. MARKUS.

1979 "Plus ça change . . . : The New CPS Election Study Panel." *American Political Science Review* 73:32–49.

CONVERSE, PHILIP E., WARREN E. MILLER, JERROLD G. RUSK, and ARTHUR C. WOLFE.

1969 "Continuity and Change in American Politics: Parties and Issues in the 1968 Election." *American Political Science Review* 63:1083–1105.

CORBETT, MICHAEL.

1982 *Political Tolerance in America: Freedom and Equality in Public Attitudes*. New York: Longman.

COVER, ALBERT D.

1977 "One Good Term Deserves Another: The Advantage of Incumbency in Congressional Elections." *American Journal of Political Science* 21: 523–541.

CRAIG, STEPHEN C.

1979 "Efficacy, Trust, and Political Behavior: An Attempt to Resolve a Lingering Conceptual Dilemma." *American Politics Quarterly* 7:225–239.

CREWE, IVOR.
1981 "Britain's New Party: Can It Make It?" *Public Opinion* 4 (June/July), 51–56.

CREWE, IVOR, BO SÄRLVIK, and JAMES ALT.
1978 "Reply to Abramson." *British Journal of Political Science* 8:509–510.

CRITTENDEN, JOHN.
1962 "Aging and Party Affiliation." *Public Opinion Quarterly* 26:648–657.

CUTLER, NEAL E.
1969–1970 "Generation, Maturation, and Party Affiliation: A Cohort Analysis." *Public Opinion Quarterly* 33:583–588.
1977a "Demographic, Social-Psychological, and Political Factors in the Politics of Aging: A Foundation for Research in 'Political Gerontology.' " *American Political Science Review* 71:1011–1025.
1977b "Political Socialization Research as Generational Analysis: The Cohort Approach Versus the Lineage Approach." In Stanley Allen Renshon, ed., *Handbook of Political Socialization: Theory and Research*. New York: Free Press. Pp. 294–326.

CUTLER, NEAL E., and VERN L. BENGTSON.
1974 "Age and Political Alienation: Maturation, Generation and Period Effects." *Annals of the American Academy of Political and Social Science* 415: 160–175.

CUTLER, STEPHEN J.
1978 "Instructional Uses of the General Social Surveys." *Contemporary Sociology: A Journal of Reviews* 7:541–545.

CUTLER, STEPHEN J., and ROBERT L. KAUFMAN.
1975 "Cohort Changes in Political Attitudes: Tolerance of Ideological Nonconformity." *Public Opinion Quarterly* 39:69–81.

DAHL, ROBERT A.
1956 *A Preface to Democratic Theory.* Chicago: University of Chicago Press.

DALTON, RUSSELL J.
1980 "Reassessing Parental Socialization: Indicator Unreliability Versus Generational Transfer." *American Political Science Review* 74:421–431.

DAVIS, JAMES A.
1975 "Communism, Conformity, Cohorts, and Categories: American Tolerance in 1954 and 1972–1973." *American Journal of Sociology* 81:491–513.

DENNIS, JACK.
1969 *Political Learning in Childhood and Adolescence: A Study of Fifth, Eighth, and Eleventh Graders in Milwaukee, Wisconsin.* Madison: Wisconsin Research and Development Center for Cognitive Learning.
1981 "On Being An Independent Partisan Supporter." Paper presented at the annual meeting of the Midwest Political Science Association, Cincinnati.

DOUVAN, ELIZABETH, and ALAN M. WALKER.
1956 "The Sense of Effectiveness in Public Affairs." *Psychological Monographs: General and Applied* 70 (Whole Number 429).

DOWSE, ROBERT E., and JOHN HUGHES.
1971 "The Family, the School, and the Political Socialization Process." *Sociology* 5:21–45.
DREYER, EDWARD C.
1973 "Change and Stability in Party Identifications." *Journal of Politics* 35:712–722.
DUNCAN, OTIS DUDLEY.
1969 "Social Forecasting—The State of the Art." *The Public Interest* 17:88–118.
EASTON, DAVID.
1965 *A Systems Analysis of Political Life*. New York: Wiley.
1975 "A Re-Assessment of the Concept of Political Support." *British Journal of Political Science* 5:435–457.
EASTON, DAVID, and JACK DENNIS.
1967 "The Child's Acquisition of Regime Norms: Political Efficacy." *American Political Science Review* 61:25–38.
1969 *Children in the Political System: Origins of Political Legitimacy.* New York: McGraw-Hill.
ERIKSON, ROBERT S.
1979 "The SRC Panel Data and Mass Political Attitudes." *Britsh Journal of Political Science* 9:89–114.
ERIKSON, ROBERT S., and KENT L. TEDIN.
1981 "The 1928–1936 Partisan Realignment: The Case for the Conversion Hypothesis." *American Political Science Review* 75:951–962.
FARRIS, CHARLES D.
1960 "Selected Attitudes on Foreign Affairs as Correlates of Authoritarianism and Political Anomie." *Journal of Politics* 22:50–67.
FEREJOHN, JOHN A.
1977 "On the Decline of Competition in Congressional Elections." *American Political Science Review* 71:166–176.
FEREJOHN, JOHN A., and MORRIS P. FIORINA.
1979 "The Decline of Turnout in Presidential Elections." Paper presented at the National Science Foundation Conference on Voter Turnout, San Diego, Calif.
FERGUSON, LEROY C.
1981 "Political Orientations." In Harben Boutourline Young and Lucy Rau Ferguson, *Puberty to Manhood in Italy and America*. New York: Academic Press. Pp. 201–224.
FIELD, JOHN OSGOOD, and RONALD E. ANDERSON.
1969 "Ideology in the Public's Conceptualization of the 1964 Election." *Public Opinion Quarterly* 33:380–398.
FINIFTER, ADA W.
1970 "Dimensions of Political Alienation." *American Political Science Review* 64:389–410.
1972 "Concepts of Alienation." In Ada W. Finifter, ed., *Alienation and the Social System*. New York: Wiley. Pp. 3–11.

FINIFTER, ADA W. and BERNARD M. FINIFTER.
1980 "Social and Political Factors in American Emigration: Preliminary Report on a Survey of Americans in Australia." In *Peace, Development, Knowledge: Contributions of Political Science*. Ottawa: International Political Science Association Secretariat, University of Ottawa.

FIORINA, MORRIS P.
1977a "The Case of the Vanishing Marginals: The Bureaucracy Did It." *American Political Science Review* 71:177–181.
1977b *Congress: Keystone of the Washington Establishment*. New Haven, Conn.: Yale University Press.
1981 *Retrospective Voting in American National Elections*. New Haven, Conn.: Yale University Press.

FOSTER, LORN S.
1978 "Black Perceptions of the Mayor: An Empirical Test." *Urban Affairs Quarterly* 14:245–252.

FREEDMAN, RONALD, PASCAL K. WHELPTON, and ARTHUR A. CAMPBELL.
1959 *Family Planning, Sterility, and Population Control*. New York: McGraw-Hill.

FRIEDRICH, ELAINE R. A.
1977 "Black Perspectives on Politics: The Emergence of an Alienated Subculture." Unpublished Ph.D. dissertation, University of Michigan.

GAMSON, WILLIAM A.
1968 *Power and Discontent*. Homewood, Ill.: Dorsey.

GANS, CURTIS.
1978 "The Politics of Selfishness, The Cause: The Empty Voting Booths." *Washington Monthly* 10 (October), 27–30.

GARCIA, F. CHRIS.
1973 *Political Socialization of Chicano Children: A Comparative Study with Anglos in California Schools*. New York: Praeger.

GERMAN, DAN B., and MARVIN K. HOFFMAN.
1978 "Differential Socialization in Legal Orientations Among Pre-adults." Unpublished manuscript, Appalachian State University.

GINSBERG, BENJAMIN, and ROBERT WEISSBERG.
1978 "Elections and the Mobilization of Popular Support." *American Journal of Political Science* 22:31–55.

GLENN, NORVAL D.
1972 "Sources of the Shift to Political Independence: Some Evidence from a Cohort Analysis." *Social Science Quarterly* 53:494–519.
1977 *Cohort Analysis*. Beverly Hills, Calif.: Sage Publications.
1978 "The General Social Surveys: Editorial Introduction to a Symposium." *Contemporary Sociology: A Journal of Reviews* 7:532–534.

GLENN, NORVAL D., and W. PARKER FRISBIE.
1977 "Trend Studies with Survey Sample and Census Data." In Alex Inkeles, ed., *Annual Review of Sociology,* Vol. 3. Palo Alto, Calif.: Annual Reviews. Pp. 79–104.

GLENN, NORVAL D., and TED HEFNER.

1972 "Further Evidence on Aging and Party Identification." *Public Opinion Quarterly* 36:31–47.

GREENBERG, EDWARD S.

1969 "Political Socialization to Support of the System: A Comparison of Black and White Children." Unpublished Ph.D. dissertation, University of Wisconsin.

GREENSTEIN, FRED I.

1965 *Children and Politics*. New Haven, Conn.: Yale University Press.

1975 "The Benevolent Leader Revisited: Children's Images of Political Leaders in Three Democracies." *American Political Science Review* 69:1371–1398.

GREENSTEIN, FRED I. and SIDNEY TARROW.

1970 *Political Orientations of Children: The Use of a Semi-Projective Technique in Three Nations*. Beverly Hills, Calif.: Sage Publications.

GREENSTEIN, FRED I., and RAYMOND E. WOLFINGER.

1958–1959 "The Suburbs and Shifting Party Loyalties." *Public Opinion Quarterly* 22:473–482.

HADLEY, ARTHUR T.

1978 *The Empty Polling Booth*. Englewood Cliffs, N.J.: Prentice-Hall.

HAGNER, PAUL R., and JOHN C. PIERCE.

1981 "Conceptualization and Consistency in Political Beliefs: 1956–1976." Paper presented at the annual meeting of the Midwest Political Science Association, Cincinnati.

HARTWIG, FREDERICK, WILLIAM R. JENKINS, and EARL M. TEMCHIN.

1980 "Variability in Electoral Behavior: The 1960, 1968, and 1976 Elections." *American Journal of Political Science* 24:553–558.

HARVEY, S. K., and T. G. HARVEY.

1970 "Adolescent Political Outlooks: The Effects of Intelligence as an Independent Variable." *Midwest Journal of Political Science* 14:565–595.

HAWLEY, WILLIS D.

1976 "The Implicit Civics Curriculum: Teacher Behavior and Political Learning." Unpublished manuscript, Duke University.

HEBERS, JOHN.

1979 "The Party's Over for the Political Parties." *New York Times Magazine* December 9, pp. 158–160, 174–175, 180, 182.

HELM, CHARLES J.

1979 "Party Identification as a Perceptual Screen: Temporal Priority, Reality & the Voting Act." *Polity* 12:110–128.

HESS, ROBERT D., and JUDITH V. TORNEY.

1965 *The Development of Basic Attitudes and Values Toward Government and Citizenship During the Elementary School Years,* Part I. Report to U.S. Office of Education on Cooperative Project No. 1078. Chicago: University of Chicago.

1967 *The Development of Political Attitudes in Children*. Chicago: Aldine.

HIRSCH, HERBERT.

1971 *Poverty and Politicization: Political Socialization in an American Sub-Culture*. New York: Free Press.

HIRSCH, HERBERT, and ARMANDO GUTIERREZ.

1977 *Learning To Be Militant: Ethnic Identity and the Development of Political Militance in a Chicano Community.* San Francisco: R & E Research Associates.

HOUSE, JAMES S., and WILLIAM M. MASON.

1975 "Political Alienation in America, 1952–1968." *American Sociological Review* 40:123–147.

HOWELL, SUSAN E.

1980 "The Behavioral Component of Changing Partisanship." *American Politics Quarterly* 8:279–302.

HUNTER, JOHN E., and T. DANIEL COGGIN.

1976 "A Reanalysis of Achen's Critique of the Converse Model of Mass Political Belief." *American Political Science Review* 70:1226–1229.

HYMAN, HERBERT H.

1959 *Political Socialization: A Study in the Psychology of Political Behavior.* Glencoe, Ill.: Free Press.

1972a "Dimensions of Social-Psychological Change in the Negro Population." In Angus Campbell and Philip E. Converse, eds., *The Human Meaning of Social Change*. New York: Russell Sage. Pp. 339–390.

1972b *Secondary Analysis of Sample Surveys: Principles, Procedures, and Potentialities*. New York: Wiley.

1978 "A Banquet for Secondary Analysts." *Contemporary Sociology: A Journal of Reviews* 7:545–549.

HYMAN, HERBERT H., and PAUL B. SHEATSLEY.

1953 "Trends in Public Opinion on Civil Liberties." *Journal of Social Issues* 9(No. 3):6–16.

IYENGAR, SHANTO.

1978a "The Development of Political Efficacy in a New Nation: The Case of Andhra Pradesh." *Comparative Political Studies* 11:337–354.

1978b "Political Crisis and Political Learning Among High School Students: The Case of India." Paper presented at the annual meeting of the Midwest Political Science Association, Chicago.

1980a "Subjective Political Efficacy as a Measure of Diffuse Support." *Public Opinion Quarterly* 44:249–256.

1980b "Trust, Efficacy and Political Reality: A Longitudinal Analysis of Indian High School Students." *Comparative Politics* 13:37–51.

JACKMAN, MARY R.

1977 "Prejudice, Tolerance, and Attitudes toward Ethnic Groups." *Social Science Research* 6:145–169.

JACKMAN, ROBERT W.

1972 "Political Elites, Mass Publics, and Support for Democratic Principles." *Journal of Politics* 34:753–773.

1977 "Much Ado about Nothing." *Journal of Politics* 39:185–192.

JANOWITZ, MORRIS.

1978 *The Last Half-Century: Societal Change and Politics in America.* Chicago: University of Chicago Press.

JAROS, DEAN, HERBERT HIRSCH, and FREDERIC J. FLERON, JR.

1968 "The Malevolent Leader: Political Socialization in an American Subculture." *American Political Science Review* 62:564–575.

JAROS, DEAN, and KENNETH L. KOLSON.

1974 "The Multifarious Leader: Political Socialization of Amish, 'Yanks,' Blacks." In Richard G. Niemi, ed., *The Politics of Future Citizens: New Dimensions in the Political Socialization of Children*. San Francisco: Jossey-Bass. Pp. 41–62.

JENNINGS, M. KENT, KLAUS R. ALLERBECK, and LEOPOLD ROSENMAYR.

1979 "Generations and Families: General Orientations." In Samuel H. Barnes, Max Kaase, et al., *Political Action: Mass Participation in Five Western Democracies*. Beverly Hills, Calif.: Sage Publications. Pp. 449–486.

JENNINGS, M. KENT, and KENNETH P. LANGTON.

1969 "Mothers Versus Fathers: The Formation of Political Orientations Among Young Americans." *Journal of Politics* 31:329–358.

JENNINGS, M. KENT, and RICHARD G. NIEMI.

1968 "The Transmission of Political Values from Parent to Child." *American Political Science Review* 62:169–184.

1974 *The Political Character of Adolescence: The Influence of Families and Schools*. Princeton, N.J.: Princeton University Press.

1981 *Generations and Politics: A Panel Study of Young Adults and Their Parents*. Princeton, N.J.: Princeton University Press.

JOHNSTON, J.

1972 *Econometric Methods,* 2nd ed. New York: McGraw-Hill.

JOHNSTON, LLOYD D., JERALD G. BACHMAN, and PATRICK M. O'MALLEY.

1980a *Monitoring the Future: Questionnaire Responses from the Nation's High School Seniors, 1977*. Ann Arbor, Mich.: Institute for Social Research.

1980b *Monitoring the Future: Questionnaire Responses from the Nation's High School Seniors, 1979*. Ann Arbor, Mich.: Institute for Social Research.

JONES, JAMES T.

1965 "Political Socialization in a Mid-Western Industrial Community." Unpublished Ph.D. dissertation, University of Illinois.

JONES, RUTH S.

1976 "Community Participation as Pedagogy: Its Effects on Political Attitudes of Black Students." *Journal of Negro Education* 45:397–407.

1979 "Changes in the Political Orientations of American Youth 1969–1975." *Youth and Society* 10:335–359.

1980 "Democratic Values and Preadult Virtues: Tolerance, Knowledge, and Participation." *Youth and Society* 12:189–220.

JUDD, CHARLES M., JON A. KROSNICK, and MICHAEL A. MILBURN.

1981 "Political Involvement and Attitude Structure in the General Public." *American Sociological Review* 46:660–669.

JUDD, CHARLES M., and MICHAEL A. MILBURN.

1980 "The Structure of Attitude Systems in the General Public: Comparisons of a Structural Equation Model." *American Sociological Review* 45:627–643.

JUKAM, THOMAS O.
1977 "The Effects of Vietnam Policy on the Decline of Political Trust in American Political Life." Unpublished Ph.D. dissertation, Michigan State University.

KATOSH, JOHN P., and MICHAEL W. TRAUGOTT.
1981 "The Consequences of Validated and Self-Reported Voting Measures." *Public Opinion Quarterly* 45:519–535.

KEITH, BRUCE E., DAVID B. MAGLEBY, CANDICE J. NELSON, ELIZABETH ORR, MARK WESTLYE, and RAYMOND E. WOLFINGER.
1977 "The Myth of the Independent Voter." Paper presented at the annual meeting of the American Political Science Association, Washington, D.C.

KENSKI, HENRY C.
1977 "The Impact of Economic Conditions on Presidential Popularity." *Journal of Politics* 39:764–773.

KERNELL, SAMUEL.
1978 "Explaining Presidential Popularity." *American Political Science Review* 72:506–522.

KESSEL, JOHN H.
1980 *Presidential Campaign Politics: Coalition Strategies and Citizen Response*. Homewood, Ill.: Dorsey.

KEY, V. O., JR.
1966 *The Responsible Electorate: Rationality in Presidential Voting 1936–1960*. Cambridge, Mass.: Harvard University Press.

KIRKPATRICK, SAMUEL A.
1976 "Aging Effects and Generational Differences in Social Welfare Attitude Constraint in the Mass Public." *Western Political Quarterly* 29:43–58.

KISH, LESLIE.
1965 *Survey Sampling*. New York: Wiley.

KLINGEMANN, HANS D., and WILLIAM E. WRIGHT.
1973 "Modes of Conceptualization and the Organization of Issue Beliefs in Mass Publics." Paper presented at the World Congress of the International Political Science Association, Montreal.

KNOKE, DAVID.
1976 *Change and Continuity in American Politics: The Social Bases of Political Parties*. Baltimore: Johns Hopkins University Press.

KNOKE, DAVID, and MICHAEL HOUT.
1974 "Social and Demographic Factors in American Political Party Affiliations, 1952–72." *American Sociological Review* 39:700–713.

KORNHAUSER, ARTHUR, HAROLD L. SHEPPARD, and ALBERT J. MAYER.
1956 *When Labor Votes: A Study of Auto Workers*. New York: University Books.

KRAUSE, MERTON S.
1972 "Schoolchildren's Attitudes Toward Public Authority Figures." Unpublished manuscript, Institute for Juvenile Research, Chicago.

KRITZER, HERBERT M.
1979 "Accounting for Strength of Partisanship: Single-Factor Versus Multi-Factor Explanations." Unpublished manuscript, University of Wisconsin, Madison.

LADD, EVERETT CARLL, JR.
1978 *Where Have All the Voters Gone? The Fracturing of America's Political Parties*. New York: Norton.
1979 "Note to Readers." *Public Opinion* 2 (October/November), 27.

LAMARE, JAMES W.
1974 "Language Environment and Political Socialization of Mexican-American Children." In Richard G. Niemi, ed., *The Politics of Future Citizens: New Directions in the Political Socialization of Children*. San Francisco: Jossey-Bass. Pp. 63–82.

LANE, ROBERT E.
1959 *Political Life: Why and How People Get Involved in Politics*. Glencoe, Ill.: Free Press.
1962 *Political Ideology: Why the American Common Man Believes What He Does*. New York: Free Press.
1969 *Political Thinking and Consciousness: The Private Life of the Political Mind*. Chicago: Markham.

LANGTON, KENNETH P., and M. KENT JENNINGS.
1968 "Political Socialization and the High School Civics Curriculum in the United States." *American Political Science Review* 62:852–867.

LAWRENCE, DAVID G.
1976 "Procedural Norms and Tolerance: A Reassessment." *American Political Science Review* 70:80–100.

LEVIN, MARTIN L.
1961 "Social Climates and Political Socialization." *Public Opinion Quarterly* 25:596–606.

LIKERT, RENSIS.
1932 "A Technique for the Measurement of Attitudes." *Archives of Psychology* (Whole No. 140).

LODGE, MILTON, and BERNARD TURSKY.
1979 "Comparisons between Category and Magnitude Scaling of Political Opinion Employing SRC/CPS Items." *American Political Science Review* 73: 50–66.

LOEHLIN, JOHN C., GARDNER LINDZEY, and J. N. SPUHLER.
1975 *Race Differences in Intelligence*. San Francisco: W. H. Freeman and Company.

LONG, SAMUEL.
1975 "Malevolent Estrangement: Political Alienation and Political [Violence] Justification Among Black and White Adolescents." *Youth and Society* 7:99–129.
1976 "Political Alienation among Black and White Adolescents: A Test of the Social Deprivation and Political Reality Models." *American Politics Quarterly* 4:267–303.
1978 "Personality and Political Alienation among White and Black Youth: A Test of the Social Deprivation Model." *Journal of Politics* 40:433–457.

LUBELL, SAMUEL.
1956 *The Future of American Politics*, 2nd ed. Garden City, N.Y.: Doubleday.

LUEPTOW, LLOYD, SAMUEL A. MUELLER, RICHARD R. HAMMES, and LAWRENCE S. MASTER.

1977 "The Impact of Informed Consent Regulations on Response Rate and Response Bias." *Sociological Methods & Research* 6:183–204.

MCCLOSKY, HERBERT.

1964 "Consensus and Ideology in American Politics." *American Political Science Review* 58:361–382.

MCCLOSKY, HERBERT, and JOHN H. SCHAAR.

1965 "Psychological Dimensions of Anomy." *American Sociological Review* 30:14–40.

MCPHERSON, J. MILLER, SUSAN WELCH, and CAL CLARK.

1977 "The Stability and Reliability of Political Efficacy: Using Path Analysis to Test Alternative Models." *American Political Science Review* 71:509–521.

MADDOX, WILLIAM S., and ROGER HANDBERG.

1980 "Children View the New President." *Youth and Society* 12:3–16.

MALIK, YOGENDRA K.

1979 "Trust, Efficacy, and Attitude Toward Democracy: A Case Study from India." *Comparative Education Review* 23:433–442.

MANNHEIM, KARL.

1952 "The Problem of Generations." In Paul Kecskemeti, ed., *Essays on the Sociology of Knowledge*. New York: Oxford University Press. Pp. 276–322.

MARGOLIS, MICHAEL.

1977 "From Confusion to Confusion: Issues and the American Voter (1956–1972)." *American Political Science Review* 71:31–43.

MARKUS, GREGORY B.

1979 "The Political Environment and the Dynamics of Public Attitudes: A Panel Study." *American Journal of Political Science* 23:338–359.

MARKUS, GREGORY B., and PHILIP E. CONVERSE.

1980 "Dynamic Modelling of Cohort Change: The Case of Political Partisanship." Unpublished manuscript, University of Michigan.

MARSH, ALAN.

1977 *Protest and Political Consciousness*. Beverly Hills, Calif.: Sage Publications.

MATTHEWS, DONALD R., and JAMES W. PROTHRO.

1966 *Negroes and the New Southern Politics*. New York: Harcourt, Brace, and World.

MERELMAN, RICHARD M.

1971 *Political Socialization and Educational Climates: A Study of Two School Districts*. New York: Holt, Rinehart, and Winston.

MILLER, ARTHUR H.

1974a "Political Issues and Trust in Government: 1964–1970." *American Political Science Review* 68:951–972.

1974b "Rejoinder to 'Comment' by Jack Citrin: Political Discontent or Ritualism?" *American Political Science Review* 68:989–1001.

MILLER, ARTHUR H. (continued)

1978 "Partisanship Reinstated? A Comparison of the 1972 and 1976 U.S. Presidential Elections." *British Journal of Political Science* 8:129–152.

1979 "The Institutional Focus of Political Distrust." Paper presented at the annual meeting of the American Political Science Association, Washington, D.C.

MILLER, ARTHUR H., THAD A. BROWN, and ALDEN S. RAINE.

1973 "Social Conflict and Political Estrangement, 1958–1972." Paper presented at the annual meeting of the Midwest Political Science Association, Chicago.

MILLER, ARTHUR H., EDIE N. GOLDENBERG, and LUTZ ERBRING.

1979 "Type-Set Politics: Impact of Newspapers on Public Confidence." *American Political Science Review* 73:67–84.

MILLER, ARTHUR H., and WARREN E. MILLER.

1976 "Ideology in the 1972 Election: Myth or Reality—A Rejoinder." *American Political Science Review* 70:832–849.

1977 "Partisanship and Performance: 'Rational' Choice in the 1976 Presidential Election." Paper presented at the annual meeting of the American Political Science Association, Washington, D.C.

MILLER, ARTHUR H., WARREN E. MILLER, ALDEN S. RAINE, and THAD A. BROWN.

1976 "A Majority Party in Disarray: Policy Polarization in the 1972 Election." *American Political Science Review* 70:753–778.

MILLER, WARREN E.

1979 "Misreading the Public Pulse." *Public Opinion* 2 (October/November), 9–15, 60.

1980 "Disinterest, Disaffection, and Participation in Presidential Politics." *Political Behavior* 2:7–32.

MILLER, WARREN E., and TERESA E. LEVITIN.

1976 *Leadership and Change: Presidential Elections from 1952 to 1976*. Cambridge, Mass.: Winthrop.

MILLER, WARREN E., ARTHUR H. MILLER, and EDWARD J. SCHNEIDER.

1980 *American National Election Studies Data Sourcebook, 1952–1978*. Cambridge, Mass.: Harvard University Press.

MITCHELL, WILLIAM C.

1959 "The Ambivalent Social Status of the American Politician." *Western Political Quarterly* 12:683–698.

MONROE, KRISTEN R.

1979 " 'God of Vengeance and of Reward?': The Economy and Presidential Popularity." *Political Behavior* 1:301–329.

MUELLER, JOHN E.

1973 *War, Presidents and Public Opinion*. New York: Wiley.

MULLER, EDWARD N., and THOMAS O. JUKAM.

1977 "On the Meaning of Political Support." *American Political Science Review* 71:1561–1595.

MULLER, EDWARD N., THOMAS O. JUKAM, and MITCHELL A. SELIGSON.

1982 "Diffuse Political Support and Antisystem Political Behavior: A Comparative Analysis." *American Journal of Political Science* 26:240–264.

NATIONAL ASSESSMENT OF EDUCATIONAL PROGRESS.
1976 *Education for Citizenship: A Bicentennial Survey.* Denver.
1978 *Changes in Political Knowledge and Attitudes, 1969–76.* Denver.

NIE, NORMAN H., with KRISTI ANDERSEN.
1974 "Mass Belief Systems Revisited: Political Change and Attitude Structure." *Journal of Politics* 36:540–591.

NIE, NORMAN H., and JAMES N. RABJOHN.
1979 "Revisiting Mass Belief Systems Revisited: Or, Doing Research Is Like Watching a Tennis Match." *American Journal of Political Science* 23:139–175.

NIE, NORMAN H., SIDNEY VERBA, and JOHN R. PETROCIK.
1976 *The Changing American Voter.* Cambridge, Mass.: Harvard University Press.
1979 *The Changing American Voter,* enlarged ed. Cambridge, Mass.: Harvard University Press.
1981 "Reply to Abramson and to Smith." *American Political Science Review* 75:149–152.

NIEMI, RICHARD G., RICHARD S. KATZ, and DAVID NEWMAN.
1980 "Reconstructing Past Partisanship: The Failure of the Party Identification Recall Questions." *American Journal of Political Science* 24:633–651.

NIEMI, RICHARD G., and BARBARA I. SOBIESZEK.
1977 "Political Socialization." In Alex Inkeles, ed., *Annual Review of Sociology,* Vol. 3. Palo Alto, Calif.: Annual Reviews. Pp. 209–233.

NIEMI, RICHARD G., and HERBERT F. WEISBERG.
1976 "Do Voters Think Ideologically?" In Richard G. Niemi and Herbert F. Weisberg, eds., *Controversies in American Voting Behavior.* San Francisco: W. H. Freeman and Company. Pp. 67–84.

NUNN, CLYDE Z., HARRY J. CROCKETT, JR., and J. ALLEN WILLIAMS, JR.
1978 *Tolerance for Nonconformity: A National Survey of Americans' Changing Commitment to Civil Liberties.* San Francisco: Jossey-Bass.

OLSEN, MARVIN E.
1969 "Two Categories of Political Alienation." *Social Forces* 47:288–299.
1970 "Social and Political Participation of Blacks." *American Sociological Review* 35:682–697.

ORUM, ANTHONY M., and ROBERTA S. COHEN.
1973 "The Development of Political Orientations Among Black and White Children." *American Sociological Review* 38:62–74.

OSKAMP, STUART.
1977 *Attitudes and Opinions.* Englewood Cliffs, N.J.: Prentice-Hall.

PAGE, BENJAMIN I.
1978 *Choices and Echoes in Presidential Elections: Rational Man and Electoral Democracy.* Chicago: University of Chicago Press.

PERCHERON, ANNICK, and M. KENT JENNINGS.
1981 "Political Continuities in French Families: A New Perspective on an Old Controversy." *Comparative Politics* 13:421–436.

PETROCIK, JOHN R.

1974 "An Analysis of Intransitivities in the Index of Party Identification." *Political Methodology* 1:31–47.

1978 "Comment: Reconsidering The Reconsiderations Of The 1964 Change In Attitude Consistency." *Political Methodology* 5:361–368.

1980 "Contextual Sources of Voting Behavior: The Changeable American Voter." In John C. Pierce and John L. Sullivan, eds., *The Electorate Reconsidered*. Beverly Hills, Calif.: Sage Publications. Pp. 257–277.

PETROCIK, JOHN R., SIDNEY VERBA, with CHRISTINE SCHULTZ.

1981 "Choosing the Choice and Not the Echo: A Funny Thing Happened to *The Changing American Voter* on the Way to the 1980 Election." Paper presented at the annual meeting of the American Political Science Association, New York.

PHARES, E. JERRY.

1976 *Locus of Control in Personality.* Morristown, N.J.: General Learning Press.

PHIZAKALEA, ANNE-MARIE.

1975 "A Sense of Political Efficacy: A Comparison of Black and White Adolescents." In Ivor Crewe, ed., *British Political Sociology Yearbook*. Vol. 2: *The Politics of Race*. London: Croom Helm. Pp. 123–154.

PIERCE, JOHN C.

1970 "Party Identification and the Changing Role of Ideology in American Politics." *Midwest Journal of Political Science* 14:25–42.

PIERCE, JOHN C., and DOUGLAS D. ROSE.

1974 "Nonattitudes and American Public Opinion: The Examination of a Thesis." *American Political Science Review* 68:626–649.

POLSBY, NELSON W., and AARON WILDAVSKY.

1980 *Presidential Elections: Strategies of American Electoral Politics,* 5th ed. New York: Scribner's.

POMPER, GERALD M.

1972 "From Confusion to Clarity: Issues and American Voters, 1956–1968." *American Political Science Review* 66:415–428.

1975 *Voters' Choice: Varieties of American Electoral Behavior.* New York: Dodd, Mead.

PRESIDENT'S COMMISSION FOR A NATIONAL AGENDA FOR THE EIGHTIES.

1980 *The Electoral and Democratic Process in the Eighties*. Washington, D.C.: U.S. Government Printing Office.

PRESTAGE, JEWEL L.

1969 "Black Politics and the Kerner Report: Concerns and Directions." In Norval D. Glenn and Charles M. Bonjean, eds., *Blacks in the United States*. San Francisco: Chandler. Pp. 538–549.

PROTHRO, JAMES W., and CHARLES M. GRIGG.

1960 "Fundamental Principles of Democracy: Bases of Agreement and Disagreement." *Journal of Politics* 22:276–294.

REITER, HOWARD L.

1979 "Why Is Turnout Down?" *Public Opinion Quarterly* 43:297–311.

1980 "The Perils of Partisan Recall." *Public Opinion Quarterly* 44:385–388.

REMMERS, H. H., ed.
1963 *Anti-Democratic Attitudes in American Schools*. Evanston, Ill.: Northwestern University Press.

REPASS, DAVID E.
1976 "Comment: Political Methodologies in Disarray: Some Alternative Interpretations of the 1972 Election." *American Political Science Review* 70:814–831.

RINTALA, MARVIN.
1979 *The Constitution of Silence: Essays on Generational Themes*. Westport, Conn.: Greenwood.

RODGERS, HARRELL R., JR.
1974 "Toward Explanation of the Political Efficacy and Political Cynicism of Black Adolescents: An Exploratory Study." *American Journal of Political Science* 18:257–282.

ROLLENHAGEN, RICK E.
1981 "Explaining Variation in Concern About the Outcome of Presidential Elections, 1960–1980." Unpublished manuscript, Michigan State University.

ROSENBERG, MORRIS.
1965 *Society and the Adolescent Self-Image*. Princeton, N.J.: Princeton University Press.

ROTTER, JULIAN B.
1966 "Generalized Expectancies for Internal versus External Control of Reinforcement." *Psychological Monographs: General and Applied* 80 (Whole No. 609).
1971 "Generalized Expectancies for Interpersonal Trust." *American Psychologist* 26:443–452.

RUBIN, RICHARD L.
1976 *Party Dynamics: The Democratic Coalition and the Politics of Change*. New York: Oxford University Press.

ST. PETER, LOUIS, J. ALLEN WILLIAMS, JR., and DAVID R. JOHNSON.
1977 "Comments on Jackman's 'Political Elites, Mass Publics, and Support for Democratic Principles.' " *Journal of Politics* 39:176–184.

SANTI, LAWRENCE.
1980 "Turnout and Trust in Government, 1964–1972." Paper presented at the annual meeting of the Western Political Science Association, San Francisco.

SCHLESINGER, JOSEPH A.
1965 "Political Party Organization." In James G. March, ed., *Handbook of Organization*. Chicago: Rand McNally. Pp. 764–801.
1975 "The Primary Goals of Political Parties: A Clarification of Positive Theory." *American Political Science Review* 69:840–849.

SCHULMAN, MARK A., and GERALD M. POMPER.
1975 "Variability in Electoral Behavior: Longitudinal Perspectives from Causal Modeling." *American Journal of Political Science* 19:1–18.

SCOTT, RICHARD R.

1981 "The Development of Political Attitudes in Segregated and Desegregated Schools." *Urban Review* 13:25–34.

SEARING, DONALD D., JOEL J. SCHWARTZ, and ALDEN E. LIND.

1973 "The Structuring Principle: Political Socialization and Belief Systems." *American Political Science Review* 67:415–432.

SEARING, DONALD D., GERALD WRIGHT, and GEORGE RABINOWITZ.

1976 "The Primacy Principle: Attitude Change and Political Socialization." *British Journal of Political Science* 6:83–113.

SEARS, DAVID O.

1975 "Political Socialization." In Fred I. Greenstein and Nelson W. Polsby, eds., *Handbook of Political Science*. Vol. 2: *Micropolitical Theory*. Reading, Mass.: Addison-Wesley. Pp. 93–153.

SEGAL, DAVID R., MARCUS FELSON, and MADY WECHSLER SEGAL.

1973 "Mortality and Political Partisanship: A Test of the Butler–Stokes Hypothesis." *Comparative Politics* 5:601–610.

SHAFFER, STEPHEN D.

1981 "A Multivariate Explanation of Decreasing Turnout in Presidential Elections, 1960–1976." *American Journal of Political Science* 25:68–95.

SHINGLES, RICHARD D.

1979 "College as a Source of Black Alienation." *Journal of Black Studies* 9:267–289.

1981 "Black Consciousness and Political Participation: The Missing Link." *American Political Science Review* 75:76–91.

SHIVELY, W. PHILLIPS.

1972 "Party Identification, Party Choice, and Voting Stability: The Weimar Case." *American Political Science Review* 66:1203–1225.

1974 *The Craft of Political Research: A Primer.* Englewood Cliffs, N.J.: Prentice-Hall.

1979a "The Development of Party Identification among Adults: Exploration of a Functional Model." *American Political Science Review* 73:1039–1054.

1979b "Rejoinder to Abramson." *Political Methodology* 6:457–461.

1979c "The Relationship Between Age and Party Identification: A Cohort Analysis." *Political Methodology* 6:437–446.

1980 "The Nature of Party Identification: A Review of Recent Developments." In John C. Pierce and John L. Sullivan, eds., *The Electorate Reconsidered*. Beverly Hills, Calif.: Sage Publications. Pp. 219–236.

SMITH, ERIC R. A. N.

1980 "The Levels of Conceptualization: False Measures of Ideological Sophistication." *American Political Science Review* 74:685–696.

1981 "Reply to Abramson and to Nie, Verba, and Petrocik." *American Political Science Review* 75:152–155.

SMITH, M. BREWSTER, JEROME S. BRUNER, and ROBERT W. WHITE.

1956 *Opinions and Personality.* New York: Wiley.

SNIDERMAN, PAUL M.

1975 *Personality and Democratic Politics*. Berkeley: University of California Press.

SORAUF, FRANK J.
1980 *Political Parties in America,* 4th ed. Boston: Little, Brown.

STIMSON, JAMES A.
1976 "Public Support for American Presidents: A Cyclical Model." *Public Opinion Quarterly* 40:1–21.

STOKES, DONALD E.
1962 "Popular Evaluations of Government: An Empirical Assessment." In Harlan Cleveland and Harold D. Lasswell, eds., *Ethics and Bigness: Scientific, Academic, Religious, Political, and Military.* New York: Harper and Brothers. Pp. 61–72.

STOUFFER, SAMUEL A.
1955 *Communism, Conformity, and Civil Liberties: A Cross-section of the Nation Speaks Its Mind.* Garden City, N.Y.: Doubleday.

SULLIVAN, JOHN L., GEORGE E. MARCUS, STANLEY FELDMAN, and JAMES E. PIERESON.
1981 "The Sources of Political Tolerance: A Multivariate Analysis." *American Political Science Review* 75:92–106.

SULLIVAN, JOHN L., GEORGE E. MARCUS, JAMES E. PIERESON, and STANLEY FELDMAN.
1978–1979 "The Development of Political Tolerance: The Impact of Social Class, Personality, and Cognition." *International Journal of Political Education* 2:115–139.

SULLIVAN, JOHN L., and DANIEL RICHARD MINNS.
1976 " 'The Benevolent Leader Revisited': Substantive Finding or Methodological Artifact?" *American Journal of Political Science* 20:763–772.

SULLIVAN, JOHN L., JAMES E. PIERESON, and GEORGE E. MARCUS.
1978 "Ideological Constraint in the Mass Public: A Methodological Critique and Some New Findings." *American Journal of Political Science* 22:233–249.
1979 "An Alternative Conceptualization of Political Tolerance: Illusory Increases 1950s–1970s." *American Political Science Review* 73:781–794.

SULLIVAN, JOHN L., JAMES E. PIERESON, GEORGE E. MARCUS, and STANLEY FELDMAN.
1979 "The More Things Change, the More They Stay the Same: The Stability of Mass Belief Systems." *American Journal of Political Science* 23:176–186.

SUNDQUIST, JAMES L.
1973 *Dynamics of the Party System: Alignment and Realignment of Political Parties in the United States.* Washington, D.C.: The Brookings Institution.

SURVEY RESEARCH CENTER.
1976 *Interviewer's Manual,* rev. ed. Ann Arbor, Mich.: Institute for Social Research.

TEDIN, KENT L.
1974 "The Influence of Parents on the Political Attitudes of Adolescents." *American Political Science Review* 68:1579–1592.

TORNEY, JUDITH V., A. N. OPPENHEIM, and RUSSELL F. FARNEN.
1975 *Civic Education in Ten Countries: An Empirical Study.* New York: Wiley.

TRAUGOTT, MICHAEL W., and JOHN P. KATOSH.

1979 "Response Validity in Surveys of Voting Behavior." *Public Opinion Quarterly* 43:359–377.

TRILLING, RICHARD J.

1976 *Party Image and Electoral Behavior.* New York: Wiley-Interscience.

U.S. BUREAU OF THE CENSUS.

1965 *Current Population Reports,* Series P-25, No. 311, "Estimates of the Population of the United States, by Single Years of Age, Color, and Sex: 1900 to 1959." Washington, D.C.: U.S. Government Printing Office.

1971 *U.S. Census of the Population: 1970, Number of Inhabitants.* Washington, D.C.: U.S. Government Printing Office.

1972 *Statistical Abstract of the United States: 1972,* 93rd ed. Washington, D.C.: U.S. Government Printing Office.

1974 *Current Population Reports,* Series P-25, No. 519, "Estimates of the Population of the United States, by Age, Sex, and Race, April 1, 1960 to July 1, 1973." Washington, D.C.: U.S. Government Printing Office.

1977 *Current Population Reports,* Series P-25, No. 704, "Projections of the Population of the United States: 1977 to 2050." Washington, D.C.: U.S. Government Printing Office.

1978 *Current Population Reports,* Series P-25, No. 721, "Estimates of the Population of the United States, by Age, Sex, and Race: 1970 to 1977." Washington, D.C.: U.S. Government Printing Office.

1979 *Current Population Reports,* Series P-25, No. 800, "Estimates of the Population of the United States, by Age, Sex, and Race: 1976 to 1978." Washington, D.C.: U.S. Government Printing Office.

1981a *1980 Census of the Population: Age, Sex, Race, and Spanish Origin of the Population by Regions, Divisions and States.* Washington, D.C.: U.S. Government Printing Office.

1981b *Statistical Abstract of the United States: 1981,* 102nd ed. Washington, D.C.: U.S. Government Printing Office.

U.S. SENATE, SUBCOMMITTEE ON INTERGOVERNMENTAL RELATIONS OF THE COMMITTEE ON GOVERNMENT OPERATIONS.

1973 *Confidence and Concern: Citizens View American Government; A Survey of Public Attitudes,* 3 vols. Washington, D.C.: U.S. Government Printing Office.

VAILLANCOURT, PAULINE MARIE.

1972 "The Political Socialization of Young People: A Panel Survey of Youngsters in the San Francisco Bay Area." Unpublished Ph.D. dissertation, University of California at Berkeley.

VALENTINE, DAVID C., and JOHN R. VAN WINGEN.

1980 "Partisanship, Independence, and the Partisan Identification Question." *American Politics Quarterly* 8:165–186.

VERBA, SIDNEY, and NORMAN H. NIE.

1972 *Participation in America: Political Democracy and Social Equality.* New York: Harper and Row.

VERBA, SIDNEY, NORMAN H. NIE, and JAE-ON KIM.

1978 *Participation and Political Equality: A Seven-Nation Comparison.* New York: Cambridge University Press.

WATTENBERG, MARTIN P.
1981 "The Decline of Political Partisanship in the United States: Negativity or Neutrality?" *American Political Science Review* 75:941–950.

WEISBERG, HERBERT F.
1980 "A Multidimensional Conceptualization of Party Identification." *Political Behavior* 2:33–60.

WEISBERG, HERBERT F., and BRUCE D. BOWEN.
1977 *An Introduction to Survey Research and Data Analysis*. San Francisco: W. H. Freeman and Company.

WEISSBERG, ROBERT.
1975 "Political Efficacy and Political Illusion." *Journal of Politics* 37:469–487.

WEISSBERG, ROBERT, and RICHARD JOSLYN.
1977 "Methodological Appropriateness in Political Socialization Research." In Stanley Allen Renshon, ed., *Handbook of Political Socialization: Theory and Research*. New York: Free Press. Pp. 45–84.

WELCH, SUSAN, and CAL CLARK.
1974 "Change in Political Efficacy: A Test of Two Hypotheses." Paper presented at the annual meeting of the American Political Science Association, Chicago.
1975 "Determinants of Change in Political Efficacy: A Test of Two Hypotheses." *Journal of Political and Military Sociology* 3:207–217.

WELCH, SUSAN, and J. MILLER MCPHERSON.
1981 "The Impact of Political Issues on Political Efficacy: A Panel Analysis." *Micropolitics* 1:71–86.

WILLIAMS, CHRISTINE B.
1980 "A Socialization Explanation of Political Change." In John C. Pierce and John L. Sullivan, eds., *The Electorate Reconsidered*. Beverly Hills, Calif.: Sage Publications. Pp. 111–134.

WOLFINGER, RAYMOND E., and STEVEN J. ROSENSTONE.
1980 *Who Votes?* New Haven, Conn.: Yale University Press.

WRIGHT, JAMES D.
1975 "Does Acquiescence Bias the 'Index of Political Efficacy'?" *Public Opinion Quarterly* 39:219–226.
1976 *The Dissent of the Governed: Alienation and Democracy in America*. New York: Academic Press.

ZELLMAN, GAIL L., and DAVID O. SEARS.
1971 "Childhood Origins of Tolerance for Dissent." *Journal of Social Issues* 27:109–136.

Index of Names

Index of Topics